International Perspectives on Vietnam

Edited by Lloyd C. Gardner & Ted Gittinger

TEXAS A&M UNIVERSITY PRESS
College Station

The paper used in this book meets the minimum requirements
of the American National Standard for Permanence
of Paper for Printed Library Materials, z39.48-1984.
Binding materials have been chosen for durability.

Library of Congress Cataloging-in-Publication Data

International perspectives on Vietnam / edited by Lloyd C. Gardner and
    Ted Gittinger.
        p.   cm. — (Foreign relations and the presidency ; no. 2)
    Includes bibliographical references and index.
    ISBN 0-89096-898-5 (c)
    1. Vietnamese Conflict, 1961–1975.   2. Vietnamese Conflict,
1961–1975—Influence.   3. Great powers.   4. World politics—1945–
I. Gardner, Lloyd C., 1934–   .   II. Gittinger, Ted.   III. Series.
DS557.7.I57   1999
959.704'3—dc21   99-31797
                                                        CIP

International Perspectives on Vietnam

NUMBER TWO:
Foreign Relations and the Presidency
H. W. Brands, General Editor

IN ASSOCIATION WITH
The Center for Presidential Studies
George Bush School of Government and Public Service

Contents

Part 3. The World System

Tables

International Perspectives on Vietnam

Introduction

LLOYD C. GARDNER

Why did it take so long to end the Vietnam War? The answer, in part, is that the war in Vietnam was really many wars. Radiating outward from the actual scenes of fighting, moreover, were a number of perceptions of what the struggle was about, and what it meant for the rest of the world. For the major powers involved, of course, Vietnam was a proxy war—part of the contest between East and West, between communism and capitalism, between democracy and tyranny. Washington and Moscow policymakers believed that how they conducted themselves went beyond the question of who won or lost, therefore, and into a set of assumptions about their role in the world. Dean Rusk put forward such a view many times, never more forcefully than during a debate in July, 1965, over the decision to send the first 100,000 combat troops to Vietnam. In answer to a doubter, the secretary of state said, "If the Communist world finds out we will not pursue our commitment to the end, I don't know where they will stay their hand."[1] Though not quite a mirror image, Moscow's fear of being dragged more deeply into the Vietnam War because of the perceived need to counter Chinese criticism led the Soviets to equivocate their role as would-be peace broker between Washington and Hanoi. Further complicating this picture, Washington and Moscow discussed a shared interest in not allowing Vietnam to prevent agreements to limit the spread of nuclear weapons. U.S. attempts to go beyond such an unstated understanding, and to encourage the Soviets to join in the effort to "contain" Beijing's presumed (in both Washington and Moscow) expansionist aims were much less successful.

In these circumstances, it was hardly surprising that Vietnam soon became a war of abstractions—or that soldiers returning to the United States talked about coming back to the world. It was thus all the more difficult to fathom a way out of an encounter that defied explanation in traditional military terms. American leaders stressed historical memory and analogy, needing to convince themselves as well as the public that it was necessary to counter the enemy's changing tactics in this global confrontation called the Cold War. Whether they understood Vietnam in terms of Munich and the folly of appeasement, or as the Greek Civil War—the first proxy struggle at the outset of the Cold War—or like the Korean example of a limited war so agonizingly difficult to end—these all provided "lessons" of how the current generation must behave in the face this new form of aggression. Secretary of Defense Robert McNamara averred, for example, that the Chinese were attempting in this new phase of the Cold War to construct a coalition in Asia against American interests. "This understanding of a straightforward security threat is interwoven with another perception—namely, that we have our view of the way the US should be moving and of the need for the majority of the rest of the world to be moving in the same direction if we are to achieve our national objectives. . . . Our ends cannot be achieved and our leadership role cannot be played if some powerful and virulent nation—whether Germany, Japan, Russia or China—is allowed to organize their part of the world according to a philosophy contrary to ours."[2] That guiding Cold War assumption provided the basis for shaping Vietnam decisions, but it was stretched thinner and thinner as the "credibility gap" widened.

Vietnam's shock waves produced different sorts of reactions, however, even in the regions nearest the fighting. China watched the fighting and participated with both material and human support, not only to aid to a "sister" communist nation, but always with one eye on Russia's activities as well. Hanoi's skill in maneuvering between the quarreling Communist powers to extract as much aid as possible for its war may well have further aggravated the "Sino-Soviet split." Hanoi's ability to make peace on its own, on the other hand, was also, at least to a certain extent, conditioned by its need not to alienate its allies. As Professor Robert Brigham demonstrates, moreover, Hanoi was not the only Vietnamese "actor" opposing the Saigon regime. The NLF was not simply a puppet of the North, as American policymakers insisted to justify intervention, a situation that further complicated efforts to find a satisfactory end to the war.

In Southeast Asia, the area where the "dominos" were supposedly most at peril from China's looming shadow, the repercussions of the Vietnam War remain a highly controversial subject. After the fall of Saigon in 1975, American policymakers consoled themselves with the thought that while the Vietnam "battle" might have been "lost," the real objectives of that conflict had been achieved. "I think that the doctrine of an unlimited world revolution by militant means is a doctrine that is so incompatible with the peace of the world," Dean Rusk testified about China's ambitions before the Senate Foreign Relations Committee in 1966, "and the system of international society that we are trying to build on the United Nations Charter, that [that] is certainly one of the largest questions, if not the largest question."[3] The new nations of Southeast Asia, emerging from a century or more of colonialism and Japanese occupation were in a fragile stage of their development, it was argued. And the American presence in Vietnam bought time for these new countries to come into their own—out of Red China's immediate reach. It was perhaps natural, then, for policymakers to see contemporary events in Southeast Asia during the war itself as further justification for the stand taken in Vietnam. President Kennedy and President Johnson both reaffirmed Eisenhower's "domino" thesis at crucial turning points in the war. Perhaps the most dramatic event of the era was the overthrow of the leftist government in Indonesia by pro-Western military forces. Hailed by "specialists" as evidence that America's presence in Vietnam had stiffened the backs of those opposing the drift into China's orbit, the events in Indonesia, it turned out, while removing a leftist regime, were determined by local issues. And the formation of a regional organization, ASEAN, which also encouraged belief that America's stabilizing influence was the key factor in promoting regionalism—may have been a response to Vietnam, but was it because the countries feared being dictated to by all the great powers? Professor Robert McMahon thinks so, and he argues the case in his essay, asking "What Difference Did It Make?"

A curious side issue to the events in Indonesia, moreover, was a concern that grew in Washington that the rightist coup and bloodbath that followed would actually make it more difficult to end the war in Vietnam, because the NLF would fear the same fate. Criticisms of the Saigon government as antidemocratic made the choices in Vietnam appear much less clear cut. Even the most hawkish of the hawks had to admit that in a postwar Vietnam, elements of the defeated National Liberation Front would have to play some role. Indonesia was not a good example if the object was to persuade the Viet Cong to lay down their arms.

Vietnam certainly made a difference to Korea and Japan. At the outset of the Vietnam War, Korea was America's mendicant client state in Asia, one that suffered from various economic and political ills with no easy cure in sight, a burden on the U.S. Treasury and a problem for State Department planners anxious about the continuing tension between Seoul and Tokyo. Because President Johnson wanted to demonstrate that America was not alone in Vietnam, Korea suddenly emerged as a newly valued ally, eligible for very special treatment. Korea was urged to make peace with Japan and take up a military role in Vietnam. The ensuing rapprochement pleased policymakers, and while not as important, perhaps, as the troops Seoul sent to fight in Vietnam, it was certainly welcome. The troops came at a high cost. Not only did the United States have to pay for these forces, as Professor Kil Yi points out, but also when it did come time to enter into peace negotiations, Washington found itself faced with objections from Korean leaders that although they had participated in the fighting—the second-largest force after the Americans—they were not given a seat at the peace table.

Economically, Korea made great gains from the Vietnam War. So did Japan. But opinion in Japan was far more sharply split than in Korea. Many Japanese feared being dragged into the actual fighting, and were upset, as Professor Hiroshi Fujimoto points out in his contribution, about the American use of Okinawa as a launching pad for B-52 bombers. Though it is hard to say exactly how important Vietnam was to Japan's emergence as the "economic giant" it would become by the end of the 1960s, on the average, writes Fujimoto, Japan profited at least $1 billion a year from the war. Johnson had also sought Israel's support for the war, not for men to fight, but as a means of influencing American Jewry, who, until the 1967 war, saw little connection between the struggle in Southeast Asia and Israel's besieged position in the Middle East amidst hostile Arab states. Judith Klinghoffer argues that the Palestine Liberation Organization took heart from the success of the NLF, and that, indeed, the Soviets also saw the situation as ripe for Russian gains in influence throughout the region. In a sense, however, these adverse developments from Israel's point of view were a result of America's involvement, if one argues that Washington's preoccupation with Vietnam, and its demonstrated inability to defeat the enemy there, prompted adventurism in the Middle East.

A similar paradox characterized the reactions to the war in Europe. Throughout the war, American policymakers worried about what the reactions there would be. At first, the view expressed by former Secretary of State Dean Acheson and others held that the Europeans were waiting to see if the United States would carry out its commitments—as something of a test case. It was not simply that the Europeans supposedly equated Vietnam and Berlin, for example, but that any sense of a weakening American resolve would undermine the United States' credibility as a world leader, leaving dangerous openings for the likes of a General Charles de Gaulle or someone else with aspirations to form some kind of "Third Force" in Europe. Hence, stalwartness in Vietnam became—it was supposed—a guarantee that the United States would not allow either the Russians or anyone else to disturb the status quo in Europe. As Frank Costigliola points out, the Western alliance was held together by an organization of meaning and belief as well as one of tanks and troops. When it became clear that the war was having the opposite effect intended, policymakers chided European counterparts for not properly understanding the stakes of the war. What the allies do not realize, Secretary Rusk lectured NATO ministers, was that "the present position of the United States amounts to a near miracle. More than half a million Americans are involved in Southeast Asia, most of them in combat. In spite of that, the United States is maintaining its forces in Europe." The willingness of the American people to continue bearing those burdens was perhaps being taken too much for granted.[4] But even such a stalwart pro-American as German Foreign Minister Ludwig Erhard found himself fretting about whether or not the Americans might, as de Gaulle warned, reduce the commitment to Europe in order not to lose in Vietnam. In the aftermath of the Tet Offensive in 1968, the so-called Council of Wise Men, led by Acheson, urged the president to find an alternative to further escalation for Europe's sake, or, rather, for the sake of America's stake in Europe.

Lyndon Johnson inherited the war in Vietnam from John Kennedy, but events leading to it actually began back in 1947. When the enabling bills for aid to Greece and Turkey were presented to the Senate Foreign Relations Committee in executive session, Senator Walter F. George, a long-time internationalist, pondered the implications of what was being labeled the Truman Doctrine. He was worried and said so. "I do not see how we are going to escape going into Manchuria, North China, and Korea and doing things in that area of the world. . . . We have got the right to exercise common sense. But I know that when we make a policy of this kind we are irrevocably committing ourselves to a course of action, and there is no way to get out of it next week or next year. You go down to the end of the road."[5] George's warnings were put aside, in part because the presidential initiative in proposing aid to Greece and Turkey put the legislators in a difficult position. If they denied Truman the authority and funds to combat the challenge, then, as Rusk would say later, they feared the communists would not stay their hand there and elsewhere. This Cold War dilemma—how to rein in executive power without appearing stultified as a nation—persisted throughout the Cold War and after. Some argue that Vietnam was bound to happen, somewhere, given the assumptions of the Cold War. Some see the war as a necessary holding operation, as discussed above. Yet all would agree that the struggle to make peace was a cruelly difficult process. The essays in this book will provoke you, we hope, and they will provide information, we believe, that will further the struggle to come to terms with the Vietnam experience.

Chapter 1

Was It All a Sideshow?

International Perspectives on Vietnam

JOHN PRADOS

The Vietnam War had reverberations throughout the world. American observers have often succumbed, however, to the temptation not to see the wider picture. The war happened to Vietnamese and to Americans, and for more than a decade it dominated our thinking and our policies. Yet today, in the post–Cold War world, the temptation remains. Memories fade of the intense divisions that surrounded the Vietnam War and of the dichotomy between pursuing that war or managing America's role in the larger world. Now the argument is heard that Vietnam represents simply one battle in the big Cold War. It is not so bad to lose a single battle, perhaps, especially if the war is won. In this view the Vietnam conflict amounts to little more than a sideshow, an accent or highlight to the Cold War competition.

The fine papers in this collection open the door to a much deeper understanding of the impact of the Vietnam conflict on the world, and on the United States in that world. The sideshow logic really flows from a certain level of analysis. With many levels of analysis, it becomes possible to appreciate a whole series of elements that place the notion of the Vietnam War as a sideshow in a radically different light. This paper will discuss three levels of analysis regarding the Vietnam War, relating the contributions scholars have made here to those levels of analysis, to reach a more nuanced perception of the historical importance of the conflict. We will proceed to draw a parallel between the Vietnam War and another conflict in the historical past and finish by making a recommendation that policymakers can take up in the endeavor not to repeat the past.

The first level of analysis has to be from the perspective of the Vietnamese. There can be no doubt that this war was no sideshow for them. Northerners dreamed of reunifying the country. Southern rebels fought for that plus a new way of life. South Vietnamese struggled to keep those changes from happening. For all of them the war represented the greatest of challenges; the conflict became the central feature of Vietnamese life. As H. W. Brands points out in his illuminating essay concluding this volume, there could be no sideshow here. In fact, it became a feature of some later explanations for why the United States lost in the Vietnam War: Vietnamese fighters had their lives suffused with the struggle, their futures dependent upon its outcome, while Americans went to Vietnam as part of a military machine.[1] Americans spent a year (in the army or air force), thirteen months (in the Marine Corps), or some other period of time in Vietnam, then went home, to the world, as they called it. The Vietnamese stayed where they were, fighting. For them the war would end only when one side went down to defeat.

That kind of involvement would be personal and societal, and on *this* level of analysis, Vietnam ultimately became much more than a sideshow for Americans also. Though not at first, and not in the Vietnamese sense of hanging suspended between victory or death, the conflict became central to America and the American people. The whys and hows of the Vietnam War came to consume this country in ways that are still being played out today and will probably continue in contention through the remainder of our lives. This issue was no sideshow; it brought about the fall of at least two presidents of the United States, as well as untold anguish for many Americans of all political persuasions.

U.S. diplomatic policy constitutes a second level of analysis. Washington clearly had a multiplicity of interests throughout the world. In today's historical view, which puts this conflict in the middle of the era called the Cold War, that very nomenclature suggests the reality that the primary U.S. foreign concern of the time lay in Washington's competition with Russia. That competition, in turn, centered mainly in Europe in the 1960s then Europe plus Africa during the 1970s. Those regional issues, along with certain global ones such as disarmament and arms control, or economic relations, held sway. So, was Vietnam about the Cold War? Or was Vietnam the Vietnam War? And was it a sideshow? A careful analysis requires disaggregating U.S. involvement in and prosecution of the Vietnam War from the ultimate effects and impact of that war. The papers presented here provide key insights in these areas.

As Robert J. McMahon points out in his paper, "What Difference Did It Make? Assessing the Vietnam War's Impact on Southeast Asia," prior to the start of this war the United States lacked major economic, military, or strategic interests in Vietnam. Judged from that standpoint, something else had to have led Washington into the Vietnam quagmire. In the internal decision memoranda of the Johnson administration, indeed, Vietnam does not loom very large in importance among justifications for the American military involvement that took place. The classic formulations of U.S. aims in the Vietnam War were those elaborated by Assistant Secretary of Defense for International Security Affairs John T. McNaughton in 1964 and 1965. These are worth examination.

One version of U.S. war aims headed a paper titled "Action for South Vietnam," of which Assistant Secretary McNaughton completed his second draft on November 6, 1964. The purposes of engagement McNaughton saw were

(a) To protect U.S. reputation as a counter-subversion guarantor.
(b) To avoid domino effect especially in Southeast Asia.
(c) To keep South Vietnamese territory from Red hands.
(d) To emerge from crisis without unacceptable taint from methods.[2]

Of this array of war aims the first thing to note is that none concerns Vietnam except tangentially. One is regional—concern for the domino effect—but here McMahon's work shows that, even after the U.S. defeat in the war, the dominos did not fall. Another aim mentions Vietnam, but in the context of a monolithic communist menace that did not in fact exist. The other aims depended directly on assumed U.S. victory in the conflict that followed. Not only did that not happen, but U.S. methods in the war were indeed condemned as unacceptable, the very opposite of what Washington presumably intended.

John McNaughton produced another version of U.S. war aims as an annex to his memorandum "Plan for Action far South Vietnam," prepared for Secretary of Defense Robert S. McNamara on March 24, 1965. This time the formulation was

70% To avoid a humiliating U.S. defeat (to our reputation as a guarantor).
20% To keep [South Vietnam and the adjacent] territory from Chinese hands.
10% To permit the people of [South Vietnam] to enjoy a better, freer way of life.
ALSO—To emerge from crisis without unacceptable taint from methods used.
NOT—to "help a friend" although it would be hard to stay in if asked out.[3]

McNaughton's new list makes clearer than before the very small degree to which Vietnam was important in U.S. purposes in the Vietnam War. The list, moreover, was created at a time when Washington had begun its cycle of major decisions that culminated in the large-scale commitment of American ground combat troops in the summer of 1965.

In terms of purposes, some of McNaughton's asserted aims dovetail with the argument favored by Secretary of State Dean Rusk, who saw the Vietnam War as being about the "credibility" of the United States. The whole question of credibility, its nature, and the use of the credibility argument in propelling decisions made on the Vietnam War has yet to be sufficiently addressed, but the papers here do touch on it. We enter the delicate question of credibility when considering John McNaughton's notion of the U.S. "reputation as a guarantor."

It is true that there was a question of credibility of the United States as a counterinsurgency guarantor in the context of the 1960s, when wars of national liberation were the rage. The focus to some degree in Moscow and to a much greater one in Washington was on what to do as a major power facing revolutions in Third World countries. There was some question about what to do in South Vietnam and what the impact of that might be in other developing countries in the throes of revolution. In some other countries, on the other hand, the United States might have had greater strategic interests or a broader rationale for intervention. In addition, given the fact that Vietnam was virtually unknown to the American people at the time, and the kind of push-pull process by which intervention actually occurred, there is reason to wonder whether it would have mattered to U.S. credibility at all if Washington had never entered the Vietnam War.

Another facet of the credibility question is that many people in Washington did not even concern themselves primarily with the contingency of the United States in Third World revolutions. Their focus was on the main game, the Cold War. In many minds in the White House and National Security Council, the issue was the credibility of U.S. treaty guarantees to U.S. allies in the face of a general war between the United States and Russia, and/or China if that nation too became involved. In that contingency, American actions in Vietnam did not matter much at all because it was a long stretch to argue that intervention or inaction in a counterinsurgency environment in an Asian nation would make any difference to the trust allies placed in the United States in the North Atlantic Treaty Organization and other alliance relationships that Washington pursued at that time.

In fact it can be argued that Asian intervention could have only a negative impact on U.S. allies in Europe. It could (and did) happen that the necessity to field an army in South Vietnam would degrade U.S. capability to fight a war against Russia in Western Europe, and the perception of that diminution in capability would affect U.S. alliance credibility much more sharply than any outcome in Southeast Asia. In addition, although *success* in a Vietnam intervention would have left U.S. credibility substantially unaffected, *failure* had to be detrimental. In sum, Washington had little to gain but much to lose by a Southeast Asian war.

The United States sent more than a half million troops to South Vietnam, spent $130 billion, and suffered 58,000 dead. That can only be seen as a substantial commitment. Yet from the policy standpoint of war aims, Vietnam was indeed a sideshow. With marginal reasons for action plus much to lose, Washington nevertheless moved in a big way. This mismatch between purposes and the extent of the U.S. commitment had a great deal to do with the floundering of the U.S. war effort and the defeat that finally eventuated.

A third level of analysis relates to the actual consequences of the Vietnam War. The papers here tell us much about these consequences, unintended and otherwise. Europe is a good place to start because we have just been discussing the credibility of the North Atlantic Treaty Organization (NATO) alliance. In his paper, "The Vietnam War and the Challenge to American Power in Europe," Frank Costigliola tells us that the war undermined two sets of beliefs, the previous Cold War paradigm of monolithic communism and the Atlanticist vision of Americans. These ideas underlay U.S. influence in Europe.

The challenge to American power would be legitimated by France under President Charles de Gaulle. De Gaulle argued, "Americans had neither the right nor the wisdom to make decisions for Europeans."[4] Not only that, but the hostility evolved as the Vietnam War became more intractable. The notion of Dean Rusk and others that U.S. actions in Asia would solidify the alliance in Europe proved exactly contrary. Frank Costigliola shows that, instead, critics of the alliance fortified their arguments by pointing to the dangers of the expanded war in Southeast Asia. Moreover, Americans as well as Europeans became more ambivalent toward the NATO alliance. This gives us another clue about credibility. In fact the pursuit of credibility in Southeast Asia damaged U.S. credibility in its area of main concern, the contingency of a general war against the Soviet Union, as Russia was then known.

European attitudes described by Costigliola are not simply the attributions of postwar historians, they were French perceptions at the time. Charles de Gaulle predicted as early as June, 1965—before Washington had even made its major decision on the intervention with ground troops—that the Vietnam War would end only when the United States withdrew, and that that would happen only when America tired of the war.[5] French Foreign Minister Maurice Couve de Murville was also quoted saying that the Soviet Union in practice exerted a moderating influence on the Vietnam conflict,[6] a point that U.S. officials consistently resisted and one to which we shall turn next. Washington's most loyal ally, the Federal Republic of Germany, which clung longest to a belief in the Rusk linkage between credibility in Vietnam and Europe, would only have that vision undermined by the hollowing out of U.S. military forces in NATO to fight the Vietnam War.

Now we turn to what became well known during the Vietnam War years as the Moscow-Beijing-Hanoi triangle, that is, the set of nations backing Washington's Vietnamese enemy. Russia, as the opposing superpower of the time, can be taken up first. In his important contribution to this collection, Russian diplomatic historian Ilya V. Gaiduk puts his main theme into the title of his paper: "Containing the Warriors: Soviet Policy Toward the Indochina Conflict, 1960–65." Where American officials frequently saw Moscow as pressing against Western interests everywhere, Gaiduk shows Russians understanding their ability to be truly limited. He portrays a conservative Soviet leadership, unlike some observers at the time and even analysts in this volume, and does so based on formerly secret documents of the Soviet government. With these solid sources Gaiduk performs the task of placing Soviet policy in Vietnam in the context of Moscow's worldwide interests, showing that the Russians preferred to avoid war in Southeast Asia and even saw positive gains to be made by mediating a peaceful solution to the Vietnam conflict. Incidentally, Gaiduk's essay here offers the finest account yet available, and the first one based on actual documentary sources of Russian diplomacy in the Geneva negotiations on Laos held during 1961 and 1962.

Lloyd Gardner picks up where Gaiduk leaves off. His paper, "Fighting Vietnam: The Russian-American Conundrum," juxtaposes Soviet and American policies with each other and covers the whole of the Johnson administration and much of the Vietnam War period overall. Gardner finds not only that the Soviet Union was encouraging a certain, more moderate, Vietnamese approach, but one that Russia and America shared an interest in; not a condominium, as it would be termed during the Nixon administration, but a way to understand each other in these Third World cockpits. Vietnam proved one example, and the Middle East, another, although some analysts may differ. The key requirement was to manage conflict in the Third World without involving the United States and Russia in ways that could not be taken back.

The basic U.S. strategy evolved around this belief, this shared desire of Washington and Moscow to avoid a direct confrontation. We see the consequences of that approach in the Middle East War of 1967, when the superpowers did in fact take steps to communicate with each other and minimize risks. In Vietnam, at some point as the war continued, Washington felt that Moscow should weigh in with Hanoi and pull it back if the situation ever neared real collision between superpower forces in Southeast Asia.

Lloyd Gardner calls this general approach the Russian road to peace[7] and, on the U.S. side, finds its main exponent to have been W. Averell Harriman, who served Kennedy as assistant secretary of state for Far Eastern affairs, and Lyndon Johnson as an ambassador-at-large for Vietnam negotiations. Chester L. Cooper, with whose account of the 1997 Hanoi conference on the history of the war Gardner begins his paper, happens to have been top aide to Harriman during the wartime period. I was myself among the American historians on the U.S. delegation at Hanoi, and Cooper's quotes are generally accurate. As we heard in great detail at Hanoi, Harriman, with Cooper at his side, tirelessly sought every avenue to open a pathway into Hanoi's politburo for Americans and Vietnamese to talk about the war. That included the Russian road but also many others—Hungarian, Polish, French, and, contrary to the impression left by Cooper's quotes, some Americans too. That Harriman proved unsuccessful in achieving the goal of opening negotiations has to do with a whole concatenation of factors from the military operations that took place, to reluctance on the part of Hanoi, to the basic lack of any real bargaining position among American leaders. The Russians *did* do their part in passing messages to Hanoi when asked, and they encouraged the Vietnamese to talk; Moscow did not simply fuel a proxy war in Southeast Asia.

So there was a conservative Soviet Union not necessarily out to start a war in Southeast Asia. That was something Washington did not perceive or did not perceive well enough. In the same article Lloyd Gardner cites at the head of his paper, Chet Cooper today harks back to the "domino theory" of the 1950s and 1960s as perhaps a good guide to American decisionmakers. But that theory was about a Russian octopus, its tentacles reaching down into Southeast Asia, directing the activities of local communist parties like the Lao Dong in Vietnam. According to the domino theory, the countries where those parties existed would fall into Moscow's orbit if America did not fight. As discussed earlier, this domino theory features in lists of reasons for the U.S. intervention in Vietnam.

Today we have ample evidence that communism was not monolithic, however, that Moscow did not in fact control all those local communist parties. Chester Cooper's opinion notwithstanding, the Hanoi conference of June, 1997, itself produced yet more evidence the Vietnamese were running their own show. And the other tenet of the theory, that Southeast Asian countries would fall like dominos if the first one (South Vietnam) went down, was also appreciated *at the time* to be an exaggeration. In June, 1964, the Central Intelligence Agency produced a report for its director that in any adverse result in Southeast Asia, enough time would pass in the evolution of that event, that the consequences of the fall of South Vietnam could be localized, restricted to that particular country. This weakens even more the rationale for United States intervention in Vietnam. We shall return to the matter of the domino theory presently.

Robert K. Brigham, an American scholar who has conducted original research in Hanoi's own archives, further strengthens this line of analysis in his paper, "Vietnam at the Center: Patterns of Diplomacy and Resistance." He describes a process by which Hanoi charted its way through the shoal waters of confrontation between the communist states Russia and China. The communist conflict, known to history as the Sino-Soviet split, sharpened throughout the period of the Johnson administration, with hostility reaching its peak during the Nixon years. The Chinese relationship with Hanoi eventually soured, and Brigham shows that much of the reason for that evolution came directly from Hanoi's relations with Russia. At the same time he shows how Hanoi, though it tried to navigate between the conflicting communist states, was finally forced to favor one side over the other.

Where Hanoi's politics have often been pictured as a struggle between certain factions—there were both pro-Soviet and pro-Chinese groups—or between Vietnamese from different regions—northerners and southerners—Brigham provides a much more sophisticated picture of the interests of individual Vietnamese politburo members and groups in the Lao Dong party. The problems, the real difficulties Vietnamese had to confront in order to carry out the war in the South, led to a shifting pattern of political alliances in Hanoi. Brigham tells us that conflict within the Lao Dong revolved especially around the compromise made at the Twelfth Plenum, in December, 1965, where the decision was that intervention by Hanoi's regular forces, plus continued people's war in the South, would make for a war of attrition that could be conducted long enough to exhaust the United States. Hanoi needed Chinese aid because Beijing could furnish masses of some types of supplies, but the Vietnamese needed Russian assistance because Moscow could give them certain types of equipment impossible for the Chinese. Hanoi's balancing act heightened pre-existing regional differences within the Lao Dong, another important factor in the developing situation. These concerns form the horns of a dilemma.

The third side of the triangle was China. It is most elegant to take together the two papers on China that are here present. Both Qiang Zhai and Xiaoming Zhang show a People's Republic of China prepared to help Hanoi within the framework of Beijing's own interests. The relationship soured as the Vietnamese continued to take an independent path, and declined particularly after 1968. In his paper, "An Uneasy Relationship: China and the DRV during the Vietnam War," Qiang Zhai shows despite common goals of resisting the United States, Hanoi and Beijing "differed in their approaches to the issues of waging war and pursuing peace," and that distrust and suspicion persisted in both capitals.[8] This point is reinforced by Zhai's recitation of the record right through the period of the Nixon administration, to the Paris Peace accords of 1973, and the paper presents for the first time a Chinese side of the story that is based on real evidence. Xiaoming Zhang's account of the "Belligerent Allies" reinforces that observation in several ways. He shows that Hanoi was completely reliant on Moscow for certain key weapons systems, including the most advanced aircraft, surface-to-air (SAM) missiles, radars, and electronics. China, on the other hand, supplied all the tanks, plus the vast majority of artillery weapons, small arms, and ammunition. Beijing's interests are shown in the fact that its shipments of military hardware peaked in 1968, but then again from 1971 to 1973.[9] American escalatory actions during the last period forced a Chinese decision to increase military aid to Hanoi even though the Democratic Republic of Vietnam (DRV) and the People's Republic of China (PRC) had by then drifted apart. Robert Brigham's study of DRV leaders underlines the thorniness of noting that "strained relations between Moscow and Beijing compelled Hanoi to accept many compromise solutions that limited its future options and may have prolonged the war."[10]

To bring this argument full circle, a demonstration of U.S. credibility by means of an intervention in Southeast Asia required a clear demonstration of dominance, in a few words, a short victorious war. But Washington's escalatory actions pressed on the Moscow-Beijing-Hanoi triangle in ways that drove them together and prolonged the Vietnam War. This miscalculation in Washington must be seen as a major error, with impact both in Southeast Asia and in the Cold War as a whole.

Finally, wars have unintended consequences. In their contributions, respectively, on Southeast Asia, Japan, and South Korea, scholars Robert J. McMahon, Hiroshi Fujimoto, and Kil J. Yi, open our eyes to a whole series of developments. In his notable analysis on Southeast Asia, McMahon directly confronts claims made in some quarters that the defeat in Vietnam actually amounts to a longer-term victory for the United States because it "bought crucial time for the economic development and political maturation of the region's non-communist states."[11] McMahon not only demonstrates the claim to have been faulty in its logic, he wrote before the real-world meltdown of the Southeast Asian and Far Eastern economies in 1997–98.

The logic is here worth emphasis because of how it figures in explanations of the Vietnam outcome. To show that U.S. intervention fostered geopolitical equilibrium in the region, for example, it is necessary to demonstrate that China posed a true national security threat in the 1960s (no, because of lack of capability and internal turmoil from the Cultural Revolution); that it ceased to be a threat due to U.S. action (no, again due to turmoil); that Southeast Asian countries were able to carve out the role they did as the result of time bought by Washington's intervention (in fact, the regional organization ASEAN flourished in spite of United States policy); and that each of these outcomes was an explicit American aim (never the case).[12] As for U.S. action sparking not merely economic development, but the soaring growth rates of the "tiger" economies, the subsequent economic crisis reveals the fragility of that claim.

The real victors of the war, Hiroshi Fujimoto tells us in "Japan and the War in Southeast Asia, 1965–67," were the Japanese. Pressures of the war forced the United States to ask, indeed help, Japan to take a greater regional role, resulting in the first international conference Japan had convened since the end of World War II, its replacing the United States as the major exporter to the Far Eastern region, supplanting the United States as the major trading partner for South Korea, and generally ending up as the "chief beneficiary" of America's longest war.[13]

Dr. Kil J. Yi adds to that perspective with his study, "A Demanding Ally: South Korea in the Vietnam War." Yi shows that South Korean involvement in Vietnam flowed not from foreign policy but from economic motives, and that by close calculation Seoul proved able to gain enormously from the American imbroglio in Vietnam. Ultimately U.S. aid funded a substantial portion of South Korean budgets, freeing investment resources to prepare Korea's industrial take-off of the 1970s and 1980s.[14]

Together, Japan and South Korea dominated trade on the Pacific rim from the 1970s, effectively supplanting United States economic primacy in the Far East. This direct effect of the Vietnam War was clearly an adverse development for Washington, and indeed for Wall Street. In fact, examination of this whole set of consequences shows a range of adverse effects, some intended, some not, of far greater importance than any interests the United States may have had going into Vietnam at the outset of the war. In summary, with a weak rationale, a miscalculation of the reaction of the Vietnamese, as well as their supporting communist powers, a misguided belief in the effects of intervention on U.S. credibility, and an impending range of adverse consequences, Washington launched itself into the quagmire of the Vietnamese War. A kick start down the road to that quagmire was the incident in the Gulf of Tonkin in the summer of 1964, which brings to mind an uncanny historical parallel.

These papers were publicly presented at a meeting that culminated on October 19, which in 1997 happened to be the 258th anniversary of the date in 1739 that Great Britain declared war against Spain, hostilities that became known as the "War of Jenkins's Ear." This is a story about diplomacy and force, peripheral interests and consequences, exactly as is Vietnam. The global conflict of that day, and it was a "cold war," existed between Britain and France. Great Britain's interest in the conflict with France did not necessarily extend to fighting Spain, but hubris and miscalculation in 1739 worked the same way they would in Southeast Asia in the 1960s.

The background concerns trade and diplomacy on Caribbean coasts—British trade, Spanish coasts. Under the 1713 Treaty of Utrecht that ended the War of the Spanish Succession, a prohibition of British trade had been replaced with the system called *"asiento,"* under which a single British ship each year (the so-called annual ship) was permitted to trade in the Spanish West Indies. In London, The City wanted, demanded, the exports; in the West Indies the Spaniards wanted slaves but Spanish ships were not allowed to carry them. British merchants were happy to supply the want, selling goods on the side, and bring home sugar and rum, calmly violating the *asiento*. The Spanish navy and its *guarda costas* in the Indies, depending upon the day-to-day state of relations with Britain and their own inclinations, could enforce the *asiento* or not. Meanwhile, at the overarching level of state diplomacy, Spain was tied to France by loose treaty relations that could be activated by hostilities with a third power. Tensions over these matters were sharpening by the 1730s and a number of incidents between merchants and *guarda costas* had occurred.[15]

Enter Robert Jenkins. A Glasgow ship captain, master of the brig *Rebecca,* Jenkins was on a smuggling voyage in the Indies when *guarda costas* overhauled him. The Spaniards stopped the *Rebecca* and boarded her; according to Jenkins, they strung him up from the yard arm, but let the skipper down before he died from hanging. Then the *guarda costas* cut off Jenkins's ear and left. The sea captain returned home, but appeared at Parliament to demand restitution, with an ear pickled in a jar of fluid. Outraged, Great Britain declared war. There was an initial success in the Indies, but the British were defeated in Florida. Hostilities continued; France entered the war, which then became a generalized European conflict, the War of the Austrian Succession. Further setbacks brought about the fall of the twelve-year-old government of Sir Robert Walpole, then the longest-serving prime minister of Great Britain. In short, for minor peripheral interests, the British initiated a conflict that their policy sought to avoid, with dire consequences for the state and the political regime of that day.

The parallel with Vietnam in its Cold War context is striking. Vietnam was Spain. France had the role of the communist powers in the cold war of that time. There were doubts about veracity of the initial incident—in 1739 Parliament had only Robert Jenkins's word, in 1964 American naval commanders in the Gulf of Tonkin sent conflicting messages about what was happening to them. If anything, in 1964 Washington had an advantage because modern tele-communication mechanisms allowed it to at least try to investigate the par-ticulars of the incident in the field. But the outcome was the same, the United States was Britain, driving Spain into the hands of the French allies (read Hanoi into the hands of Moscow and Beijing), with danger of the very general war that it was the object of United States policy to avoid. Both for the British in 1739, and for Washington in 1961 or 1964, there was a serious mismatch be-tween the importance of the interests invoked in a local incident, and the ex-tent of the commitment made, not to say its consequences.

Incidents are like streetcars, which is to say the timing will always be such that another will be along presently. If so, a power should be careful which streetcar it jumps aboard. In the post–Cold War world in particular, every lo-cal incident will demand attention, offering the potential to engage the inter-ests of the superpower. American policymakers lately have put their attention on whether, prior to entering one of these local situations, they have elabo-rated an "exit strategy." That flows from a different lesson of Vietnam, valid in its own way, but not a measure that can prevent Washington's overextending itself. More attention needs to be devoted to the *entry* strategy, to the match between interests and allowable commitment, to prevention of situations where peripheral interests predominate, to the analysis in advance of the adverse con-sequences probable in the case of an outcome other than the one expected. Along this path lies the responsibility of power.

Part 1

North Vietnam and Its Allies

Chapter 2

Fighting Vietnam

The Russian-American Conundrum

LLOYD C. GARDNER

The persistent efforts of the United States to enlist Moscow's support in reaching a "satisfactory" solution to the Vietnam War are not unknown to scholars, though not yet fully appreciated for their import. Former Defense Secretary Robert McNamara's journey to Hanoi in June, 1997, with a contingent of scholars and Vietnam policymakers, however, gave us glimpses of the North Vietnamese reaction at the time. Team member Chester Cooper reported in the *Washington Post* that his repeated attempts to probe the Vietnamese representatives about how their responses to American "peace overtures" were formulated met with almost total silence. This veil fell away only once, when a former Foreign Ministry official asked a question in return, "Why did you always rely on third parties? Were you just making propaganda? Why didn't you try to contact us directly?" "Why, indeed," mused Cooper, who replied that although Washington had made some effort, "It may be fair to say we could have tried harder, been more persistent."[1] In a related story on the Hanoi discussions, a former deputy foreign minister, Tran Quang Co, detailed the reasons why such a failure to deal directly with the DRV led to misunderstandings and prolonged the war. "The U.S. failed to understand the objective of our war. It was only for our own national liberation and reunification." Hanoi, he insisted, was not a tool of world communism.[2]

There are really two questions here, as Cooper implies, intertwined around a Cold War philosophy and set of assumptions. One could say without much research at all that the reason the United States attempted to work through Moscow was because Hanoi was presumed to be acting with Kremlin approval and aid. That, after all, was the centerpiece of the U.S. Cold War belief system. But the original reasons for seeking Russia's aid to end the war evolved into the search for an entryway into an overall "understanding" about rules for managing Third World conflicts. And thus Vietnam became a testing ground for whether Soviet-American relations could be stabilized despite such conflicts, enough so that pressing business elsewhere could be conducted in almost normal fashion. The arms race, in particular, was one such issue, both as a bilateral question and as a problem in coming to terms with the end of the postwar era in Europe. The war in Korea had frozen Cold War positions. Vietnam, regarded in many ways as another Korea, began the search for détente.

Hopes the "Russian card" could be played were a major factor shaping Washington's policy decisions almost from the beginning. Like other tantalizing "solutions" to the Vietnam "puzzle," the Moscow answer proved illusory. What kept American policymakers in lively pursuit were intimations and promptings from Soviet leaders, which at first seemed to confirm Cold War assumptions, but which also reinforced confidence that the war was within the nation's capabilities—politically as well as militarily. Until, say, the middle of 1966, Vietnam appeared to Washington policymakers as another problem in "crisis management," following lessons learned in the Cuban missile crisis. When those assumptions began to be questioned, the quest for Russia's intercession did not end—instead, it took on even greater urgency. But how could one play the Russian card without risking the cohesiveness of the ideological construction of the Cold War itself? Cold War rhetoric from the time of the Truman Doctrine to Ronald Reagan's anathematizing of the Soviet Union as the "Evil Empire" made it difficult to reconcile public stance with private signals. Presidents from Truman to Reagan all used similar terms to describe the conflict, as a famous historian once put it, as a "presumably mortal antagonism" waged without a thought of compromise "between two rigidly hostile blocs."[3] So while there were ongoing bilateral talks on various important questions throughout the Cold War era, national leaders constantly worried about creating a dilemma for themselves. Any hint of moral equivalency, even any suggestion of commonality, risked undermining the ideological consensus behind definitions of the national interest.

Korea had been a bitter lesson in this regard for politicians and pundits alike. It strained the consensus nearly to the breaking point. No more Koreas meant no more stalemates, no more exhausting treks up and down a remote peninsula only to settle for the status quo. Republican leader Richard Nixon declared in the August, 1964, *Reader's Digest* that confidence in (and within) America would soon slip without a "will to win" in Vietnam. "Our present situation constitutes an unparalleled opportunity to roll back the Communist tide," he wrote, "not only in South Vietnam but in Southeast Asia generally, and indeed in the world as a whole." Yet even amidst all this tough talk about the will to win, Nixon advocated the Russian card to expose divisions in the communist world. "Soviet Russia and Red China are not merely rivals, they are bitter enemies. Moscow does not want to see Peking [Beijing] grow strong and expand in Southeast Asia. On the contrary, Khrushchev has every reason to hope that China's ambitions can be held in check. This deep division between our enemies reduces the danger that the war in Vietnam will escalate into nuclear war."

However, exploitation of those differences, in Nixon's offering to *Digest* readers, did not countenance the possibility of achieving only the "decent interval" for which he was later happy to settle—or anything less than the military victory. Thus it was not surprising that following a White House discussion on Vietnam policies in late November of 1964, one participant voiced his concern that gradual escalation of the war in the expectation of a negotiated settlement—inevitably less than perfect—might not be a sound approach. Could it be carried out, he asked his colleagues, "under the klieg lights of a democracy, in view of its requirement that we maintain a credible threat of major action while at the same time seeking to negotiate, even if quietly?"[4]

Policymakers frequently asked themselves that question without a good answer in mind. All the while Lyndon Johnson kept reminding his advisers of the Korean "lesson," seeking reassurance that Vietnam was not going to become another disaster for the Democrats. In the event, of course, Vietnam proved much worse than Korea. At least in Korea the enemy was out in the open, both in the sense of terrain—and in the more important sense of providing an antagonist capable of being seen as a credible menace. Even so, as the war dragged on inconclusively during seemingly pointless arguments over protocol matters at Panmunjon, it took Eisenhower's cleverness to rescue the endangered consensus. Adlai Stevenson could never have made such a peace and kept peace at home.

In Vietnam the situation was bad from the beginning. The American military command only caught glimpses of the enemy in firefights, while the public at home struggled with a fragmented picture of what the war was about. Upon his entrance into the White House Lyndon Johnson boldly declared that he would not be the president who lost Vietnam—even though he would admit to doubts about the original decisions to go off into the rice paddies of Southeast Asia, and he openly scorned what he called the "cops and robbers" shenanigans that preceded the overthrow of President Ngo Dinh Diem.

He had not anticipated that he would inherit the dire results of those mal-adroit conspiracies, and he justifiably resented the predicament Diem's murder left hovering over his presidency. But he was told—and he believed—that the United States, once committed, could not just back out of Vietnam. A cascading tsunami would sweep out of Vietnamese waters, alarmists warned, inundating all in its path to Berlin. But less excitable Cold War professionals also spoke of serious consequences. The struggle in Vietnam began to appear dangerous to American interests, after all, at a time when a sense of falling behind the communist "bloc" occasionally tugged at the sleeve of the national consciousness—and steadily gnawed away at the self-image of the New Frontiersmen. While these fears had something to do with such imaginary dangers as the "missile gap," and something more to do with the growing realization that long-submerged racial "matters" threatened white domestic tranquillity, there were quivery feelings in the land, whispering that Sputnik and Castro foretold American decline.

True, Kennedy had stared down Khrushchev in the Cuban missile crisis, but the world was waiting to see, it was believed in the editorial rooms of the *New York Times* and in the corner offices of NSC acolytes laboring over position papers, whether JFK's bravura performance could be repeated when the threat reappeared in a more subtle, if ultimately no less dangerous, guise. "War comes," Eugene Rostow once explained why Vietnam had to be fought to the end, "when people feel the moorings slipping, when the *situation is getting out of hand* and there's a slide toward *chaos* which threatens their safety."[5] Rostow was talking about a supposed slide toward nuclear war should the "Communist" challenge be ignored. The need for intervention arose in Rostow's typical formulation out of a rope of ideas that held things together, and which stretched between past and present into the future. Dean Rusk offered a deceptively simple response to Republican Senator Bourke Hickenlooper's comment during the Gulf of Tonkin "crisis." Asked the Iowa senator, is there "a comparison between Cuba and this? No one knows what would have happened had we not reacted. Is it possible this follows the same route?" Rusk assured him that American resolve still burned with the same intensity as the eternal flame that glowed day and night over Kennedy's hillside grave in Arlington cemetery. "What the Russians learned in Cuba," Rusk said, "could have an influence on the entire world."[6]

But that was not the simple response it might have seemed. Vietnam was six thousand miles away, not sixty, and the Russians had not anted nuclear-capable missiles into this new "game." As Russian historian Ilya Gaiduk has demonstrated, moreover, the thesis that Moscow was sending Ho Chi Minh forth as the new communist "champion" throughout Southeast Asia has little to recommend it.[7] Rusk's answer to Senator Hickenlooper bespoke something more involved than a quick showdown where the other fellow blinks. The American response to the shadowy events in the Tonkin Gulf, he explained, was a different sort of crisis management: "For months and months we have been trying to get to them a signal."[8] The primary objective was not to warn off Ho Chi Minh but to alert Moscow that Hanoi's behavior had put in jeopardy promising post-Cuba efforts to re-imagine Cold War rules of engagement. It was up to them both, the signal was meant to convey, to keep their client "states" on tight leashes.

A brief review of pre-Tonkin events illustrates the argument. The final decision to "intervene" against Diem, it will be remembered, had come hard on alarming reports that the once-honored "George Washington" of Southeast Asia was engaged in secret negotiations with communist contacts to end the war.[9] Independent actions of that sort were held to be doubly dangerous, for the precedent they would set, and for the concomitant threat they posed to "free world" unity. What good were promises of American aid, for example, if local rulers took it upon themselves to decide when to surrender? Critics called South Vietnam an army without a state. The response to that charge held that although that might be so at present, it was only a stage in nation-building. Thus Diem could not be allowed to leave the American-trained cadres without a country to defend.[10] Conversely, attempts to carry a war outside superpower-imposed boundaries also could not be tolerated.[11] If Washington stepped in to prevent Diem from betraying the cause, it proved equally determined to prohibit his successor from launching an invasion of the North.[12]

In anticipation of something like the Gulf of Tonkin events, American officials prepared detailed "instructions" for Canadian diplomat Blair Seaborn to use in his discussions with the North Vietnamese. Canada was one of three nations represented on the International Control Commission to watchdog the 1954 Geneva Agreement ending the first Vietnam War. Long defunct in terms of its original mission, the ICC found a minor role as a postal service, carrying messages back and forth. Thus Seaborn was asked to convey a tough message to Hanoi. The United States, he was to say, viewed "the problem" in South Vietnam "as something which affects its policies and its stature throughout the entire world." Furthermore, it held Hanoi directly responsible for the guerrilla activities plaguing the South, and, should it become necessary, the United States would not hesitate to escalate military actions and direct pressure on the Democratic Republic of Vietnam. On the other hand, Seaborn was also to impress upon those he addressed that "we do generally accept the practice of peaceful co-existence and that we do tolerate 'national Communism' as a fixture which it is not our purpose to subvert." He could go further if he wished, to point out that "our policy encompasses the occasional provision of economic assistance."[13]

Lyndon Johnson's personal message to Nikita Khrushchev in the aftermath of the American attacks on North Vietnamese PT-Boat bases similarly urged the Soviet leader to consider the "heavy responsibility which we both bear for keeping the peace and for preventing incidents anywhere in the world from starting a chain of dangerous and irreversible developments." Anything the Russian leader could do to restrain Hanoi—or Beijing—"from further reckless action . . . will be most helpful to peace." These were not simply "White Paper" public relations letters Johnson was writing to make a defensible record for escalating the war. Subsequent events would demonstrate that, given the options Americans faced in Vietnam, Russian involvement in bringing about peace was deemed more and more important. It was impressed upon Moscow in later "pen pals" correspondence that the United States and the Soviet Union had other matters of great significance for the world to consider, including especially arms control, which could be facilitated by cooperation to end the war. As would also become apparent, however, Russian-American correspondence and other exchanges concerning Vietnam, while frustrating to its superpower authors, proved downright alarming to allies—whether North and South Vietnam, or West Germany and Israel—fearful of being asked to sacrifice vital interests.

At the very outset of Johnson's presidency there were hints that Khrushchev and the Soviet leadership had indeed absorbed the "lesson" of the Cuban missile crisis. In place of Khrushchev's blustery dismissal of JFK's complaints about Castro at the 1961 Vienna summit, there seemed to be a greater willingness to consider the late president's argument that upheavals around the world had to be handled in a way "to avoid direct contact between our two countries so as not to prejudice the interests of their national security."[14] The first word LBJ heard from the Russians was a message via Drew Pearson from Ambassador Anatoly Dobrynin. Dobrynin had pointed out that the change in the presidency offered a good opportunity to "demonstrate United States–Russian friendship" by attempting to resolve the Cuban issue. With Deputy Premier Anastas Mikoyan in Washington for the funeral, it was "an opportune time to explore the subject." The ambassador then pointed out, Pearson added, "that Castro was as much a problem to Khrushchev as he was to the United States."[15] When Johnson met briefly with Mikoyan on November 26, 1963, the president did indeed open a discussion of the Cuban "problem." Twice he repeated that "we were not planning to invade," but the Cuban question remained "the biggest with our people" because of Castro's efforts at subversion throughout the hemisphere. Mikoyan responded that it was the other way around: Cuba was being subverted. The Soviet Union believed "all subversion should be ended everywhere." That discussion closed with an exchange of vague invitations "for further meetings."[16]

Four days later, Rusk met with Dobrynin and repeated Johnson's complaints about Cuban activities, but he also tried out a bid to isolate China. War could come over Cuba or Berlin, the secretary said, but also because of China. Dobrynin bit. Why over China? he asked. Rusk explained, "If China were to pursue a policy of militancy involving countries in the Far East to which we had commitments, this might bring about a confrontation between us which could ultimately lead to war." He understood, the ambassador replied.[17] Then it was McGeorge Bundy's turn. The national security adviser tried to put Dobrynin's mind to rest about reported re-examinations of the Cuban policy, assuring him again that "we had no intention of provoking a war in that area." Cuba was like Berlin was to the Soviet Union, Bundy went on. Probably Russian planners ask themselves "continuously what could be done to improve the situation in Berlin without provoking a war."[18] With the subject shifted to Berlin, Bundy offered his views on the German question. To Dobrynin's expressions of deep concern about the proposed Multilateral Force (MLF), Bundy remarked that the idea of German participation in a sea-going nuclear fleet "took account of the German [political] right in a way in which his government's policy did not." Bundy noted that the ambassador did not attempt to offer any response. His notes of their tête-à-tête ended with a strong affirmation: "We parted with a final toast to peace. On the whole this was the most searching and instructive conversation I have yet had with a Soviet diplomat. Somewhere in the middle of lunch, we switched from formal address to first names."[19]

Dobrynin also felt very good about the conversation. On New Year's Eve he called on Bundy with some "further reflections" on their discussion, which turned out to be in the form of a proposal for a summit meeting to allow Khrushchev and Johnson to get to know one another—even if there were no big results to present to the world.[20] In Dobrynin's memoirs, the idea of an early summit seemed to come from Bundy, at Johnson's request. The ambassador also recalled that Bundy had warned him not to expect a pullout from Vietnam, because "this would be equivalent to Johnson's political suicide."[21]

So how did matters stand as the United States wrestled with the Vietnamese imbroglio through 1964? Whether warranted or not, Washington believed that for a variety of reasons Moscow shared its desire to avoid a direct clash in Southeast Asia. It is not too much to say that the basic politico-military strategies adopted in Vietnam were largely shaped around this belief—and the further expectation that at some point Moscow would weigh in to force Hanoi to come to terms. If anything, American strategy counted too much on such an eventuality. The bombing strategy, Rolling Thunder, for example, was never designed to win the war, but had political and psychological objectives as its targets—first, South Vietnamese morale, and then leverage for the Russians to use to persuade its little "sister socialist state" to cease making war against Saigon. Rolling Thunder began, of course, when Soviet Premier Alexei Kosygin was in Hanoi—an insult he took to heart and complained about for a long while afterward.[22] Mac Bundy, just back from Vietnam, was full of fire about the raid on the American base at Pleiku, the ostensible reason for initiating a bombing campaign. Kosygin's visit should play no role in the decision, he declared. "If we take no action, the Soviets may think we are in fact a paper tiger."[23] Here was an interesting analysis of the Vietnamese conflict that postulated that it was necessary to bomb North Vietnam so as to give the Russians arguments to use in Hanoi—arguments that demonstrated reasons for restraint and excused the Soviets from extending additional aid to conquer South Vietnam.

Dean Rusk was prepared to argue, however, that Moscow was being dragged into the conflict as a somewhat unwilling ally—forced to meet the challenge of its commitments to Hanoi, as well as to fend off a bid by Beijing for supremacy in the world communist movement. If Moscow did nothing about the bombing, it would lose face in the communist world. At another briefing of congressional leaders, the secretary of state flatly stated that the Soviets did not want "to tangle with us over Southeast Asia." But more than that, he explained, it was American policy not to confront Moscow "with the harshest choices. . . . This is one of the reasons we haven't taken this question to the Security Council of the United Nations. We don't want to force them into the role of an advocate, when it might be they might wish to be somewhat more in the role of a middleman."[24]

Rusk was often accused by critics of failing to see the Sino-Soviet split when it had become as plain as the nose on his face. To the contrary, there is more than abundant evidence that the secretary hoped he could use that conflict as an inducement to Moscow to become more involved—not less—in Vietnam. In a backhanded fashion, and despite his doubts, the secretary of state could see how bombing Vietnam while Kosygin was present in Hanoi actually served such a purpose. Paraphrasing Bundy, if the Soviets did nothing, the Vietnamese might think *they* were a paper tiger and turn more to Beijing.[25]

Averell Harriman, not surprisingly, eventually became the principal advocate of the Russian road to peace in Vietnam, and he came to despise Rusk's fixations on various Cold War analogies (particularly the Greek Civil War analogy), but both men thought Washington and Moscow shared a common goal of peace and order in Southeast Asia. Harriman, especially, thought that the major task for diplomacy was to maneuver things so that Moscow became

Hanoi's principal ally and supplier of weapons. That way it would have the leverage necessary to persuade Hanoi when it was time to come to the peace table. The permutations on this theme thus unwound one after another, always offering Washington hope, after the initial military phase of crisis management proved unavailing, that peace was a matter of fifteen minutes more of willpower. Why the Russians should be impressed with the volume of American firepower in Vietnam if it did not bring results on the ground, was never fully explored.

Yet another variation on this theme came from Mac Bundy's office. Troubled, his memorandum said, by a lack of clarity inside as well as outside the government with respect to American objectives in Southeast Asia, he had "come up with a rationale which, long-range and egg-headed as it is, has convinced me, at least, that I am on God's side." America was not in Vietnam because the Vietnamese wanted us there but because the West was at a crossroads where its civilization clashed with the greatest challenge it had faced since the Reformation. It was not nuclear war that threatened:

> I am talking about a new polarization of the world, which will, in its early manifestations, see the poor, restless, non-white peoples, led or pushed by China, isolate themselves from Europe (East and West) and America (North, but probably not South) economically if they can, but certainly culturally and politically. In a subsequent stage this isolation will develop into active pressure to the point where, in a sense, we will find ourselves in a virtual stage of siege. . . .
>
> It may be impossible for a people, no matter how well led, to change the course of history. But it is possible, at a minimum, to delay, ward off, mitigate threats to our society and the way of life of immediately following generations. . . . And, at long last, this is where Vietnam comes in.
>
> In the last analysis, the West must preserve (or at least not willingly and voluntarily default) its access to, communication with, and benign influence on the peoples of Asia and Africa. . . . China has chosen to slam shut its doors, at least for the present. We and other peoples of the world cannot afford to see any more doors close, for every door that closes quickens the pace of the rich-poor, colored-white, North-South division of the world.[26]

This dark Spenglerian view of the "Decline of the West"—with its implied argument for incorporating Russia into the last-ditch stand against an alien world momentarily excited intellectually by the Marxist heresy, but with a Conradian heart full of darkness and hatred for the West—is more frequently associated not with Bundy, but with his ultimate successor, Henry Kissinger. Such forebodings and ruminations can be found in policymakers' writings throughout the Vietnam era, for they served a variety of purposes—like putting down pros and cons on a yellow pad.[27]

But the time for philosophizing could not be prolonged in search of still more reasons why the Russians should want to cooperate to protect, or join up with, the White Man's Burden in Southeast Asia. Averell Harriman believed the bombing had had enough time to sink into Soviet consciousness by mid-summer of 1965. Policymakers had kept a careful watch on Ambassador Dobrynin's growing anguish about the "collision course" the bombing threatened for Soviet-American relations. When was the bombing going to be stopped? Dobrynin asked everyone he met. Undersecretary George Ball noted the Soviet ambassador's distress sympathetically. "Dobrynin is very much under pressure," Ball told reporter Chalmers Roberts, "and concerned that his function has been . . . one of the fellow(s) to improve things and he finds himself where events are moving against his own objective . . . this confirms what we have been getting from a lot of sources."[28] On July 1, 1965, Dean Rusk advised Ambassador Foy Kohler in Moscow that Harriman had expressed an interest in attending the Moscow Film Festival later that month, and that Dobrynin had responded that he would be received for a "courtesy call" by Premier Kosygin. Kohler responded that he was always delighted to see Harriman, but there was little likelihood of the Soviets' budging on Vietnam unless the former governor of New York brought new proposals on the air strikes or for a direct approach to Hanoi.[29] Kohler's pessimism was countered in reports of speeches Kosygin delivered recalling statements by Roosevelt and Eisenhower about the value of Soviet-U.S. "wartime collaboration."[30] Tearing himself away from the film festival, Harriman had two lengthy conversations with the Soviet premier on July 15th and 21st. At both Kosygin warned him about playing China's game: "You are responsible for tensions in the area and the peoples of the East are turning against you. You have only your puppets there and by your actions and resistance to national liberation movements you only prove the Chinese point that war is inevitable."[31]

Kosygin even interrupted Harriman's efforts to explain Johnson's readiness to accept Vietnamese self-determination "once the war is over" with a derisive outburst, "You don't believe what you are saying." Taking this as a slur on LBJ's motives, and his own honesty, Harriman appealed to the Soviet leader to believe in Johnson's sincerity just as Stalin had accepted his word during the war, because he, Harriman, had "come to the Soviet Union in the 20's in order to help the Soviet people." It was a marvelous moment in the Cold War, surely, with Harriman asking current Russian leaders to accept Stalin's validation of his credentials! The second conversation (which ranged over issues of nuclear disarmament and the future of Germany as well as Vietnam), brought out a different side of the Russian position. There were still the ritual condemnations of American policy on humanitarian grounds and more ironic warnings about how Washington was pursuing a pro-Chinese policy, but this time there were words near the end that caused the special envoy and his note-taker to put Kosygin's statements in direct quotation marks and even to include the Russian words he had used. He had no authority to negotiate for the Vietnamese "comrades," Kosygin began, but as he had "previously said, the Vietnamese comrades do not exclude a political settlement, even one bypassing the Chinese *(Pomimo Kitaitsev)."* Study Hanoi's four points, he urged, and make counterproposals. "Think them over, turn them around and send them back to the North Vietnamese. You have the means to do so." Harriman pressed for more detail. Kosygin had hinted at significant differences between Hanoi and Beijing. What might this mean for future U.S.-DRV discussions? "In all confidence, I can only repeat that our Vietnamese comrades do not rule out a political settlement," the Soviet premier said. "That is all I can say but this, it seems to me, is very important. Naturally, this would be on the basis of the retention of the 17th parallel."[32]

While Kosygin may have had no good reason to think that Hanoi would look at Washington's efforts to re-do the famous "Four Points"—calling for a settlement on NLF terms—at the very least his discussion indicated that Moscow would not hold out for immediate reunification.[33] In between the first and second Harriman-Kosygin conversations, Dean Rusk had a meeting with UN Secretary-General U Thant. Thant noted that Moscow reports of some things Harriman had said in public were to the effect that North and South Vietnam should "settle their own affairs." Caught a bit off guard, Rusk replied that "we have had frank talks with Moscow," but the Soviet Union is "unable to take the initiative [and] so is being dragged along. Washington and Moscow are unable to strike a relevant bargain, since Moscow cannot deliver. Nor can we talk bilaterally with Hanoi, without involvement of the Saigon Government."[34]

It was taboo to speak of bilateral negotiations of any kind at this stage of the war. Rusk apparently meant that the Russians should deliver Hanoi to a larger peace conference, or, preferably, let them just fade away, as they supposedly had the Greek Communists in the early years of the Cold War. After the second conversation, however, Rusk did make several attempts to see if it were not possible to deal with the Vietnam problem *sotto voce.* He even told a close aide that he believed the DRV's four points were subject to "dickering." This burst of activity was probably triggered by the imminent decision to send the first 100,000 men to Vietnam—which would put American intervention beyond the point of no return. Mac Bundy was not happy about this late complication. Although himself a proponent of enlisting Moscow's aid, he thought the moment not especially propitious. American ground forces should be in place first. He had been instrumental in the struggle to convince Johnson of the logic of the bombing campaign and was now skewing the troop debate so as to prevent any last-second hitches. There was little new in the Harriman reports, he claimed, although he had before him two memoranda by the State Department's director of intelligence and research that suggested there were several noteworthy points to consider. Besides, he told Rusk, the problem had become so immense it would be difficult to play it in a low key.[35]

American policy had achieved its objective with Russia, Harriman would claim after his Moscow conversations. It—and he personally—had persuaded the Kremlin that it must intercede; Kosygin had talked about possible terms; and the Russian leader himself had developed the theme that the Chinese bid for power had to be turned back. But Harriman's free-wheeling left many perturbed. John J. McCloy, for example, had also become alarmed by reported Harriman statements, including one in Russian newspapers to the effect that he favored some sort of neutral status for a reunited Germany. Harriman claimed he had been misquoted, but that did not really satisfy the diplomat-banker. "It's in his bones," McCloy claimed. "We don't want an alliance especially at a time we're sending troops to the Far East." McCloy did not really care a fig about Vietnam, but he *did* worry about how such questions knit together.[36] For his part, Harriman felt big-time grievances against those in the State Department who tossed aside his accomplishment because they apparently believed that Russia had it in mind only to keep the United States bogged down in Southeast Asia. But he had to wait until the excitement of going to war died down, and Vietnam revealed what it was really going to be like.[37]

Bundy reinjected himself in the Russian dialogue at the end of November, 1965, spending two hours with Ambassador Dobrynin going over the German question with reference to their joint concern to see that Bonn never got independent control of nuclear weapons. Vietnam came up at the end, but the ambassador's statement that a previous bombing pause had not given Moscow any opportunity to influence Hanoi's response caught at Bundy's sleeve. The Russians still probably could not "deliver" the North Vietnamese, as Rusk had put it, but the idea of a long pause had many things to recommend it—most particularly the need for repair work on the consensus at home before a new escalation. Critics of a pause, like Clark Clifford and Abe Fortas, were warning Johnson that when it failed to produce results he would be faced with the decision to resume, having pleased neither doves nor hawks. Dobrynin's urgings were something Bundy could use to persuade Johnson that a pause was the right step to take. Forwarding a memorandum of their conversation to the president, the national security adviser wrote, "I continue to think that the considerations are very evenly balanced, but I now think there is just a little more to be said in favor of the pause than has yet been fully presented to you."[38]

Against his better judgment, Johnson would say, he accepted the arguments Bundy and McNamara made for a bombing pause. He added flourishes to the pause by sending American diplomats to the far corners of the world to proclaim his good intentions and readiness to open negotiations, "We will meet at any conference table, we will discuss any proposals—four points or fourteen or forty—and we will consider the views of any group." Though obscured by all the pointless frenetic activity Johnson had set in motion, the American position had changed slightly. There was now a gray tinge on what had been an adamant black-and-white refusal to consider serious negotiations that would include Saigon's nemesis, the National Liberation Front.[39]

No direct appeal was made to the Soviets, but Harriman on his rounds as "ambassador for peace" met with several bloc country leaders, relating to them his belief stemming from the July sessions in Moscow that Kosygin wanted peace. The Soviets did send a politburo member to Hanoi, Alexander Shelepin, who presented the case for negotiations. But Ho Chi Minh's public letter to heads of state nixed any thought that Russia had bought a right to speak thus with its increasing supplies of arms and advisers. Nothing could happen, the Vietnamese leader insisted, as he no doubt had in private admonitions to his Russian visitor, until there was an unconditional halt to the bombing of North Vietnam.[40] After reading Ho's "message," Johnson wanted to know if the Russians were retreating from what Dobrynin had "told us." Not formally, came the answer from Bundy, but then they "don't assert they have tried to get Hanoi to the table."[41]

The exchange with Bundy was somewhat perplexing to Johnson, or should have been, because his national security adviser had clearly intimated a much stronger commitment on the Russian side, and much firmer confidence they could get things moving. It was Bundy who was retreating, not Dobrynin. Either that, or Bundy had misled the president. The exchange was not clarified because it came during a meeting to overcome objections to resuming the bombing at the end of January, 1966. At another meeting with the so-called "Wise Men"—former policymakers of senior rank from government and business—on January 28, 1966, Secretary of Defense McNamara, and others, described the situation as a test of wills. Early victory was out. The best he could offer was a doubling of American military forces and resumption of the bombing. If that were done, it "might be sufficient to break their will." Bombing involved risks, especially the possibility of a Chinese response, but he could not believe "the American people will long support a government which will not support by bombing [its] 400,000 troops there." Dean Rusk talked about Russia's predicament in frank terms. Were it not for the Chinese, he now argued, Moscow would be happy to go back to a "Geneva" solution to the problem. As for the bombing, he asserted that they did not object to bombing in the South—only in the North, because of their problems with Beijing as rival for leadership of the communist world.[42]

In effect, policymakers had reversed themselves. The bombing had been initiated, at least in part, to give Russia an excuse to put pressure on Hanoi—according to crisis-management logic—now it was admitted that Moscow was helpless because the DRV could enlist China's support. John J. McCloy delivered a harsh verdict on the pause. It sent the wrong message. The pause was undertaken largely for political purposes at home, he said, but all it succeeded in accomplishing was to convey the impression that "we've been too excited, too panicky—an indication of weakness to the enemy. . . . they are confirmed in their estimate that we are weak and feeling the pressures at home." Clark Clifford agreed, The "only way to get out of Vietnam is to persuade Hanoi we are too brave to be frightened and too strong to be defeated." As for China, Beijing will become bolder if we do not bomb. If we keep the strength of our air force before them, he went on, and make them feel we can destroy them—they will not.[43]

These remarks were similar in mood to written comments submitted to the public by a member of the Wise Men group not present that day, former Secretary of State Dean Acheson—who often served as their unofficial chairman, and who had played a key ancillary role in 1965 when they had been summoned to give their blessing to the decision to send the first 100,000 troops. Acheson had grown weary of Johnson's hand-wringing about his bad treatment by the "Harvards," who supposedly dominated the media, and who had never forgiven him for succeeding John Kennedy. "I blew my top," Acheson recalled, "and told him he was wholly right on Vietnam. . . . he had no choice except to press on. . . ."[44] Writing in the Detroit News, Acheson again saw it his duty to put some iron in LBJ's backbone. The article was entitled, "Vietnam an Asian 'Greece?'" and its subtitle told much of the story: "Reds Must Learn the Cost of Aggression." Acheson rehearsed a familiar pedagogical exercise in Cold War America: At a time when many thought Greece was lost to communism, President Harry Truman had stepped forward to halt the messianic force emanating from Moscow and turned it back in its tracks. Ever since, the communists had been seeking to outwit the West with variations on the Greek method. Vietnam was the latest. But fortunately in Saigon and Washington there was the same determination to "suppress the belligerency" Truman had displayed two decades earlier. Acheson's article concluded with a frightening citation of evidence from a leader of the other world—with the same purpose in mind as Bundy's memo a year earlier: "The Communist Chinese minister of defense, Marshal Lin Piao, in a speech on Sept. 3, referring to North America and Western Europe as the 'cities of the world' and to Asia, Africa, and Latin America as the 'rural areas,' declared that 'contemporary world revolution also presents a picture of the encirclement of cities by the rural areas.'"[45]

Back in the Cabinet Room, Johnson had reached his decision. "I was the first Congressman to speak up for the Truman Doctrine," he closed the proceedings. "I am not happy about Vietnam but we cannot run out—we have to resume bombing."[46]

While the Russian "connection" on Vietnam was once again in abeyance, other negotiations were underway on nuclear weapons. One purpose these negotiations served—regardless of their immediate outcome—was the implied enlistment of the Soviet Union on the side of the "cities" against the Chinese-sponsored "rural" revolution. Another indication of Russian "maturity" as a world power was Kosygin's successful mediation of an India-Pakistan dispute. Thus, at the same time Johnson was girding up his loins to resume bombing, he wrote a pen pal letter to Kosygin, congratulating him on the Tashkent agreement and outlining the American position on a nuclear nonproliferation treaty.[47]

New National Security Adviser Walt Rostow told Johnson that the expectations for Russian action on the Vietnam question had gone the wrong way. Harriman's efforts, and others, had been influenced by the idea that American pressure on Hanoi would convince the Russians to use their influence to bring about negotiations out of concern for the general state of East-West relations. It had been hoped, moreover, that an increased Russian military "presence" would add to Moscow's leverage. It was not going to work that way. Hanoi welcomed the Russians as a counterweight to Beijing, yes, "but only we—not Moscow—can push them over the hump into negotiations."

And to do that required a still greater military effort: "It is not, Mr. President, that I'm bloody-minded or a hawk. But the strain of trying to do the job principally by attrition of main force units places almost intolerable burdens on the political life of our country and on the war-weary South Vietnamese. *We've got to try to shorten this war without doing unwise or desperate things.*"[48]

There was a growing feeling, nevertheless, that Moscow had somehow let the Western side down in Vietnam. Despite Kohler's and Harriman's predictions that Moscow could not be used the way Washington wanted—or as cover for American mistakes, as the conversations on ending the pause implied—there was a tendency to blame the Soviets for not pulling their weight. Here was an odd variation on the idea that Russia had prompted Ho to act, blaming the Kremlin for succumbing to instant gratification instead of obeying the Weberian rules for capitalist success. Thomas Hughes, the director of intelligence and research in the State Department, who had called attention to the noteworthy developments in Kosygin's final discussion with Averell Harriman, now pretty much agreed with the skeptics. "The troublesome thing about how Brezhnev and Kosygin have handled themselves," he wrote Rostow, "is that they do not seem to have thought much beyond current profit to the time when their willingness to hitch their cart to Hanoi's horse may lead them into a direct confrontation with us that can no longer be glossed over, like their present involvement in some of Hanoi's air defense. Perhaps the time has come to get that message across more clearly."[49]

Even though he professed a belief that the Russian option was a will-o'-the-wisp, Rostow drafted a letter to Kosygin for Johnson's signature that used the Tashkent agreement as argument for Kremlin recognition of the common interest the two countries had in persuading Hanoi to respect the 1954 Geneva and 1962 Laos Accords. "Looking back over the past year," this surprising draft read, "I believe both our governments have cause for satisfaction in the progress made towards stabilizing an important region where conflict would be contrary to the interests of the Soviet and American peoples." Congratulations on Tashkent were followed by, "It appears to me to be now urgently in our common interest to persuade the authorities in Hanoi to end this violation of the 1962 Accords and bring the issue of Vietnam to the negotiating table at the earliest possible time."[50]

Dean Rusk took up the question with Dobrynin directly, asking why the Soviet Union could not "lift a finger" to help with the question of North Vietnamese violations of Cambodian neutrality? That could be a starting point and then things could move on to re-establishing the framework of the 1954 and 1962 agreements. The ambassador was not encouraging. He had talked with Brezhnev and Kosygin while back in Moscow, and all they had said was that the bombing was creating a dangerous situation. Rusk agreed, but during the last pause the North Vietnamese had insisted the United States accept the NLF as the sole representative of the South Vietnamese people. "We could stop the bombing again, but not on a unilateral basis, while the infiltration was stepped-up." This remained the American position until Johnson's March 31, 1968, speech. Rusk's offer to "go back to" Geneva had been debated within the Johnson administration, with some officials pointing out that Geneva probably would not be acceptable to Saigon because of the still-unfilled requirement for all-Vietnamese elections. Vietnamese specialist Robert Komer had pointed out to LBJ's confidant Jack Valenti that Geneva did not have a good smell in Moscow or Hanoi, either. "The Russians appear to recognize that their leverage with Hanoi is very tenuous on such questions as negotiations (Hanoi still harbors, with good reason, the feeling that Moscow sold out the Viet Minh at the 1954 Geneva Conference)."[51]

From time to time, in addition to Rusk's suggestions that the two powers get behind a push to reopen the Geneva agreements to take into account the current situation, American officials communicated to their Russian counterparts, and through foreign leaders, the message that the United States wanted no permanent military bases in Vietnam. Over the summer of 1966 a stream of reports was directed to the Kremlin concerning American desires to connect Vietnam with the successful negotiation of the German question, and a nuclear nonproliferation treaty, which had languished because of the various schemes advanced for allowing the Bonn government a role, as in the now-defunct MLF plan. The Soviets wanted an airtight pact that would prohibit any sort of "transfer" of nuclear capabilities to German hands by virtue of its membership in NATO. The American response continued to be that the United States did not have authority to rule on East German participation in Warsaw Pact consultations, so how could Moscow expect the United States to yield on NATO? Hungarian sources in Washington, meanwhile, had heard that the United States was willing to go further than in the past on all East-West questions if the Soviets proved more forthcoming on Vietnam.[52] When the Soviet delegation at the United Nations suddenly came forward with a proposal for using a routine visit to the opening session of the UN General Assembly to initiate high-level negotiations, Averell Harriman snapped to attention. Here was an opportunity—perhaps the last, he warned—to engage the Soviet Union in "constructive action." Afraid that Dean Rusk would prove unequal to the task, Harriman directed his memos to the Oval Office as well as to the secretary's office. It was the first glimmer of light in many months, he urged. "Dean's talk could end it, or be the beginning of positive discussions."[53]

Harriman also submitted a lengthy memorandum on talking points that held out the possibility that this could be the beginning of a new relationship with the Soviet Union, not just on Vietnam, but on other issues. Indeed, he would take out the "hardware participation" option for Germans and compensate them by concessions on the offset agreements (payments to the United States for troop costs). Few Germans, Harriman wrote Johnson and Rusk in yet another memorandum, really believed a nuclear role would ever happen anyway, but offset concessions could sweeten the disappointment. It would add to the dollar drain, but it would be worth it to end hostilities in Vietnam: "In sum, I believe that we will have to agree on some arrangement affecting Germany if we are to induce Moscow to act in Vietnam. I recognize the political difficulties in Germany at the present time, but our interests are so overwhelming to get the war over in Vietnam, that I cannot help but feel we should move as rapidly as feasible."[54]

These were breathtaking proposals. For several months John McCloy had headed a special mission to reach agreement on offset payments, as part of his ongoing sense of obligation to the welfare of American-European relations. Such a proposal would not go down well with him. And, as noted, McCloy had always seen Vietnam through Eurocentric eyes. Now, Harriman was boldly declaring that Vietnam took precedence—Vietnam and Soviet-American détente. Rusk's talks with Andrei Gromyko at UN headquarters did not move the nuclear nonproliferation treaty much closer to reality. And there was no talk of a "deal" involving Vietnam. The Soviet foreign minister traveled to Washington a few days later to meet with Johnson. Interesting things happened there. Gromyko opened the meeting by professing his profound confusion about American foreign policy. If the United States were ready to promote international détente, however, it would find the Soviet Union ready to go forward.[55] Johnson rambled on at length about his Vietnam policy, reviewing the usual arguments, and adding only that he was ready to pull out the troops and convert the bases. He concluded this presentation saying that he "had difficulty resisting pressures" to do more against North Vietnam, but it was not his purpose to "destroy" the DRV or change its government. Gromyko said the Soviet government paid attention to American statements desiring an end to the war but did not see it take any steps in that direction. Although the Soviet Union did not engage in the Vietnamese negotiations, it did not deny having "influence" among its friends. "The Soviet Union was in favor of ending the war in Vietnam and believe(d) this was in the interests of the great powers, including the United States. The first of first steps was to stop the bombing. . . . He could not say what North Vietnam or the NLF would do, but the reaction would be a different one. He repeated he was prepared to say that the behavior of the other side would be different if the United States ended the bombing of North Vietnam."[56]

Johnson brought up Soviet assurances about the earlier bombing pause. He had heard this all before—but through Mac Bundy's ears as we have seen, when the national security adviser wanted an additional reason to have a bombing pause to satisfy domestic opinion. Gromyko did not deny that the Soviets had previously pushed the idea—but the United States had attached conditions to the halt. The second thing Johnson must do, Gromyko went on, was to make a concrete statement about the withdrawal of American forces, not just talk generally. This might be of use in Hanoi. "He said that the Soviet Union was not holding anything back and was acting in good faith. They would like to see the end of the war."

There was a short discussion of the nuclear nonproliferation treaty that did not seem to move the question forward at all, but Gromyko left the White House to tell reporters that he felt both sides were anxious to reach an agreement. The press declared that the impasse had been broken. Somewhat alarmed, Ambassador-at-Large Llewellyn Thompson spoke with Dobrynin about the impression Gromyko had left. Was Thompson particularly disturbed by the press reports? Dobrynin asked. Thompson said only that both sides realized remaining problems were difficult. It was a very interesting exchange. Gromyko's "misleading" statements to the reporters may have carried a message about Soviet bona fides relating to the idea of a settlement in Vietnam, or it may not, and it may well have been intended to mobilize American opinion to support a nuclear arms agreement satisfactory to the Kremlin, but it certainly suggested a desire to work with the United States across a spectrum of issues.[57]

When President Johnson traveled to Manila a short while later to attend a conference of nations participating in the Vietnam War, he tried to meet one of Gromyko's "conditions" by setting a date for American withdrawal six months "after"—but after what? His deliberate vagueness led to criticism in several quarters, especially from Richard Nixon, who claimed that such an unwise commitment would leave the South Vietnamese unprotected against renewed subversion and would thus spell disaster for the whole Vietnam effort. Johnson had to be vague. The question here was one of "timing," not how long it would take the United States to evacuate the various installations such as Cam Ranh Bay but how Washington would decide that the time was right to go. Americans would not leave until—it was pointed out in official commentaries—"the level of violence . . . subsides." That meant some time *after* a negotiated agreement, and *after* confirmation the insurgency had come to an end. Johnson put a friendly face on this crucial caveat during a press conference in early November, 1966: "Why would we want to stay there if there was no aggression, if there was no infiltration and the violence ceased? We wouldn't want to stay there as tourists. We wouldn't want to keep 400,000 men there just to march up and down the runways at Cam Ranh Bay."[58]

The promise, therefore, was really an assurance to Moscow that the United States would not use South Vietnam as a jumping-off place to attack North Vietnam or some other member of the "socialist" bloc. It in no way met the issue of the future of South Vietnam, although the president had attempted to convey to Moscow in a variety of ways that the United States was prepared to allow genuine self-determination for the Vietnamese. Indeed, American policy in 1967 was shaped in part by a desire to prepare postwar South Vietnam for ways of settling issues with its internal opposition. The emphasis on at least a

semblance of democratic rule, the private memoranda on who could participate in South Vietnam's political life after the war ended, all pointed in such a
direction. But more could not be talked about with anyone outside the
president's circle without risking a terrible disintegration at home as well as
abroad.[59]

The delicate nature of this kind of maneuver was underlined by a draft letter to Kosygin that was heavily edited—and apparently never sent—stressing
the connection between negotiations on nuclear questions and Vietnam. The
idea for the letter emanated in late December, 1966, from a State Department
committee assigned to explore negotiation possibilities and headed, inevitably, by Averell Harriman. The "Harriman Committee" suggested that newly
appointed Ambassador Llewellyn Thompson be given broad latitude to "pursue the question of negotiations" with the Russians—a probable attempt to
get around Dean Rusk's supposed lack of flexibility. One deleted passage from
the draft reiterated Johnson's belief in the special responsibility that Moscow
and Washington shared for the "peace of the world." After a typical rehearsing
of the American version of the history of the Vietnam War, the letter said that
the "sole objective" of American policy was to permit the Vietnamese to "decide their own future" within the framework of the 1954 and 1962 accords.
Repeating that there was nothing that could force the United States to abandon its commitment to that objective, the letter suggested that there were two
alternatives: negotiations or a gradual tapering off of military action (the fa-
vorite Rusk solution) by both sides.

There were several ways negotiations could be started, the letter went on,
but the aim would be to permit self-determination for South Vietnam, and
then this interesting deleted passage, "and assurance against any further attempt
to take over that country by force." The letter closed with an appeal that mutual respect for treaty commitments was really at the heart of what the war was
about. "We fully recognize and respect the interest of the Soviet Union in the
security of North Viet-Nam. We must suppose that you understand our interest in and our treaty commitments to the security of South Viet-Nam. Surely
it is to the best interests of both of us as well as both South and North Viet-
Nam to find a way to stop the fighting and let any outstanding questions be
settled by peaceful means."[60]

The heavy editing of the draft letter indicates why it was never sent. It was
impossible to devise a letter that would meet all the requirements of this very
top-secret discussion within the Johnson administration—which brought out
obvious differences without easy resolution—so the problem was attacked in
an entirely different manner. Ambassador Thompson was given a letter dealing solely with nuclear issues, and it was decided to send a separate letter to

Ho Chi Minh. The letter to the North Vietnamese leader went through several drafts, and became enmeshed in one of the most Byzantine episodes of the entire war. In brief, the confusion resulted from separate negotiations going on in Moscow and London, involving, in the latter case, Kosygin and British Prime Minister Harold Wilson. The Moscow negotiations had left the impression that the United States was prepared to stop the bombing, with the expectation of an early North Vietnamese response accepting talks and a collateral scaling down of its side of the war. For a variety of reasons, LBJ backed off that position and in messages to Wilson—who had led Kosygin to believe the American position was as stated above—and in his letter to Ho, the president offered to end the bombing only after he had been assured infiltration had ceased. The episode was so ringed with conflicting messages and competing urges that it almost defied explication; it was, therefore, the Vietnam imbroglio in microcosm. Unraveling all the threads is a fascinating exercise, but a very time-consuming one.[61]

For our purposes here, it is sufficient to say that both Wilson and Kosygin felt deeply aggrieved, all the more so because the North Vietnamese had actually asked Moscow—for the first time, really—to sound out the Americans. Kosygin may have read more into Hanoi's communications than was there and missed signals that the North Vietnamese were downgrading the idea of negotiations, but he had gone to London convinced that he could repeat his success in the Tashkent negotiations with India and Pakistan. Washington's apparent reneging on its own terms may have been no more deflating than Hanoi's recalcitrance, but it appeared so even to American diplomats who were trying to keep up with their constantly changing instructions. Faced with sharp criticism from the British prime minister, Johnson actually relented just a bit, but his offer to halt the bombing if he received an assurance from Hanoi that "all movement of troops and supplies into South Vietnam will stop at that time" was in some respects even stiffer than his letter to Ho—especially as Kosygin was given less than twenty-four hours to get a reply from the North Vietnamese.[62]

Kosygin was "vexed by the whole proceeding," Anatoly Dobrynin has written, all the more so because Johnson had previously "passed word to us that when Kosygin appeared at a televised press conference . . . , he hoped the premier would find 'the right wording' for his answers so as not to provoke the increasingly bellicose right in the United States."[63] Dobrynin's recollection is less than the full story. The American account of his conversation with Deputy Undersecretary of State Foy Kohler records the latter cautioning Dobrynin that the whole range of issues, including discussions of limitations on ABM (antiballistic missile) deployment, the Consular Convention and Outer Space Treaty, and East-West "legislation" in general, as well as Vietnam peace efforts, would suffer if the Russians complained too loudly. Kohler hoped that Kosygin would not "let himself be pressed into statements which might complicate matters here or be injurious to the process of solution of some of the problems between us." Ambassador Dobrynin said he understood.[64]

Kosygin responded to this remarkable request by informing his ambassador in Washington that it was fruitless to pursue the diplomatic route, and the Soviet Union would do its duty in terms of "proletarian internationalism" by sending arms to Hanoi and leave it at that.[65] Harriman tried hard to convince Johnson that the Soviet leader could hardly do otherwise, if he wanted to escape Chinese accusations that he was a "stooge" of American imperialism. "You may have noticed," Harriman wrote Johnson, "the Red Guard have gone so far as to call him a traitor who should be 'burned.'"[66]

Keep in mind, he went on, it is what the Communist leaders tell us privately that really matters. "I doubt if a peaceful settlement can be made with Hanoi at the present time unless it is underwritten by the Soviet Union. Hanoi needs 800,000 to 1,000,000 tons of rice to eat, not to speak of other supplies."[67] When Kosygin and Ambassador Thompson reviewed the events of the London "week," later in February, Thompson tried to emphasize American restraint in the face of constant provocation. During the bombing stand-down for the Tet holiday, he asserted, the North had shipped down as much as 25,000 tons of supplies—more than they usually were able to move in a month's time. Kosygin was scathing in his reply. For the first time, he replied, Hanoi had said that it was willing to negotiate if the bombing was stopped unconditionally. What was really gained by restarting the bombing without waiting three or four more days? Twenty-five thousand tons of supplies, he scoffed. What about the American reinforcements during the same period? Probably as much as 100,000 tons. Thompson attempted to rebut this accusation with the argument that the Americans were in South Vietnam by invitation, but Kosygin was already on to the next point. The United States was ignoring China, a grave error. For all the American insistence that it was fighting China in Vietnam, it was China, and only China, that profited from the American-Russian failure to get the Vietnam problem resolved. Kosygin's pleas in favor of negotiations had drawn a furious reaction in Beijing. That alone should testify to the seriousness of his efforts. Then he elaborated: "Chinese want extension of [the] war, and this is why they reacted the way they did to his statement in London. US was helping those forces by its actions; US left USSR open vis-à-vis China, it also left North Vietnam open vis-à-vis China. Net result is that Chinese view has triumphed, and Chinese can now say that all those efforts were nothing but a masquerade."[68]

Ambassador Thompson reiterated for the thousand and first time that the United States did not see Vietnam as one country, which was, apparently, the basis for Russian arguments that "infiltration" was a two-way problem—and a defensive one at that on the part of the Vietnamese "people" to combat American intervention. And he repeated Johnson's promise that Americans would close all their bases and come home once the fighting was over. Kosygin reverted to the China question. Did the United States not understand that China stood perched to exploit the situation throughout Asia? In India, Pakistan, the Philippines, Thailand, etc.? "[The] Saigon regime was sitting on [an] island surrounded by [a] sea of civil war. Its situation could be compared to that of Kolchak or Denikin during [the] Russian civil war. Also, it could be compared to position of Archangel Gov't, against which he himself had fought. US, as well as others, had sought to make use of those governments but all that ended in failure."[69]

Kosygin's tirade against the shortsightedness of American policy, laced with reminders of Allied intervention in the Bolshevik Revolution, was hardly a pleasing way to convey a not-very-disguised message that *neither one of them* could rely on the Saigon regime to block Chinese expansion in Southeast Asia—or beyond. A strongly nationalist Vietnamese government, led inevitably by Ho Chi Minh and his presumed successors, the Soviet leader was saying, would serve as a much more reliable bulwark. The conversation took an odd turn at the end. Requesting Thompson's indulgence, Kosygin asked if the Chinese had approached Washington about the possibility of negotiations! Obviously it could not be ruled out, from his point of view, that he had been undercut in London in order to make way for a Chinese-American settlement to Russia's disadvantage. How else, perhaps, to explain an American policy that on the surface seemed to be playing into Beijing's hands, unless there was some devious, secret game afoot.

Imagine for a moment, if you will, the impact the leaking of this document would have made on Congress and the public—with its obvious refutation of a crusade to humiliate the United States and advance the world revolution. Kosygin made it clear that it was the *United States* that was advancing the revolutionary cause by making China's predictions come true! In his ever-optimistic fashion, National Security Adviser Walt Rostow took Kosygin's "preoccupation with China" and his final inquiry as good signs that American policy had started a bidding game between the Communist giants.[70] A few days later, Johnson was ruminating about the state of diplomatic play with Drew Pearson. "When I talked to Gromyko [in October]," the president said, he "promised to throw his weight on our side for peace, and I am sure he did his best. But he just didn't have the same weight that apparently the Chinese have. When the

Chinese get a little weaker and the Russians stronger, we're going to have a peace."[71]

Johnson's conclusion appears to have been made up of equal parts of Averell Harriman's reasoning, Rostow's optimism, and his own belief that Moscow would be moved by American ability to hold up or further agreements that were of crucial importance to Soviet leaders in their anxiety to keep nuclear weapons out of German hands and slow down the arms race. Ambassador Thompson had written an analysis of the Russian situation the previous December that would have led LBJ to think along those lines: "Given the economic problems which the Soviets already face in the allocation of their resources, which are insufficient to meet their goals, I believe that their civilian leaders would welcome an opportunity to avoid incurring the enormous expenditure which the deployment of a major ABM system would entail, at least over the next few years."[72]

It is unlikely, however, that Johnson ever really thought he had the Russians over a barrel on Vietnam. There were too many troubles plaguing American policy for that to be the case. There was, for example, the French defection, dating back to 1964, when France announced at a SEATO meeting that it could not support American policy in Vietnam and issued a separate statement from the communiqué supporting Washington's defense of the Saigon government. Two years later, Charles de Gaulle had separated France from NATO, ordering the organization to close its offices on French territory. Although he promised that France would always stand with the West, his overtures to Moscow were more than slight irritations, for they seemed to threaten the integrity of the alliance. And then there was de Gaulle's challenge to the suzerainty of the dollar, a weak spot in Johnson's ability to go on enlarging the floating debt of paper to finance the war and the Great Society.[73] At a NATO council meeting in December, 1967, Secretary of State Rusk appealed for understanding of the American position. There were those in Washington who wanted to bill de Gaulle for the relocation of NATO headquarters; indeed, there were those who wanted to reopen the question of French debts from World War I. What the allies do not realize, Rusk went on, was that "the present position of the United States amounts to a near miracle. More than half a million Americans are involved in Southeast Asia, most of them in combat. In spite of that, the United States is maintaining its forces in Europe." The willingness of the American people to continue bearing those burdens was perhaps being taken too much for granted.[74]

When Rusk and others talked to the Europeans bilaterally, it was about the need for support in maintaining force levels, in helping with "offset" payments for American forces, and so on, but never about abandoning a "lost cause" in

Vietnam. This was a difficult situation, to say the least, for while the secretary of state continued to insist that European capitals had a great stake in a successful end to the war, it now seemed that they were being called upon to "pay" for American credibility—a reversal from the original idea that Europe "profited" from American willingness to stay the course. Added to these woes, Kosygin's promises of increased aid to North Vietnam were now evident to American observers. Harriman once more insisted that there was a silver lining to Moscow's determination to prevent a North Vietnamese collapse. It may well give the Russians more leverage in Hanoi. They are humiliated, he added, that they cannot prevent the "destruction of our intensified air and naval attacks," but they still are not "greatly concerned by what happens in the South. . . . I believe it is still possible to find a way to get the Soviet Government to participate actively in obtaining a settlement in Vietnam."[75]

The open record of American diplomacy in encouraging a Russian "mediatory" role had begun to present a problem, however, in dealing with European leaders beyond the offset question. As if reading Harriman's mail, German Chancellor Kurt Kiesinger's "defensive attitude" raised the question of whether America's "global responsibilities" in Vietnam would not force Washington "to some degree to sell out German interests." The president must convince him, Walt Rostow urged, "You are not counting on Moscow's bailing us out in Vietnam." And that, "Anything we have ever gotten from Moscow was because of our strength and unity in the West."[76]

Whatever the peril of further defections in the Western alliance, Johnson initiated a new appeal to Kosygin on May 19, 1967, citing not only Vietnam, but also the darkening situation in the Middle East, and supposed Cuban involvement in the internal affairs of South American countries. "I would wish you to consider if—whatever our differences—our common interests do not now require concerted or parallel action to bring these situations under control."[77] In a somewhat circuitous fashion, this correspondence led to the "Glassboro Summit" the following month. Kosygin traveled down the New Jersey Turnpike from the Soviet mission to the United Nations to what was then Glassboro State College, now Rowan University, a site selected because it would not allow critics in the Communist world to say that he had gone all the way to Washington to pay a call on the president of the United States—a doubly humiliating exercise, supposedly, because Moscow's client states in the Middle East had just lost the Six-Day War to Israel, and the Soviet Union was still unable to protect North Vietnam against American bombers. How accurate this assessment was is hard to tell, but certainly Johnson and Rostow wanted to balance their approach to insure that Kosygin was neither humiliated nor made to feel he had the upper hand.[78] As Rostow wrote to the president, the approach should be "that we welcome the Soviet Union as the other 'older child' in the family of nations and look to the Soviet Union as a partner in setting a framework which will avoid hostility between ourselves and by the other members of the family."[79] Ambassador Thompson cabled from Moscow that there was more to say at the first "summit" of the Johnson administration about the joint interests of the two countries with the most power in the atomic age: "Unfortunately, more than one government [is] trying to cause trouble between us in short-sighted view of their narrow selfish interests. Important that we be frank with each other and have the kind of relations which will enable us to frustrate efforts of troublemakers. We believe in real co-existence and not mere absence of war between us. We must find way to prevent quarrels between other countries from involving us. . . . Essential that we not devote our energies to working against interests of the other or to let other small countries try to solve their problems by engaging the two of us in a head-on collision."[80]

The line-up of "small countries" Thompson had in mind probably started with the Middle East, but it would have to include, by this reasoning, pretty much the rest of the world. However that may be, McGeorge Bundy, called to the White House to consult on the summit, thought it important that the president clear up one point at the outset—the bombing of North Vietnam while Kosygin was in Hanoi. "I think you ought to tell him—in a wholly private word—that you had no intention of involving him in any way—you had long since determined that you would *have* to react at once to the next direct attack on US installations there—and your hand was forced by the people who hit Pleiku. (I believe this quite personal concern of his is entirely separate from the general question of bombing.)"[81] What a turnaround this was for one who had urged the attacks to demonstrate that nothing the Russians could do would save North Vietnam from the wrath of the righteous!

Everyone who sent in advice recommended that LBJ show a friendly, but firm, face to this "old pro" Kosygin. Probably not since FDR welcomed Stalin to the "family circle" at Tehran had there been so much talk about older brothers and the rest of the world, about the great responsibility that fell on their shoulders to keep order, about mutual respect for one another's vital interests.[82] At their first meeting, on June 23, the Russian premier opened the discussion with an apology for having caused the president such difficulty in finding a suitable place to meet. Johnson waved that aside and segued neatly into a "family" discussion. How many children were there in Kosygin's family? he asked. Just two, the premier said, he and his sister. Well, said Johnson, there were five in his. Often he—the oldest brother—and the oldest sister "had to take special pains in order to avoid disputes and differences between them so as to set a good example for the other children in the family." While he did not want to appear paternalistic toward the Soviet Union, LBJ went on, he thought that if the two could work together, they could multiply their resources to help their peoples—and the rest of the world, no doubt—to a better life. Kosygin responded that whenever they discussed problems on a global scale, there seemed to be complete agreement on goals. But whenever they began to discuss specifics, "then a great many difficulties and differences arose." And right away, discussing the Middle East, the differences did appear about who was responsible for the events leading to the Six-Day War and its aftermath. Johnson quickly put the Middle East alongside the issues of ABM deployment and Vietnam, suggesting that all were the kind of responsibility that belonged to older brothers to resolve. Kosygin kept pressing, however, on Israel's responsibility for the continuing tension in the area until the two broke for lunch.[83]

After lunch, Kosygin took the initiative to inform Johnson "in strictest confidence" that in anticipation of their meeting he had contacted Hanoi to ask what he could do to help bring about an end to the war. Pham Van Dong's reply had come in just as they were eating. In substance, it said that if the United States stopped the bombing, they would immediately go to the conference table. Kosygin thought this opened a real opportunity to move forward toward peace. Remember, he said, that General de Gaulle had fought the Algerians for seven years and still wound up at the conference table. Johnson put the obvious next question. Suppose we went to the conference table this very minute, he said, would that mean fighting would continue as it did during the Korean peace negotiations? Kosygin could not guarantee the war would end, of course. But he was not done with history lessons. "With great emphasis he made the point that while the President thought he was fighting the Chinese in North Korea, Mr. Kosygin had to tell him that he was actually helping the Chinese in achieving their very worst designs."[84]

The president then countered that of course China presented a danger to both countries, and he certainly did not want to aid them in their designs. But he would be "crucified" if he took the decision to stop the bombing, and the five divisions the North Vietnamese had poised immediately north of the DMZ moved into action against American troops. Kosygin suggested that Johnson set one condition: that representatives of the two countries meet within two days. But the president still demurred. Would the Soviets provide "assistance at the conference table" to obtain "self-determination for the people of South Viet-Nam?" Here, of course, was the real difficulty. After all the effort, the casualties, the expenditure, the administration's insistence that its critics were wrong, how could the United States take part in a peace conference that merely turned over South Vietnam to the enemy? Now it was Kosygin's turn to demur. He could not decide such a question without "advice" from Hanoi. Johnson elaborated. He had told Gromyko, he said, that if the Soviet Union could help obtain such an agreement, then the United States would "ultimately" withdraw its forces. Free elections in South Vietnam, under the auspices of the co-chairs of the 1954 Geneva Conference, would fulfill "the conditions of such an agreement." Undoubtedly wary of what was being said so fast—for example, the idea of free elections in the South was not part of the duties of the co-chairs of the 1954 conference—Kosygin suggested that Johnson reduce all these things to a paper, which he would then transmit to Hanoi. Johnson proposed they meet again in two days, presumably so such a document could be prepared. Kosygin closed with a statement that he "felt very strongly that Viet-Nam destroyed much that had developed between the United States and the USSR and had given China a chance to raise its head with consequent great danger for the peace of the entire world."[85]

The message was duly prepared and handed over to Kosygin. It stipulated that there be immediate discussions, and that neither side take military advantage of a bombing halt. In an "oral" message so that Kosygin would understand "what is in my mind," Johnson further stipulated that if the talks did not lead to peace or if protracted talks were used to gain a one-sided advantage, "we shall have to resume full freedom of action."[86] Kosygin promised that as soon as he heard anything from Hanoi, he would let Johnson know at once.

There never was a reply. Once again, it appears that the premier exaggerated his ability to get peace talks under way. He may have assumed that he could obtain from Johnson a statement that the bombing would be ended unconditionally, and from Hanoi, a promise to go to the peace table within a few days. He wagered on both ends—and lost.[87] To broker a successful ending of the Vietnam War was highly advantageous to the Soviet leadership. Their estimates of Saigon's weakness were confirmed by LBJ's inquiry about Russian help at the peace conference to insure that the South would have self-determination through free elections. If the peace conference proceeded in any other way, it would merely confirm the combined power of the NLF/DRV to set the agenda for future reunification. Kosygin thought the stakes were high enough: new prestige for the Soviets as peacemakers (and for himself personally), a satisfying triumph over China and its supporters in the Third World, and over the United States.

How he weighed those traditional ambitions and sympathies against American efforts to engage the Soviet Union as a partner in the American-ordered world is hard to say. At the conclusion of the Glassboro talks, he reported to Moscow, "Johnson and his associates treated us in a friendly manner, paid us much attention and tried to show their eagerness to find solutions to crucial problems."[88] One small sign emerged from a comment French leader Charles de Gaulle made to the American ambassador concerning Kosygin's stopover in Paris. The Russian premier told de Gaulle that Moscow did not intend to rearm Egypt and other Arab states to the same extent as previously. Unfortunately, Kosygin opined, the United States was too preoccupied with Vietnam to do anything about steps to limit Israeli actions![89]

But the Russian-American talks on Vietnam had still produced no breakthrough. When Rusk probed Dobrynin about an answer to Johnson's message, the reply he received was what Kosygin had told General de Gaulle: Moscow believed that America's attitudes on both the Middle East and Vietnam "precluded" any Soviet efforts to assist in the latter matter. Irritated, Rusk said that was not what he asked. He had asked if there had been a reply. Dobrynin said that he had said all he could say.[90] Rusk repeated the question at later sessions, with no more luck.

The Russians did claim that American steps in the direction of expanding the war during the summer months had put the DRV in the position that it could not conceive of the Glassboro message as conveying anything new. "Furthermore," an official scolded Ambassador Thompson, "it is not the first time that it has happened that immediately following upon a sounding taken by the USA a new buildup of military actions against the Vietnamese people and an intensification of the bombing of the territory of the DRV have occurred." One could only express regret that American actions did not contribute "at all" to a peaceful settlement.[91]

Rusk responded mildly that he felt regret that there was no sign of any willingness on Hanoi's part to think about a mutual deescalation—an indication that he believed the only avenue open to peace now was the Greek analogy. Johnson, meanwhile, had taken heart from what were claimed to be victories in the "other war" in Vietnam—the progress toward a constitutional government that would enlist the hearts and minds of the South Vietnamese on Saigon's side in the battle with its enemies. "There is no stalemate," he told a television commentator. "There is no failure militarily in Vietnam." No Democrat and no Republican would ever receive a mandate to sell out Vietnam. "I do think we can build a nation. Korea did it. I think that South Vietnam is doing it now." Even so, he wanted "so badly" to sit down and talk. And he still got the feeling that Kosygin "is trying to help." All America wanted was to prevent a takeover by force. "If they take it by votes, that's a different matter, okay."[92]

In September, Johnson told an audience in San Antonio that he would halt the bombing if the DRV agreed to early talks and to not "take advantage" of the situation. Few thought this marked much of a change in American policy, even though LBJ no longer called for a cessation of infiltration as in his letter to Ho the previous February. Hanoi labeled the offer "sheer deception." It had to await explication by a new secretary of defense, Clark Clifford, but the San Antonio "formula" did eventually play a part in getting talks started.[93] By late fall Johnson felt compelled to summon the Wise Men to another meeting on Vietnam. One impetus for the meeting had been the growing disillusionment of Secretary of Defense McNamara. Led by Dean Acheson, the Wise Men squelched all talk of quitting—no matter its source. He was an even greater advocate of the Greek analogy than Dean Rusk, predicting that there would be no negotiations, "because that's not how the Communists operate." When he said this at lunch with Johnson, all the rest, save one or two, nodded in agreement.[94]

Interestingly, after listening to the Wise Men, Johnson once again defended the Soviet Union's performance in the war to a gathering of Democratic members of the House of Representatives. "She supplies them equipment just like you'd supply your brother. That doesn't mean that she's out there with her guns shooting at us herself. And that's a lot of difference. Lot of difference."[95]

The debate over sending another 200,000 men to Vietnam in the aftermath of the Tet Offensive brought big changes in the attitudes of the Wise Men, with Dean Acheson again leading the way, but this time toward disengagement. Averell Harriman, who stood less in awe of these performances by his old Yale compatriot, had meanwhile sought out Dobrynin for another go at getting Moscow involved in peace talks. He invited the ambassador to lunch at his home on N Street in Georgetown. Dobrynin stayed for three and a half hours. Did the Soviet Union want to see the war end? Harriman asked him bluntly, or did the Kremlin believe its interests were served by having the United States enmeshed in the conflict? Dobrynin insisted that his government wanted to see the war end because there were so many bilateral matters in more important areas to be settled. Sounding very much like Edward "Colonel" House during World War I talks with the Kaiser's advisers about the need for cooperation in the "waste areas" of the world, Harriman then suggested that "we might work together on reconstruction and development of Southeast Asia as a whole." Dobrynin was noncommittal, Harriman recorded, "but he did not take issue with my statement that we were working in a parallel line, attempting to strengthen the subcontinent against possible advances of Red China in that area."[96]

Harriman then tried a little different line, suggesting that it would be better if the Soviet Union were directly involved in getting Hanoi to the peace table, rather than leaving it up to contacts the United States had established with one or more of the satellite countries of Eastern Europe. After more desultory talk on these lines, Dobrynin asked why the United States did not take the chance, stop the bombing and see what would happen? Harriman was in the midst of giving the usual response when an idea occurred to him: "I then asked him whether he thought it would help the Soviet Union if we should stop the bombing of North Vietnam except for the southern part north of the DMZ?" "You mean," he inquired, "this would be in place of the assumption of 'no advantage'?" "Well," said Harriman, "it might be interpreted as that." Dobrynin showed interest but did not give a definite reply. Walt Rostow marked this passage in Harriman's memorandum of the conversation; he and Harriman met privately with the Soviet ambassador late in the afternoon of March 31, to show him a copy of the dramatic speech Johnson was about to give announcing a partial bombing halt. Then the ambassador was ushered into the president's office to hear what Johnson now expected of his government. Going back to Geneva, Johnson began, the Soviet Union had been directly involved in Vietnam questions, and now it was up to Moscow, as a major arms supplier, to bring its influence to bear for a conference and the making of peace. He had hoped after Glassboro that Premier Kosygin wished to be helpful, but nothing had come of it. But now the time had come, if there was ever to be a chance of Soviet-American cooperation. "In South Vietnam itself the contending parties must give up war and seek a one-man, one-vote solution." He was not being pushed into a corner by the "doves," LBJ insisted, but by the forty percent of Americans who wanted him to do more. "That was the problem with which he had to deal. . . . The President had great concern about Southeast Asia as a whole, not only Vietnam. He feared a much wider war that would be contrary to both our interests and the Soviet [Union]'s interests. He thought perhaps the Chinese were getting 'cocky' and 'chesty.' Their aggressive ambitions should not be encouraged. It was up to the U.S. and the U.S.S.R. to end the war in Vietnam soon and prevent hostilities from spreading."[97]

Dobrynin asked a few questions and departed. Johnson then went before the television cameras to shock the nation—not so much with his announcement of a partial bombing halt—but with his announcement that he would not stand for election to another term as president. The Soviet ambassador was as surprised as anyone. Harriman again invited him to lunch, to see if he had grasped the significance of all that had taken place. In the American's mind, the basic outline of a settlement had already taken shape. With Moscow's help, Hanoi and Washington would get together to figure out how to bring to an end their "part" of the war. When that was settled, it would be up to the factions in South Vietnam to settle things among themselves. He was pleased at the ambassador's reactions: "Dobrynin indicated that from the Soviet standpoint, if we left North Vietnam alone, they were not as concerned about events in South Vietnam."[98]

From that point, Harriman went on to set forth practically a whole agenda for peace talks, including full representation of the NLF. Dobrynin said someone had told him that the United States would only allow the NLF to sit behind the North Vietnamese delegation and whisper in their ears. Who told him that nonsense? Harriman challenged. President Johnson had promised that the NLF could be present and have their views considered. This was, of course, to be a major sticking point, but Harriman brooked no objections in his determination to get things moving. Did that mean, the ambassador queried, that the NLF could sit at the same table? "Well," came the answer, "if it is a round table with no question of the status of anyone present, yes." Washington could not recognize the NLF as a government, however, or as the representatives of the Vietnamese people.[99]

Harriman got the job as chief negotiator for the Paris talks—though Rostow tried hard to limit his role to the opening sessions. The national security adviser argued that there were two reasons for calling him home once things got underway. There was his health to consider. But there was also his lack of sympathy for the South Vietnamese.[100] Despite his doubts about Harriman's self-defined role as peacemaker—and what it might cost the national reputation—Rostow himself thought that the likely outcome of the peace negotiations would hinge upon an ability to convince the North Vietnamese to have "a member" of the NLF meet with a Saigon representative to go to work on a southern settlement. These talks could go on while the Paris negotiations settled the other questions. "We could then press Thieu to offer a one-man-one-vote solution which would permit the NLF, disguised as a popular front party, to run if—repeat if—it accepts the constitution as the basis for political life."[101]

In Paris, meanwhile, Harriman lost no time in getting in touch with the Soviet ambassador to France, Valerian Zorin, perhaps best remembered for his duel with Adlai Stevenson during UN debates at the time of the Cuban missile crisis. The North Vietnamese had said that no progress could be made until Washington ended all the bombing of DRV territory. When the American appealed to Zorin for help, the answer he got was that Hanoi had sent a delegation to Paris not on the basis of the U.S. president's March 31 speech, but on the basis of their own declaration of April 3, stating that they were sending a delegation to talk only about a complete halt.[102] Undaunted, Harriman asked if they could keep in touch—but it was going to be a long summer. In Washington, the new secretary of defense, Clark Clifford, pushed the president to recognize that there were "no real plans to win the war"—at least not under the limitations placed on the military. "Our hopes must go with Paris."[103]

In early June a letter from Kosygin arrived in Washington. It required "careful consideration," Walt Rostow advised the president. The Soviet premier wrote that he and his colleagues had reason to believe that a complete cessation of the bombing would produce a breakthrough in the Paris talks, leading to a peaceful settlement. He also assured Johnson that such a step would neither harm American troops nor damage American prestige. "For a great world power the ultimate positive result of one or other act outweighs many times all other considerations to which an excessively exaggerated meaning is sometimes given."[104] The letter was a perfectly ironic climax to years of trying to achieve Russian participation in the peace process. Its immediate impact was to further exacerbate the already divided counsels around the president. Instead of offering the prospect of reconciliation—either in America or Vietnam—Johnson feared it promised the final undoing of all that he had tried to accomplish. Already the presidential campaign had revealed the Democratic party in disarray, threatening the final breakdown of the New Deal coalition, which, with the partial exception of the Eisenhower years, had ruled the country all his political life. The foreign policy consensus established by Harry Truman was also imperiled. And, finally, as Johnson wrote in his memoirs, he remembered Kosygin's earlier assurances that had dissolved into the Vietnamese jungles like the NLF under pursuit by Westmoreland's soldiers.

"What was Moscow saying now that it had not said two and a half years earlier?" Johnson asked readers of his memoirs. The slightly patronizing tone of the letter, which lectured him about "exaggerated meanings," also seemed to portend a growing Soviet confidence in the ultimate outcome of the Cold War. Perhaps this was as hard to take as any of the other considerations that led the president to respond with a question. What steps did the Soviets guarantee the DRV would take toward deescalation? He would be willing, he said, to accept Kosygin's word, if given "privately and with precision," that such steps would be taken.[105]

There were many recriminations voiced about the affair of the Kosygin letter, as Dobrynin continued to insist to all who would listen that a great opportunity had been missed. Moscow cared little about what happened in South Vietnam, he repeated, but it could do nothing about the war until America acted in accordance with Russian advice. And Rusk kept repeating in reply that "it was most unfortunate that the two countries on whose shoulders rested the responsibility for destroying humanity or not could not communicate on vital subjects without being ambiguous."[106] That ambiguity Rusk decried was, of course, at the heart of the attempt to manage the Cold War as it shifted into the Third World after the Chinese Revolution. It concealed many things, some of which, if confronted directly, threatened the *raison d'être* of the conflict, some which threatened self-perceptions, and some which allowed problems to be resolved safely without destroying humanity.

In mid-July Johnson's Russian experts, Charles Bohlen and Llewellyn Thompson, asked him to reconsider his response to Kosygin's letter. This time they were joined by Walt Rostow, who drafted such a message, using an apparent lull in the ground fighting as the reason for the new communication. It was still being discussed at the end of the month as Russian forces prepared to move into Czechoslovakia to put an end to what has been called "Prague Spring."[107]

Besieged by the turmoil that was 1968, Johnson complained to his advisers as they considered this draft that, "I believe the International Communists have a movement under way to get me to stop the bombing. What is the situation on infiltrators?" This last was unintended (or perhaps intended) *double entendre*. The infiltrators from North Vietnam, the infiltrators who ran the Peace Movement, who controlled the media, who abused his hospitality as Kennedy "spies," they had all become one in his mind.[108]

August was filled with Soviet assurances that its promulgation of the "Brezhnev Doctrine" did not portend future moves into Rumania or actions in Germany to threaten Berlin's status. Johnson had hoped for a crowning accomplishment in arms limitation. But Moscow's Czech "incursion" ruined that prospect—and, not surprisingly, brought on a hail of criticism from Beijing. America's allies also presented a problem. If efforts to enlist Russian support at the Paris talks continued, critics were certain to point out that concessions in Germany or at Israel's expense were sure to be on the table.[109]

At the end of the first week of October, Gromyko pressed Dean Rusk on the question of South Vietnamese participation in the peace talks. Was it an essential precondition for ending the bombing? The secretary assured him that it was, indeed, an essential requirement. Over the next few days word came from a Soviet official in Paris that the DRV had agreed that Saigon could be represented at peace talks that would begin immediately. Russia had at last delivered the North Vietnamese, albeit too late. Johnson, however, could not deliver the South Vietnamese![110] A complete bombing halt was announced by the president on October 31, 1968. The next day Dean Rusk told a press conference, "The decision of last evening was not the end of a struggle." Others were now expected to help with managing Hanoi. "Now, I am also saying to all of those who have said, oh, things will be wonderful if you stop the bombing, we are saying to them, all right, get busy, get busy. See what you can do. We have made our move now you make yours."[111]

For five years the United States had attempted to involve the Soviet Union in a solution that would preserve the Cold War "order" and allow the superpowers to negotiate other vital matters to both sides. Moscow was pinioned between three posts: Washington, Beijing, and Hanoi. And while Soviet leaders always insisted that Saigon had no legitimate standing and was nothing more than an island bastion surrounded by civil war—one that could not hold out for a minute without American support—the "Vietnamization" phase of the struggle would go on for five more years. Johnson's successors played the "China card" with considerable skill, but in the end it would be the Vietnamese who decided their own fate. And soon after it was over, Russia would face its own "Vietnam" in Afghanistan.

Chapter 3

Containing the Warriors

Soviet Policy toward the Indochina Conflict, 1960–65

ILYA V. GAIDUK

It is a great temptation for a historian who for many years has studied the history of the Cold War, after having read recently published books on the problem based on archival documents from other countries, to exclaim: "We now know!" If only it were true. Undoubtedly we now know much more about the Cold War than we did, say, twenty or even ten years ago. But we discover with some uneasiness that our knowledge is still far from complete, even after many documents have been released in Russia and other Eastern European countries and have been studied and interpreted by the ablest scholars of our time. The reason lies not only in the selectivity of the declassification process in many countries, where only some documents relating to a problem or some aspect of it are opened, but not the whole complex of materials. This happens everywhere, in Russia as well as in the United States. We should also keep in mind that archival documents have their own limits and cannot educate us on many factors that influenced the decision-making process, such as the psychology of political leaders, their mood in a specific moment of this process, the inner argumentation which helped them to convince themselves of the righteousness of their decisions or actions. This is what we probably will never know.

However there is another problem, that of the selectivity of scholarly interest itself, which concentrates on some aspects of the Cold War or on some countries or regions, while putting others aside. This has an especially negative effect on the study of the period when the world was becoming a real complex of interactive tendencies and events; what was happening in one corner of it had its effect on developments in many other places, and the other way around. In this sense, the study of Soviet policy toward the conflict in Indochina is suffering most of all.

What are the problems in Soviet foreign policy that attract the most attention of historians? These are, of course, the German question, Soviet relations with its Eastern European allies, Soviet policy toward the leading Western countries (the United States, Great Britain, France), and the Soviet-China rivalry. Among the international crises during the Cold War, Berlin, Cuba, and the Middle East occupy the foremost positions in the works of scholars. And only now has the Vietnam War elbowed a place into this front row, though in Russian historiography it happened quite recently. One can search in vain for books or articles on the Soviet position during the crises in Indochina in 1954 or in Laos in 1961, although those positions probably reflected Soviet foreign policy priorities and were influenced by developments in the international arena. Recall, for example, the problem of the European Defence Community during the Geneva Conference in 1954, and the Kennedy administration's adventure in the Bay of Pigs just on the eve of the Geneva Conference of 1961.

I put forward these arguments in order to make clear my intention to place Soviet policy toward the Indochina conflict in the years preceding the Vietnam War within the general context of Moscow's relations with the outside world. I will try to explain the actions of the Kremlin leaders in the sphere of Soviet–North Vietnamese relations both on the basis of new documents from Russian archives, and by drawing attention to events in the international arena that affected, in one way or another, those actions.

I have chosen as a starting point the year of 1960 for a number of reasons. It was a year marked by several significant events that had far-reaching implications for Soviet foreign policy. It is very difficult to rank them in accordance with their importance. They were not, of course, equal in the eyes of the Soviet leaders. Because priorities for them lay undoubtedly in relations with the principal rival, the United States, I would begin with the U-2 spy flight incident in May, 1960, and Soviet Premier Nikita Khrushchev's walkout at the Paris summit. Tension between the two countries grew, coinciding with mounting problems in the Kremlin's relations with Communist China, in this case, a Soviet ally. Moscow's decision to recall all Soviet experts working in the People's Republic of China, adopted in July, 1960, was a crucial step toward the breakdown of the Sino-Soviet alliance.[1]

It is striking that exactly midway between these two events there occurred another that, at first glance, had no relationship whatsoever to Soviet problems with the Americans and the Chinese. This was a visit of the First Secretary of the Central Committee of the Workers' Party of Vietnam, Le Duan, who came to Moscow at the end of May to discuss with the Kremlin a draft of his report to the forthcoming Lao Dong Party Congress. And probably that first glance would have been correct, if during the previous year the Fifteenth Plenum of the Lao Dong Party had not adopted a decision that tended to change the whole situation in the region of Indochina.

According to a resolution of the plenum and a special meeting of the party politburo several months later, Vietnamese Communists should be oriented toward a military struggle for the reunification of Vietnam. Hanoi believed there was a "revolutionary situation" in South Vietnam. As a result, it was decided to intensify military efforts in the South combined with an "offensive against the enemy on the political front." The North Vietnamese central committee adopted a concrete plan of action to fulfill the task.[2]

At the same time Hanoi undertook steps to test the reaction of its socialist allies to the proposed change in policy, and to prepare them for the eventual translation of the new course into action. Thus in the period just before Le Duan's visit to the Soviet Union and China, high North Vietnamese officials began meeting with their socialist counterparts, hinting at a new situation in South Vietnam and possible measures necessary for adjusting to it. One such meeting took place in April, when Deputy DRV Foreign Minister Ung Van Khiem informed ambassadors of the socialist countries that "[i]n a situation of repressions and every possible persecution, the population of the South in recent months has begun to go over from a political and economic struggle to armed struggle." He complained that it had become difficult for the communist cadres in the South "to restrain the population from resumption of the large-scale guerrilla struggle."[3]

Another conversation took place during a visit of DRV Minister of Defense Vo Nguyen Giap to Moscow in May. Giap astonished his Soviet hosts with an open declaration that the activity of the International Control Commission (ICC) in Vietnam, though still important for preserving peace in the region, "practically became disadvantageous for us in some respects. *From the military viewpoint* [Emphasis is the author's throughout the article], the Agreement on the Cessation of Hostilities [the Geneva Agreements] imposes on the DRV significant restrictions (for example, prohibition of air forces)."[4] In other words, Giap demonstrated Hanoi's dissatisfaction with the Geneva agreements and called for their revision, particularly concerning the ICC's existence.

Hence the spirit and substance of the report that Le Duan brought to Moscow for consideration of his Soviet colleagues were hardly a surprise for them. Still it was not a welcome development for Moscow. The Foreign Ministry prepared an evaluation of the draft, in which diplomats from the ministry's

Southeast Asian department paid the most attention to the section entitled "Struggle for Unification of the Motherland, for Completion of the National Democratic Revolution all over the Country." They emphasized the fact that "[t]heses of this section represent, in essence, a direct task to develop in South Vietnam a military struggle with the purpose of overthrowing the Ngo Dinh Diem regime, to create during its course liberated areas with the establishment there of the people's power." This declaration from the podium of the party congress would mean, reasoned the Soviets, an open acknowledgment by the DRV of its inspiration and support of guerrilla activities in the South. It would lead the Saigon regime and the United States with the help of SEATO to undertake "the most extreme measures" in order to suppress the "revolutionary movement" in South Vietnam.[5]

The Soviets emphasized that the ideas of this section were a development of secret decisions of the Fifteenth Plenum of the Lao Dong Party, and a public declaration of them at the congress "would undermine the correct tactical course which the Vietnamese friends are following and which provides them necessary political advantages. This course was, and so far is, based on the premise that the DRV has no connection with armed guerrilla activities in South Vietnam which are a result of the mass discontent of the South Vietnam population." The ministry drew attention to the fact that Hanoi's report neglected the importance of the Geneva agreements, although from a tactical viewpoint it would be to the advantage of the DRV to emphasize that the struggle for the unification of Vietnam was a struggle for the implementation of the Geneva agreements, which were in turn supported by world public opinion.[6]

All these points were touched upon during meetings of the Soviet leaders with Le Duan, who had come to Moscow via Beijing, where he had discussed the draft of the report with his Chinese colleagues. It is impossible to tell, without appropriate documents from Chinese archives, whether Le Duan enjoyed more understanding in China than in the Soviet Union. But in one conversation with a Soviet chargé d'affaires in Hanoi, N. I. Godunov, after Le Duan's visit, Deputy Foreign Minister Ung Van Khiem shared with his Soviet counterpart the report which Le Duan presented to the North Vietnamese leadership about his trip and the positions of the DRV allies. According to Duan, the Chinese and Soviet "comrades" fully agreed with the ideas of the sections that formulated the problems of internal policy of the Lao Dong Party. "As to the foreign policy problems, and especially the issue of prospects of the development of the situation in South Vietnam, there are some differences in the viewpoints of the Chinese and Soviet communists, though they are not of the character of principle."[7]

Let us not be deluded by these words of a polite Vietnamese. It is worth noting that the conversation between Godunov and Ung Van Khiem started with the latter's expressing certain misgivings on the part of the "Vietnamese friends" with regard to the differences between the positions of the Soviet and Chinese parties on issues of international politics. Khiem emphasized that "our Central Committee was always inclined to the necessity for all Communist parties to have identical views on the main problems of our time, which is a strong guarantee against committing mistakes in practical activity and the rise of deviationist tendencies."[8]

North Vietnamese concern over developments in Sino-Soviet party relations was also apparently stimulated by events that took place at the Bucharest meeting of the communist and workers' parties in July, 1960, also attended by Le Duan. This meeting, as Communist Party of the Soviet Union (CPSU) Central Committee Secretary Frol Kozlov reported to a CPSU plenum, was devoted "to the discussion of the erroneous views of the Chinese comrades on a number of principal issues of social development in the present situation, on the issues of strategy and tactics of the world communist movement."[9] According to the Soviets, the Chinese leadership underestimated the "great changes" that were taking place in the correlation of forces in international relations; they denied the possibility of preventing wars, understood incorrectly Lenin's principle of peaceful coexistence, and regarded as utopian the idea of general and complete disarmament before a complete victory of socialism in the world was achieved. In addition to these sins Beijing did not believe in the peaceful communist takeover of any particular country. The Chinese also had erroneous opinions on neutral countries and national bourgeoisies, and they violated a number of Leninist principles of socialist buildup in committing leftist mistakes in reforms in China.[10]

Moscow also criticized the Chinese for their advocacy of Korean-style "local wars," putting forward instead their own concept of "revolutionary wars of liberation." The Soviet Communists "regard civil wars against rotten regimes, against capitalism, and wars for national independence as just wars. We always supported such wars, and not by words, but by deeds, by sending arms to the people as well," declared Kozlov at the plenum.[11] His statement helps explain the Soviet position during Le Duan's visit to Moscow in May–June, 1960, and why the Kremlin did not support a course toward beginning an open war between the North and the South, but instead emphasized the necessity of keeping the war at the level of an internal struggle between Diem's regime and local guerrillas.

Thus even after the crisis in Soviet-American relations after the U-2 incident, Khrushchev and his colleagues were not ready to abandon their policy of détente with the West. Moreover, in the summer of 1960 they were uneasy about the course that Soviet-American relations would take. The forthcoming presidential elections in the United States only added to their uncertainty, because the Kremlin could not exclude the possibility that a Democratic president would come to the White House and, they believed, U.S. policy toward the Soviet Union might undergo a favorable modification.

Regardless of the outcome of U.S. presidential elections, the Soviets understood that Southeast Asia occupied an important place in the strategic plans of American policymakers. Moscow realized that Washington could not be reconciled to any changes in the balance of power there in favor of the communist bloc. Any open declaration by the Vietnamese "friends" of their support of the armed struggle in the South, let alone their direct involvement in military operations there, was likely to initiate a strong reaction by the United States, with grave consequences for international relations.

It was in this vein that the Southeast Asian department of the Soviet Foreign Ministry put forward its arguments against the spirit and principles of Le Duan's Party Congress report. A memorandum of the department reads, "[I]t is necessary to regard as little corresponding to reality a premise that the U.S.A. and the bloc of SEATO could allow without resistance unification of Vietnam on the democratic basis and thus agree with the loss, in favor of the socialist camp, of such *a first-class strategic position* in Southeast Asia like South Vietnam. Thus the issue of the unification of Vietnam in the ways envisioned by the Vietnamese friends *is a part of the issue of correlation of forces between the two world camps* [i.e., capitalist and socialist]." Furthermore, the Soviets analyzed the internal situation in the South and came to the conclusion that "[t]he present situation in South Vietnam does not furnish a basis to talk about a favorable internal revolutionary situation, about a possibility to overthrow the Diem regime and to establish the people's regime. Along with this . . . it is unlikely that the U.S.A. would agree to the loss of such an important military strategic springboard like South Vietnam, and would not intervene in the internal situation in South Vietnam. Preservation of political domination in Indochina is not unimportant for the U.S.A., and it would be lost in case of the loss of South Vietnam. Therefore it should be expected that if an attempt to overthrow the Diem regime by means of revolution is undertaken, the U.S.A. directly or through the mechanism of the SEATO treaty would turn to military intervention in South Vietnam."[12]

Apparently the Soviets were worried that Hanoi's open support of the civil conflict in the South would lead to an international conflict, with the involvement of the United States and eventually the Soviet Union. Such a development would run directly contrary to Moscow's plans for détente and cooperation with the West.

Still another factor complicated the growing dilemma of the Kremlin concerning the conflict in Indochina. As early as 1959 Soviet diplomats noted Hanoi's growing political, economic, as well as ideological dependence on Communist China. The Soviet leaders themselves helped to create this dependence in the 1950s with their policy of sharing responsibilities with Beijing in the sphere of cooperation with North Vietnam. It was the Kremlin's position after the 1954 Geneva Conference that the main burden of assistance to the fledgling communist state of Vietnam should be assumed by Beijing.[13] Chinese Communists, Moscow reasoned, knew better the situation in the neighboring region, and the history, traditions, and way of life of the Vietnamese people. China was closer to the DRV geographically and had direct lines of communication with it. The Chinese could therefore better and with more timeliness respond to the needs of Hanoi. Of course there was another reason for such a policy of the "Soviet comrades": They did not want to be overextended in resources and energy that they believed necessary to preserve for use in the European theater.

This division of labor created a basis for the gradual strengthening of ties between the DRV and the People's Republic of China, and when a conflict loomed large in the sphere of Sino-Soviet relations, it was too late for Moscow to try to save the situation. Indeed the Soviets did not undertake any efforts to this end at the time, probably because they still hoped to find ways for reconciliation with Beijing. Besides, they apparently believed that Ho Chi Minh, whom Moscow regarded as a loyal pro-Soviet leader, would be able to prevent his country's full alignment with the Chinese Communists.

Nevertheless, in a memorandum prepared soon after Le Duan's visit to Moscow in May–June, 1960, the Southeast Asian department drew attention to the close cooperation that existed between the DRV and the PRC. Soviet diplomats noted that between the Workers' Party of Vietnam (WPV) and the Chinese Communist Party (CCP) there existed "permanent ties" in the form of consultations and exchange of information. In the sphere of foreign policy, both sides regularly shared opinions on all principal problems in the international situation and rendered each other active assistance, especially concerning relations with the countries of Southeast Asia and the Far East. "The closest coordination of foreign policy actions undertaken by the two countries exists on issues of struggle for the fulfillment of the Geneva agreements on Vietnam and Laos."[14]

This was in striking contrast to the lack of interest on the part of the Vietnamese in sharing their views on South Vietnam with their Soviet counterparts. The Southeast Asian department complained in a memorandum prepared that same July that "the issue of the unification of Vietnam is . . . especially delicate because of the apparent tendency of the Vietnamese friends to avoid its discussion with Soviet representatives at all levels," and that "the Vietnamese friends are informing our embassy in Hanoi on the issue of South Vietnam only from the viewpoint of propaganda."[15]

All these complex considerations made the Kremlin very cautious with regard to Hanoi's new attitude toward prospects for the struggle in South Vietnam. As the Soviet leaders met with Le Duan, they evidently tried to convince him that such a reversal of Hanoi's policy in the South was not appropriate. It is known that the DRV leadership followed the advice of the Soviets to the extent that they softened the wording of the part of the report to the Third Congress that concerned the situation in the South and the position of Hanoi.[16] However, this was obviously only a temporary and cosmetic concession. By the end of the year, when the crisis in Laos burst out, Hanoi seized it as an opportunity to promote its new policy in South Vietnam.

The crisis in Laos developed throughout the period after the 1954 Geneva Conference on Indochina, but reached its peak in the last months of 1960. The Soviets followed attentively all the twists and turns of the confrontation between the neutralist government of Souvanna Phouma and the opposition to it, both from the right and the left. Soviet concern over the course of affairs in Laos grew in the months that followed Captain Kong Le's successful coup d'état in August and the formation of the new neutralist government of Souvanna Phouma. In November Moscow noted the worsening of the Laotian situation as a result of the right-wing revolt against the neutralist government. Soviet diplomats believed one of the reasons for the growing isolation of Phouma was the uncompromising stance that the procommunist Pathet Lao took while negotiating with the neutralists on a future coalition government. Such a position of the "Laotian friends," as Veniamin Likhachev, the head of the Southeast Asian department, wrote to Deputy Foreign Minister Georgii Pushkin, undermined Phouma's prestige in the army and among the national bourgeoisie. Likhachev predicted that the result would be civil war, with Laos becoming "a factor that would be undoubtedly used by the imperialist circles of the U.S.A. to the detriment of our struggle for relaxation of international tension, disarmament, etc."[17]

The Soviets could do little to influence developments in Laos, though in October, 1960, they established diplomatic relations with that country and started to provide economic assistance to the regime of Souvanna Phouma, whom they regarded as an "authoritative feudal-bourgeois leader oriented toward peace, neutrality and national concord."[18] Meanwhile the Pathet Lao were under the strong influence of Hanoi, which saw no harm in strengthening its allies in the neighboring country.

In fact the situation developed according to the scenario described by Soviet diplomats. The confrontation between Souvanna Phouma and his rightist opposition, headed by Phoumi Nosavan, led to the creation of two governments and two armies on the territory of Laos. While the Soviet Union, China, and North Vietnam supported Phouma, the United States undertook to dispatch arms, money, and advisers to Nosavan. Neither superpower ceased to accuse the other of violating the principles of the 1954 Geneva agreements on Laos, and to warn of the unpredictable consequences of such a policy. Finally, after an abortive coup d'état against the neutralist government on December 9, 1960, Souvanna Phouma left Vientiane and went to Cambodia. Three days later, on December 12, the National Assembly of Laos declared Phouma's government resigned and approved a new government headed by Boun Oum, who represented right-wing forces. The king of Laos approved this decision of the National Assembly.

In those hectic days of December the communist supporters of Phouma tried to reverse this unfortunate turn of events. It seems that the lead in this matter was taken by the Chinese and their Vietnamese allies, not by the Soviets. Already on December 4, during a conversation with the counsellor of the Soviet embassy in Hanoi, I. Kiselev, DRV Prime Minister Pham Van Dong emphasized the necessity of accelerating the pace of sending assistance to Laos: "[I]f we are late," he said, "such a situation can arise when nobody is to be helped."[19]

Several days later a similar conversation occurred between a Soviet diplomat and Chinese Foreign Minister Chen Yi, who met with the Soviet chargé d'affaires Nikolai Sudarikov and, in anticipation of decisive developments in Laos, urged the Soviets to prepare the necessary assistance for that country. "One cannot be late with the assistance," warned Chen Yi.[20] Apparently the Chinese leader was anxious to be ready for any eventuality, so as not to lose the initiative. The next day Sudarikov talked to Zhou Enlai, who, like Chen Yi, urged Moscow to accelerate dispatching arms, ammunition, and gasoline to Souvanna Phouma.[21] Zhou promised all possible assistance from Beijing in providing transit of these dispatches through the territory of China.

It was not necessary to push Moscow too hard in the direction of assisting Phouma and the Pathet Lao. The Soviet leadership understood that the crisis in Laos had ceased to be a local civil war with little or no consequence for the outside world. Now it was developing into an international problem that, in the context of the Cold War, might affect the international balance of power. Even as Vietnamese and Chinese leaders talked about the need to accelerate the delivery of Soviet aid, there were already eleven railway cargoes of weaponry and thirty-five of oil and gasoline at the Soviet-China border, ready for transport to Laos.[22] Nevertheless, unlike their Asian allies, the Soviet leaders did not want a protracted war in Laos. Almost from the outset they favored the possibility of resolving the conflict at a Geneva-like international conference.

On December 22, 1960, the Soviet Union sent a diplomatic note to the government of Great Britain. In it Moscow drew the attention of the British co-chairman of the 1954 Geneva Conference to the grave situation in Laos and raised the possibility of a conference with participation of the countries that had taken part in the Geneva Conference in 1954. On January 7, 1961, Khrushchev sent letters to Sukarno, Souvanna Phouma, Nehru, Norodom Sihanouk, U Nu of Burma, and de Gaulle, followed on January 9 by a letter to Pham Van Dong, with an appeal to convene such a conference as soon as possible. The Soviets supported Sihanouk's initiative to convene a conference with the participation of fourteen countries; that is, in addition to the Great Powers, those that bordered Laos and/or were involved in the conflict.

The Soviet desire for an early and peaceful settlement of the crisis in Laos was in accord with the hopes of the Kennedy administration. This was not the case, however, with Moscow's Asian allies. Although Beijing and Hanoi supported the Soviet initiative on the conference and approved resumption of the activities of the International Control Commission in Laos, they had their own views on the situation there, and on the prospects for an international conference, which differed from those of Moscow. In a conversation between Soviet Ambassador to the DRV Leonid Sokolov and Vo Nguyen Giap on January 27, 1961, the North Vietnamese leader admitted that his colleagues in the politburo thought it necessary to prevent the broadening of the conflict in Laos. "But this, to a significant degree, depends on the military situation in Laos," stressed Giap. "New victories of the patriotic forces will certainly accelerate the convening of a conference to discuss the issue of Laos."[23] Pham Van Dong, during his meeting with the Soviet ambassador several days later, was likewise outspoken. "The convening of the conference," he declared, "depends on the military situation in Laos; the achievement of new successes by the Kong Le forces and Pathet Lao can accelerate this conference."[24] In other words, Hanoi favored a conference, but only when the Pathet Lao and their allies could negotiate from a position of strength.

The reasons for the reluctance of the "Vietnamese friends" are quite understandable. Laos served Hanoi as a convenient channel through which they sent cadres, supplies, and armed units to the South in support of the guerrilla struggle there. According to the Soviet estimates, during the summer of 1961 alone the DRV dispatched to South Vietnam, through provinces controlled by the Pathet Lao, three fully equipped infantry battalions and enough cadres for twenty battalions, which they planned to organize by enlisting local recruits. Hanoi also sent to the South arms and ammunition originally delivered for the Pathet Lao by Soviet planes. At the same time the North Vietnamese undertook to establish and strengthen guerrilla bases in the jungles of South Vietnam.[25]

The Chinese regarded the problem of Laos more in the context of the international situation. With Hanoi, they were in no hurry to see a diplomatic solution of the Laos crisis. Instead they were eager to use it to create difficulties for "American imperialism" throughout the world. Zhou Enlai, for example, linked the U.S. fiasco in the Bay of Pigs with the situation in Laos in his conversation with Soviet chargé Sudarikov and confessed that "it would be not bad" if the situation became a little more tense. According to Zhou, "since the U.S.A. created tension in Cuba, it is appropriate [for us] in response to create tension in other places. . . ." In addition to Laos, Zhou Enlai spoke of the Congo and Algeria. He added pointedly, "We also have the Taiwan Straits."[26]

Moreover, Beijing considered Indochina ripe for revolution and was against stabilization in this part of the world. Describing Chinese views on the eve of the international conference on Laos, the Soviet Foreign Ministry noted, "the Chinese comrades speak against settlement in that country on the basis of complete unification as well as against its neutrality. They emphasized a possibility of resumption of the armed struggle in Laos later on. . . . Along with this the Chinese comrades underestimate consequences of the continuing foreign interference in the developments in Laos and believe it will not do any harm if the international conference does not take place at all, since the progressive forces of Laos will develop in any case."[27]

Such an attitude could not be accepted by Moscow without reservation. Although the Kremlin was not totally unreceptive to the prospect of creating difficulties for its principal rival in the Cold War confrontation, it recognized certain limits in pursuing such a policy, the situation in Vietnam being not the least of them. In view of the development of the guerrilla struggle in the South and the bellicose pronunciations from Hanoi, the Soviet leadership was worried about the conflict in Laos becoming a match to fire the whole of Indochina. Therefore they regarded a peaceful solution of the Laos problem both as a means of preventing the spread of armed conflict in the region and as an example for a similar settlement in South Vietnam. Furthermore, a neutral Laos, controlled by the government of Souvanna Phouma with a broad participation of representatives of the procommunist Pathet Lao, did not contradict plans for undermining the U.S. position in the region, while guaranteeing the existence of at least one pro-Soviet neutral country there. Therefore the long-range Soviet goals were not at variance with those of China and North Vietnam, though Moscow tried to reach them by other, more moderate and peaceful ways. That is why the USSR Foreign Ministry, in its instructions to the Soviet embassy in

Laos, defined the task Moscow tried to fulfill as "the struggle for the extermination of the hotbed of international tension in that region and the neutralization of that country. In this connection we are based on the need, on the one hand, to render all-out assistance to the patriotic forces of Laos, and on the other hand, to fight actively in searching for ways of peaceful settlement of the Laotian problem."[28]

Directives for the Soviet delegation at the Geneva Conference on Laos, which started its work on May 17, 1961, were formulated by the Soviet leadership in the same vein. As Deputy Foreign Minister Pushkin put it later in his report on the conference for his superiors,

> The principal goal of the Soviet delegation at the international conference was to seek achievement of mutually acceptable international agreements which would help the restoration of peace in that country and would guarantee its true independence and neutrality, while fully taking into account the interests of national-patriotic and democratic forces in Laos. *With this it was taken into consideration that the neutralization of that country will give an opportunity to avoid international military conflict in the region of Southeast Asia, to put an end to the involvement of the U.S.A. and other Western countries in the internal affairs of Laos and thus to create favorable conditions for the further strengthening and developing of democratic forces in that country* [italics added]."[29]

It was not easy for the Soviets at the conference to fulfill their instructions. They had to overcome the resistance of their Chinese and Vietnamese allies, who regarded every concession to the "Westerners" as a betrayal of the common cause. Pushkin, as the actual head of the Soviet delegation in Geneva, encountered enormous difficulties in heading off steps by his Asian counterparts that could have endangered the successful outcome of the negotiations. When, for example, the Chinese decided to raise the issue of the withdrawal from Laos of former Nationalist Chinese troops who fought on the rightist side, Pushkin tried to persuade them that they should not do this, because at the conference "much will depend on what questions and in what form they are posed by the socialist countries." The Soviet deputy foreign minister argued against the Chinese inclination to regard the negotiations only from the point of view of the struggle against imperialism. "To make the Western countries agree on a settlement favorable for socialist countries, for the democratic forces of Laos," he argued in a conversation with his Chinese colleague Zhang Hanhfu, "is not only a struggle, but also a victory. The whole problem is how to wage this struggle, what tactical line to follow." The issue of the Chiang Kai-shek bands in Laos could have become a serious obstacle even if all other issues concerning Laos had been settled by the negotiators.[30]

Likewise Pushkin undertook efforts to "contain" his Vietnamese colleagues, who also pursued their own agenda during the conference, often to the detriment of the settlement of the crisis. Hanoi was not pleased with any requirement to withdraw its troops from Laos as part of an agreement. The North Vietnamese leaders wanted to find some way to leave behind at least some forces, apparently with the purpose of assisting insurgents in South Vietnam. Hanoi was supported in this by the Chinese, who expressed to the Soviets their opinion on the expediency of retaining Vietnamese troops in Laos, whose number was about eight thousand, organized into thirteen battalions.[31] Pushkin resolutely opposed the idea, calling it "dubious." He argued that the purpose of the socialist countries should be political work in Laos—internal democratic reforms, not a military solution. When acting chief of the Vietnamese delegation Nguyen Co Thach attempted to placate the feelings of his Soviet counterpart by saying that he was actually talking about Vietnamese engineers and specialists, Pushkin still opposed it, because, from his point of view, it would undermine any agreement. It would be more advantageous, he said, for the Communist countries to reach a peaceful settlement in Laos. According to him, this would annul SEATO by undermining U.S. credibility in the eyes of "reactionary elements" in South Vietnam and Thailand, who would regard the agreement on Laos as a defeat of the United States. "This is why we should not stick at trifles," he insisted.[32]

Thus while overcoming the reluctance, and even the resistance of their Chinese and Vietnamese allies, the Soviets moved toward a peaceful resolution of the Laos crisis. Their efforts eventually proved to be successful, and the Geneva Conference on Laos ended in July, 1962, with documents on neutrality, reconciliation, and national unity, and the independence of Laos, signed by all its participants.

Encouraged by the successful outcome of the Geneva Conference on Laos, which Moscow regarded as a U.S. defeat,[33] the Soviets began to consider prospects for a peaceful settlement of the Vietnam problem as well, in particular opportunities for arranging a Laotian-type international conference as proposed by Prince Sihanouk. Although this idea was attractive to the Soviet leaders, who as before believed that "the interests of the Soviet Union and the socialist camp demand preservation and strengthening of peace both in Vietnam and in the whole of Indochina,"[34] they decided that conditions were not propitious for such a conference; at least, Moscow was not inclined to be its initiator.[35]

Why were the Soviets, who followed developments in Vietnam with apprehension, skeptical with regard to the prospects of convening a conference similar to the one on Laos? Their attitude was influenced by a number of factors that may be explained by certain documents of the Soviet Foreign Ministry relating to the year 1962. These papers drew attention to the increasingly serious aggravation of the situation in South Vietnam, caused by the growing U.S. involvement in the struggle against Vietnamese "patriots," as well as by Hanoi's increased support of Southern insurgents. As to the former, analysts in Moscow spoke of the "military intervention of the U.S.A., aimed against the liberation movement of the South Vietnamese people,"[36] and they interpreted U.S. moves as a part of a plan to transform South Vietnam into a military springboard in Southeast Asia, an "important strategic link in the chain of military bases that encircle socialist countries in the south and east." According to Moscow, the United States intended South Vietnam to become one more U.S. satellite in the Cold War rivalry, along with Japan, the Philippines, Okinawa, Taiwan, Pakistan, and Turkey.[37]

One would expect that in this situation the urgency of finding a solution to the Vietnam problem by neutralizing South Vietnam, and thus excluding it from the military plans of American strategists, would push the Soviet leadership to undertake resolute steps in that direction. However, Moscow apparently did not feel its position in the region firm enough to do so. In fact, Moscow hesitated to pursue any definite policy toward the Vietnam conflict unless it was sure that this policy was acceptable in Hanoi. The situation was complicated by the widening gap between the views of Moscow and Hanoi on the armed struggle in South Vietnam. While the Soviets continued to regard such a struggle as undesirable, because it seemed sure to spur U.S. involvement in the conflict and in Diem's internal position, the North Vietnamese grew more firmly wedded to a military solution.

Hanoi's attitude was at least partly a result of the growing influence of Beijing on the North Vietnamese leadership. Moscow knew from various sources that the majority in the politburo of the Lao Dong Party agreed with the Chinese on problems of war and peace, the correlation of forces in the world, and the prospects of the national liberation movement; the Soviets stood in disagreement on all counts. Among the North Vietnamese leaders who expressed sympathies with respect to the Chinese Communist Party and spoke for closer rapprochement between the DRV and the PRC were members of the politburo Truong Chinh, Hoang Van Hoan, Nguyen Chi Thanh as well as members of the Central Committee Xuan Thuy and Tran Tu Binh.[38]

Soviet analysts noted that there were limits to Chinese influence in the DRV—the group of pro-Chinese politicians was counterbalanced by such influential leaders as Ho Chi Minh and Pham Van Dong, who constantly emphasized the necessity of strengthening ties with the Soviet Union.[39] Even so,

Beijing possessed enough leverage to consolidate its position in the DRV. First of all, the Chinese demonstrated their open support for Hanoi's plans for an armed struggle to unify Vietnam. According to the Soviet Foreign Ministry, they organized a campaign that was not limited to the PRC's veiled criticisms of Soviet policy from time to time, but which also took on the character of a broad daily propaganda in the mass media.

Furthermore, in December, 1961, Beijing sent to Hanoi a high-ranking military delegation that, according to Soviet observers, was a demonstration of the readiness of the Chinese to render resolute military support to the DRV.[40] Although there is no other information on this visit in the documents available in Russian archives, it is tempting to guess that a demonstration of support was not its sole purpose. During the visit the Asian Communist allies could well have discussed practical methods of military cooperation.

The Chinese reinforced their propaganda and moral support for the DRV with significant economic aid. This was part of China's general strategy to strengthen its influence in the friendly countries on its borders which, along with the DRV, included North Korea and Mongolia. According to the Soviet embassy in Hanoi, in the sphere of trade, aid, and credits, as well as in rendering technical assistance to North Vietnam, the People's Republic of China occupied the leading position among socialist countries.[41] Furthermore, Chinese economic and technical aid was concentrated in the most important areas of DRV industry. China helped the North Vietnamese build up their largest factories in both heavy and light industry and also helped to improve the railway system and the irrigation systems.

Soviet analysts believed these Chinese efforts were aimed at establishing a material basis for Beijing's ideological influence in neighboring countries. In September, 1961, the Soviet embassy in China warned Moscow that China, as an "incomparably larger and economically more powerful country" than its small neighbors, could strengthen economic ties to them and "thus an economic basis will be formed that the Chinese comrades will be able to exploit, in case of necessity, certain possibilities for spreading their ideological influence in them." To support this view, Soviet diplomats drew the attention of their superiors to "elements of hesitation in the positions of the DRV and the KPDR [Korean People's Democratic Republic]."[42]

What was a prognosis in 1961 became reality the next year. Notwithstanding some differences in the views of the Chinese and North Vietnamese leaders,[43] there was growing rapprochement between them, especially regarding the problem of South Vietnam. Soviet observers noted that stopovers in Beijing of North Vietnamese delegations on their way to other socialist countries, with the purpose of coordinating their positions with those of the "Chinese comrades," became a usual practice, one in contrast with Hanoi's behavior with respect to the "Soviet friends." The Soviet Foreign Ministry observed that the North Vietnamese neither wanted to coordinate their actions in South Vietnam with the Soviets, nor inform Moscow of their plans for the struggle to reunify the country. Moreover, they tried to deprive Moscow of information that would help the Kremlin complete its knowledge of developments there. The Foreign Ministry explained that "the Vietnamese comrades are afraid that we can oppose their course toward a fast acceleration of the armed struggle against the Diem regime, in view of the present international situation. Perhaps under Chinese influence they believe that the Soviet Union pays more attention to European problems and, to some extent, underestimates the problem of Vietnam."[44] The Foreign Ministry drew the pessimistic conclusion from these facts that in spite of the sympathies toward the Soviet Union among some North Vietnamese leaders, "the influence of the Chinese friends in the DRV remains strong."[45]

In such circumstances the Soviet leadership adopted an extremely cautious attitude toward developments in Vietnam. Not only were they reluctant to undertake diplomatic steps to resolve the conflict by peaceful means; Moscow rejected any suggestions even to consider rendering assistance to the communist struggle in South Vietnam as well. When the Soviet embassy in Hanoi suggested discussing "preliminarily" the question of what kind of arms, ammunition, and other equipment could be sent to South Vietnamese "patriots" through the DRV,[46] Moscow rebuked the embassy for having "tacitly" admitted that the DRV course on the development of armed struggle in the South was justified, and then drew the attention of Soviet diplomats in North Vietnam to the fact that in U.S. governing circles "the issue of the possibility of intervention aimed at preventing any attempts to liberate South Vietnam with the help of the [North] Vietnam People's army" was being discussed. Moscow believed that an open armed struggle against Ngo Dinh Diem's regime would endanger the "revolutionary forces" in the South and would lead to a deeper U.S. involvement that could make South Vietnam a "sharp knot of international tension." In this light, the Soviets questioned the expediency of the embassy's proposal about arms and equipment for the patriots.[47]

The only actions that Moscow leaders found acceptable in their predicament were efforts to secure international recognition of the National Liberation Front (NLFSV)—created by Hanoi in December of 1960 to coordinate actions of the socialist countries with respect to South Vietnam—and to keep trying to obtain information on developments there.[48] This was virtually a passive policy on the part of the Soviet Union. On the one hand, the Soviet leaders found nothing intrinsically bad in an insurgency in South Vietnam and even nourished hopes for a Communist takeover there. On the other, they preferred to see this victory achieved by the southerners themselves, without the open involvement of their allies in Hanoi, let alone other socialist countries. The latter case could become, Moscow feared, a pretext for direct U.S. intervention and would result in the transformation of the region of Indochina into an arena of international conflict. Therefore the Soviets tried to curb the militancy of their Vietnamese allies, even as Hanoi was being encouraged by Beijing to take more active steps in resolving the Vietnam problem.

Obviously the consequences of such a cautious policy could prove to be negative for Moscow. The USSR Foreign Ministry Southeast Asian department was worried that the restraint of the Soviet Union with regard to the conflict in Indochina might be perceived by Washington as unwillingness to get involved and might create an illusion among American policymakers that as long as their actions were not directed against the DRV, Moscow would remain reluctant to undertake any decisive steps in that region. In the meantime, the United States could suppress the Communist insurgency in the South and achieve "pacification" of the country, while avoiding a major crisis in its relations with the Soviet Union. But the ministry officials' misgivings did not change their superiors' stance.

At the same time, Moscow's attempts to contain its North Vietnamese allies inspired only irritation among the DRV leaders. They questioned the Soviet policy of peaceful coexistence, which they found contrary to their goal of reunifying their motherland. Soviet arguments did not make much sense to the policymakers in Hanoi, who resisted sacrificing the lives of their compatriots in the South for the sake of vague prospects of an East-West détente. Consequently the years that preceded the beginning of the Vietnam War were marked by a growing estrangement between Moscow and Hanoi.

In an effort to save the situation, Moscow felt it necessary to approve in 1962 a token of military assistance to the NLFSV.[49] During the period preceding 1965, the Soviet Union sent to the southern "patriots" through the DRV 130 recoilless guns and mortars, 1,400 machine guns, 54,500 rifles, and ammunition for them.[50] This aid fell far short of the needs of the communist guerrillas in the South. Such reluctant support led only to the further dissatisfaction of the Vietnamese with their Soviet "friends." Guerrillas in the South wondered why the Soviet Union sent arms to India for the struggle against a "friendly communist country," that is, China, and refused to send them to South Vietnam in support of a national liberation movement against "American imperialism."[51]

Encouraged by the coup against Diem in November, 1963, which had been tacitly approved by the United States, and the following chaos of kaleidoscopic changes of governments in Saigon, North Vietnam increased its support of the guerrilla struggle south of the demilitarized zone and began preparations for a protracted war. The Ninth Plenum of the Lao Dong Party in December, 1963, worked out a strategy of the Vietnamese Communists for this struggle.[52] According to information obtained by the Soviets in Hanoi, the North Vietnamese were ready to fight against the Americans and their "Saigon puppets" until complete victory, even if this would mean a war lasting many years.[53] But after the October, 1962, missile crisis, which almost led to nuclear war between the superpowers, Khrushchev was much more reluctant to plunge into adventures that promised dubious dividends in the Cold War confrontation. The conflict in Vietnam fell into this category. The position of the Soviet "friends" perplexed Hanoi and strengthened misunderstanding between the two countries.

Meanwhile China bolstered its position in Vietnam. Chinese sympathizers consolidated their faction in the Lao Dong politburo, where such centrists as Ho Chi Minh and Pham Van Dong remained in the minority.[54] The Sino–North Vietnamese alliance was strengthened when in December, 1964, a Chinese military delegation visited Hanoi to discuss the struggle for the reunification of Vietnam. This delegation signed a formal military agreement with the DRV, with a view to the introduction of Chinese troops on the territory of North Vietnam.[55]

Thus Moscow failed to contain the warriors and so prevent the escalation of the crisis in Indochina into an open armed struggle between the North and the South, and between the Democratic Republic of Vietnam and the United States. Many factors contributed to this failure. First, Indochina and the situation there remained on the periphery of Soviet policymakers' attention. After the settlement in Laos, they were more preoccupied with events in other parts of the world, particularly in Europe and in Cuba. In a sense, Chinese accusations were partly justified. This negligence was typical of Moscow's foreign policy ever since the Geneva Conference, when the Kremlin decided to divide responsibilities with China in matters related to Vietnam. So long as China remained a faithful Soviet ally, this division of labor made sense. But the Kremlin proved to be unprepared for a situation in which China became more a rival than a partner of the Soviets in the world communist movement, with its own views on the international situation that conflicted with those expounded by Moscow. Furthermore, the Soviet leaders had to contend not only with Asian allies but with the United States, whose policy, inherited by Lyndon Johnson from his predecessor, reluctantly led to a growing U.S. involvement in the conflict. In both cases Moscow's actions were marked by a lack of resoluteness and strength, for the Soviets had also to fight with their own convictions and prejudices, formed by the Cold War. One might say that there simply were too many difficulties confronting Moscow for it to overcome. In some cases the Soviets could not act because it was either too late or not within their political and diplomatic ability. In other cases they deliberately chose not to act, because of their convictions and phobias. As a result, they helped make the war in Vietnam a historical fact and an example of missed opportunities.

Chapter 4

Communist Powers Divided

China, the Soviet Union, and the Vietnam War

XIAOMING ZHANG

Throughout the Vietnam War, the two dominant Communist powers, the People's Republic of China (PRC) and the Soviet Union, were allied with the Democratic Republic of Vietnam (DRV) against the United States and the Saigon regime. This Communist coalition proceeded even though the two Communist powers were often at loggerheads over communist ideology and over the question of whether leadership of the world revolutionary movement should come from Moscow or Beijing. From the beginning of hostilities in Vietnam, this dispute was more significant to Chinese leaders, especially Mao Zedong, than any others. Almost from the founding of the PRC in 1949, the Sino-Soviet dissension affected Beijing's strategy, policy, and overall involvement in Vietnam. Although both Chinese and Soviet involvement in Vietnam were permeated by competing security concepts and national interests, these elements, though important, were often overshadowed by personal experience and perceptions on the part of their leaders toward their respective competing communist societies and within the context of the global Cold War environment. To some extent, therefore, the Vietnam War should be seen not only as one element in the Sino-American confrontation but also one element in the Sino-Soviet rivalry.

The Sino-Soviet dispute has been an important subject to the scholarship of those who have studied various international dimensions of the Vietnam War.[1] The ideological competition and geopolitical struggle between the two

Communist powers has been recognized as an overriding determinant of Beijing's and Moscow's involvement in the Vietnam War. Yet the perceptiveness of the Chinese Communist Party (CCP) leaders as they sought to relate their Vietnam policies to Sino-Soviet relations has been studied less thoroughly. Students of the CCP's foreign relations need to pay attention, for example, to the underlying ideology, personal beliefs, and experience that shaped China's relations with the Soviet Union through the twists and turns of the 1950s and 1960s as the partnership of the two Communist powers transformed into a deadly rivalry. This study will look in some depth at the extremely intricate course of China's involvement in the Vietnam War in the context of the Sino-Soviet relationship. To be more specific, it argues that CCP leadership's political vision and values—especially Mao's personal attitude toward the Soviet leaders in the Kremlin and the Soviet Union in general—complicated China's decisions and activities to support the DRV in its resistance to American aggression. As a result, China's involvement in the Vietnam War brought about adverse consequences for both Beijing and Hanoi during the following decade.

China's initial involvement in Vietnam began at the time when a new relationship evolved between the Chinese and Soviet Communists in the late 1940s. During the immediate post–World War II years, Moscow adopted a minimalist position with respect to supporting Asian communist revolutions. The Chinese Communist war against Jiang Jieshi's Nationalist government had only marginally benefited from nominal assistance from the Soviet Union. To the Soviet leader, Joseph Stalin, Asian communist leaders such as Mao Zedong and Ho Chi Minh seemed uncontrollably independent, likely to become an Asian hybrid of Titoism.[2] Because of the descent of the "iron curtain" in Europe and an imminent communist victory in China, the Soviet attitude toward the Chinese revolution altered. When Liu Shaoqi, second in the leadership of the CCP, secretly went to Moscow in July and August, 1949, in order to seek a new strategic relationship between the two parties, Stalin spoke with feeling of the international impact of the Chinese revolution on other countries and revolutionary movements, noting that the center of world revolution had gravitated from Europe to East Asia, and that the Chinese Communists must play a more active role in promoting world revolutionary movements there.[3]

Stalin's view about China's leading role in Asian revolutions was based on a Soviet fundamental assessment of the world situation prefaced in the late 1940s. Moscow was preoccupied by its European interest; any incident there might lead to direct confrontation with the United States and its allies. A powerful Soviet Union required a relatively long period of peace to develop its socialist economy. In Asia, the Chinese experience presented the opportunity for a communist revolutionary movement that would not involve the Soviet Union directly.[4] When Ho Chi Minh asked Stalin to provide substantial Soviet assistance for the Vietnamese Communist revolution during his 1950 secret visit to Moscow, the Russian leader directed him to the Chinese. To Stalin, China had many contacts with Vietnam historically and contemporarily, due in large part to its contiguous location. As a result, a new triangular relationship was forged, in which the Soviets would concentrate in giving their assistance to China, while the Chinese, in turn, could assist the Vietnamese Workers Party (VWP).[5]

Oddly enough, Stalin's strategic plan for the sphere of responsibility coincided with plans of the Chinese. With a revolutionary victory at hand in China, Mao Zedong and other CCP leaders had to reconsider the nature and significance of their own revolution in relation to a much broader anti-imperialist Asian, even world, revolution. Although the Bolshevik revolution had provided momentum for a world proletarian revolutionary movement, the Chinese revolution offered another model in a backward, largely rural country to other peoples who were struggling for national liberation. China's assistance to the Viet Minh would afford an opportunity for the CCP leadership to make Vietnam the first nation to launch an Asian revolution based on the Chinese model.[6]

Perhaps more importantly, playing a preeminent role in Asia would enable the CCP leaders to act independently while maintaining initiative in their own hands in terms of Beijing's new strategic partnership with Moscow. In 1949, the CCP leadership adopted a leaning-to-one-side policy, which theoretically submitted the CCP to Moscow's supremacy in the world communist movement. To many Chinese Communist leaders, the leaning to the Soviet Union policy was merely a measure of expedience to secure China from a possible U.S. invasion while using Soviet assistance to gain strength. In the minds of Chinese leaders, they never accepted the idea that China's political status was an inferior one. Although China was a lesser military and economic power, its involvement in Vietnam demanded that the international community recognize China's equal status as a great world power.[7]

Indeed, intense Chinese national pride could not acquiesce in a dependent relationship with the Soviet Union for a lengthy period. The traditional Middle Kingdom mentality often served as an inspiration for Chinese regional and even global ambitions.[8] The fate of the Sino-Soviet alliance and its effect on Vietnam would ultimately be determined by the question of how long the CCP leadership would continue to subordinate itself to Soviet supremacy in the world communist movement. Throughout his remaining years in the Kremlin, Stalin held to a noncommittal policy toward the situation in Indochina, while the Chinese helped the Viet Minh troops resist the French in battlefields across Vietnam. Not until the 1954 Geneva Conference did the Soviet leadership enter into its first venture in Indochina. However, the Soviet role remained strictly limited.

The Geneva Conference was initiated by the Soviet call for finding ways of reducing international tensions in the Far East.[9] Nonetheless, the Chinese capitalized on Geneva as an opportunity to elevate China's status and prestige in the international arena following three years of waging a bloody war in Korea. Chinese diplomacy, not the Soviet's, became the center of attention at the conference. The Chinese, as Professor Qiang Zhai has noted, not only succeeded in playing "British and French realism off the rigidity and inflexibility of American Cold War policies," but also cooperated with the Soviets to press the Viet Minh to accept a compromising settlement in Southeast Asia.[10] Nothing else out of Geneva appeared more significant than an emerging perception of China by the Chinese leadership as the champion of the Afro-Asian nationalist cause against the oppression and exploitation of the West.

Nonetheless, Chinese delegates operated at the conference within a benevolent partnership of the existing Sino-Soviet relationship. Beijing's inexperience at international meetings and uncertainty about the conference made it all but necessary for the Chinese to seek Soviet guidance. In April, 1954, Zhou Enlai made three visits to Moscow, where he consulted with Soviet leaders concerning goals, position, and strategy at the conference. At Geneva, Soviet leadership on the communist side was unquestionable. Meetings between Zhou Enlai and Vyacheslav Molotov, Soviet foreign minister, were held almost daily at the residence of the Soviet delegation. The Chinese were particularly cautious in speaking, as well as in drafting documents, along the same lines as the Soviets.[11] On the other hand, the Soviet foreign minister often intervened when issues between China and the other powers became acrimonious, urging the Americans to seek accommodation with Beijing and facilitating an improvement of the Sino-British relationship.[12] Close consultations and near harmonious cooperation between China and the Soviet Union characterized Communist diplomacy at Geneva.

Geneva opened a new chapter for the PRC's diplomacy. At the end of 1953, the Beijing leadership adopted the principles of peaceful coexistence as the basic norms governing China's foreign relations.[13] Although the PRC would continue to provide the DRV with economic and military assistance, the Beijing leadership would not encourage any quick revolutionary transformation in the South. During his meeting with Ho Chi Minh and Pham Van Dong in November, 1956, Zhou Enlai repeatedly emphasized that "the unification should be regarded as a long-term struggle," and that "only when the North had been consolidated with extensive efforts, would it become possible to talk about how to win over the South and how to unify the country."[14]

China's promotion of peaceful coexistence and noninterference in the internal affairs of Asian countries witnessed a more independent Chinese diplomacy in the international arena. Participation in the 1955 Bandung conference was the first occasion for the PRC to conduct its diplomacy at an international conference in the absence of any Soviet guidance. At about the same time, Nikita Khrushchev assumed the leadership in the Kremlin, which granted Beijing a chance to reconsider Sino-Soviet relations on more equal terms. Khrushchev's 1954 visit to Beijing cast serious doubt on the quality and ability of the new Soviet leader in the minds of Chinese leaders. For example, recalls Mao's translator, Shi Zhe, Khrushchev appeared to the Chinese as neither prudent nor well behaved.[15]

In early 1956, Chinese leaders began to free themselves from the Soviet model and explore China's own way to socialism.[16] Such an effort reflected the burgeoning unease among Chinese leaders. Mao was particularly discontented with the unequal relationship between Beijing and Moscow. He had personal respect for Stalin as a great leader who managed to transform the Soviet Union into a Communist superpower, but at the same time he was agonized by his bitter experience with the Russian dictator.[17] If Mao somehow had allowed himself to bow to Stalin, he certainly would not do so to his successor. Not too long after Khrushchev took over the Kremlin, differences emerged between the Chinese and Soviet parties and governments over issues ranging from Khrushchev's criticism of Stalin and the general principles underlying the relations among "brotherly parties and states" to the Soviet Union's attitudes toward the Chinese revolution.[18]

Beginning in 1958, drastic differences between Mao's and Khruschev's perceptions of the world situation became publicized. The focus of this disagreement was on how to handle their relations with the West and how to prevent a world war in a nuclear age. Mao Zedong believed that the international situation had come to a turning point as the balance of power between the East and the West had changed fundamentally. The United States was in a passive, defensive position, whereas the Soviet-led Communist movement was in a position of active offense. To Mao, the Soviet leadership, however, seemed too scared of war, especially nuclear war, and pursued a policy of accommodation or even of compromise with the West, while reducing support of national independence movements in order to avoid a Soviet-U.S. confrontation.[19]

This discordance was reflected in Mao's Vietnam policies. In the late 1950s, the Hanoi leadership asked Moscow's advice about the strategies for its future struggle. The Soviet response was to encourage peaceful coexistence between the North and South, and "the use of peaceful means for national unification on the independent and democratic basis." Beijing, however, wanted the Vietnamese to abandon any illusion for unification through plebiscite, in accordance with the Geneva agreement, and to prepare for a long-term struggle.[20] The Soviet Union's assistance to the DRV was largely economic. Three thousand World War II German weapons symbolized the only military supplies from the Soviet Union to the DRV, and Ho was very unhappy about this.[21]

The Soviet attitude toward Hanoi's unfinished revolution after Geneva left the DRV leadership to continue depending solely on China for development of its own military prowess. In October, 1958, Vo Nguyen Giap headed a Vietnamese military delegation to Beijing, discussing their military plan and Chinese aid. In the summer of 1958, Ho Chi Minh went to Beijing and Beidaihe, a summer resort in North China, talking with Zhou Enlai and Deng Xiaoping about Chinese assistance to Vietnam.[22] Following these talks, China stepped up its efforts to equip and train North Vietnamese soldiers. For example, China immediately supplied North Vietnam with 50,000 Soviet-designed AK-47 assault rifles even before Chinese soldiers were equipped.[23] In 1959, the Hanoi leadership readopted the strategy of armed struggle in the South. Developments in the South, such as heavy losses of communist personnel and controlled areas and increasing discontent among key social and political groups might have been crucial to Hanoi's decision, but assured Chinese support could not be ignored.

The year 1960 was marked by a fast-paced rupture between the two Communist allies. Beginning in April, Beijing published "Long Live Leninism," followed by two other articles critical of the current Soviet leadership. In response, the Soviets first organized fellow communist parties to attack the CCP's domestic and foreign policies at the Bucharest conference on June 20, and then about a month later declared the withdrawal of all Soviet experts working in China.[24] The intensified Sino-Soviet ideological disputes further radicalized the Chinese position in international affairs. As early as 1959, Mao had realized that Khrushchev's détente policy had betrayed the Marxist proletarian cause and turned the Soviet Union into the first victim of John Foster Dulles's strategy of "peaceful evolution."[25] In 1962, an ethnic riot instigated by the Soviet Union broke out in China's Xinjiang region. Simultaneously, U.S. military involvement in South Vietnam increased, culminating in the formal establishment of the Military Assistance Command in Vietnam. Jiang Jieshi and the Chinese Nationalists in Taiwan also actively engaged in commando attacks against the mainland. These developments greatly alarmed Beijing authorities. As Mao's secretary for foreign affairs, Lin Ke, recalled later, the Chinese leader began to think of "the possibility of joint U.S.-Soviet efforts to attack China."[26]

In Mao's view, war was inevitable, and imperialism was the root of war. Having realized the cruelty of war, the Chinese leader certainly did not want a war fought in China or a world war. However, he believed that fear would not impede war. The prevention of an outbreak of war, particularly nuclear war, depended on the development of China's own strength and the support for national independence movements in other countries. To the Chinese leader, Vietnam was one area that would thwart U.S. imperialism, deterring the United States from launching a world war.[27] After the summer of 1962, China redoubled its efforts to support the guerrilla warfare in South Vietnam by supplying the DRV with 90,000 rifles and guns for equipping 230 infantry battalions. In March, 1963, senior military officers from China met with North Vietnamese generals to discuss Chinese assistance and cooperation in the event of a U.S. invasion.[28] In December, the deputy chief of staff of the People's Liberation Army (PLA), Li Tianyou, was sent to help the Vietnamese set up strategic defense and battlefield preparations.[29]

China's policy toward Vietnam must be understood within the context of the rapidly deteriorating Sino-Soviet relationship. The rise of Khrushchevism in Moscow meant the abandonment of Soviet legitimacy as the leader of the socialist countries and the ongoing world revolution. Beijing desperately needed supporters in its ideological disputes with Moscow. Giving China's support to North Vietnam would guarantee Hanoi's obligation to stand on China's side and would demonstrate that the center of world revolution had shifted to Beijing. On the other hand, Chinese leaders could not afford to give any impression that China also had failed to support revolutionary liberation movements when PRC leaders were sharply criticizing Moscow's failure to do so. Victory in North Vietnam's war of national liberation could also demonstrate Mao's political correctness in adopting a more militant approach toward the United States.

Deteriorating relations between China and the Soviet Union placed Hanoi in an awkward position. Ho Chi Minh had regarded the Soviet Union and China as Vietnam's "big brother and big sister," always finding himself bewildered by the Sino-Soviet quarrels. Hoping for united Sino-Soviet support for his revolutionary cause in Vietnam, Hanoi initiated a mediation between Beijing and Moscow. In 1962, Ho proposed to convene an international conference of Communist parties to resolve their differences. This proposal brought Chinese and Soviet party leaders together at a negotiation table in Moscow in July, 1963. Unfortunately, no healing of the breach resulted; instead, the gap widened.[30] Yet Ho continued to urge a Sino-Soviet dialogue. After receiving several letters from Ho, on December 27, 1963, Mao answered that he agreed to have another round with the Soviets but did not feel it necessary to have such a meeting within the immediate future because there would be nothing new to discuss. The dispute, as Mao continued, could not be resolved by three or four meetings, and it would take years and even more than ten years to achieve an outcome that was "favorable to revolution and to a true solidarity."[31]

What made Mao feel most gratified at the time was that the VWP had just convened the Ninth Plenum of the Central Committee, at which the Hanoi leadership adopted an antirevisionist platform. Although the VWP leadership still wanted to achieve the unity of the world communist movement, it began to be concerned that the Soviet détente policy might place "maintenance of world peace above unification of Vietnam."[32] To win their armed struggle in the South, the North Vietnamese needed substantial assistance from their Communist allies. For the time being, however, only Beijing was offering the necessary commitments. An antirevisionist rhetoric would please the Chinese and likely would realize more support, while sending a message to the Soviet leadership that détente with the West could very well threaten the revolutionary cause of Vietnam.

In January, 1964, a party delegation headed by Le Duan, the new secretary-general, was dispatched to Moscow to expound the VWP's position and views. Probably worried about a misinterpretation by the Chinese, the delegation was instructed not to make a joint statement with the Soviets. However, an internal dichotomy occurred among Hanoi's leaders. Le Duan violated the politburo's decision and signed a joint statement while in Moscow even though its content appeared incompatible to the party's antirevisionist line.[33] Le Duan's visit did not alter Soviet policy toward Vietnam during Khrushchev's last year in the Kremlin. His pro-Russian attitude began to cast a shadow over future Sino-Vietnamese relations. Shortly after his return from Moscow, Le Duan warned the chief editor of *Nhan Dan,* Hoang Tung, not to publish any more antirevisionist articles.[34]

How the Chinese read this change is unknown. In 1964, the Chinese leadership increasingly worried about the U.S. threat to China and decided to prepare the nation for war. Considering China's vulnerability in such a conflict, Beijing adopted a three-front strategy.[35] This strategy called for a heavy investment in the remote provinces of southwestern and northwestern China, while requiring every first and second front province to set up its own munitions industry.[36] The Tonkin Gulf incident in August, 1964, greatly alarmed Chinese leaders. The thought could not have escaped Mao's mind that a massive war of invasion against China was imminent, and U.S. military escalation in Vietnam was perceived to be the prelude of the larger conflict. Beginning in the fall of 1964, preparing for war became a dominant national theme, penetrating every cell of Chinese society.[37]

While Beijing's attention focused on the south, awaiting a possible U.S. invasion, the deteriorating relationship with Moscow continued to be a pervasive concern for China's security. In early 1963, Beijing authorities started to worry about China's long frontier with the Soviet Union. Between July and October, 1963, Luo Ruiqing, PLA's chief of staff, traveled to Northeast China and Xinjiang, organizing Chinese frontier defenses. Perceiving an invasion from the north against the capital area, on July 2, 1964, Mao ordered the construction of three defense lines around Beijing and Tianjin.[38] Nevertheless, in Beijing's strategic thinking at the time, U.S. imperialism was treated unequivocally as China's chief potential threat. The ouster of Khrushchev in October offered the Chinese an opportunity to heal the breach between the two communist allies.

Beijing's response was cautious but one of elation. Chinese leaders speculated that Khrushchev's fall from power was probably due either to the failure of his internal and external policies that led to grievance inside the party, or to his arbitrary style of leadership, or maybe both. They, however, believed that the change of leadership in Moscow would benefit the Soviet Union in its relationship with other socialist countries as well as the entire world.[39] Prior to receiving a Soviet invitation, Mao proposed to send a Chinese delegation headed by Zhou Enlai to participate in celebrations for the forty-seventh anniversary of the October Revolution in Moscow. The primary purpose of this trip was to explore whether Soviet policy had actually changed under the new leadership and to seek communist unity against real and perceived enemies. Particularly, the Chinese leadership wanted to persuade the new Soviet leaders to cancel a scheduled international communist meeting that Khrushchev had programmed for criticizing the CCP.[40]

Despite a Chinese desire for improving the Sino-Soviet relationship during their mission, the Chinese leaders found themselves disappointed in Moscow. During a Soviet reception on November 6, 1964, Marshal Rodin Malinovsky suggested to Zhou that the Chinese should overthrow Mao just as the Russians had ousted Khrushchev. Although new Soviet leader Leonid Brezhnev later apologized for this, Zhou and other Chinese at the scene came away convinced that Malinovsky's provocation represented a continuation of Khrushchev's thought and policy by the current leadership in the Kremlin. During the following discussions between Zhou and Soviet leaders, remaining hopes, if any, of the Chinese for improving Sino-Soviet relations evaporated. The Soviet leaders insisted on convening the international communist meeting. Anastas Mikoyan, a Soviet politburo member, declared that with reference to Soviet policy toward China the new Soviet leaders were acting in no way different from Khrushchev.[41]

Having not been satisfied with Moscow's policy toward Vietnam, the Hanoi leadership also regarded the ouster of Khrushchev as an opportunity to acquire

Soviet concrete support for their war of national unification. During their participation in the Soviet October Revolution celebrations, Pham Van Dong and Le Duc Tho recommended that the new Soviet leadership send a delegation to Vietnam, one that would express Soviet readiness to provide assistance, including military assistance, to the Vietnamese in their war against the United States. According to Hoang Van Hoan, the DRV leaders pointed out to the Soviet leaders that any Russian assistance would reduce the Chinese influence in Vietnam.[42]

This timely proposal was welcomed by the new Soviet leadership. Russian historian Ilya Gaiduk has noted that after the Tonkin Gulf incident the Soviet Union "faced a problem of reconciling its communist prestige with its geopolitical interest." As war between Hanoi and Washington appeared inevitable in Southeast Asia, Soviet leaders became aware of the serious risk to their influence in the world communist movement if they remained inactive toward North Vietnam. A continuing refusal to provide assistance to the DRV would make Moscow a target for sharp criticism from China. On the other hand, Moscow's assistance of the DRV would strengthen Soviet positions in Southeast Asia, while its failure to support the North Vietnamese would raise questions about Soviet ability to defend other socialist countries, especially those in Eastern Europe.[43]

During the months of November and December, 1964, two meetings of the Presidium of the Soviet Communist Central Committee convened for the purpose of discussing the issue of Soviet military aid to Vietnam.[44] No details are available about these meetings. Somehow a new Soviet policy toward the conflict in Vietnam emerged. On February 6, 1965, new Soviet Prime Minister Alexis Kosygin visited Hanoi. Following a series of negotiations between the Soviets and Vietnamese, a joint communiqué declared that measures would "be taken to strengthen the defensive potential of North Vietnam."[45] Indeed, the direction and forms of Soviet assistance were later confirmed during Le Duan and Vo Nguyen Giap's April, 1965, visit to Moscow. After that, the DRV began receiving Soviet MiG fighter planes, surface-to-air missile (SAM) systems, and other supplies. Soviet pilots and military specialists were also sent to operate the Soviet weapons in North Vietnam.[46]

These Soviet gestures to Hanoi were regarded negatively in China. During Kosygin's stopover in Beijing on February 11, Chinese leaders declined a Soviet proposal to coordinate their assistance to North Vietnam; instead, they warned the Soviet leader not to use the Vietnam strife to bargain with Washington.[47] To the Hanoi leadership, a joint effort by two Communist allies would be in the best interest for their national liberation at a time when the United States was escalating the war in Vietnam. Soon after Kosygin's visit to Hanoi, the DRV proposed a joint statement by the socialist countries to condemn the United States for waging a war against Vietnam.[48] Viewing the new Soviet-Vietnamese relations as Moscow's attempt to gain ascendancy over China in Vietnam, the Chinese rejected this proposal. On February 28, 1965, Zhou traveled to Hanoi, explaining to Ho Chi Minh and Le Duan that "the new Soviet leaders are pursuing just Khrushchevism and will never change it."[49]

The year 1965 also marked an escalation of Chinese involvement in Vietnam. Washington's gradual increase in its air attacks on the DRV and the introduction of combat units into South Vietnam in March, 1965, convinced Beijing that the United States was bent on invading North Vietnam and possibly also China. On April 14, 1965, the CCP Central Committee dispatched a directive to the party's county and military regimental organizations, calling them to prepare for fighting together with the Vietnamese people against the United States. While closely watching the development of an expanding military situation in Vietnam, the directive stated that all party cadres at county level and above should also "prepare for the U.S. imperialists to bombard our country's military facilities, industrial bases, key transportation places, and big cities, and even to expand war operations into our land." The directive also warned that they should be ready for not only a small- or medium-scale war, but also a large one. Subsequently, the Central Military Committee (CMC) alerted the Chinese air force, navy, and the military regions of Guangzhou and Kuanming into combat readiness.[50]

Although Chinese leaders perceived a serious possibility of war with the United States, they calculated that it was in China's best interest to resist the Americans in Vietnam. Following Hanoi's invitation, on April 17 the CMC swiftly ordered the organization of Chinese troops to assist in defending North Vietnam. Beginning in June, 1965, Chinese troops crossed the border, taking over the air defense of areas north of the twenty-first parallel; operating and maintaining two rail supply lines between China and Hanoi; constructing defense works along the northeast coast and in the Red River delta area; and building highways in North and Northwest Vietnam. Beijing, sensitive to Vietnamese national pride and their sensitivity about self-sufficiency and self-reliance, also agreed that all Chinese troops in Vietnam would be commanded by the Vietnamese with Chinese assistance. Meanwhile, China increased the supplying of arms, munitions, and other materials sent to the DRV, and made every effort to satisfy the Vietnamese with the sinews of war. China's own security interests underlined the deployment of Chinese troops and the extensive aid to the Vietnamese.[51]

With regard to the continuing Sino-Soviet dispute, Beijing's attempt to maintain Hanoi in its orbit was obvious. Beijing became more and more concerned about Soviet moves in Vietnam, which were easily perceived as undercutting the Chinese self-promoted leading role in the current world struggle against U.S. imperialism, and also as an effort to resume Moscow's former domination of the communist world. On April 3, 1965, the Soviets sent a secret letter to Beijing suggesting a Sino–Soviet–North Vietnamese conference at Beijing to discuss achieving a unified action to aid Vietnam. Two weeks later Moscow made further requests for Chinese cooperation with Soviet assistance to the DRV: (1) the transit of 4,000 Soviet troops through China to Vietnam; (2) the use of one or two airfields in southwest China to allow the Soviet planes to defend North Vietnam; and (3) an air corridor for Soviet free traffic in China's airspace.[52]

The Chinese did not respond until July 10 and this time repudiated all Soviet appeals under the accusation that the Soviet proposal was an attempt to control China "under cover of aid." In this letter the Chinese claimed that their observations during the past few months indicated that the Soviet appeasement of the United States would have the effect of selling out the interest of the Vietnamese people's liberation cause, and the so-called "united action" was designed to "subordinate the fraternal parties to the order of your patriarchal party" and "to turn them to the tool of the Soviet-U.S. collaboration for world domination."[53]

Beijing's understanding was to relate the Sino-Soviet rift to Hanoi's war against the United States, but such would be hardly apprehended by the Vietnamese because they critically needed assistance from *both* Communist powers. While the Beijing leadership would have rejected such a Soviet proposal from the very beginning, it did not want to give any inkling to the Vietnamese that its ideological dispute with Moscow would compromise Chinese support to Hanoi. The month of April, 1965, became crucial to China's policy toward Vietnam. It was during this period that the Chinese made their own concrete commitment to the DRV and deployed troops to defend North Vietnam. Two points should be elaborated upon here. First, a delayed refusal would show Hanoi that Beijing's ideological dispute with Moscow had little to do with Chinese assistance to North Vietnam. Second, within three months the Chinese would get themselves organized and become the first country to send troops in defending North Vietnam. Thus, China demonstrated that it was a more reliable and sincere ally than a remote Soviet Union.

In the fall of 1965 Hanoi brought Moscow's request to Beijing about the air shipment across China of three Soviet surface-to-air missile regiments for North Vietnam. No longer able to throw road blocks, the Chinese consented to the transfer of the Soviet troops by trains but not by air. In order to preserve complete secrecy over the entire operation, 160,000 Chinese soldiers were mobilized to provide security and assistance to the Soviet troops and equipment traveling through China to North Vietnam. This apparently set a precedent that future transfers of Soviet materials and personnel through Chinese territory would only be conducted under the condition of China's direct control and would be considered as Beijing's favor to Hanoi.[54]

During the Vietnam War, the passage of Soviet war materials via China to North Vietnam remained a major issue throughout Sino-Soviet assistance to Hanoi. The Soviets repeatedly accused the Chinese of obstructing the transit of Soviet military equipment bound for North Vietnam. These Soviet allegations against China, as Douglas Pike summarized, included delay of Soviet shipments; harassment of Soviet military personnel en route to Vietnam; unloading of Soviet missiles from trains for pirating purposes; and even theft of Soviet equipment, including airplanes.[55] Beijing denied all Soviet charges, while raising questions about why Moscow could not ship Soviet aid materials by sea to North Vietnam.[56] To Chinese leaders, it was just a Soviet conspiracy to use their transits to bring pressure on the already overloaded Chinese rail system so that any delay could be translated into a Chinese lack of sincerity to help North Vietnam. Claiming that the Soviet transits contained obsolete military equipment and damaged weapons, Beijing then asked both the Vietnamese and Lao communists to send their own representatives to the Sino-Soviet border to determine which Soviet shipments should be transferred and which should not.[57]

The onset of the Proletarian Cultural Revolution in 1966 placed China in an ever more intractable position to handle Soviet materials. Normal rail transportation was frequently interrupted by civil violence between the rival factions of the so-called "revolutionary rebel organizations." Since the first half of 1967 looting and robberies of supplies destined for Vietnam from trains and military warehouses occurred frequently. By the end of that year the Chinese found it difficult to defend themselves against Soviet accusations.[58] Nevertheless, the Chinese claimed that 630,000 tons of aid materials from the Soviet Union and other Eastern European countries were transported to North Vietnam between 1965 and 1975, and China had made no charges for these transits.[59]

While Beijing and Moscow were competing with their assistance for North Vietnam, Hanoi had no more shortage of military supplies. The Vietnamese still demanded that Beijing ship aid in amounts that actually extended beyond their consuming and shipping capacity. Each year, large quantities of military materials were overstocked in Chinese rail yards and warehouses, while others lay idle inside Vietnam.[60] However, Beijing continued its generosity, giving highest priority to supplying arms and military equipment to

Hanoi. During the Vietnam War, the North Vietnamese forces received more of certain equipment such as howitzers, antiaircraft guns, and mortars than did the PLA.[61]

The North Vietnamese were fighting their war with ever increasing supplies from both China and Russia. A general assumption with respect to Soviet and Chinese military aid was that most of the Soviet assistance consisted of heavy and sophisticated military equipment such as planes and surface-to-air missiles, while China mainly provided a large number of light weapons and logistic supplies. According to recently available Chinese and Soviet sources, tables 4.1 and 4.2 show details of the support provided from both the Soviet Union and China to Vietnam. Chinese military aid to Hanoi appeared categorically far more extensive and substantial. Any evaluation of China's involvement in Vietnam should not ignore the facts that China had much less industrial capacity than the Soviet Union, and that during the Vietnam War, China itself was in a state of chaos due to the Cultural Revolution.

China's contribution to Hanoi's war against the United States proved significant. But the Soviet involvement might have compelled Beijing's leaders to take a second look at their earlier promise to provide air cover for Hanoi. In April, 1965, Le Duan told Liu Shaoqi that North Vietnam needed "volunteer pilots" to restrict U.S. bombardment to areas south of the twentieth or nineteenth parallels, while providing air defense for Hanoi and major transportation lines. The Vietnamese leader emphasized that the presence of the Chinese air force would have the effect of elevating the Vietnamese people's morale. In June, the form of Chinese air support was further arranged between the two countries' chiefs of staff, Van Tien Dung and Luo Ruiqing, to the effect that: (1) China could send volunteer pilots to fly Vietnamese planes in combat; (2) Chinese planes could operate from Vietnamese air fields; or (3) Chinese planes could take off from air bases in China to engage Americans over Vietnam. So far there is no evidence about any Chinese volunteers having flown combat missions in North Vietnam, except for a few cases of overflight.[62] The Vietnamese *White Book* of 1979 revealed that in July Beijing refused Hanoi's request to send Chinese pilots to Vietnam because the Chinese did not believe that the timing was appropriate. Beijing did not make any denial of this allegation. Obviously, China failed to keep Liu Shaoqi's promise: "what PLA units they (the North Vietnamese) want to come into Vietnam, and Beijing will send them only at Hanoi's request."[63]

A mounting Soviet involvement in North Vietnam drove a wedge between Beijing and Hanoi. Beginning in 1966 Chinese leaders appeared to feel offended by the changing mood of DRV leaders toward the Soviet Union. In March, without joining Beijing's boycott of the Soviet Party's Twentieth-third

Table 4.1. Chinese Military Supplies to North Vietnam, 1965–75

Type	1965	1966	1967	1968	1969	1970	1971	1972	1973	1974	1975
Aircraft	18	2	70	—	—	—	—	14	36	—	20
Artillery	4,439	3,362	3,984	7,087	3,906	2,212	7,898	9,238	9,912	6,406	4,880
Small Arms	220,767	141,531	146,600	219,890	139,900	101,800	143,100	189,000	233,500	164,500	141,800
Small Arms Ammunition	11,401	17,812	14,700	24,792	11,917	2,901	5,719	4,000	4,000	3,000	96.5
Artillery Ammunition	180	106.6	136.3	208.2	135.7	39.7	189.9	221	221	139	—
Tanks	—	—	26	18	—	—	80	220	120	80	—
Navy Vessels	7	14	25	—	—	—	24	71	5	6	—
Automobiles	114	96	435	454	—	—	4,011	8,758	1,210	506	—
Radio Transmitters	2,779	1,568	2,464	1,854	2,464	950	2,464	4,370	4,335	5,148	2,240
Telephone Sets	9,502	2,235	2,289	3,313	4,424	1,600	4,424	5,909	6,447	4,633	2,150
Uniforms	—	40	80	100	120	120	120	140	140	140	—

Note: ammunition is in hundred thousands of rounds; uniforms in hundred thousand pieces. In 1973, China also supplied North Vietnam with three surface-to-air missile systems, along with 180 missiles.

Source: Li and Hao, *Wenhua dageming zhong de jiefangjun.*

Table 4.2. Soviet Military Assistance to North Vietnam, 1965–72

Type	1965	1966	1967	1968	1969	1970	1971	1972
Aircraft	82	63	57	44	36	26	18	14
FA Guns	127	116	114	177	119	90	78	—
AD Missile Systems	10	12	14	—	14	10	10	10
Small Arms	16	17	22	18	14	18	16	10
Small Arms Ammunition	17	18	12	12	12	13	10	10
Artillery Ammunition	29	16	16	17	19	16	11	8
Radars	31	—	43	16	22	18	16	10
Food	124	116	137	122	118	113	106	110
Medical supplies	3.5	4.2	6.3	5.0	8.0	11.0	10.0	5.0

Note: ammunition is in thousands of cases; small arms in thousands; food and medical supplies in tons.
Source: Oleg Sarin and Lev Dvoretsky, *Alien Wars*.

Congress, the VWP sent a delegation headed by Le Duan to Moscow. When Chinese leaders learned that Le Duan reportedly called the Soviet Union his "second motherland," they were shocked.[64] During Le Duan's overstay in Beijing after flying from Moscow, Zhou Enlai brought up two incidents to the Vietnamese leader illustrating Beijing's resentment toward Hanoi's improving relationship with the Soviet Union. First, the Chinese leader wanted Duan to explain why Vietnam had given the Soviet cargo ship an unfair priority over a Chinese ship, which had arrived at the Haiphong port first but received no permission to dock inside the port and thus suffered severe damage during an American air raid.[65] Second, Zhou questioned the Vietnamese leader about Hanoi's real intention in view of recently published accounts in Vietnamese journals of China's historical invasion of Vietnam. The Chinese leader declared that the central concern for Vietnam and China must be their common struggle against American imperialism.[66]

Clearly, Chinese leaders were unhappy about Hanoi's lack of interest in keeping a proper distance from Moscow. They were unable to do anything besides complain. In July, 1966, Hanoi requested one Chinese engineering unit to stay longer after its completion of its original mission. Beijing responded negatively and ordered the unit to return home in September as a move to demonstrate its anger. Even so, because Vietnam was such an important symbol in the world Communist movement, Beijing's ideological commitment to a world revolution left China no other choice but to remain an adamant supporter for Hanoi during the war. Later that year China dispatched another military unit to North Vietnam as a fulfillment of Hanoi's request.[67]

Indeed, the most distressing Soviet influence in Vietnam was its effort to reach a political settlement of the Indochina conflict. Prior to 1966, Soviet leaders found themselves unable to persuade the North Vietnamese to negotiate with the Americans. With an increasing Soviet involvement in North Vietnam, the Hanoi leadership began to divide between pro-war and pro-peace groups. After the Twelfth Party Plenum of the VWP in December, 1965, Le Duan and the pro-peace group appeared to persuade other Hanoi leaders to support negotiations within the limited war strategy.[68] It was during this period that Duan started to advertise to the party and the country that although the war with the Americans was a "long and arduous" struggle, Hanoi would "achieve a decisive victory within a short time to solve the problem." Duan's solution for a decisive victory, according to Hoang Van Hoan, was to be negotiations with the United States.[69] Beijing was well aware of this development in Hanoi all the while, publicly criticizing Moscow's assistance as trying to push the Vietnamese toward "another Munich,"[70] and privately admonishing the Vietnamese leaders not to expect anything at the negotiation table without winning victories on battlefields.[71]

Despite Chinese efforts to influence Hanoi during the course of the war in Vietnam, Beijing was caught off guard in the spring of 1968. On April 3, Hanoi announced its readiness to send a delegation to talk with the Americans. Since the early 1950s, the VWP leaders had routinely consulted with the CCP leadership about their revolutionary strategy and moves. But this time they did not. Zhou Enlai complained to Ho Chi Minh, who was receiving medication in Beijing, asking whether Chairman Ho knew about this or not, and even suggesting to the Vietnamese leader that the hiding of such a move from China might be a conspiracy of Le Duan. Although Ho was also surprised by this news, he soon accepted Duan's explanation that Hanoi's new peace talk approach was what the VWP had simply learned from the CCP's experience of *"bianda biantan"* [fighting while negotiating] during China's civil war.[72]

Nevertheless, Beijing's disappointment continued with a silence by the Chinese media about the Paris peace talks between May and October, 1968. Not until November did the Chinese leadership reluctantly accept Hanoi's peace talk. During his conference with Pham Van Dong on the 17th of that month, Mao, however, still cautioned the Vietnamese leader that "it is difficult to get the U.S. to withdraw from Vietnam through negotiations." In the meantime, Mao informed the Vietnamese leader that China would like to pull their troops out of North Vietnam too.[73] Hanoi's unilateral decision to proceed with negotiations with the Americans ostensibly had a chilling effect on Sino-Vietnamese relations.

By 1968, however, it became evident to the Chinese that Hanoi was growing closer to Moscow than to Beijing. Initially, Hanoi had made every effort to keep troops from the two belligerent allies cooperative during their operations in North Vietnam. Later, the Chinese discovered that Soviet surface-to-air missile units were given priority to redeploy themselves in order to avoid U.S. retaliations, while Chinese antiaircraft artillery units were asked to move into a position previously occupied by the Soviets.[74] When conflicts did occur between Chinese soldiers and Soviet military personnel, the Vietnamese authorities would side with the Soviets, and even accused the hostility of the Chinese soldiers toward the Soviets as somehow impinging "upon Vietnam's sovereignty."[75] It was under this kind of atmosphere that Chinese troops began to depart Vietnam in early 1969.

While the North Vietnamese zagged to the Soviet Union, Chinese leaders were also pondering their own strategy and security. Evidence of the Soviet buildup in the Far East was ample between 1965 and 1969. The signing of a twenty-year treaty of friendship between Moscow and Ulan Bator in 1966 brought Soviet troops to the Chinese-Mongolian border, only a few hundred miles distant from Beijing. Soviet forces in its Far Eastern region grew significantly from approximately seventeen divisions in 1965 to twenty-seven divisions by 1969. Moscow's deployment of nuclear missiles to the Far Eastern military districts in 1967 brought even more pressure on China's security.[76] Since 1964, border incidents had doubled, culminating with the first open fire clash between Chinese and Soviet border patrol units over the Zhen Bao/Damansky Island in March, 1969.[77] Moscow's August, 1968, invasion of Czechoslovakia provided evidence to the Beijing leadership that the "socialist imperialist" Soviet Union might be more perilous than the United States to China's security.[78]

In early 1969, Chinese leaders, however, found themselves needing to prepare their country to fight both superpowers—the United States and the Soviet Union—in either separate wars or a joint war. President Lyndon B. Johnson's 1968 decision to halt the bombing of North Vietnam gave Chinese leaders only a modest breathing space. Although Washington had already engineered a peace approach in Asia, what the Chinese perceived during this period was a more dangerous and threatening United States under the new president, Richard Nixon. In the spring of 1969, the Ninth CCP Congress adopted the platform to prepare for a war with both the United States and the Soviet Union.[79] While still wondering whether the war would come from the south or the north, Mao in February asked four recently deposed PLA marshals—Cheng Yi, Ye Jianying, Xu Xiangqiang, and Nei Rongzhen—to conduct a study on the international situation, and then to make suggestions on policy to the party leadership. Between May and September, the four marshals held several discussions and submitted four reports to the party center. The reports analyzed the triangular relationship among China, the Soviet Union, and the United States from a strategic perspective, noting that the real conflict of interests was between U.S. imperialism and Soviet revisionism, and the contention between them was constant and acute. As a result, the reports argued, it was quite unlikely that the United States and the Soviet Union, either individually or together, would start a massive war of invasion against China.[80]

Unfortunately, this view had little effect on Beijing's policy-making nucleus. China's strategic thinking and security concerns were dominated by Mao's bitter experience and ideological disputes with the Soviet leadership. Escalating Soviet anti-China propaganda along with an increasing Soviet military presence in the Far East, and eventually border clashes, confirmed to the Chinese leadership that the Soviet Union was the more dangerous enemy of China. Beijing's strategic focus steadily shifted to the north. In June, 1969, Mao approved a new national defense plan with an emphasis on "three-north" regions (North China, Northeast China, and Northwest China).[81]

With an ascending belligerency on the Soviet-China border, Kosygin's September meeting with Zhou Enlai in Beijing's airport was an effort to reduce tensions between the two countries. However, Beijing never responded to Moscow's proposals for conclusion of a treaty renouncing aggression and war in Soviet-Chinese relations.[82] Instead, Beijing interpreted the recent Kosygin visit as a smoke screen. Chinese leaders at the time were extremely concerned about a possible Soviet nuclear strike against China, a hot topic in everyday news reports at home and abroad. Yet, during his Beijing airport talks with Kosygin, Zhou received no such promise from the Soviet prime minister that Moscow would not use nuclear weapons to attack China. Beijing was also suspicious of Kosygin's influence inside the Kremlin. When Chinese leaders noted that Kosygin's return received low-key treatment at the Moscow airport, they simply inferred that whatever commitment he had made to the Chinese in Beijing would not constitute the opinion of the Soviet politburo.[83] In October, China entered into an immediate war status with the Soviet Union.[84]

Without access to archives in Hanoi, it is difficult to evaluate the North Vietnamese reaction to such a strategic turn in China.[85] Given the reality that Hanoi continued to regard Washington as the dangerous enemy, it is plausible that the Vietnamese realized that their dependency on China's support to win the war was at stake. According to Chinese sources in table 4.1, the year of 1970 marked a decline in China's military assistance to North Vietnam to the lowest level since 1965, while the last Chinese units returned to China in July.[86] Hanoi's fear of a less-committed Chinese support was further aggravated after Henry Kissinger's trip to China in 1971. A Sino-American détente forced Beijing to assure Hanoi that it was not losing interest in the war and would never allow its other interests to betray Vietnam.[87]

China's détente policy with the United States in the early 1970s placed Beijing in a vulnerable position to remain a champion in a self-projected world revolution, particularly in Vietnam. Thus, the Chinese leadership found itself trapped in a paradoxical situation. While China urgently needed to defend itself from an expected Soviet attack, Beijing still had to respond positively to Hanoi's request for additional military assistance when President Nixon commenced still another round of air raids and mining in North Vietnam. By this time Hanoi's demands often exceeded China's production capability, so Beijing transferred arms and equipment directly from the PLA to Hanoi's inventory.[88] Even while Beijing at the time believed that Hanoi should have asked Soviet assistance against U.S. mining operations, the Chinese leaders had to commit their own poorly equipped navy to Haiphong harbor.[89] Too much had been promised for too long, and any reduction or a hesitated response to Hanoi's request could have undermined China's credibility and prestige in Vietnam.

For the last years of the war, China continued to support the North Vietnamese cause of national unity with substantial assistance. However, it was conducted in a completely different context. With the danger of a U.S. presence in Vietnam dramatically reduced, the years of rivalry with the Soviet Union for dominance in Vietnam also came to a halt. Chinese influence on Hanoi appeared drastically curtailed as the North Vietnamese were no longer compelled to consult and discuss their strategy and policy issues with the Beijing leadership as they had done earlier. With an increasing threat on its northern frontier from the Soviets, China certainly wanted to negate the possibility of a two-front conflict. Nevertheless, the Beijing leadership had to continue to support Hanoi's war efforts in the South for the sake of its commitment to international anti-imperialist struggles. But this stimulus was short lived. After the Vietnamese Communists won the war in 1975, conflicting interests between Hanoi and Beijing began to eclipse their common bond of Marxist-Leninist ideology and eventually gave rise to a new round of confrontation in Southeast Asia.

In summary, both China and the Soviet Union played important roles in the Vietnam War. The driving forces behind China's involvement in Vietnam were Chinese security concerns and national interests, which, however, were often entangled with Sino-Soviet relations and influenced by Chinese perceptions of that relationship. Chinese leaders, particularly Mao, had pondered over a less-than-equal relationship for the PRC with the Soviet Union. Stalin's remarks that the center of revolution had shifted to Asia seemed to legitimize China's claim for a leading role in the Asian, and eventually the world, revolutionary movement. Vietnam offered an opportunity for the new occupants of the Forbidden City to carry this mandate. Perhaps most important, China's involvement in Vietnam demanded that the international community acknowledge its equal status as a great world power at a time when China remained a lesser military and economic power. When the Chinese leadership perceived Khrushchev's détente policy toward the United States to be a threat to China's Asian revolution programs, Vietnam became a central focus of the Sino-Soviet dispute. Beijing's support of Vietnam would not only discourage a possible U.S. aggression against China, but it would also demonstrate China's political correctness in adopting a more militant policy toward the United States. Furthermore, a resolute Chinese commitment for North Vietnam's war of national liberation could ensure that Hanoi, in turn, would stand at Beijing's side.

The Soviet leadership, aware of its weak position in North Vietnam vis-à-vis China, began pursuing an active policy toward the conflict after the fall of Khrushchev in 1964. Although Hanoi desperately needed support from both Communist allies, Beijing resented Soviet involvement, especially its call for a united action, Moscow's attempt to regain control of North Vietnam and China. Fear of Soviet domination served as an inspiration for China's objection to common support actions. However, China's ideological commitment to other countries' national liberation movements could not justify Beijing in reducing assistance to Hanoi. When China's ideological dispute with the Soviet Union presented the Chinese with a new security problem, Beijing's leaders found themselves in an awkward position to make a policy adjustment. The CCP's championship of Hanoi's national unification conflicted with China's new national security concern. By the time China's Indochina policy had to yield to this reality, Hanoi saw a huge gap existing between Beijing's word and deeds, despite China's continued effort to provide military and material support to Vietnamese communists. As a result, one of the great ironies of the Cold War and of communism occurred. After many years, during which China's resources were committed to Hanoi's war effort, the Chinese had created for themselves a new adversary in the event. For both China and Vietnam the tragedy of the Vietnam War continued as the two erstwhile "brotherly comrade" socialist nations engaged in a decade of sabre-rattling and contentious dialogue.

Chapter 5

Vietnam at the Center

Patterns of Diplomacy and Resistance

ROBERT K. BRIGHAM

"We had problems with our own allies," a former senior diplomat from Hanoi explained after the war. "We needed Soviet and Chinese support as a deterrent against further U.S. aggression, but we never wanted to depend on Moscow or Beijing."[1] Indeed, throughout the Vietnam War, the Lao Dong, Vietnam's Communist Party, skillfully charted a course between its two powerful allies. Lao Dong leaders purposefully avoided taking sides in the Sino-Soviet dispute and played one side off the other to gain increased aid and support. It was not until 1968, and the opening of peace talks, that Hanoi finally took a decisive step toward the Kremlin. There were times, however, when leaders in Hanoi could not avoid the pitfalls of being a small nation caught in an international and ideological struggle. There was a price for using Soviet technology and Chinese forces as a deterrent. Occasionally, Vietnam's leaders had to subordinate their own revolutionary interests to the needs of their useful confederates. Furthermore, the Sino-Soviet dispute caused considerable problems for Hanoi, striking at the heart of regional disagreements within the Lao Dong itself.

This paper, using the latest Vietnamese-language sources available to scholars, suggests that Lao Dong leaders operated in a diplomatic world of dependency and resistance. They needed Chinese and Soviet support for revolutionary survival but feared foreign domination and ideological corruption. Party officials in Hanoi also feared that their revolution "could become a pawn" in the ideological conflict between Moscow and Beijing.[2] Hanoi's top leaders therefore gambled on a diplomatic ploy that utilized regional differences within the Lao Dong to assuage Moscow and Beijing. The Lao Dong adopted a Janus-faced policy that created the illusion of revolutionary fidelity to both Communist superpowers. This was indeed a dangerous gambit, and at times, the Lao Dong came perilously close to regional disintegration. "We had no choice but to try to play one side off the other," a Lao Dong official explained after the war, "we had suffered at Geneva for being a small nation with large friends and we had to watch out for our own national interests."[3] For the Lao Dong, however, surviving the ideological split between the Soviets and the Chinese meant exacerbating party regionalism and factionalism.

Regional differences first surfaced within the Lao Dong after the 1954 Geneva Accords. The division of Vietnam forced the party to accept twin revolutionary goals: developing socialism in the North and liberating the South. At times, these objectives were mutually exclusive, and they led to two distinct camps. Most northerners favored granting primacy to consolidating the northern economic experiment, while at the same time, working toward reunification of the country through political means. Some northern Lao Dong leaders, such as National Assembly leader Truong Chinh, feared that an offensive strategy in the South threatened northern interests and provided a pretext for the United States to intervene militarily.[4] They feared that American war planes would target key industries in the North, making economic development impossible. Most southerners, on the other hand, wanted the party to use its limited resources for a complete military victory over the American-backed Saigon regime. During the late 1950s, they favored armed violence to liberate Vietnam south of the seventeenth parallel. Southerners, such as Nguyen Chi Thanh, leader of the party's Southern Directory (COSVN), believed that military victory could come "in a relatively short period of time."[5] The political division of Vietnam, therefore, was an important determinant of subsequent revolutionary national behavior.

During the 1950s, the Lao Dong's regionalism mirrored the Sino-Soviet dispute. The key question in this contest remained: Should revolutionaries transform their societies by parliamentary means or wars for national liberation? In 1956, at the Soviet Union's Twentieth Party Congress, Premier Nikita Khrushchev denounced Josef Stalin and declared that the capitalist and socialist worlds could co-exist peacefully.[6] He added that anti-imperial countries could make the transition from capitalism to socialism through political means alone.[7] Even after Khrushchev's ouster in 1964, Moscow favored the political line through what it called "united action."[8] This policy relied on the combined political power of the socialist bloc countries in eastern Europe to move the

United States toward a less aggressive policy in Vietnam through pragmatic negotiations. Revolutionaries in China, on the other hand, called Khrushchev's policy change "dangerous revisionism," and pledged their continued support for bloody wars of national liberation.[9] "The Soviet revisionists had turned their backs on the Vietnamese revolution," one Beijing propaganda piece proclaimed, "and had left the battlefield in disgrace."[10] Above all else, Beijing feared a Soviet-American accommodation at its expense. Chinese leaders correctly predicted that the 1959 Camp David meeting between Khrushchev and President Eisenhower represented a rapprochement between the Cold War rivals. While Moscow tried to lessen the tensions with Washington, Beijing tried purposefully to foment anti-Americanism in the developing world.

Between 1954 and 1958, the Lao Dong favored the political struggle, moving briefly into Moscow's camp. Party leaders in Hanoi held out hope that the International Control Commission would enforce the political provisions of the 1954 Geneva Accords and that national unity would come through the ballot box. Most political observers agreed that the Lao Dong would win any national election held in Vietnam.[11] Even after elections looked unlikely, the DRV favored the political line. In April, 1956, shortly after the Soviet Union's Twentieth Party Congress, Deputy Premier A. I. Mikoyan and Ho Chi Minh delivered a joint declaration in Hanoi. They concluded that the DRV should consolidate its economy and "achieve reunification of Viet Nam by peaceful and democratic means."[12] For the Lao Dong, the political struggle offered the nascent party a respite from its long military conflict against the French and the time necessary to develop the northern economy. According to official Lao Dong reports, Hanoi's first priority was to "raise the living standard of the people" and "diversify the economy."[13] At its Ninth Plenum in April, 1956, the Lao Dong confirmed its commitment to the political struggle. Truong Chinh, the outgoing secretary-general, reported that "the view of the Soviet Union and the 20th Congress . . . has provided us with new reasons to be confident in the correctness of the policy of the Lao Dong . . ."[14] The political struggle also favored the party's emphasis on the moral superiority of its social revolution compared to South Vietnam's political program.

Hanoi's ideological and strategic position was never static, however, and the Lao Dong often embraced Soviet and Chinese philosophies simultaneously. Ngo Dinh Diem, president of the Republic of Vietnam (RVN/South Vietnam) disrupted this balancing act when he began a series of anticommunist campaigns that threatened to destroy the Lao Dong's infrastructure south of the seventeenth parallel. Diem and his secret police arrested thousands of suspected communists, and, as a result, cadre levels dropped off dramatically. Diem's harsh and repressive policies eventually forced southerners to adopt a more militant line. In 1956, Le Duan, then the leader of the Nam Bo [Southern] Regional Committee, issued a report calling for armed violence against Diem. In this document, "The Path of Revolution in the South," Le Duan argued that the time had come to take up arms to liberate Vietnam south of the seventeenth parallel, because "the U.S.-Diem clique are determined to destroy the Communists." In a now famous declaration, the Lao Dong leader claimed that "there is no other path for the people of the South but the path of revolution."[15] In 1959, the party accepted Le Duan's recommendations and presided over the birth of the National Front for the Liberation of South Vietnam (NLF). By 1962, the NLF's mission was to overthrow Ngo Dinh Diem by force.

On the surface, the move toward armed rebellion in the South was a clear refutation of Moscow's policies. The creation of a revolutionary front meant that the party had granted primacy to violence over the political struggle. In Hanoi, however, the highest ranking officials in the government still spoke the language of revisionism. Party Premier Pham Van Dong argued publicly that the best way to help the South was to strengthen the North economically and socially. In a speech before the National Assembly he proclaimed, "our brothers in Moscow still lead the Socialist camp. We need their guidance and assistance."[16] Several other party leaders echoed these comments, suggesting that "China wants to keep Vietnam divided and weak. They would like to see us enter into a long battle with the Americans to make us all bleed."[17] According to one official postwar polemic from Hanoi, "China did not want an early end to the Viet Nam War because they wanted not only to weaken the Vietnamese revolutionary forces, but also to avail the longer the better, of the publicity obtained by aiding Viet Nam . . ."[18] More importantly, Ho Chi Minh called on Moscow to assume leadership of the socialist world.[19]

In 1963, the internal contradictions within the Lao Dong intensified. Shortly after the Buddhist uprisings in southern Vietnam, *Hoc Tap,* the party's theoretical journal, editorialized: "The modern revisionists represented by the Tito group and their followers are spreading a smoke screen about the method of seizing state power . . . They are doing their utmost to peddle pacifism and misrepresent Marxist-Leninist theory on the role of violence in history."[20] That same summer, Nguyen Chi Thanh and other southern leaders continued their barrage against the revisionists. Thanh criticized party leaders who favored the political struggle alone, arguing that "if we feared the United States and had no faith in the success of our struggles against it, we would have called on the people of southern Viet Nam to wait and coexist peacefully with the U.S.-Diem clique."[21] Thanh concluded, "we are not afraid of the United States . . . the building of the north itself cannot replace the resolution of the inherent social contradiction of South Vietnam."[22] These regional differences were not based on psycho-cultural distinctions between northerners and southerners, as some social scientists have suggested.[23] Instead, they represented the problems associated with Vietnam's twin revolutionary goals and the Sino-Soviet dispute.

The conflict within the Lao Dong increased dramatically with the Johnson administration's decision to escalate the war. In March, 1965, Johnson introduced American ground troops and expanded the air war over northern Vietnam. By July, the American mission had changed from a "defensive" posture to an offensive war of attrition. These changes forced the Lao Dong to reexamine its revolutionary priorities. Party leaders concluded that American military intervention had precipitated a crisis in Vietnam that made the old debate between the political versus military lines irrelevant. Furthermore, Hanoi decided that economic consolidation was no longer feasible given the Johnson administration's willingness to wage war. How could Hanoi build a diversified industrial infrastructure with regular American bombing raids? At its regular meeting in September, 1965, the Lao Dong's politburo discussed the latest military developments. Party leaders understood that the changing nature of the war required a new strategy and suggested using the upcoming December plenum to consider their options.

At the Lao Dong's Twelfth Plenum, several new strategies surfaced. Truong Chinh and those who had favored the political line in the 1950s now called on the party to embrace the Chinese concept of people's war. According to this revolutionary theory, villagers and cadres fought with local resources and in a limited fashion. "You won the countryside one village at a time through a protracted war concept," one party military official explained, "ultimately using the enemy's technological superiority against them."[24] People's war was self-reliant, allowing the party to make a limited overall commitment to the southern battlefield. "We can only win through people's war," Truong Chinh argued, "the peasants are our greatest weapon."[25] Chinh saw continuity, therefore, between his two positions. "It did not matter that Truong Chinh and the others embraced the political line of the Soviets in the 1950s and China's people's war concept in the 1960s," one party official explained, "there was a certain consistency in this approach."[26] Indeed, the overall goal for Truong Chinh and most northerners was to secure a unified Vietnam under the socialist banner with as little damage to the North as possible.

There was a significant distinction, however, between Truong Chinh and Beijing. While Beijing supported a protracted people's war, it never favored negotiations with the Americans. The Soviets, on the other hand, saw their policy of "united action" as a conventional military struggle that was eventually settled at the bargaining table. In a strange twist of political thinking therefore, Truong Chinh and many northerners supported a Maoist people's war in the South *and* Soviet-sponsored negotiations. The protracted war promised to limit the conflict to the South and was self-reliant, allowing the DRV to continue its socialist revolution. Negotiations also benefited the North, reducing tensions in the international arena and restraining the war. "We embraced the protracted war and negotiations," one northern party leader recently commented, "because these two tracks served our needs best. Throughout our long revolutionary history, we always adapted outside thoughts to our local conditions. Our revolution was always a mixture of Marxist-Leninism, Maoism, and foremost Viet patriotism."[27] In a postwar memoir, one of the party's leading journalists, Bui Tin, explained the Lao Dong's position this way: " . . . we campaigned to obtain modern weaponry from both the Soviet Union and China, whereas our struggle was eventually resolved through negotiations initiated under the guidance of Ho Chi Minh and the party leadership."[28]

Truong Chinh's position at the Twelfth Plenum no doubt angered many southerners, including Nguyen Chi Thanh, who saw no substitute for battlefield victory. Thanh warned that a protracted war favored the United States. He suggested that Washington was already committed to the battlefield, and therefore, the Lao Dong had to match that commitment or face serious consequences. Furthermore, Thanh concluded that the only way to victory was a Clausewitzian military offensive.[29] He believed, like Clausewitz, in a decisive military encounter that approached total war. Thanh also opposed any negotiations with the Americans until they withdrew from southern Vietnam. Other southerners may have differed with Thanh in his support of a conventional military strategy, but few shared Truong Chinh's desire to settle the conflict at the bargaining table. "We were disgraced at Geneva," one disgruntled southerner complained, "and we were not about to have our fate decided at the negotiating table again."[30] Another southerner explained, "we would never, never enter into any meaningful talks with the Americans until they withdrew from our country."[31] During the Johnson years, therefore, the NLF remained hostile to negotiations.

The ideological contest continued at the Twelfth Plenum until Le Duan, then the Lao Dong's secretary-general, suggested a compromise. In a party declaration now known as Resolution 12, Le Duan outlined the concept of a protracted war strategy. According to this new proposal, the Lao Dong would "endeavor to limit the enemy's war and defeat the enemy in that limited war, inflict heavy casualties on them, and force them to become bogged down and heavily defeated."[32] At the same time, Hanoi would increase the number of regular PAVN[33] infantry units fighting in the South.[34] The Communist Party resolved to fight a protracted war of attrition until the Americans withdrew, but it would also "go all out to highly concentrate the forces of both regions . . . to win a decisive victory in a relatively short period of time."[35] The Lao

Dong correctly understood that the United States could simply overwhelm the southern revolution if the NLF was not supported by northern troops and supplies. Furthermore, the party concluded that the village war was entering a different phase as the Americans introduced new weapons to the battlefield. The goal therefore was to fight a protracted war of resistance, relying on both people's war and conventional forces. Hanoi believed that in combining these two military strategies it could wear down the Johnson administration's resolve to fight the war, and at the same time, win international support for its cause.

Once the Lao Dong approved Resolution 12, it had to "sell" it to Moscow and Beijing. Because the protracted war strategy favored neither benefactor directly, Hanoi had to devise a diplomatic program that promised to deliver continued Soviet and Chinese support. By the spring of 1966, it was clear that the Lao Dong's politburo had decided to use regional differences within the party to promote the Soviet and Chinese lines simultaneously. In a bold move, Hanoi sent DRV and NLF diplomats to socialist capitals, pledging loyalty to the Soviets' "united action" and Beijing's people's war. The Lao Dong could provide ample evidence to each ally, and regional delegates truly represented the various ideological viewpoints captured by the Sino-Soviet dispute. "We sent the NLF delegation to Beijing," one Foreign Ministry official explained, "and our more moderate diplomats to Moscow."[36] Indeed, only the skillful Le Thanh Nghi, a politburo member and DRV vice premier, could handle both positions simultaneously. Between 1965 and 1968, he made over six trips to Beijing and Moscow, seeking favor in both capitals.[37] On several occasions, Vice Premier Nghi had to explain the Lao Dong's protracted war strategy to his hosts. "He told the Chinese that the protracted war was really the people's war of Mao and Lin Piao," a Foreign Ministry official later commented, "and to the Soviets he said that the protracted war opened the way for negotiations with the United States to end the conflict. He was very clever."[38]

Le Thanh Nghi was a skilled and able diplomat, but the changing positions of the Soviet Union and China forced the Lao Dong to rely more heavily upon their two-track strategy. In 1966, Hanoi went on the diplomatic offensive by launching a propaganda campaign to impress the leaders of the Soviet Union and China with its revolutionary devotion. Le Duan made several public statements condemning China's Cultural Revolution, claiming that the Vietnamese revolution was not a copy of Beijing's.[39] General Hoang Minh Thao dismissed China's claim that it was the model for Vietnam, suggesting that "the people's war outlook of our party is a new, creative development of the Marxist-Leninist ideas of revolutionary violence and revolutionary war."[40] In September, *Hoc Tap* editorialized that the Vietnamese struggle was unique in the history of liberation movements and was based on Vietnam's past experiences with foreign invaders.[41] The Lao Dong also attacked China's Cultural Revolution by chiding national leaders, such as Mao, who had become deified "to the detriment of close Party relations with the masses."[42]

At the same time, southerners condemned the Soviets' more moderate position. Thanh claimed that Moscow's willingness to engage the United States in a peaceful dialogue was counter-revolutionary. He challenged other nations to "pick up the banner of national liberation" and flatly reject "the revisionist policies of those who help the imperialists through their naive talk of peaceful coexistence."[43] In a public radio address aired in China, Thanh concluded that "if the United States can be defeated in South Viet Nam, it will be possible to defeat it anywhere in the world."[44] The NLF also condemned the Soviets' position, claiming that "negotiations with the United States were tantamount to surrender."[45] The front also published several short books condemning Soviet-style revisionism.[46]

As the propaganda war continued, the Lao Dong launched the second phase of its diplomatic program. In 1966 and early 1967, the DRV and the NLF sent their various representatives to Moscow and Beijing, promoting solidarity between Vietnam and the Communist superpowers. In December, 1966, on the sixth anniversary of the founding of the NLF, Nguyen Xuan Long and Tran Van Thanh led a delegation of NLF diplomats on a seven-city tour of China. Thanh was the NLF's official diplomatic representative to Beijing, a post he occupied in 1964 following years of diplomatic service in Cuba. Long was a Saigon intellectual and one of the more outspoken critics of negotiations. On December 20, the anniversary date, Long delivered a scathing attack against Soviet revisionism in the southern Chinese city of Kwangchow. "The Soviets," he claimed, "were working in the service of U.S. imperialism . . . peddling America's peace fraud."[47] In Beijing, Thanh joined Chen Yi, China's foreign minister, in condemning the revisionists and those who supported negotiations with the United States. Yi declared that the Chinese people were fully prepared to march against the United States any time the Vietnamese people required it.[48] *Renmin Rabao* [The People's Daily], the Chinese Communist Party's newspaper, welcomed the NLF delegation and warned the Johnson administration and the Soviets that their "conspiracy of forcing peace talks . . . would be futile."[49] Within the year, China would officially recognize the NLF and grant it full diplomatic standing. The front, in turn, established a permanent and fully staffed mission in Beijing.[50]

As NLF officials toured China, condemning negotiations and Soviet-styled revisionism, the DRV sent its representatives to Moscow. In March, 1966, Le Duan led a DRV delegation to the Soviet Union for Moscow's Twenty-third Congress. During the proceedings, Le Duan called Russia his "second motherland."[51] In addition, the Lao Dong secretary-general stated that Vietnam's protracted war strategy was faithful to the most important teachings of Marx and Lenin.[52] China had boycotted the Soviet Congress, refusing to send a delegation and censoring news from Moscow. When word of Le Duan's support for the Soviet line reached Beijing, Chinese leaders refused to allow a division of their best combat engineers to extend their stay in Vietnam.[53]

There were other problems for the Lao Dong's dual-track diplomatic strategy. By mid-year, Hanoi began to notice a significant decrease in Chinese aid, and there were reports that Beijing had not allowed some Soviet material to pass overland through China on its way to Vietnam.[54] In addition, Beijing required that all aid traveling through China be placed under its control "and be interpreted as a favour from Beijing to Hanoi."[55] In early 1966, a Chinese cargo ship, the *Red Flag*, entering the Vietnamese port city of Haiphong was made to wait while a late-arriving Soviet ship docked first. As a result, the *Red Flag* was left exposed and suffered tremendous damage from an American bombing raid.[56] DRV officials traveling to China shortly after the incident received a stern lecture from Premier Zhou Enlai.[57] Following the visit, China condemned Vietnam's "growing reliance on Soviet strategy and material."[58] By the end of the year, Hanoi's duplicitous diplomatic gamble began to unravel.

Still, Le Duan's trip to the Soviet Union was important because it established a credit relationship between Hanoi and Moscow. For the remainder of the war, the Lao Dong received long-term credits to purchase sophisticated Soviet war weaponry. Further meetings in 1967 produced over $1 billion in pledges to the Lao Dong from Moscow and its satellite countries.[59] "We needed the Soviet aid," General Tran Van Quang explained, "but we also depended on China as a fraternal ally . . . it was a very difficult situation."[60] A party publication summarized the Lao Dong's dilemma: "the Soviets want us to go to the peace table," and China is "determined to help us fight until the generations of our sons and grandsons."[61]

By the end of 1967, however, Hanoi was firmly planted in Moscow's camp. Two important events brought the Lao Dong into the Soviet realm: the death of General Nguyen Chi Thanh in the early summer of 1967, and the Lao Dong's decision to launch the Tet Offensive. In June, an official report from Hanoi claimed that the outspoken Thanh had died of a heart attack in the DRV capital.[62] Thanh had steadfastly opposed all efforts to negotiate with the United States and was especially hostile to the various secret peace contacts. With him gone, northerners in Hanoi reclaimed control of the Southern Directory (COSVN), creating a triumvirate of sympathetic leaders. "Thanh was the last obstacle to negotiations," one former Lao Dong official later commented, "with him gone the move to Paris was easy."[63]

Perhaps an even more important factor in Hanoi's evolution toward Moscow was the party's acceptance of the Tet strategy. In early April, 1967,[64] the Lao Dong approved plans to launch a major offensive in key southern cities, provincial capitals, and district towns.[65] The main objective was to force the Americans to the bargaining table. The tactical effort and the final strategic objective were clearly in line with Moscow's thinking. For several years, the Soviets had urged Hanoi to create favorable conditions to end the military conflict at the negotiating table. The Tet Offensive would show the world that the balance of forces south of the seventeenth parallel had shifted in favor of the communists and that the Americans had no alternative but to negotiate. By May, 1968, with peace talks underway in Paris, China withdrew all combat engineers from Vietnam and reduced its overall aid package significantly.[66] These actions, of course, ended Hanoi's balancing act. Relations between Hanoi and Beijing remained cool for the remainder of the war, and the former allies would be at war in 1979.

The Lao Dong's dual-track diplomatic strategy failed to deliver Vietnam from the Sino-Soviet dispute. Instead, Hanoi's policies heightened pre-existing regional tensions within the party and forced the Lao Dong to make some hard decisions. The Lao Dong was in a precarious position. It needed Soviet and Chinese aid and support, but these came with ideological strings attached. Throughout the Johnson years, therefore, the Lao Dong balanced its needs with the ideological demands of its powerful Communist allies. Strained relations between Moscow and Beijing compelled Hanoi to accept many compromise solutions that limited its future options and may have prolonged the war. Eventually, the Lao Dong's strategy of *vua Dan, vua dam* [fighting while negotiating] brought it a hard-won victory, but at enormous cost.

Chapter 6

An Uneasy Relationship

China and the DRV during the Vietnam War

QIANG ZHAI

During the Vietnam War, and especially between 1965 and 1968, Beijing invested substantial amounts of time, energy, and money in the Democratic Republic of Vietnam (DRV) to assist Hanoi in its struggle against the United States. But by the time the war ended in 1975, Sino-DRV ties were very much strained. Four years later, the two former allies went to war with each other. How did this happen?

A close examination of the Beijing-Hanoi interactions during the Vietnam War indicates that despite the common goal of resisting the United States, the two communist states differed in their approaches to the issues of waging war and pursuing peace and that despite the rhetoric of "comrades plus brothers," distrust and suspicion existed on both sides. This chapter will draw primarily on newly released Chinese materials to chart the course of the evolution of Chinese-DRV relations during the Vietnam War and will analyze the reasons for the fluctuations in the relationship. It argues that it was primarily China's insensitivity to the needs of the DRV and Mao's sense of superiority and arrogance that contributed to the final breakdown of the Sino-DRV friendship.

During the First Indochina War, China played an important role in Ho Chi Minh's victory over the French by providing military advisers and weapons to the Viet Minh.[1] In the decade after the 1954 Geneva Conference, Beijing continued to assist the DRV in consolidating its power and reconstructing its economy. When the Sino-Soviet dispute emerged in the late 1950s, Ho tried to remain neutral for fear of losing support from either of the two Communist powers.

Between 1962 and October, 1964, however, Hanoi looked primarily to Beijing for support in resisting the United States and carrying out its goal of unifying the South, given Khrushchev's indifference to the conflict in Indochina. During this period, Moscow remained primarily an onlooker regarding events in Southeast Asia. This role suited Khrushchev's purpose of seeking peaceful coexistence with the United States and avoiding clashes similar to the Cuban missile crisis of 1962.[2] As the major provider of military hardware to the DRV during this period, China supplied Hanoi with 90,000 rifles and machine guns, 446 pieces of artillery, 21 million bullets, and 76,400 artillery shells.[3]

Coping With the U.S. Escalation of the War, 1964–65

During the first half of 1964, Washington's attention was increasingly focused on Hanoi. This trend reflected a mounting U.S. concern over the infiltration of men and supplies from the North and growing dissatisfaction with a policy that allowed Hanoi to encourage the insurgency without punishment. The Johnson administration expanded its covert operations against North Vietnam, including intelligence overflights, the dropping of propaganda leaflets, and OPLAN 34A commando raids along the North Vietnamese coast.[4]

At the same time, tensions were also increasing in Laos. In April, a right-wing coup shook the Lao government, prompting Prime Minister Souvanna Phouma to reorganize the government by excluding the communists. Considering the 1962 Geneva Accords irrelevant, the Pathet Lao attacked the pro-government forces on the Plain of Jars in May. Souvanna permitted unarmed U.S. reconnaissance flights over the Plain of Jars. After communist antiaircraft guns shot one down on June 6, the United States retaliated three days later by using F-100s to strike the communist antiaircraft battery at Xieng Khouang. Apparently without U.S. authorization, Thai-piloted Royal Lao Air Force T-28s attacked the Pathet Lao headquarters at Khang Khay and hit the Chinese Economic and Cultural Mission there, killing one Chinese and wounding five others.[5]

Leaders in Beijing watched these developments closely and with apprehension. At a diplomatic reception hosted by a visiting Tanzanian delegation in Beijing on June 16, Chinese Premier Zhou Enlai condemned the U.S. bombing of the Pathet Lao headquarters and the Chinese Mission as a violation of the Geneva Accords and an escalation of the conflict in Indochina.[6]

To confront the increasing American pressure in Indochina, the Chinese Communist Party (CCP) stepped up its coordination with the Vietnamese and

Lao communists. On June 21 and 22, 1964, General Van Tien Dung, chief of staff of the People's Army of Vietnam (PAVN), visited Beijing, where he talked with Zhou Enlai about China's military aid to the DRV.[7] Mao told Dung: "Our two parties and two countries must cooperate and fight the enemy together. Your business is my business and my business is your business. In other words, our two sides must deal with the enemy together without conditions."[8]

During July 5–8, Zhou Enlai led a CCP delegation to Hanoi, where he discussed with representatives from the Vietnam Workers' Party (VWP) and the Pathet Lao the situations in South Vietnam and Laos. The Vietnamese and Lao leaders briefed the Chinese on how the United States was using South Vietnam as a base to attack socialism and as a test ground for its "special warfare." After noting that Southeast Asia was the area in the world where "contradictions are most concentrated, struggle most fierce, and revolutionary conditions most ripe," Zhou pointed out two possible military developments in the region: (1) the United States might intensify the "special warfare"; (2) it might turn the "special warfare" into a local war with a direct deployment of American troops in South Vietnam and Laos, or with bombing or invasion of the DRV. No matter what approach the United States adopted, Zhou said, China would surely intervene to support the struggle of the Southeast Asian people. As to concrete measures that the VWP and the Pathet Lao might take, Zhou suggested a combination of political and military struggles: on the political front, to adhere to the two Geneva Accords, exploit Franco-American contradictions, and organize a broad international united front to lay bare U.S. violations of both Geneva Accords; in the military area, to strengthen armed forces, consolidate base areas, and win battles of annihilation. "Our principle for the struggle," Zhou continued, was "to do everything we can to limit the war to the current scale while preparing for the second possibility" of American intervention. Should the second possibility occur, Zhou said, China would match American actions: if the United States sent troops, China would also send troops.[9] Zhou confirmed the agreement made between China and the DRV in 1963 that Beijing would send combat soldiers into North Vietnam if the United States used ground troops to invade the DRV. Clearly Chinese leaders did not want war with the United States; at the same time they had to be prepared for the worst scenario.

Immediately after the Gulf of Tonkin incident, Zhou Enlai and Luo Ruiqing, chief of staff of the People's Liberation Army (PLA), cabled Ho Chi Minh, Pham Van Dong, and Van Tien Dung on August 5, asking them to "investigate the situation, work out countermeasures, and be prepared to fight."[10] In the meantime, leaders in Beijing instructed the Kunming and Guangzhou Military Regions and the air force and naval units stationed in South and Southwest China to begin a state of combat readiness. Four air divisions and one antiaircraft division were dispatched into areas adjoining Vietnam and put on a heightened alert status.[11] In August, China also sent approximately 15 MiG-15 and MiG-17 jets to Hanoi, agreed to train North Vietnamese pilots, and began to build new airfields near the Vietnamese border, which would serve as sanctuaries and provide repair and maintenance facilities for Hanoi's jet fighters.[12] Beijing intended to deter the United States from expanding the war in South Vietnam and from attacking the DRV.

The first months of 1965 witnessed a significant escalation of the American war in Vietnam. On February 7, 9, and 11, U.S. aircraft struck North Vietnamese military installations just across the seventeenth parallel, ostensibly in retaliation for Viet Cong attacks on American barracks near Pleiku and in Qui Nhon. On March 1, the Johnson administration stopped claiming that its air attacks on North Vietnam were reprisals for specific communist assaults in South Vietnam and began continuous bombing of the DRV. On March 8, two battalions of marines armed with tanks and eight-inch howitzers landed at Danang.[13]

Worried about the increasing U.S. involvement in Vietnam, Zhou Enlai during his visit to Pakistan on April 2 asked Pakistani President Ayub Khan, who was scheduled to visit the United States later in the month, to convey to President Johnson a four-point message:

(1) China will not take the initiative to provoke a war with the United States. (2) The Chinese mean what they say. In other words, if any country in Asia, Africa, or elsewhere meets with aggression by the imperialists headed by the United States, the Chinese government and people will definitely give it support and assistance. Should such just action bring on American aggression against China, we will unhesitatingly rise in resistance and fight to the end. (3) China is prepared. Should the United States impose a war on China, it can be said with certainty that, once in China, the United States will not be able to pull out, however many men it may send over and whatever weapons it may use, nuclear weapons included. (4) Once the war breaks out, it will have no boundaries. If the United States bombards China, China will not sit there waiting to die. If they come from the sky, we will fight back on the ground. Bombing means war. The war cannot have boundaries.[14]

Ayub Khan did not deliver the Chinese message. Just nine days before his arrival in the United States, President Johnson, dismayed by Ayub's flirtation with China, suddenly canceled his invitation.[15] On June 8, Zhou Enlai asked

President Julius Nyerere of Tanzania to forward the same four-point message to the United States.[16] This was the most serious warning issued by the Chinese government to the United States, and given the caution exercised by Johnson in carrying out the "Rolling Thunder" operations against the DRV, it was one that Washington did not overlook. Clearly, U.S. leaders had drawn a lesson from the Korean War, when the Truman administration's failure to heed Beijing's warning against crossing the thirty-eighth parallel led to a bloody confrontation between the United States and China.

The U.S. escalation in early 1965 made the DRV desperate for help. Le Duan and Vo Nguyen Giap rushed to Beijing in early April to ask China to increase its aid and send troops to the DRV. Duan told Chinese leaders that Hanoi needed "volunteer pilots, volunteer soldiers as well as other necessary personnel, including road and bridge engineers." The Vietnamese envoys expected Chinese volunteer pilots to perform four functions: to limit U.S. bombing to the southern part of the country, to defend Hanoi, to protect several major transportation lines, and to boost morale.[17] On behalf of the Chinese leadership, Liu Shaoqi, vice chairman of the CCP Central Committee, replied to the Vietnamese visitors on April 8 that "it is the obligation of the Chinese people and party" to support the Vietnamese struggle against the United States. "Our principle is," Liu continued, "that we will do our best to provide you with whatever you need and whatever we have. If you do not invite us, we will not go to your place. We will send whatever part (of our troops) that you request. You have the complete initiative."[18]

During April 21 and 22, Vo Nguyen Giap discussed with Luo Ruiqing and Yang Chengwu, first deputy chief of staff, the arrangements for sending Chinese troops to the DRV.[19] In May, Ho Chi Minh met with Mao in China, where he asked the Chinese leader to help the DRV repair and build twelve roads in the area north of Hanoi. Mao accepted Ho's request and instructed Zhou Enlai to see to the matter.[20]

In discussions with Luo Ruiqing and Yang Chengwu, Zhou said: "According to Pham Van Dong, U.S. blockade and bombing has reduced supplies to South Vietnam through sea shipment and road transportation. While trying to resume sea transportation, the DRV is also expanding the corridor in Lower Laos and roads in the south. Their troops would go to the south to build roads. Therefore they need our support to construct roads in the North." Yang suggested that because assistance to the DRV involved many military and government departments, a special leadership group should be created to coordinate the work of various agencies. Approving the proposal, Zhou immediately announced the establishment of the "Central Committee and State Council Aid Vietnam Group" with Yang as director.[21]

In early June, Van Tien Dung held discussions with Luo Ruiqing in Beijing to flesh out the general Chinese plan to assist Vietnam. According to their agreement, if the war continued as it was, the DRV would fight by itself and China would provide various kinds of support as the Vietnamese needed it. If the United States used its navy and air force to support a South Vietnamese attack on the North, China would also provide naval and air force support to the DRV. If U.S. ground forces were directly used to attack the North, China would use its land forces as strategic reserves for the DRV and conduct military operations whenever necessary. As to the forms of Chinese-Vietnamese air force cooperation, Dung and Luo agreed that China could either send volunteer pilots to Vietnam to operate Vietnamese aircraft, station both pilots and aircraft in Vietnam airfields, or fly aircraft from bases in China to join combat in Vietnam and only land at Vietnamese bases temporarily for refueling. The third option was known as the "Andong model" (a reference to the pattern of Chinese air force operations during the Korean War). As to the methods of employing Chinese ground troops, the two military leaders agreed that Chinese forces would either help to strengthen the defensive position of the North Vietnamese troops while they prepared for a counteroffensive, or launch an offensive themselves to disrupt the enemy's deployment and win strategic initiatives.[22]

But despite Liu Shaoqi's April promise to Le Duan and Luo Ruiqing's agreement with Van Tien Dung, China in the end failed to provide pilots to Hanoi. According to the Vietnamese "White Paper" of 1979, the Chinese General Staff on July 16, 1965, notified its Vietnamese counterpart that "the time was not appropriate" to send Chinese pilots to Vietnam.[23] China's limited air power may have caused leaders in Beijing to have second thoughts. Beijing's hope to avoid a direct confrontation with the United States may also have played a role. Whatever the reasons for China's decision, the failure to satisfy Hanoi's demand must have greatly disappointed the Vietnamese and undoubtedly contributed to North Vietnam's decision to rely more on the Soviet Union for air defense.

Beginning in June, 1965, China sent ground-to-air missiles, antiaircraft artillery, railroad, engineering, mine-sweeping, and logistical units into North Vietnam. The total number of Chinese troops serving in North Vietnam between June, 1965, and March, 1968, amounted to over 320,000.[24] Participation peaked in 1967, when 170,000 Chinese soldiers were present.[25] They operated antiaircraft guns, built and repaired roads, bridges, and rail lines, and constructed factories. They enabled the PAVN to send large numbers of troops to South Vietnam for the fighting. When the last Chinese troops withdrew from Vietnam in August, 1973, 1,100 soldiers had lost their lives and 4,200 had been wounded.[26]

Both Mao and Zhou Enlai followed events in Vietnam closely and issued directions regarding China's aid to the DRV. After reading a report by a group of Chinese journalists about the difficult living conditions of the Vietnamese Communist troops in the southern mountain regions, Mao announced in November, 1965, that China "must give mosquito nets, cloth, canned food, dried meats, medicine, water-proof cloth, hammocks and other materials in large quantities" to the Vietnamese.[27] Zhou Enlai directed that Chinese equipment sent to South Vietnam should be designed so as to be "easy to use, easy to carry, and easy to hide." For this purpose, he demanded specifically that each piece of equipment should not weigh over thirty kilograms, so that Vietnamese women would have no difficulty in carrying it on head or shoulder.[28]

To supervise the transport of materials to the DRV, Beijing in 1965 established a special leadership group. Luo Ruiqing was appointed director. Materials provided by China, the Soviet Union, and other socialist countries were shipped by rail to cities near the Vietnamese border, where they were transported into the DRV either by rail or by trucks. The North Vietnamese transport system was soon overwhelmed, and an overstocking of supplies occurred at Chinese railway stations and warehouses. Beginning in 1967, China employed over 500 trucks to help carry supplies into the DRV.[29]

To facilitate the infiltration of supplies into South Vietnam, China created a secret coastal transportation line to ship goods to several islands off Central Vietnam for transit to the South. A secret harbor on China's Hainan Island was constructed to serve this transportation route.[30] Beijing also operated a costly transportation line through Cambodia to send weapons, munitions, food, and medical supplies to the National Liberation Front (NLF) in South Vietnam.[31] Between 1965 and 1967, Chinese weapons for 50,000 soldiers arrived by ship via Sihanoukville.[32]

Why did Mao choose to commit China's resources to North Vietnam? Mao's decision to aid Hanoi involved his perception of U.S. threats to China's security, his commitment to national liberation movements, his criticism of Soviet revisionist foreign policy, and his determination to transform the Chinese state and society. These four factors are mutually related and reinforcing.

Between 1964 and 1965, Mao worried about the increasing American involvement in Vietnam and perceived the United States as posing a serious threat to China's security. The CCP leader viewed the United States as "the most ferocious enemy of the people of the world," pursuing neocolonialist aggression against Asian, African, and Latin American countries and seeking "peaceful evolution" against socialist states. In Asia, Mao contended, the United States was occupying Taiwan, turning South Korea and South Vietnam into its colonies, exercising actual control and partial military occupation of Japan, undermining Laotian neutrality and independence, plotting subversion of the Cambodian government, and interfering with other Asian countries. Mao believed that American escalation of the war in Vietnam constituted a link in Washington's chain of encirclement around China. For him, support for North Vietnam was a way to counter U.S. containment. A communist success in South Vietnam would prevent the United States from moving closer to the Chinese southern border.[33]

To counter the American threat and to break out of China's isolation from the world, Mao sought to form a broad international united front. He viewed national liberation movements in the Third World as the most important potential allies in the coalition he wanted to establish. For Mao, the Vietnam conflict was part of a broader movement across Asia, Africa, and Latin America that represented a challenge to imperialism as a whole.

Envisioning China as a spokesman for the Third World independence cause, Mao believed that the Chinese revolutionary experience was relevant to the struggle of national liberation movements in the underdeveloped areas. By firmly backing the Vietnamese struggle against the United States, he hoped to demonstrate to Third World countries that China was their true friend. Victory for North Vietnam's war of national unification would vindicate the political wisdom of Mao's militant strategy for coping with U.S. imperialism, and by the same token would refute Khrushchev's policy of peaceful coexistence.

Mao intervened in the Indochina conflict to define China's place in the world. The Vietnam War would test and validate the adopted PRC self-image as champion of Third World national liberation movements. The U.S. intervention in Indochina helped Mao to answer with ease and clarity his perennial dictum for the Chinese revolution "to unite with real friends in order to attack real enemies." The Vietnam War provided the exogenous trigger for national identity mobilization and confirmed for the national self and "others" that China would stand up for the integrity of its national identity as a supporter of national liberation movements against imperialism and colonialism.[34]

Finally, Mao found the tensions in Indochina useful in mobilizing the Chinese population to follow his radical domestic programs. The problem of succession preoccupied Mao throughout the first half of the 1960s. His acute awareness of impending death contributed to his sense of urgency. The U.S. escalation of the war in Vietnam made him all the more eager to put his own house in order. He was afraid that if he did not nip in the bud what he perceived to be revisionist tendencies, and if he did not choose a proper successor, after his death China would be in the hands of Soviet-like revisionists, who would "change the color" of China, abandon support for national liberation struggles, and appease U.S. imperialism. Mao was a man who believed in dialectics. Negative things could be turned into positive matters. Thus while the American presence in Indochina was a threat to the Chinese revolution, Mao found that he could use the threat to intensify domestic anti-imperialist feelings and to mobilize the population against revisionists. Mao had successfully employed that strategy during the civil war against Chiang Kai-shek. Now he could apply it again to prepare the masses for the Great Cultural Revolution that he was going to launch. Accordingly, in the wake of the Gulf of Tonkin incident, Mao unleashed a massive "Aid Vietnam and Resist America" campaign across China.

The newly available Chinese documents clearly indicate that Beijing provided extensive support (short of volunteer pilots) for Hanoi during the Vietnam War and risked war with the United States in helping the Vietnamese. As Allen S. Whiting has perceptively observed, the Chinese did not take pains to conceal their deployment of troops in Vietnam. Chinese troops wore regular uniforms and did not disguise themselves as civilians. Their presence was easily confirmed by U.S. intelligence through aerial photography and electronic intercepts. This deployment, along with the large base complex that China built at Yen Bai in Northwest Vietnam, provided credible and successful deterrence against an American invasion of North Vietnam.[35]

The specter of Chinese intervention in a manner similar to the Korean War was a major factor in shaping President Johnson's gradualist approach to the Vietnam War. Johnson wanted to forestall Chinese intervention by keeping the level of military actions against North Vietnam controlled, exact, and below the threshold that would provoke a direct Chinese entry. This China-induced U.S. strategy of gradual escalation was a great help for Hanoi, for it gave the Vietnamese Communists time to adjust to U.S. bombing and to develop strategies to frustrate U.S. moves. As John W. Garver has aptly noted, "By helping to induce Washington to adopt this particular strategy, Beijing contributed substantially to Hanoi's eventual victory over the United States."[36]

Sino-Vietnamese Friction, 1965–67

Signs of Chinese-Vietnamese differences emerged even upon the beginning of China's intervention in the Vietnam conflict. Two major factors complicated Sino-Vietnamese relations. One was the historical pride and cultural sensitivity that the Vietnamese carried with them in dealing with the Chinese. The other was the effect of the Sino-Soviet split.

Throughout their history, the Vietnamese have had a love-hate attitude toward their big northern neighbor. On the one hand, they were eager to borrow advanced institutions and technologies from China; on the other, they wanted to preserve their independence and cultural heritage. When they were internally weak and facing external aggression, they sought China's help and intervention and downplayed their inherent differences with the Chinese. When they were unified and free from foreign threats, they tended to resent China's influence and paid more attention to problems in the bilateral relationship.

This pattern certainly applied during the 1950s and the first half of the 1960s. The Vietnamese Communists during this period confronted formidable enemies, the French and the Americans, in their quest for national unification. Ho Chi Minh avidly sought advice and weapons from China. But sentiments of distrust were never far below the surface. Friction emerged between Chinese military advisers and Vietnamese commanders during the First Indochina War.[37] Vietnamese distrust of the Chinese manifested itself again when Chinese support troops entered Vietnam in the mid-1960s.

When Chinese troops went to the DRV in 1965, they found themselves in an awkward position. The Vietnamese leadership wanted their service in fighting U.S. aircraft and in building and repairing roads, bridges, and rail lines. But the Vietnamese made a point of restricting the Chinese troops' contact with the local population. When a Chinese medical team offered treatment to save the life of a Vietnamese woman, Vietnamese officials blocked the effort.[38] Informed of incidents like this, Mao urged the Chinese troops in Vietnam to "refrain from being too eager" to help the Vietnamese.[39] While Chinese soldiers were in Vietnam, the Vietnamese media reminded the public that China had invaded Vietnam in the past. The journal *Historical Studies* published articles in 1965 describing the history of Vietnamese resistance against Chinese imperial dynasties.[40]

Increasing animosity between Beijing and Moscow also hampered Sino-DRV cooperation. Chinese and Soviet efforts to win Hanoi's allegiance put the Vietnamese in a dilemma. On the one hand, the change of Soviet attitudes toward Vietnam from reluctant to active assistance in late 1964 and early 1965 made the Vietnamese less willing to echo Chinese criticisms of Soviet "revisionism." On the other hand, Hanoi still needed China's assistance and the deterrence it provided.

Meanwhile, Mao's rejection of the Soviet proposal for "united action" on Vietnam ruled out the possibility of a closer coordination within the international communist camp in support of the DRV. During Soviet Premier Alexei Kosygin's visit to Beijing in February, 1965, he proposed to Mao and Zhou Enlai that Beijing and Moscow end their mutual criticisms and cooperate on aid to Vietnam. Mao dismissed Kosygin's suggestion that polemics be suspended, asserting that China's argument with the Soviet Union would continue for another nine thousand years.[41] The Chinese also rejected Soviet requests for an "air corridor" through which an airlift could be conducted and for the cession of a base in Yunnan where hundreds of Soviet military personnel could be stationed to assist Hanoi's war effort. Instead they accused the Russians of taking advantage of the war in Vietnam to violate Chinese sovereignty. While rejecting this kind of coordination, Beijing did allow the Soviet Union to transport its aid to the DRV through the Chinese rail corridor, which remained a major supply route for the Vietnamese war effort during 1965–68.[42]

On April 3, 1965, Moscow proposed to Beijing the convocation of a DRV-Chinese-Soviet summit meeting, but China rejected the suggestion. In a reply to the Soviet Communist Party on July 10, the CCP Central Committee, with Mao's approval, retorted that on the Vietnam issue the Soviet Union had adopted appeasement toward the United States. Moscow's proposal for "united action" on Vietnam, according to the Central Committee, was designed to subordinate fraternal parties to the Soviet party and to turn those parties into Russian tools as the Soviet Union sought to dominate the world jointly with the United States.[43] Mao's arrogance and strongly held ideological convictions eliminated any possibility of reconciliation between Beijing and Moscow.

During February and March, 1966, a Japanese Communist Party delegation led by Secretary-General Miyamoto Kenji visited China, the DRV, and North Korea to encourage "joint action" by China and the Soviet Union to support Vietnam. Miyamoto first discussed the idea with the CCP delegation, led by Liu Shaoqi, Zhou Enlai, Deng Xiaoping, and Peng Zhen in Beijing. The two sides worked out a communiqué that included only points of agreement between the two delegations. The communiqué condemned U.S. aggression in Vietnam and pledged support for the Vietnamese people. On the issue of attitudes toward the Soviet Union, the two parties emphasized the importance of the struggle against modern revisionism in fighting U.S. imperialism but failed to mention the Soviet Union by name. When Miyamoto came to see Mao in Shanghai on March 28, the chairman flew into a rage, insisting that the passage of the communiqué must mention the Soviet Union by name. Miyamoto disagreed, and the Beijing communiqué was torn up.[44] Clearly by this time Mao had connected the criticism of Soviet revisionism with the domestic struggle against top party leaders headed by Liu Shaoqi and Deng Xiaoping. It was no wonder that these officials soon became leading targets for attack when the Cultural Revolution swept across China a few months later. Again Mao's ideological intransigence closed the door on Sino-Soviet cooperation in international politics.

In the meantime the Vietnamese made their divergent attitude toward Moscow clear by deciding to send a delegation to attend the Twenty-third Congress of the Communist Party of the Soviet Union, which was held between March 29 and April 8. The Chinese had chosen not to participate in the congress. The Vietnamese were walking on a tightrope, relying on the vital support of the advanced weapons from the Soviet Union but not wanting to damage their ties with China. Thus they made a special point of refuting Moscow's accusations that Beijing was blocking Soviet weapons shipments to the DRV. Pham Van Dong, speaking before the North Vietnamese National Assembly, praised China for its "devoted help in the transit of the aid from the Soviet Union and other fraternal East European countries according to schedule."[45]

By carefully navigating among the shoals of the Sino-Soviet rivalry, Hanoi eventually succeeded in getting Beijing and Moscow to agree, in early 1967, on a new arrangement for transporting Soviet arms through China to the DRV. The agreement provided that the North Vietnamese would receive the shipments at the Sino-Soviet border and escort them through Chinese territory. This arrangement had the advantage of minimizing the chance of Chinese-Russian quarrels over weapons transportation and was undoubtedly meant by both powers as a gesture of support for Hanoi's war effort rather than as a prelude to a Sino-Soviet rapprochement.[46]

Chinese leaders persisted in their efforts to undermine Soviet credibility by reminding the Vietnamese of Moscow's perfidy in its support for the Chinese revolution in the 1940s. In a meeting with Pham Van Dong in Beijing on April 11, 1967, Zhou Enlai declared solemnly:

> We believe that you will surely win the final victory. We will mobilize the people of the whole world to support you to achieve victory. The Soviet Union, however, surely wants you to stop halfway. It has done such a thing during the Stalin period. After the surrender of Japan in 1945, the United States supported Chiang Kai-shek. At that time, the Soviet Union had suffered a great deal in the war. It concluded the Yalta agreement, dividing spheres of influence with the United States. The Yalta agreement is wrong. As a tactic, the agreement is all right; but as a policy, it is incorrect. The explosion of the two atomic bombs in particular shocked the Soviet Union. The Soviets were eager to sign an agreement with Chiang Kai-shek, recognizing the fact that the United States enjoyed the greatest sphere of influence in China. The Soviet Union in return wanted to maintain Russian special interests in the Northeast and Xinjiang and keep the People's Republic of Mongolia. At the time, Stalin fired off a cable to Comrade Mao Zedong stating that the CCP should cooperate with Guomindang instead of starting a civil war and that if the CCP launched a civil war, the Chinese nation would be destroyed. Clearly the Soviet Union had been intimidated by the atomic bomb.[47]

The emphasis on Russian untrustworthiness remained a familiar theme in Chinese criticism of the Soviet Union throughout the Vietnam War.

1968: A Turning Point

In 1968 China's strategic environment changed drastically. Sino-Soviet relations took a decisive turn for the worse. In the meantime Washington made its first tentative moves toward disengagement from South Vietnam. In this new situation, Beijing's strategic interests began to differ fundamentally from those of Hanoi. Whereas the Chinese would come to regard the United States as a potential counterbalance against the Soviet Union, their Vietnamese comrades continued to see Washington as the most dangerous enemy.

The year began in South Vietnam with the Tet Offensive. VWP leaders hoped that the general offensive and uprising would set in motion a chain of developments that could bring about a withdrawal of American troops and the creation of a coalition government dominated by the NLF. The operation highlighted the crucial importance of the cities in the VWP's strategy for victory. The party's calculations about the significance of the urban sector were based not only on its careful consideration of the class nature and problems in the cities, and of the steady weakening of the Saigon regime but also on its historical memory of the August Revolution in 1945, when it seized power swiftly by combining urban and rural resistance.[48] Ever since the early 1960s, the idea of the general offensive and uprising had preoccupied the thinking of party strategists as they concentrated on the struggle in the South. Throughout 1965–67, the party had persisted in viewing the urban role as both decisive and promising.[49]

The Tet Offensive, however, contradicted Mao Zedong's theory of protracted people's war in several respects. Mao's doctrine envisioned three stages in conducting people's war. In the first stage the revolutionary forces would assume the strategic defensive against the strategic offensive launched by the reactionary forces. In the second stage, a strategic parity or equilibrium would exist. It would be the period of the enemy's strategic consolidation and the revolutionary forces' preparation for the counteroffensive. In the third stage the revolutionary forces would wage a strategic offensive against the enemy. During the first and second stages, the revolutionary forces would leave the cities in the hands of superior enemy forces and conduct extensive guerrilla warfare in the countryside against the increasingly dispersed and static enemy forces. In the course of the long and difficult second stage of strategic stalemate, the revolutionary forces would consolidate and expand their control of the countryside while the enemy would try to protect the cities. Mobile warfare would be progressively introduced to supplement guerrilla operations. During this phase the balance between the revolutionary and reactionary forces would gradually change. Political mobilization of the rural population would be crucial in facilitating this change. This was to be the principal strategic aim of the revolutionary forces during the first and second stages. Rural organizations of all kinds, under party leadership, were to be established to supply manpower and support the front. As larger and larger guerrilla units were formed, they would be hardened by combat against dispersed enemy outposts. The strength of the reactionary forces would be gradually depleted by this continuous attrition, and by psychological weariness stemming from factors like homesickness and antiwar sentiment. Eventually the strength of the revolutionary forces would exceed that of the reactionary forces and accordingly the war would proceed to the third stage, in which mobile war, supplemented by positional and guerrilla war, would become the primary method, and the revolutionary forces would carry out a general offensive to capture the cities.[50]

The Tet Offensive diverged from Mao's teaching of people's war. It shifted the focus of revolutionary struggle from the rural to urban areas well before the third stage and committed the revolutionary forces to positional war prematurely. It involved a large-scale strategic offensive by the communist units before the strategic balance between the revolutionary and counter-revolutionary forces had tipped in favor of the former. It exposed the underground infrastructure of the revolutionary forces to an enemy that still held the military advantage. In the process it undermined the mass base of the revolutionary forces, the single most important element in prosecuting the war.[51]

Not until 1968 did policymakers in Beijing begin to talk about large-unit operations in Vietnam. Mao advised Ho Chi Minh that the DRV should organize large formations to carry out battles of annihilation in the South.[52] On February 7 of that year, Zhou recommended to Ho a similar approach of employing large units in mobile warfare:

> Given the development of the Vietnam War to the current moment, why not consider the organization of one to two or three field corps, each including thirty to forty thousand troops. Try to annihilate in each battle the enemy's complete unit of four to five thousand soldiers. These corps should be able to operate far from the home base and to fight from this theater to another theater. Engage isolated enemy units. Adopt the methods of digging open-air tunnels to get close to the enemy and conducting night and close-range combat so as to render ineffective the firepower of the enemy's aircraft and artillery. Construct open-air tunnels from three to four directions. These tunnels are different from

underground ones. They should be capable of facilitating the movement of troops and the transportation of ammunition. Employ also some forces to intercept the enemy's reinforcement units.[53]

Despite Mao and Zhou's encouragement of the use of large units in mobile operations, they stopped short of urging Ho to launch the sort of general offensive against cities that the North Vietnamese had undertaken.

In general, Chinese leaders preferred a low- to mid-intensity war in Vietnam. They perceived several advantages in emphasizing a limited and protracted war: (1) to keep the United States bogged down in the war and maintain the importance of China's aid to the DRV; (2) to reduce the incentive for the United States to expand the war, thus avoiding a potential Sino-American confrontation; (3) to help China opt out of a hopeless competition with Moscow to provide large amounts of advanced military hardware. But when the VWP adopted General Vo Nguyen Giap's strategy of general offensive and positional warfare, which relied on the employment of modern heavy weaponry, the importance of Russian weapons shipments increased.[54]

The VWP's decision to launch the Tet Offensive in contradiction of Mao's military doctrine revealed the independent nature of decisionmaking in the DRV. Hanoi's move toward negotiations with the United States in April, 1968, further demonstrated the limitations of China's influence over the DRV. On April 3, in response to Johnson's dramatic March 31 speech, Hanoi announced its plan to send a delegation to talk with the Americans. According to Hoang Van Hoan, after hearing Hanoi's announcement, Zhou Enlai immediately asked Ho Chi Minh, who was in Beijing for medical treatment at the time, about the VWP's decision. Stunned, Ho said that he knew nothing about it.[55] In making the decision to begin negotiations with the United States, the VWP politburo under Le Duan's leadership had neither reported to Ho in Beijing nor consulted with the Chinese.

The strains in Sino-DRV relations as a result of Hanoi's decision to open negotiations with Washington were clearly revealed in the discussions between Zhou Enlai and Pham Van Dong in Beijing during April 13–20. The Chinese premier criticized Hanoi for making two major compromises: (1) accepting Johnson's partial bombing halt instead of adhering to its previous position of demanding a complete and unconditional end to the bombing before entering into any negotiations, and (2) agreeing to Paris as the site for talks and abandoning its own proposed sites of Phnom Penh and Warsaw. By making these concessions, Zhou continued, the DRV was helping Johnson solve his difficulties. Zhou listed the low votes for Johnson in the primary elections, Congress's refusal to approve General William Westmoreland's request for additional troops, and the dollar crisis as indications of the president's problems. He even drew a strange connection between Hanoi's April 3 announcement and the assassination of Martin Luther King on April 4, claiming, "Had your statement been issued one or two days later, the murder might have been stopped."[56]

In his May 7 discussion with Xuan Thuy, minister of international liaison of the VWP, Zhou complained: "We feel that you have responded too quickly and too impatiently, perhaps giving the Americans a misperception that you are eager to negotiate. Comrade Mao Zedong has told Comrade Pham Van Dong that negotiation is all right but you must assume a high posture." Contending that what counted most was military victory, Zhou advised the Vietnamese envoy that Hanoi should not let the Americans obtain through negotiations what they had failed to obtain on the battlefield.[57]

The DRV-U.S. negotiations that began in Paris on May 13 quickly ran into a deadlock. So long as the balance of forces in the battlefield remained unfavorable, Hanoi had no intention of engaging in substantive talks. It used the Paris negotiations primarily to advance the goals of securing the cessation of U.S. bombing, encouraging antiwar sentiment in the United States, and widening the gap between Washington and Saigon.[58]

Beijing, however, remained unenthusiastic about the Paris talks. Between May and October, 1968, the Chinese media remained silent about the DRV-U.S. negotiations. Beijing refrained from sending any correspondents to cover them in Paris. Chinese newspapers criticized France for providing a place for the talks.[59] Finally on November 17 Mao told Pham Van Dong in Beijing that he was in favor of Hanoi's policy of fighting while negotiating. But he cautioned the Vietnamese that it was difficult to get the United States to withdraw from Vietnam through negotiations and that the Americans did not keep their word.[60]

Between 1968 and 1970, China refrained from intervening in the talks between the DRV and the United States. The active Soviet involvement was a major reason for Beijing's indifferent and negative attitude. In a meeting with Ion Gheorghe Maurer, chairman of the Council of Ministers of Romania, in Beijing on September 7, 1969, Zhou Enlai made this point clear: "With regard to the Paris talks, we have never intervened partly because the DRV makes decisions and partly because the Soviet Union has intervened. [Because of the Soviet factor] we are even more unwilling to intervene. We have not paid attention to the progress of the talks. The Soviet Union is using the Vietnam issue, the Middle East issue, the West Berlin issue, and the China issue as trump cards in its bargaining with the United States. All these issues have been subordinated to their foreign policies. Their international policies are nothing but the unity of the two superpowers to dominate the world."[61]

After the opening of the Paris peace talks and the suspension of the American bombing of the DRV in November, 1968, China began to pull its support troops out of the DRV. The withdrawal of Chinese antiaircraft artillery units was completed in March, 1969. By July, 1970, the rest of the Chinese support troops had returned home.[62]

At the same time Beijing also began to reduce its military aid to the DRV. In a review of international situations with Pham Hung, secretary of the Southern Bureau of the VWP, and Hoang Van Thai, deputy defense minister of the DRV, in Beijing on April 21, 1969, Zhou Enlai stressed the principles of independence and self-reliance.[63] In 1969 China's supply of military equipment to the DRV sharply declined. According to one Chinese account, in 1969 Beijing provided Hanoi with 139,900 rifles, 3,906 pieces of artillery, 119.2 million bullets, and 1.36 million artillery shells as compared to 219,899 rifles, 7,087 pieces of artillery, 247.9 million bullets, and 2 million artillery shells in 1968.[64] Hanoi's preference for more sophisticated Soviet weapons may be partly responsible for the reduction of the Chinese aid.

Sino-U.S. Rapprochement and Vietnam, 1969–72

Developments in both Soviet and American policies in 1968–69 caused Mao and his associates to reassess their "dual enemy" approach in world affairs. In July, 1968, Brezhnev announced the doctrine of "limited sovereignty," arrogating to the Soviet Union the right to intervene in any socialist countries when socialism was deemed "in danger." In August, Soviet tanks rolled into Czechoslovakia to crush the "Prague Spring." Serious fighting flared up in March, 1969, when Chinese troops ambushed a Russian patrol unit on the island of Zhenbaodao (Damansky) in the Ussuri River, claimed by both China and the Soviet Union. During the rest of the year, about four hundred border clashes occurred between Chinese and Soviet forces.

In the meantime, the Nixon administration announced its intention to withdraw from Indochina and to retrench throughout Asia. In July, 1969, Nixon lifted restrictions on U.S. trade and travel in China that had existed since the Korean War. Through Pakistani and Rumanian leaders, the American president informed Beijing that the United States opposed the Soviet proposal to establish a collective security system in Asia and was interested in opening dialogues with China.[65]

Although Beijing's public statements still emphasized the alleged "collaboration" between the United States and the Soviet Union in seeking domination of the world, Chinese leaders realized that Moscow posed a much more serious threat to China than Washington. Within the changed strategic environment, they began to consider the possibility of playing the United States against the Soviet Union. In 1969, a group of four marshals, Chen Yi, Ye Jianying, Xu Xiangqian, and Nie Rongzhen, proposed to thaw relations with the United States in order to achieve "strategic effects."[66]

As a first step toward Sino-American rapprochement, Beijing and Washington resumed their ambassadorial talks in Warsaw in January, 1970. But the overthrow of Prince Sihanouk in March and the U.S. invasion of Cambodia in early May disrupted the tentative process. Sihanouk had tried to remain neutral in the Vietnam conflict by walking a tightrope between Hanoi, Beijing, Moscow, and Washington, but in March, 1970, his balancing act collapsed. While he was visiting the Soviet Union, the Cambodian Assembly deposed him as head of state.[67] The prince went on to Beijing on a planned visit, where Zhou Enlai still treated him as the Cambodian chief of state and expressed China's intention to support his struggle.[68]

In late April, the Summit Meeting of the Indochinese Peoples was held in southern China. Sihanouk, Souphanouvong of Laos, Pham Van Dong of the DRV, and Nguyen Huu Tho of the Provisional Revolutionary Government of the Republic of South Vietnam (PRG) attended the conference. At the meeting, the Indochinese delegates promised mutual assistance for each other's war. China, for its part, pledged to provide a "rear area" and "powerful backing" for the struggle against U.S. aggression.[69] On April 25, Zhou Enlai hosted a banquet in honor of the four Indochinese delegations. Congratulating them on the success of the meeting, the Chinese premier also announced the successful launching of China's first satellite the previous day.[70] Clearly Zhou wanted to impress his listeners with China's latest achievement. By sheltering Sihanouk and sponsoring the summit meeting, China had stolen the diplomatic show from the Soviet Union. China's influence in Indochina had been reasserted for the moment.

Nixon's decision to invade Cambodia in early May prompted a strong reaction from China. On May 11, Mao met with Le Duan in Beijing. According to Lu Huixiang, who served as a note-taker in the Mao-Duan conversation, the CCP chairman said that the main tendency in the world was revolution and that small countries should not be afraid of U.S. imperialism.[71] On May 18, the Chinese government announced the cancellation of the Warsaw talks scheduled to open two days later. At a mass rally in Tiananmen Square on May 20, Mao issued a statement expressing support for Sihanouk and denouncing U.S. aggression.[72] It is important to note that Mao's statement, despite its rhetorical shrillness, lacked substance. It did not make any concrete commitments to the struggle in Indochina.[73] The address was primarily a propaganda gesture designed to serve three purposes: (1) to remind Third World countries that

China remained their friend; (2) to embarrass the Russians by highlighting that nearly twenty countries had recognized the Royal Government of National Union of Cambodia led by Sihanouk, which the Soviet Union had not done; (3) to send a message to Nixon that Sino-U.S. rapprochement must be based on a reduction of American involvement in Indochina.

China did not resume negotiations until Washington completely withdrew from Cambodia in June and initiated renewed contacts. Mao invited Edgar Snow, his old friend from Yan'an, to appear on the high balcony at Tiananmen for the National Day celebration on October 1. For the first time, the CCP leader was publicly identified with the still tentative opening to the United States. Through the Pakistani channel, Nixon conveyed to the Chinese government that he was prepared to send a high-ranking envoy to Beijing. In November, Zhou Enlai replied that China would welcome a presidential emissary in Beijing.[74]

In February, 1971, the United States directed and supported a South Vietnamese invasion of Laos. Nixon immediately reassured China in a news conference on February 17 that "this action is not directed against Communist China. It is directed against the North Vietnamese who are pointed toward South Vietnam and toward Cambodia. Consequently, I do not believe that the Communist Chinese have any reason to interpret this as a threat against them or any reason therefore to react to it."[75]

China strongly condemned the invasion, but at the same time indicated that it would do nothing more. Deputy Foreign Minister Qiao Guanhua told Ole Aalgard, the Norwegian ambassador in Beijing, that China was conscious of a new trend in U.S. policy and that it was just putting off, not canceling, talks with Washington. He asked the Norwegian diplomat to inform the Americans of their conversation.[76] Between March 5 and 8, Zhou Enlai traveled to the DRV to reaffirm China's support for the struggle of the Indochinese peoples.[77] At the same time, however, Zhou indicated that China had no intention of intervening over Laos and that he was convinced that Washington was serious about disengaging from Vietnam. Both Moscow and Hanoi viewed China's reaction to the invasion of Laos as much less forceful than its reaction to the incursion into Cambodia a year before, when it was less certain about U.S. intentions.[78]

To demonstrate China's commitment to the improvement of Sino-American relations, Mao in early April decided to invite a U.S. national table tennis team to visit China. Meeting with the American ping-pong players on April 14, Zhou Enlai said: "Your trip to China has opened the gate for friendly visits by people of the two countries." The U.S. table tennis team's visit speeded up the process of Sino-American rapprochement. Between April and May, the two countries agreed that Nixon's national security adviser, Henry Kissinger, would visit Beijing in July.[79]

To seek rapprochement with the United States while North Vietnam was still locked in a desperate struggle with the Americans, however, created serious implications for Sino-DRV relations. China's détente with the United States might push Hanoi further into the arms of the Soviet Union, a development that would run counter to the very objective that underlay Beijing's opening to America. Improving relations with the United States required difficult adjustments in China's relations with the DRV. How would Hanoi react to China's opening to America? Chinese leaders fully considered the implications of a new relationship with the United States for Sino-Vietnamese relations. There were officials within the party who believed that a rapprochement with Washington would undermine the war in Vietnam and the Paris peace negotiations.[80]

To clarify thoughts within the party on the eve of Kissinger's visit, the politburo convened a meeting on May 26, 1971, discussing the implications of the forthcoming Sino-U.S. negotiations. Among the issues discussed was the Vietnam War. The meeting concluded that while the Sino-American negotiations might cause a short-term "ripple" in the Indochina war and the Paris peace talks, the progress in Sino-U.S. discussions would eventually benefit the struggle of the Indochinese people by facilitating the withdrawal of American troops from Vietnam and promoting the peace negotiations in Paris, because Nixon had realized that the focus of Soviet-American contention was in Europe and the Middle East rather than in the Far East. The report of the May 26 politburo meeting became a major policy guideline underlying China's approach to the coming Sino-American negotiations.[81]

To convince the North Vietnamese that China's opening to America would not undermine their war effort, the Chinese leadership in 1971 substantially increased DRV weapons shipments, which had declined in 1969–70. Beijing's aid reached record levels during 1972 and 1973.[82] The North Vietnamese, however, later called this increase an attempt by Chinese leaders "to cover up their betrayal and to appease the Vietnamese people's indignation."[83]

Vietnam was one of the issues that Kissinger raised during his secret talks with Zhou Enlai between July 9–11, 1971. In addition to using China to offset Soviet power, the Nixon administration wanted Beijing to make Hanoi more amenable to U.S. suggestions for ending the war. In his talk with Zhou Enlai on July 9, Kissinger attempted to wed China's interest in resolving the Taiwan issue to Washington's interest in closing the Vietnam War. After informing Zhou that the United States sought to end the war in Vietnam through negotiations and was preparing a timetable for the withdrawal of U.S. forces from Vietnam and Indochina, Kissinger stressed that Washington hoped to find an honorable solution that would preserve U.S. prestige. As to the Taiwan issue, Nixon's envoy stated that the United States planned to withdraw two-thirds of its troops from the island within a brief period after the conclusion of the war in Indochina. In response to Kissinger's emphasis on protecting American honor in Indochina, Zhou Enlai pointed out that the Americans always liked to stress their prestige and honor. It would be the greatest honor and glory for the United States, the Chinese premier concluded, if it completely withdrew its forces from Indochina.[84]

After talking with Kissinger, Zhou immediately went to brief Mao. Informed of the U.S. intention to withdraw its forces from Indochina, the CCP chairman noted that "the United States should make a new start and . . . let the domino fall. The United States must withdraw from Vietnam. We are in no hurry on the Taiwan issue because there is no fighting on Taiwan. But there is a war in Vietnam and people are dying there. We should not invite Nixon to come just for our own purposes."[85] In the end, the Chinese leaders ignored Kissinger's request that they pressure Hanoi to change its policy toward the Paris peace talks and prisoners of war.[86]

Immediately after Kissinger left China, Zhou Enlai rushed to Hanoi on July 13 to inform Le Duan and Pham Van Dong of his meetings with Kissinger.[87] After mentioning Kissinger's principle of linking the settlement of the Taiwan issue with the resolution of the Indochina problem, Zhou assured the Vietnamese that China had pointed out to the American negotiator that the withdrawal of American troops from South Vietnam had priority over the question of Chinese representation in the United Nations.[88] Clearly the Chinese wanted to dispel doubts in the minds of their Vietnamese comrades that China had abandoned its commitment to their cause. Mao did not want to alienate Hanoi in the Sino-Soviet competition within the communist world. He was also nervous that his opening to the United States might tarnish China's self-image as a firm supporter of the anti-imperialist movement in the Third World.

Despite China's reassurances, the North Vietnamese had drawn the inescapable conclusion that China valued its relationship with the United States more than its revolutionary unity with the DRV. They believed that Beijing's opening to the United States undermined their interests and objectives. Specifically, they felt that the July 15 announcement of Kissinger's secret trip to China and Nixon's planned visit to Beijing significantly undercut their new peace offensive. On July 1, 1971, Nguyen Thi Binh, foreign minister of the PRG, had just unveiled the Seven-Point Proposal, which demanded that the United States set a date for the complete withdrawal of its troops from South Vietnam, coupled with the release of prisoners, and that the United States respect the South Vietnamese people's right to self-determination by ending its support for the Nguyen Van Thieu government, allowing the South Vietnamese people to establish an administration favorably disposed to peace and democracy with which the PRG would be willing to negotiate. Leaders in Hanoi and the PRG concluded that in view of Nixon's continuing unilateral withdrawal of U.S. troops from South Vietnam amid the ongoing antiwar campaign in the United States, and the defeats of Thieu's troops, Washington might be receptive to a political change in South Vietnam that could prepare the ground for settling the conflict through negotiations. They expected that when they made their terms known, the American public would exert pressure on the White House to get negotiations underway. But the spotlight on the sudden and dramatic change in Chinese-American relations seriously weakened the impact of the Seven-Point Proposal on the American public and made it easier for Nixon to ignore the public support initially elicited by the publication of the proposal.[89]

Xuan Thuy, Hanoi's chief negotiator at the Paris talks, called Nixon's forthcoming trip to Beijing a "perfidious maneuver" and a "false peace offensive" designed to split the socialist world.[90] The Hanoi media remained silent about the July 15 announcement until late in 1971 when it informed its people of the American president's impending visit to Beijing.[91]

China's changing attitude toward a negotiated disengagement of the United States from Indochina also strained Sino-Vietnamese relations. Beijing's proposal for a Geneva Conference on Indochina brought into sharp relief the incipient disagreement between Beijing and Hanoi over the execution of the war. After returning to Australia from China on July 14, 1971, Australian Labor Party leader Gough Whitlam announced that Beijing now favored a Geneva Conference on Indochina that would include non-Asian countries. *Nhan Dan* responded immediately, reminding the world that Hanoi's long-standing opposition to a new conference on Indochina remained unchanged. The party organ contended that "decisive voices belong only to those who are defeating" U.S. aggression and that the "most important cause of our victories is our correct and creative independent and sovereign line."[92]

In the wake of Kissinger's visit to Beijing, *Nhan Dan* (People's Daily), the official organ of the VWP, carried an editorial titled "'The Nixon Doctrine' Is Bound to Failure," which implicitly criticized the Sino-American talks. After reading the piece, Zhou Enlai on July 20 wrote to Zhang Chunqiao and Yao Wenyuan, two party officials in charge of propaganda, that "the editorial reveals the apprehension and estimation of the Vietnamese comrades. I think the whole text can be published. Do not excerpt passages from it." In this way, Zhou continued, China could demonstrate its "attitude of being open and aboveboard. The progress of events will prove that China under Chairman

Mao's leadership has always supported the resistance war of the people of the three Indochinese countries to the end." However, Zhang Chunqiao, apparently afraid of the negative impact of the Vietnamese article, opposed its publication in China. As a result, the *Nhan Dan* editorial was not made available to the Chinese public.[93] Zhang's veto of Zhou's proposal clearly demonstrated the power of the ultra-leftist officials, who controlled ideological matters.

In November, 1971, after Kissinger's second trip to China, Pham Van Dong visited Beijing. He had turned down an earlier invitation, issued shortly after Kissinger's first visit. During his stay in Beijing between November 20 and 25, the DRV premier held one meeting with Mao and three talks with Zhou Enlai. In his conversation with Mao on November 22, Dong asked the Chinese government to cancel the planned Nixon journey to China. Mao refused his request.[94]

In his talks with Zhou, Dong recounted developments in the Paris peace negotiations, requesting China's continued support for the DRV's war against the United States, especially in the area of transport. Zhou explained the basic principles of the United States toward negotiations with the DRV as described by Kissinger.[95] According to an account by Wang Youping, China's ambassador to the DRV between 1969 and 1974, at the close of their first formal talk on November 21 Dong reminded Zhou that North Vietnam had made a contribution to the recent return of the PRC to the United Nations. The DRV premier was referring to the official statement released by the DRV Foreign Ministry back in August of that year in support of the admission of the PRC into the United Nations. Embarrassed by his omission of this subject during the just-completed meeting, Zhou hurried to express his thanks for Hanoi's effort.[96] The message Dong was trying to deliver was that the DRV had supported the PRC on the international front but that Beijing had betrayed Hanoi by its attempt to improve relations with the United States.

Washington was persistent in trying to use Beijing to turn up the heat on Hanoi. Preparations for the Nixon visit to China provided another opportunity for U.S. officials to seek Beijing's help in ending the war in Vietnam. In January, 1972, General Vernon Walters, U.S. military attaché in France, in the course of preparing for the Beijing summit, asked Chinese diplomats in Paris to use their influence to moderate Hanoi's negotiating position. The Chinese turned down his request. When Walters asked whether China would arrange a meeting between Nixon and the Vietnamese official Le Duc Tho in Beijing, the reply was again negative.[97]

General Alexander Haig, Kissinger's deputy on the National Security Council staff, encountered similar Chinese reluctance to become involved in the Vietnam peace process when he led the U.S. advance team for the summit to

Beijing in January, 1972. Unwilling to discuss the Vietnam peace negotiations, Zhou Enlai defended Hanoi's position in the war. Responding to Haig's charge that the DRV had "insulted" the United States by its recent attack on American forces, Zhou said that North Vietnam was a victim of the latest U.S. bombing and that China had no choice but to support the DRV. If the United States really wanted to end the war and completely withdraw its forces from Vietnam, Zhou went on, it had no reason to reject the reasonable demands of the DRV.[98] The Chinese premier, nevertheless, also showed displeasure with Soviet–North Vietnamese cooperation, adding that China's assistance to Hanoi was the minimum required to avoid a deterioration of Sino-Vietnamese relations.[99]

There are indications that China was prepared to face a worsening of Sino-Vietnamese relations and closer ties between Hanoi and Moscow. When Haig told Zhou Enlai on January 4 that the continuation of the war in Southeast Asia could only give the Soviet Union an opportunity to increase its influence in Hanoi and to implement its plan to encircle the PRC, the Chinese premier replied that the Soviet intervention in Indochina was an "inevitable reaction" by Moscow to the improvement of Sino-American relations and that China was prepared to "bear the consequences of the Sino-American accommodation."[100]

Indochina was one of the topics Nixon brought up in his discussions with Zhou Enlai in February.[101] Nixon said that while the United States wanted to end the war through negotiations, it would react strongly if Hanoi launched a major offensive in 1972. After noting that the only correct solution to the Indochina problem was U.S. withdrawal from Vietnam, Zhou asserted that "so long as you continue your practice of Vietnamization, Laotianization, and Cambodianization, and so long as the Vietnamese, the Laos, and the Cambodians continue to fight, we will not stop supporting them for a single day."[102] Zhou's remarks were clearly for the record for the North Vietnamese (a copy of the discussion might be sent to Hanoi), given the fact that Beijing seemed to have agreed with Washington that the war in Indochina no longer should come between them. Nixon and Kissinger drew the impression from the talks that the Chinese gave highest priority to advancing their relations with Washington. In the words of Kissinger, "We indeed understood each other; the war in Vietnam would not affect the improvement of our relations."[103]

On March 4, within days of Nixon's departure from China, Zhou Enlai flew to Hanoi to brief the North Vietnamese on the Beijing summit and to reassure them of China's continued support. Zhou first apologized for China's failure to endorse Hanoi's decision to begin negotiations with the United States in May, 1968. He admitted that China had made a misjudgment at the time in insisting that the conditions were not ripe for Vietnamese-American negotiations.[104] Zhou then reassured the Vietnamese that in talking with the Americans China had consistently placed the settlement of the Vietnam problem above the resolution of the Taiwan issue.[105]

The North Vietnamese, however, remained unconvinced by Beijing's repeated reassurances. They later charged that China "at heart wants to make use of the Viet Nam question for the settlement of the Taiwan issue first."[106] The Chinese embassy in Hanoi immediately felt the cool attitudes of the Vietnamese. On February 21, 1972, the embassy hosted a party to celebrate the Spring Festival, a common holiday for both the Chinese and the Vietnamese. As it had done for many years, the embassy invited Vietnamese guests to attend. But to the surprise of the Chinese diplomats, not a single Vietnamese showed up this time. They soon discovered the reason: that was the day when President Nixon arrived in Beijing.[107]

China and the Spring Offensive of 1972

Since the Tet Offensive of 1968, the Hanoi leadership had been preparing for a general offensive in the early 1970s. Vo Nguyen Giap contended in late 1971 that the only effective means to win over the United States was to return to the strategy of main force warfare and general uprising. In his calculation, a decisive military victory would convince the Nixon White House and the American public that there were only two alternatives to a negotiated withdrawal: further escalation or defeat.[108]

International pressures were also a factor in Hanoi's decision. DRV leaders were nervously watching the progress of Washington's relations with both Moscow and Beijing. Uncertain over how the emerging U.S. détente with Moscow and Beijing would affect them, the North Vietnamese began to favor a military showdown. Given the interest of China and the Soviet Union in improving relations with the United States, policymakers in Hanoi had reason to worry that their two allies were susceptible to American pressures on Vietnam and their support for the DRV might diminish if the war dragged on much longer. Furthermore, the planned withdrawal of U.S. troops and a presidential election approaching in the fall of 1972 seemed to provide an opportunity to achieve a "decisive victory."[109] Therefore a general offensive in 1972 might be the DRV's last chance to force a settlement on its own terms.

On March 30, 1972, North Vietnam launched the Spring Offensive across the demilitarized zone into South Vietnam. Nixon reacted to Hanoi's attack by authorizing an extensive bombing of military targets across North Vietnam and the mining of the DRV's harbors. For the first time in the war, U.S. troops employed high-tech "smart bombs" to hit their targets with accuracy.[110] Evidently U.S. détente with Beijing and Moscow had made Nixon less worried about the reactions of the two major Communist powers.

In a meeting with Nguyen Tien, DRV chargé d'affaires in Beijing on April 14, Zhou Enlai reiterated China's support for Hanoi to carry the war to the end.[111] On May 9, the day when the United States began to lay mines in North Vietnam's harbors, the DRV ambassador met with Zhou, requesting China's assistance in mine-clearing. The Chinese premier summoned naval commanders that night, asking them to prepare for the task. The next day he conducted further discussions with Pan Yan and Lai Guangzu, chief and deputy chief of staff of the navy, respectively, to flesh out the plan for detecting and clearing mines.[112] In the meantime, the Chinese government issued a statement on May 12 condemning the U.S. mining of Haiphong and other North Vietnamese ports and promising Chinese support for the Vietnamese until "final victory" was achieved.[113]

In late May, a Chinese Mine Investigation Team arrived in Haiphong. With the help of the North Vietnamese, the Chinese team collected information regarding the types and characters of the American mines. Two months later, Chinese mine-sweeping vessels began to operate in the DRV. Between July, 1972, and August, 1973, Beijing sent altogether twelve mine sweepers and four support vessels to North Vietnam. In total, they cleared forty-six mines.[114] Given the unprecedented scale of the U.S. action in the wake of the DRV's Spring Offensive, however, Beijing's reaction was rather restrained.

On April 18, 1972, Nixon met with a visiting Chinese table tennis team in the White House, demonstrating that rapprochement was on track despite Hanoi's offensive and Washington's bombing retaliation.[115] Clearly China was in a serious dilemma. On the one hand, it had to continue its support for the DRV to avoid pushing the latter completely to the side of the Soviet Union and to maintain its self-image as a staunch supporter of national liberation movements. On the other hand, it wanted to preserve its improved relations with the United States.

The Soviet leadership suspected that China and the DRV had cooperated in launching the Spring Offensive in order to sabotage the upcoming U.S.-Soviet summit in Moscow. Leonid Brezhnev informed Kissinger in April that the Soviet Union was not behind the North Vietnamese offensive and that Beijing and Hanoi were trying their best to undermine détente between his country and the United States. Brezhnev also told Kissinger that Hanoi had requested the cancellation of the Moscow summit.[116] In fact, China was not involved in North Vietnam's decision to launch the Spring Offensive. Beijing's ignorance was confirmed by the Albanian ambassador to the DRV, who had met with the Chinese military attaché in Hanoi a few days after the offensive began and had been informed that China knew nothing about the attack.[117]

To maintain its influence in the DRV and to drive a wedge between China and North Vietnam, the Kremlin in the spring of 1972 proposed to bypass the U.S. bombing of Haiphong by sending weapons shipments to the DRV overland through China, including unloading Soviet ship cargoes in Chinese ports. While Hanoi approved the proposal, Beijing turned it down, creating an opportunity for Moscow to reproach China.[118]

The results of the Spring Offensive were disappointing to the Hanoi leadership, who had miscalculated Washington's ability and willingness to react. North Vietnam received the most sustained bombing of the war. This harsh reality, along with the realization that Nixon was likely to be reelected, convinced the North Vietnamese that circumstances dictated a quick solution. In late August, Le Duc Tho offered a new proposal in Paris, calling for the establishment of a coalition government including elements of both the PRG and the Thieu regime, as well as neutral representatives chosen by each side. For the first time, the DRV had proposed a settlement that left Thieu in power. When the United States rejected the notion of a coalition government in any form, Hanoi in October made a further concession by abandoning the demand for a coalition and agreeing to a cease-fire, followed by the complete withdrawal of U.S. troops and the exchange of prisoners of war.[119]

Hanoi's concession on the treatment of the Thieu regime came primarily as a result of intense American military pressure and the realization that there might be four more years of war if an agreement was not concluded before the U.S. presidential election. China had also advised the DRV to compromise on this issue. According to Vietnamese sources, in his talk with Pham Van Dong on November 22, 1971, Mao urged the North Vietnamese to postpone the liberation of South Vietnam: "As our broom is too short to sweep the Americans out of Taiwan, so yours is too short to do the same in South Vietnam."[120] Mao told French Foreign Minister Maurice Schumann in July, 1972, that he had advised Nguyen Thi Binh to stop insisting on Thieu's removal as a precondition for a settlement with the United States.[121]

Despite the Vietnamese claim that they had not been affected by the changes in Sino-American and Soviet-American relations, the unfolding U.S. rapprochement with China and the Soviet Union undermined Hanoi's interests. The limitations of both Chinese and Soviet aid seriously constrained Hanoi's approach to Washington. As Raymond Garthoff has observed perceptively, "At the very least, neither the Soviet nor the Chinese leaders had been prepared to subordinate or sacrifice their own interests in improving relations with the United States to support socialist North Vietnam in a crucial struggle with the leading imperialist and interventionist power."[122]

The Beijing leaders were now eager to see the Vietnamese-American negotiations in Paris succeed. They urged Hanoi to be flexible and to allow Washington a face-saving withdrawal. Mao and Zhou Enlai reminded visiting Vietnamese leaders in the winter of 1972–73 that because the United States had made up its mind to withdraw, Hanoi should conduct serious negotiations with the Americans. Mao told Nguyen Thi Binh on December 29, 1972, that if the Paris talks were successful, not only the PRG but also the DRV could "achieve [a] certain degree of normalization with the Americans."[123]

Zhou said to VWP politburo member Truong Chinh on December 31 that because "Nixon does intend to disengage," the DRV "ought to approach the negotiations seriously in order to produce results."[124] The Chinese premier, in a conversation with Le Duc Tho in Beijing on January 3, 1973, reiterated his belief that Nixon wanted to withdraw from Vietnam: "The U.S. effort to exert pressure through bombing has failed. Nixon is facing many international and domestic problems. It seems that he intends to retreat from Vietnam and Indochina. During the negotiations, you should both adhere to principles and show necessary flexibility. Let the Americans leave as quickly as possible. In half or one year the situation will change."[125] Compared to its position in 1968, China's stance on the Paris peace talks had undergone a sea change.

Mao and Zhou viewed with satisfaction the conclusion of the Paris peace agreement. In a conversation with Penn Nouth, prime minister of the Royal Government of National Union of Cambodia, on February 2, 1973, Zhou quoted Mao as saying that the Paris agreement was a "successful" one because it brought the departure of the American troops.[126]

The Chinese leaders' reaction to the Paris peace agreement indicates that they were happy to see the disengagement of the United States from Vietnam and expected a communist victory over Saigon. Beijing differed from Hanoi over strategy, not the goal. The Chinese policymakers wished to see the United States out of Vietnam and supported Hanoi's plan to unify the South, but they preferred concessions permitting the Americans to withdraw and allowing a period of several years before a renewed effort was made to defeat Thieu's regime. This position was clearly indicated in Zhou Enlai's conversation with Hoang Van Hoan in May, 1973. The Chinese premier compared the situation in Vietnam with that in China after the surrender of Japan in 1945. For about two years the CCP negotiated with the KMT and retreated before starting a counteroffensive and defeating Chiang Kai-shek's forces "without a halt." The DRV, Zhou went on, should also "win a spell of time to get prepared and, when it begins to fight, should eliminate the Nguyen Van Thieu administration without a halt. For after a period of armistice, it would be difficult for the United States to barge in."[127]

In talking with the North Vietnamese about the settlement of the Vietnam conflict, the Chinese leaders adopted a subtle approach. While they advised Hanoi to give the Americans face-saving concessions, they shied from overt arm-twisting to achieve that purpose. As John W. Garver has observed, Beijing "apparently distinguished between urging Hanoi to compromise with the United States and actively applying pressure to achieve this. While such a distinction might seem sophistic, it can also be seen as an attempt to synchronize the contradictory objectives of minimizing the influence of *both* superpowers in Indochina while creating optimal conditions for using U.S. power to check Soviet moves elsewhere in the world."[128] The Chinese leaders refrained from actively exerting pressure on the North Vietnamese because they wanted both to minimize the opportunities for the Russians to exploit the Sino-Vietnamese contradictions and to preserve China's self-image as a loyal friend of national liberation movements.

Conclusion

The Beijing-Hanoi relationship included both converging and diverging interests. The two countries shared a common ideological outlook and a common concern over American intervention in Indochina, but leaders in Hanoi wanted to avoid the danger of submitting to a dependent relationship with China. As long as policymakers in Hanoi and Beijing shared the common goal of ending the U.S. presence in the region, such diverging interests could be subordinated to their points of agreement. But when the common fear of the United States that bound China and the DRV closely together disappeared, disagreement overweighed agreement in Sino-DRV relations. In the absence of a common threat, cordial relations soon gave way to tensions and division.

During the Vietnam War, the DRV was a small power caught in the fight of three giants. It had to confront not only the military might of the United States but also political and ideological pressure from China and the Soviet Union. While Washington wanted Hanoi to cease its effort to unify the South, the Chinese and the Russians pressed the Vietnamese Communists to follow their respective international lines. Both Beijing and Moscow approached the Vietnam conflict with their own self-interests in mind.

Glenn Snyder's description of the alliance security dilemma can be usefully applied to illuminate the problems in the alliance between China and the DRV. According to Snyder, the alliance security dilemma involves a choice between support or nonsupport of allies and tension between fears of entrapment and abandonment.[129] In the late 1950s and early 1960s, Ho Chi Minh was afraid of being entrapped by China in the emerging Sino-Soviet dispute. He did not want to be dragged into a conflict over China's interests that he did not share.

Therefore, he visited both Beijing and Moscow in 1960 in an attempt to mediate the difference between Mao and Khrushchev and to promote unity in the international communist movement. In the late 1960s and early 1970s, the Vietnamese Communists began to fear that China would abandon the DRV in its search for rapprochement with the United States. Thus Pham Van Dong came to Beijing in November, 1971, asking Mao not to invite President Nixon to China.

While policymakers in Hanoi constantly feared betrayal by their big allies, they were not the submissive puppets of Beijing or Moscow. In fact, they were highly self-willed and independent actors, who were able to make their own strategic choices, often without consulting China or the Soviet Union. They were weak but not meek. They made the world, too.

Mao and his associates often ignored the interests, priorities, and needs of the VWP. Their advice to the DRV not to rely on Soviet support and their disapproval of Hanoi's strategy of fighting while talking clearly demonstrated this tendency. For the Hanoi leadership, the Russian connection was crucial. Moscow provided not only advanced weaponry but also international contact for the DRV. The Soviet Union was a member of the UN Security Council, maintained diplomatic relations with the United States, and enjoyed a wide contact with the global community. Especially in the early stage of the war between 1965 and 1967, the Soviet Union played the role of Hanoi's envoy in its dialogue with the West. Soviet officials and diplomats informed their counterparts in Washington, Paris, London, and other Western capitals of Hanoi's stance on various issues regarding the settlement of the war. They also supplied the North Vietnamese with information on Western views.[130] Chinese leaders were jealous of this Soviet role in Vietnam.

Realizing that Vietnam was a small and underdeveloped country facing an industrialized foreign power and that the resistance could not end in a total military victory over the enemy, leaders in Hanoi finally had to accept negotiations with the enemy as a fact of life and an integral component of their struggle for national reunification. They needed a period of peace in which to consolidate military and political strength. To them, negotiations were an extension of warfare rather than an alternative to it. What they sought in direct negotiations with Washington was a way to improve their chance of winning the war, not a way of preventing or ending it. Negotiations served as a tactic of warfare. Hanoi often employed the lure of negotiations as a way to win friends in the international arena, to disrupt support for the war in the United States, and to drive a wedge between Washington and Saigon.[131]

At times, especially before the launching of a major military operation, Hanoi would express an interest in conducting talks with the United States simply to trick Washington into halting its bombing and enmesh the United States in a negotiating trap. DRV Foreign Minister Nguyen Duy Trinh's declaration on the eve of the Tet Offensive of Hanoi's willingness to hold discussions with the Americans was a case in point.[132] Officials in Beijing, however, often failed to appreciate the importance of negotiations in Hanoi's strategy. They kept urging the DRV to wage a protracted war against the United States.

Since the late 1950s when the Sino-Soviet dispute erupted, policymakers in Beijing had habitually judged the VWP in light of the doctrine of opposition to Soviet revisionism, which distorted far more than it illuminated. The tendency to evaluate fraternal parties through the prism of antirevisionism also manifested itself in China's relations with Cuba in the 1960s. Just like the later deterioration of Beijing-Hanoi relations, the worsening of Chinese-Cuban ties in the mid-1960s derived primarily from Mao's dissatisfaction with Castro's flirtations with Moscow. Mao and his lieutenants were too much prisoners of their competition with the Soviets.

In a deeper historical sense, the Sino-Vietnamese conflict was caused by the clash of the competing visions held by leaders in the two countries regarding their respective roles in Indochina. These visions or self-images were informed by historical memory as well as concerns for national prestige and destiny. What Mao and his comrades sought in their commitment to revolutionary struggle was not just the rescue of China from the clutches of perennial poverty, warlord rule, and imperialist penetration but also the rejuvenation of the Chinese nation and the restoration of its historical greatness in East Asia. Historically speaking, the Chinese held a Sinocentric view of the world, regarding other countries as inferior. The Celestial Emperor in the Forbidden City considered small nations on China's periphery, including Vietnam, as within the orbit of China's influence and kept those countries within the tributary system.

Despite his claims of adherence to Marxism and Leninism, Mao fully inherited China's historical legacy. His strong belief in the absolute correctness and universal relevance of his revolutionary practice and theory for the oppressed peoples of the world against colonialism and imperialism was reminiscent of the claims of Chinese imperial rulers about the superiority of Chinese models and institutions. He felt perplexed and indignant when the Vietnamese Communists refused to echo the Chinese line in the Sino-Soviet quarrel after 1965, and when Hanoi defied his wish in entering into negotiations with the United States in 1968.

Ho Chi Minh and his associates were also conscientious students of history. What they sought in their struggle against the French and the Americans was not just the end of Vietnam's suffering under colonialism but also the reconstruction of their motherland and the re-establishment of its leading role in Indochina. Since the restoration of independence from Chinese control in the tenth century, Vietnamese imperial rulers had created hegemony over their neighbors to the west and introduced a tributary system in mainland Southeast Asia. After the establishment of the Indochinese Communist Party (ICP) in 1930,[133] party strategists saw Indochina as a single strategic space and assumed a leading role for Vietnam in guiding the revolutionary struggle in Laos and Cambodia. Although the ICP was dissolved in 1951 and separate Communist organizations were established in Laos and Cambodia, Vietnamese strategic thinking remained unchanged.

The CCP's attempt to assert China's influence over Indochina was at loggerheads with the VWP's effort to maintain its "special relationship" with Laos and Cambodia. At the 1954 Geneva Conference, Zhou Enlai, apprehensive about Vietnamese intentions to create a military bloc of all three Indochinese countries after the defeat of the French, criticized Hanoi's tendency to subordinate the interests of Laos and Cambodia to those of Vietnam. In the mid-1960s when Beijing dispatched an advisory team to Pathet Lao territory, the Vietnamese advisers there defended their superior position by minimizing the role of their Chinese competitors.

In the end, it was not just the United States who lost the Vietnam War. China also failed in Vietnam. It shed blood and spent enormous amounts of material resources in Vietnam but did not secure the gratitude and goodwill of the Vietnamese. The Chinese-Vietnamese contradiction was determined not only by contemporary conflicts between their national interests but also by historically rooted mutual distrust and suspicion.

Part 2

Allies of the United States

Chapter 7

The Vietnam War and the Challenges to American Power in Europe

FRANK COSTIGLIOLA

The Western alliance is an organization of meaning and belief as well as an organization of tanks and troops. Especially during the Cold War, the participation of Western European leaders and citizens in NATO meetings and exercises reinforced a world view that made U.S. predominance in European affairs seem normal and natural. The U.S. war in Vietnam, however, shook this world view by undermining two sets of beliefs: the Cold War paradigm and the Atlantic axioms. The Vietnam War accelerated questioning of the Cold War paradigm, which held that undifferentiated communism was the aggressor and that the struggle with communism was unavoidably the governing principle in the foreign policy of the Western nations. The Vietnam War also challenged what I term the Atlantic axioms, a set of beliefs that regarded U.S. leadership of the Western alliance as necessary, democratic, wise, moral, and popular. The challenge to these belief systems—a challenge legitimated by French President Charles de Gaulle—had political consequences at both the top levels of government and in the streets of Western Europe.

The extraordinary authority de Gaulle enjoyed stemmed from his wartime and postwar rescues of France, from his regal manner and six-foot-six-inch height, from his seniority among Western leaders, from his unquestioned anticommunism, from his incisive rhetoric, and, not least, from his often superior political analysis. De Gaulle challenged the Cold War paradigm and the Atlantic axioms because he believed that international politics had changed fundamentally from the situation at the beginning of the Cold War. With the Soviet Union's humiliation in the Cuban missile crisis, with the superpowers' nuclear stalemate, with France's nuclear capability, with Europe's growing wealth, and with America's overextended global ambitions, these sets of beliefs had become outmoded and were no longer advantageous to European—particularly French—interests. The disastrous, unwavering course of U.S. policies in Vietnam gave credence to de Gaulle's argument that Americans had neither the right nor the wisdom to make decisions for Europeans. De Gaulle suggested not just alternatives to American policies in Europe and in Asia, but also alternatives to the language and categories with which Europeans should interpret and understand those American policies.

De Gaulle's challenge was a well-articulated and widely publicized expression of what had become by the late 1960s a pervasive dissatisfaction with U.S. hegemony. The blossoming of détente in Europe weakened the unity and purpose of the alliance as Americans and Western Europeans each reached out for closer ties with Moscow and other Eastern European capitals. U.S. policy was wrenched by efforts to fight the communists in Asia while negotiating with the communists in Europe. The strains in the Western alliance during the Johnson administration marked a crucial stage in the transition from the period of the late 1940s–50s, when Washington exercised relatively easy predominance in Europe and held to a broad, Atlanticist definition of U.S. self-interest, to the post-1971 era, when Washington faced tougher economic problems and viewed U.S. national interests more narrowly. The Vietnam War accelerated this transition. Many Europeans resented the Americans for getting involved in a costly, senseless war that could ensnare them, while many Americans resented the Europeans for doing so little to help.

Americans as well as Europeans became more ambivalent about the alliance. Although American leaders sought closer links with Western Europe so as to enlist European financial help with the U.S. agenda in Vietnam and elsewhere, they also felt hemmed in by the ties that already bound America to Europe. When Johnson laid out his Great Society agenda in 1965, former Secretary of State Dean Acheson, once more a key adviser on European policy, reminded the president that "this country is not and cannot be, in John Donne's phrase, 'an iland intire of itselfe.'" The United States had to remain "'a part of the maine' because Europe can make the Great Society . . . possible, or by narrow policies, slow it or prevent it."[1] Yet in discussing Atlantic partnership, Acheson commented acidly that "only those who have never been members of a partnership regard it as a happy relationship."[2] Acheson and other U.S. officials resented Europe's growing autonomy. Irritated at the French and other Europeans "now talking of European independence," Dean Rusk complained that the "US has already surrendered its independence and because of its worldwide responsibilities and commitments today is one of [the] world's least sovereign nations."[3] "Surrendered," "least sovereign"? Rusk's exaggerated language is striking; for him and for others in the Johnson administration, any diminution in autonomy was magnified into near total loss. Such grumbling about the pinching of alliance ties recalled America's preference before the 1940s—and after the 1960s—for more unilateral diplomacy.

The slipping of U.S. predominance in Europe made the Atlantic axioms still more important to Johnson administration officials. The Atlantic axioms were assumptions that cohered during the Truman years, that Acheson, John J. McCloy, and other influential elder statesmen still propounded, and that Johnson, for all his focus on Vietnam and on domestic affairs, accepted as basic. In the State Department, these beliefs had the general support of Rusk and the fervent advocacy of Undersecretary George Ball, Walt Rostow, Eugene Rostow, Counselor Robert Bowie, Assistant Secretary William R. Tyler, and Ambassadors to NATO Thomas Finletter and Harlan Cleveland. These were also the concepts from which arose many of the ostensibly new policy initiatives of the Kennedy and Johnson years. Finally, these ideas marked the boundaries around what even skeptics, such as Secretary of Defense Robert S. McNamara and National Security Adviser McGeorge Bundy, considered as "sound" and "responsible" policy toward Europe.

The first Atlantic axiom was that the United States had to, and could, direct the Western alliance. As Acheson told Johnson, "American leadership is vital to constructive forward motion. . . . The European countries will move in response to leadership—not otherwise."[4] The second tenet was that despite the worsening gold drain and balance of payments gap, America could still spend huge amounts overseas to pay for the war in Vietnam, to station troops elsewhere in the world, and to purchase lucrative investments. Moreover, the belief ran, the European allies had a moral obligation to help finance—through weapons purchases, loans, and accumulation of dollars—the U.S. payments deficit. The third belief recognized that multilateral organizations, particularly NATO, facilitated U.S. predominance. As Eugene Rostow perceived, "NATO was a façade to conceal the extent of U.S. influence in European affairs."[5] Until challenged by de Gaulle, a pattern of language, what some observers called NATO theology, helped maintain this façade. In the parlance of numerous NATO communiqués, the allies were always "improving" consultation and "progressing" toward shared policymaking. In practice, however, the United States retained control of the important decisions. NATO's many meetings, committees, projects, and earnest declarations helped obscure the perennial, institutionalized gap between the ever elusive goal of democratization and the ongoing fact of U.S. dominion. Former U.S. diplomat Harold van B. Cleveland alluded to this gap when he remarked that an "Atlantic strategic entity *evolving* in a supranational direction . . . looks best for the United States because it *maintains* U.S. control, while meeting some of the desires of Europeans."[6] The fourth belief regarded the particular utility of multilateral organizations such as NATO, the European Economic Community, and the abortive Multilateral Force in containing and providing a creative outlet for West Germany. A major challenge, Johnson stressed to British Prime Minister Harold Wilson, was to "submerge . . . any latent nationalistic drives" of West Germany "in a larger European unity."[7]

Johnson's remark pointed to the final Atlantic axiom, the key importance and the underlying instability of Germany. Johnson and his advisers viewed almost every major problem in Europe—the nationalist challenge of de Gaulle, the faltering of British power, the financing of America's payments deficit, the need to rally support for the Vietnam War, the issue of nuclear proliferation, and the management of détente—as revolving around the Federal Republic of Germany. Shortly after the assassination of John F. Kennedy, Acheson laid out for the new president in primer style with "Do's" and "Don'ts": the reasons why "the major consideration in making political and military judgments affecting Europe should be their effect on the German people and the German government."[8] Johnson did not need the lesson; he understood that West Germany figured as America's trophy from World War II, as the chief prize in the Cold War, as the front line in the Cold War, as an ally with a powerful army under U.S. command, as a key customer and business partner, as the creditor that helped cover America's payments deficits, as an appreciative acolyte of American culture, and as the ally dependent enough on Washington to be most "responsive" to America's wishes and actions.[9] West Germany's dependence stemmed from its exposed position across the border from massive Soviet armies, from its non-nuclear status, and, this a rising concern during the Johnson years, from Germany's potentially explosive position status as a divided, dissatisfied nation.[10]

Keeping Germany and the other European allies firmly in the American camp was a prominent consideration in the minds of Kennedy and Johnson administration officials as they plunged deeper into the Vietnam War. The argument was, as it had been at the onset of the Korean War, that meeting U.S. commitments—or what could be perceived as U.S. commitments—in Asia would bolster the confidence of the allies in Europe and strengthen them vis-à-vis the Soviet Union. As Johnson commented about the allies in June, 1965, "if they wanted us to get out of Viet-Nam we can get out and they'll be in a fix."[11] U.S. leaders also believed that honoring commitments in Asia lessened the chance that the European allies, particularly West Germany, might, out of fear or opportunism, cut a deal with Moscow. The extraordinary tenacity with which U.S. officials clung to the belief that military action in Vietnam would enhance U.S. nuclear credibility in Europe was illustrated by Eugene Rostow's absurd argument to Johnson that the 1965 bombing of North Vietnam gave "a firm answer" to the question posed by de Gaulle and other Europeans: "would we risk war for our allies?" In a gross distortion of both the U.S.-Soviet nuclear deterrence relationship and the military situation in Vietnam, Rostow asserted that American bombing of North Vietnam showed "that we would risk bombs on New York in order to protect Saigon, and that Moscow would not bomb New York to protect Hanoi." As if either the Americans or the Soviets would risk nuclear destruction over Vietnam! Rostow, however, assured the president that the bombing of the North "should greatly fortify our system of alliances."[12]

Although Rostow was right that America's global alliances constituted a "system" in which U.S. actions in Asia affected ties elsewhere, he was wrong that war in Vietnam would "fortify" the alliance in Europe. Instead, critics of the alliance like de Gaulle fortified their arguments by pointing to the dangers of the expanded war. Despite their appreciation of American resoluteness, most European leaders and opinionmakers opposed any war that could widen into a conflict on their territory. Hence the usual European preference, in armament and in strategic thinking, was for deterrence over war-fighting options. As the Vietnam conflict escalated into a war involving the United States and potentially China and the Soviet Union, Europeans grew increasingly uneasy. Beginning in 1965, the squeeze on leaders in Britain, West Germany, and Italy tightened as their populations turned against the war while the Johnson administration urged them to send to South Vietnam visible support for the U.S. effort.

Johnson administration officials pressured the European allies because they wanted to have "more flags appear in South Vietnam."[13] In response to a request from McGeorge Bundy, John McNaughton in December, 1965, drew up "an Optimist's View of where we can get combat forces for Vietnam." McNaughton found difficulty, however, in even pretending optimism. Almost any additional combat forces would require "pressure," lots of money, "deliveries of cumshaw," "selling our souls and raising hob in various ways"—and even then the maximum from Europe would be a fighter squadron from Greece, a division each from Germany and Spain, and a battalion from Britain.[14] In fact, none of these troops or fighter squadrons would ever appear in Vietnam.

The war was weakening rather than strengthening Washington's global system of alliances. Rusk and other officials degraded the alliance by pushing harder. When the British faced the threat of having to devalue the pound sterling, Robert McNamara suggested that "he would give them an extra billion dollars for one brigade" sent to South Vietnam.[15]

Although Ball thought this plan of "making Hessions [sic] out of [British] soldiers" would backfire, Rusk leaned on the Germans to "send considerable numbers of people to South Vietnam." German Foreign Minister Gerhard Schroder protested that although his government ranked second only to the United States in economic aid to Saigon, Germans refused to volunteer for noncombatant duty there because "they are under the impression that all of South Vietnam is a war zone." Desperate to "get some Germans into the field," Rusk urged that German military or police units be compelled to do noncombatant duty in South Vietnam.[16] The refusal, however, of Germany and other European allies to send more than token forces further embittered Johnson and other U.S. officials. Johnson hinted that the United States might abandon such ungrateful friends. The president passed word to Europeans that "it has been costly that Europe has tended to 'disassociate' itself from the Viet Nam problem. . . . the concept of disassociation . . . can cut both ways."[17] Yet as European leaders realized, the threat of disassociation rang hollow. The Western alliance remained essential to America's global position. As Vice President Hubert Humphrey noted, "the dissolution of the alliance means the loss of our diplomatic cards in dealing with the Russians."[18]

The crosscurrents of resentment that beset transatlantic relations in the 1960s fueled the disputes between the United States and France. U.S. and French officials differed on both policies and on how to describe and interpret those policies. In May, 1964, a journalist close to de Gaulle reported that the French government felt itself engaged in a "cold war of ideas" with the United States. In the French view, an increasingly independent France would offer other nations a "guiding light" and alternative to U.S. domination.[19] While the French overestimated the glow of their intellectual "light," the Americans underestimated the credibility of French conceptions. They dismissed France's proposals as not worthy "ideas," "illusions" that were "totally false and dangerous."[20]

As the Cold War paradigm and the Atlantic axioms broke down in the mid-sixties, U.S. officials paid lip service to a diversity in ideas while trying to sustain U.S. leadership. Responding to what they termed the "doubts and ambiguities" of "apparent détente" and the "discordant" impact of French alternatives, State Department analysts sought the "psychological effect of a clear and unwavering American approach"—that is, a reaffirmation of the Atlantic axioms.[21]

In January, 1964, when de Gaulle called for the neutralization of Vietnam without being specific as to whether both Vietnams or just South Vietnam was to be neutralized, U.S. officials became upset for at least two reasons. First, de Gaulle's advocacy of neutralization dared challenge U.S. policy. In a hyperbolic reaction, Ambassador to South Vietnam Henry Cabot Lodge blamed de Gaulle for the low morale in South Vietnam. Lodge argued that "conditions are fundamentally much worse in North Viet-Nam than they are here [in South Vietnam]. Yet, due in large part to de Gaulle's public utterances this community is concentrated on itself and its own fears instead of taking the initiative against" the North.[22] Americans also found threatening the very indeterminacy of de Gaulle's neutralization proposal. Lyndon Johnson worried that de Gaulle was causing "great uncertainties" in South Vietnam at the time when the United States was trying to create psychological and political certainties in that nation. When Johnson complained to Ambassador to France "Chip" Bohlen about the "speculation and suspicion" and "confusion and mistrust" arising in South Vietnam from de Gaulle's proposal, Bohlen commiserated that French "ambiguity and vagueness" had a "very damaging effect."[23] U.S. officials also found disturbing the nature of de Gaulle's intervention: vague suggestions, based on "mystification and concealment," and yet with a "larger than lifesize effect."[24] Although Americans, in their forthright anticommunism, objected to the style of de Gaulle's intervention, that style had political purpose. While the Americans sought to impose the simplifying clarity needed to fight a war, the French aimed at the blurring of categories needed to begin negotiations. When de Gaulle did clarify his stance, however, White House officials found that "on Southeast Asia, there is no common ground."[25]

The absence of common ground became obvious in a late February, 1965, conversation between Johnson and French Foreign Minister Maurice Couve de Murville. When Couve argued that "the basic problem in South Vietnam . . . is a political one," Johnson replied that the Viet Cong had just "killed a number of our boys. The President was not going to send them a thank-you note for this." When Couve stressed that "the essential problem was: how to get out," Johnson emphasized that "he wasn't about to run out," and that "we intended to stay out there as long as necessary." While Johnson invoked the misjudgment of "Hitler and the Japanese," and George Ball declared that the "Chinese are aggressive and land hungry," Couve suggested that these analogies to the 1930s were misplaced. The French believed that the Chinese and Vietnamese preferred to negotiate and were preoccupied with internal problems, not external aggression. Further challenging the Cold War paradigm and the Atlantic axioms, Couve told Johnson that "the Russians had the same evaluation as the French, and that they constituted a moderating element."[26]

A few days later, when British Prime Minister Harold Wilson requested a meeting with Johnson to talk about ending the conflict in Vietnam, the president heatedly told Ball that "he had received the last Prime Minister he wanted to receive. He is not ready to talk for peace machinery or for conferences. He is decidedly not ready to be used as a floor mat by Wilson as he was used by the French Minister the other day."[27] Let us consider Johnson's language "as a floor mat": like Acheson, Rusk, and Lodge, Johnson felt outrage at the thought that Europeans might restrict U.S. freedom of action. The readiness of U.S. officials to exaggerate such possible restrictions pointed to a basic American assumption: that the Western alliance, despite its façade of democratic decisionmaking, was and should remain an instrument of U.S. foreign policy.

Differences with the French over Vietnam soured almost all of U.S.-French relations because, as Bohlen noted, Vietnam "runs like an endless thread through all French thinking on world affairs."[28] The differences with the French government also became acrimonious. Johnson resented de Gaulle's comment that "the United States was the greatest danger in the world today to the peace."[29] Meanwhile, much of the French public, responding to its historic sympathies for the Vietnamese and to the antiwar perspective of the French media and government, declared to poll takers that Johnson ran a close second to Mao (30 percent to 32 percent) as the worst danger to world peace.[30] Bohlen warned Couve that Americans who had lost a son or daughter were asking the simple question, "who was with us and who against?"[31]

Although aggravating to both sides, such jibes between the Americans and the French were not unusual. Since World War II, France, especially when led by Charles de Gaulle, had been the ally that had most often differed with the United States. More worrisome to U.S. leaders was the prospect that other allies—particularly Germany, the chief prize in both the U.S.-Soviet and the U.S.-French Cold Wars—would heed de Gaulle's subversive questioning of U.S. leadership. In 1963–68, as U.S.-French tensions increased due to the Vietnam War, France's blocking of British admission to the Common Market, France's exit from NATO's integrated military command, and differences over monetary and trade policy, the Federal Republic of Germany struggled to remain close to both Washington and Paris. Although the Germans valued ties with France, they believed that the link to the United States was vital to bolster their position against the Soviet Union. In 1965–66, while the stirrings of détente complicated U.S., German, and French relations with Moscow and with each other, the Christian Democratic government of Chancellor Ludwig Erhard—and most German citizens—tried to hold onto their faith in the wisdom and necessity of U.S. leadership.

De Gaulle, however, tried to destroy this faith by pointing to the spectacle of the Vietnam War. The day after the Viet Cong attack at Pleiku, de Gaulle lectured to a group of German political leaders: "Here are the United States, the Soviet Union, and Red China engaged in a major political confrontation, and Europe, which would be directly affected by an East Asian war, has no say in the matter."[32] While West Germans looked to the United States to safeguard them from a war, de Gaulle argued that American actions in Asia could spark a war in which Germany could suffer a Soviet invasion. Because de Gaulle's subversive argument violated the basic world view of most Germans, they initially found it difficult to accept.

Meeting with de Gaulle in June, 1965, Chancellor Erhard poignantly explained why Germans needed to support the U.S. war in Vietnam and, more importantly, why Germans needed to *believe* that American actions fit the righteous model of the Cold War. Erhard said that "the Americans are fighting there for reasons of treaties and solemn obligations. Should the Americans leave that area . . . there will be an inevitable reaction from the German people, because then the Germans would say to themselves, that just as the Americans were not able to hold South Vietnam, they would not be able to hold onto . . . Berlin if it were seriously threatened. Unavoidably, it came down to the question: Could one generally trust America? Erhard wanted the German people to have trust, and therefore he had to tell the Americans to stay in South Vietnam, because otherwise anxiety and doubt would erupt in Germany—with immediate effect on the internal political situation."[33] In other words, German belief in the Cold War paradigm and in the efficacy and morality of U.S. leadership had become dependent on belief in the U.S. commitment to the war in Vietnam. The urgency in Erhard's language suggested a portending crisis of belief: he spoke of an "inevitable reaction" by the German people; it came down "unavoidably" to the question of trust in America; there would be an "immediate effect" in Germany from a U.S. pullout.

In reply to Erhard's delineation of how the Vietnam War had become incorporated into the Germans' structure of meaning, de Gaulle tried to tear down that structure. The French leader recalled that in 1964 he had promoted the neutralization of Indochina as an alternative to a wider war. Now, however, the United States was plunging deeper into war. Speaking in June, 1965, de Gaulle accurately predicted that the war would end only when the United States withdrew, having concluded that "it had had enough, that the war was too expensive, that it was absurd, that there was too much domestic opposition, and perhaps also because of economic and monetary difficulties." In contrast to Erhard, de Gaulle said nothing about solemn obligations, treaties, the 1930s, or communism. Nor did the French leader believe that victory was a matter of American will, or even possible. He talked instead about the circumstances of an inevitable defeat by Asians who could not be coerced. In addition to undermining these major tenets of the Cold War paradigm, de Gaulle also aggravated German anxiety about U.S. leadership. When Erhard fretted about the repercussions in Germany of a withdrawal from South Vietnam, de Gaulle described a worse nightmare. He warned that when "the Americans did pull out of Vietnam, they might well also pull out of Europe. The Americans would leave Europe in the context of a deal with the Soviets to maintain the status quo in Europe"—that is, the status quo that kept Germany divided.[34] Since the Federal Republic had first formulated a foreign policy in 1949–50, Germany had tried to stay close to the powerful United States as a means toward bringing about eventual reunification. Now de Gaulle was arguing that America's war in Vietnam might lead to the abandonment of Germany and its cause.

The U.S. Congress's discussion of the Mansfield amendment to withdraw significant numbers of troops from Europe amplified de Gaulle's warning. In early 1966, the German foreign minister worried that American "emotional" reactions from the Vietnam War could badly affect Europe.[35] Doubts about Cold War criteria and about U.S. leadership spread. President Giuseppe Saragat of Italy was "very worried about the war in Viet Nam," the British ambassador in Rome reported. The United States had gone to war in large part to uphold the Cold War principle of resistance to communist aggression. Yet this principle meant little to the Italian president, whose "pre-occupation is not so much with the outcome" of the war. Saragat was apprehensive instead about the Americans, "who are becoming divided, confused and exasperated and he fears the consequences of this unhappy state of mind throughout the whole range of American policy."[36]

Couve further undercut faith in U.S. leadership and policy in a conversation following de Gaulle's June, 1966, trip to Moscow. When Schroder asked "whether North Vietnam or China was in the driver's seat of the war," Couve answered that "it was neither China nor North Vietnam but solely the United States." Couve argued that not only was America's anticommunist policy responsible for the continuation of the war but that that policy had lost its sense and its legitimacy. "One could well ask," Couve told the German, "what kind of policy did the United States pursue? what were its goals? Did it become involved without a precise goal; was U.S. policy just a theoretical notion of fighting communism that understood as communism all that did not fit with American views? This amounted to no policy at all!"[37] Although Schroder could reply that Couve's views no doubt reflected what the Frenchman had gathered in Moscow, he could not deny the persuasive force of the critique.

Although it is difficult to measure the exact vectors of influence, it is probable that the French critique fed the increasingly vocal sentiment in Europe, particularly among younger people, against America's war in Vietnam. The views of the French government were widely publicized in French media and were picked up by other European media outlets. One consequence of the 1963 Franco-German treaty was an influx of young Germans into France as part of an extensive exchange program for high school and university students.

Whether influenced by French media or by simply observing the Vietnam War for themselves, young Germans and other Europeans fixated on the war with fascinated horror. They had grown up with images of America as the paragon democracy, the model for new fads and factories, the liberator from the Nazis, the defender from the Red Army—the engine of Western liberal capitalism. Now they saw television screen images of well-built, heavily armed GIs destroying villages of helpless Asian peasants. Many Europeans questioned the made-in-America Western alliance and the very legitimacy of their postwar societies, which also bore the imprint of American hegemony. Beginning in 1966, U.S. embassies, consulates, libraries, and military bases in Europe reported a wave of antiwar and anti-U.S. demonstrations. In London, local police described as the "worst riot in memory" an attempt by demonstrators to "storm the U.S. Embassy."[38] In Heidelberg, the Amerika Haus became a fortress under siege.

Although U.S. officials had believed that the war in Vietnam would bolster American leadership in Europe, they found that the war undermined European faith in the wisdom, morality, and utility of that leadership. The combination of war in Asia and détente in Europe made the Cold War paradigm and the Atlantic axioms seem increasingly outmoded. Although the Vietnam War enabled some success by France in its "cold war of ideas" with the Americans, the war also stimulated a more radical critique of all Western societies, including that of France. In May, 1968, this radical critique combined with economic discontent to produce an explosion that destroyed much of de Gaulle's power. A related combination of antiwar feeling and monetary crisis undercut Johnson's power in March, 1968.[39] Noting the lessons of the Berlin wall and the Vietnam War, German leaders such as Willy Brandt charted a more independent course toward Ostpolitik and eventual reunification. But that goal was not achieved for another two decades, in large part because the Soviet Union put the brakes on evolution in Eastern Europe with the August, 1968, invasion of Czechoslovakia. Although Johnson administration officials were disappointed by this temporary setback to détente with Moscow, they also welcomed the Czech crisis as an opportunity to reassert U.S. leadership within the Western alliance.[40]

Chapter 8

The U.S.-Korean Alliance in the Vietnam War

The Years of Escalation, 1964–68

KIL J. YI

In the fall of 1965, for the first time in its history, South Korea intervened in a foreign war by dispatching its combat soldiers to South Vietnam.[1] The Korean government justified this momentous decision by reasoning that it could not "sit on its hands and see one of its friendly allies become prey to [a] Communist threat."[2] Thereafter, until its withdrawal from the war in 1973, more than 300,000 Korean soldiers experienced the war in Vietnam. In the peak years of its involvement, from 1966 to 1970, South Korea maintained a combat force in Vietnam of 50,000, which constituted nearly 10 percent of its entire armed forces. Five thousand, or 1.6 percent of those who served in the war lost their lives in that war. This casualty rate is as high as America's: 1.7 percent killed, or 58,000 out of 3,000,000 who were sent to South Vietnam. South Korea's casualty rate testifies to the fact that South Korea's role in the Vietnam War was as intense as America's. South Korea was certainly not a "token" ally whose main utility to the United States was in reinforcing the image that the free world was fully behind America's involvement in South Vietnam.

South Korea's intervention in the Vietnam War, materialized at the request of the Johnson administration over the initial reluctance of the South Vietnamese government, defied logical foreign policy and strategic calculations. It seemed so illogical that when the Johnson administration decided to solicit

Korean combat forces in the spring of 1965, Winthrop Brown, the U.S. ambassador to Seoul, filed a report that virtually questioned his superiors' ability to think logically. South Korea, Brown wrote, was a "divided" nation with a "weak" government that required "large scale external aid." The South Koreans lived under the "shadow of [the] two most powerful Communist countries." Korea's relations with Japan, its "nearest free world neighbor," were just being restored to normalcy with "difficulty." Furthermore, South Korea had trouble winning recognition as the "only legitimate government" of the Korean people.[3] South Korea, whose archenemy, North Korea, was perched just over a four-mile-wide demilitarized zone was justifiably preoccupied with immediate, existential problems. Brown concluded that Korea was not "psychologically prepared" to play a large role on the international stage.[4]

On top of these problems, South Korea's president, Chung Hee Park, had an entrenched political opposition. The leader of a military *coup d'état* that successfully toppled a civilian government only four years before, Park's legitimacy was still in question even though he had won an election supervised by his own junta. Brown feared that Park's political enemies, who were many, would "bewilder [the] general public and generate uneasiness and fear" about intervening in a "distant [and] undeclared war."[5] Rather than forcing Park into an adventure he was not equipped to undertake, Brown urged the administration to help him "build the public confidence which [Park] now lacks."[6]

Brown's assessment must be studied in order to fully understand America's seemingly illogical solicitation of South Korea's intervention in the Vietnam War. In the middle of the 1960s, South Korea remained one of the most burdensome postwar American clients. One student of South Korea's modern history noted that between 1945 to 1965, "in the space of just one generation," it had suffered "a nearly unparalleled series of political, social, military, and economic upheavals." They included "the first division of the country in 12 centuries, a major and extremely destructive war, 4 very different governments in the South," and the state of war between North and South Korea that still exists even today.[7]

The analysis of Korea's problems must start with the threat posed by North Korea. When World War II ended in 1945, the victors of the war against Japan, the United States and the Soviet Union, created their respective occupation zones, the former in the South, and the latter in the North. The *de facto* border was the thirty-eighth parallel. When the two occupiers failed to form a single Korean government, the North and South established separate governments, each calling the other illegitimate and in need of liberation. At the same time, the former became Moscow's "satellite" while the latter become Washington's "client." In the summer of 1950, North Korea attempted to unify Korea by invading the South. By early winter, China and the United States were fighting in the Korean peninsula. In 1953, the war came to an inconclusive end with the two sides agreeing to a demarcation not too different from the one that existed *ante bellum*. The parties to the war—South Korea and the UN forces led by the United States on one side, and North Korea and China on the other—failed to sign a peace treaty, which meant that the parties to the conflict agreed simply to halt military actions. The continuing state of war forced the South Korean government to maintain a force of 600,000, and the United States to maintain nearly 50,000 American soldiers in South Korea to deter another North Korean push toward the South. This military burden deprived South Korea of necessary resources for social and economic development. Consequently, South Korea became "heavily dependent on American aid."[8]

In the early 1960s, U.S. officials began to voice concerns about South Korea's "grossly inadequate progress toward self-sufficiency or self-sustained growth," which contributed to "poverty, unemployment, . . . discontent, unrest and all-pervading corruption."[9] In other words, the nearly $4 billion in aid America provided between 1945 and 1965 had only minimal effect on Korea's development. Nevertheless, largely because of Korea's strategic importance, the United States continued to extend assistance. By 1965, the United States allotted 9 percent of its total foreign economic aid (and 14 percent of its military aid) for South Korea. Even with the help of such magnitude, U.S. officials lamented that South Korea remained an "unstable U.S. stepchild."[10] This poor, backward, threatened, and uncertain child-like nation, however, was recruited into the position of the third-largest combatant on the free world side in the Vietnam War after South Vietnam and the United States. What were the motivating forces behind the U.S.-Korean alliance in the Vietnam War? What resources were used to maintain the alliance? What caused it to deescalate? These questions will be addressed here.

South Korea became America's largest third-country ally in the Vietnam War because of the Johnson administration's inability to mobilize America's allies in Southeast Asia who had more immediate interests in keeping South Vietnam communist-free. The United States had also pledged to uphold Saigon's independence. In the spring of 1964, as Viet Cong campaigns intensified in South Vietnam, the Johnson administration turned to its allies in the Southeast Asia Treaty Organization (SEATO) for help. Johnson reasoned legitimately that SEATO's pledge to assist South Vietnam from an external threat warranted the member nations' military contributions. This "more flags" campaign turned out to be a failure. According to the State Department's report, America's SEATO allies, as well as its traditional friends were "reluctant to provide military assistance, and where it has been given[,] it has been of a largely token character." They did not show the "evidence of enthusiasm for a more direct involvement." Johnson was dismayed to the point that he cabled his ambassadors in the capitals of America's major allies that he was "gravely disappointed by the inadequacy of the actions by our friends and allies. . . ."[11] The failure of the more flags campaign targeted at America's treaty partners forced Johnson to move out of the SEATO framework in his efforts to internationalize the war and seek an untested, but willing partner, South Korea.

The government of Chung Hee Park in Korea turned the Johnson administration's desperation into an opportunity for Korea.[12] Park took Johnson's risk-filled invitation to intervene in the Vietnam War to reverse what he perceived as America's planned disengagement from South Korea in light of its increasing responsibilities in Southeast Asia. Park found concrete signs of America's weariness in two policies that Washington proposed as "appropriate action" to make South Korea more productive and less dependent: downsizing of Korea's conventional military forces and accepting Japan as South Korea's economic patron.

Since the end of the Korean War, the United States had supported Korea's conventional military buildup to deter another North Korean attack. As Johnson's policy planners outlined, "For years we [the United States] have maintained [an] almost 600,000 man ROK army, plus two U.S. divisions against the threat of a resumed Chicom [Chinese Communist]/North Korean attack." According to America's strategic calculations, this force size was "far larger than needed to meet the North Koreans alone." What about the threat of a North Korean invasion supported by the Chinese forces? "We do not regard [the] threat of overt Chicom aggression as high," wrote Johnson's advisers. South Korea was no longer "a high priority target as to tie up a large proportion of U.S. assets."[13] The Johnson administration insisted on a 25-percent reduction of Korea's existing armed forces.[14]

In conjunction, Washington now endeavored to transform Korean soldiers into nation builders. The United States wanted them to acquire "skills and vocations" that could contribute to "internal security, civil works and economic growth."[15] In essence, the United States hoped to ship bulldozers, rather than howitzers, and train the soldiers to build roads and bridges rather than to demolish them. Park, a former army general, found this shifting emphasis incompatible with his ambition to build military forces that could neutralize North Korea's threat to "liberate" the South. The United States hoped to assuage Park by rationalizing that America had enough man- and firepower in and around the Korean peninsula to compensate for a downsizing of Korea's conventional military capabilities, and to deter possible North Korean attacks. Dismissing Park's protest, U.S. officials came to a conclusion at the end of 1963 that "now is the time to move."[16]

Another sign of America's desire to reduce its commitment to defend and support South Korea was Washington's insistence on the normalization of relations between Japan and Korea. The central rationale of American postwar policy in Asia has been that Japan should serve as the economic locomotive of Asia's Third World economies. Edwin O. Reischauer, the most illustrious postwar U.S. ambassador to Japan, noted that America's Asian policy "must start with" Japan: "What it is, the role it chooses to play in Asia . . . will . . . influence the nature of [America's] relationship with the rest of Asia."[17] To America's foreign policy planners, Japan, with the strongest economy in Asia, qualified as the natural patron to its less-developed neighbors. South Korea, geographically and culturally closest to Japan, was in the best position to benefit from Japan's economic prowess by trading with its former colonial master and attracting investments. More close economic ties first required normalizing the relations between the two countries. Therefore, despite their bloody history, Johnson's aides insisted that Korea and Japan were "natural allies."[18] William Bundy, assistant secretary of state for the Far East, optimistically noted that Japan's economic patronage would "afford real hope for progress in the Korean economic and social system."[19] Others in the Johnson administration envisioned that friendly relations with Japan would "most certainly open the door to the economic progress and industrial development of South Korea," and encourage "reparations" in the form of "private and governmental loans." Even the notoriously staid Rusk confided that "so great" was the advantage of cooperation between Japan and Korea that "one can taste it."[20] The Johnson administration that considered Japan's patronage over South Korea as its only realistic chance to build a viable economy elevated the rapprochement as a "top priority" foreign policy goal.[21] Chester Cooper, Johnson's special assistant in Far Eastern Affairs, summed up his boss's feeling toward America's patronage over Korea: the United States "should not get stuck with" it "forever."[22] To Park, however, Japan's patronage over Korea meant the withdrawal of U.S. commitment over Korea.

In the spring of 1965, as the United States crossed the Rubicon in the Vietnam War by dispatching large contingents of combat forces, the Johnson administration scored a diplomatic victory that the postwar U.S. presidents had previously sought unsuccessfully. South Korea and Japan finally established formal diplomatic ties after Japan agreed to extend $800 million in developmental aid and loans. Johnson's elated aides noted that South Korea had finally found its "place in the world economy."[23] South Koreans, including Park, however, were gripped with the feeling that the United States was "abandoning Korea to Japanese control," and that Korea would, again, be forced to play a subservient role to Japan.[24]

Diminishing American aid and Washington's wish to promote Japan as South Korea's economic patron deepened Korea's insecurity. At this juncture, the Johnson administration, sliding toward the quagmire in South Vietnam, sought Korea's intervention. America's desperate call for Korea to accompany its soldiers into the jungles of South Vietnam offered an opportunity for the Park government to force the United States to maintain its commitments to Korea. In mid-May, 1965, upon Johnson's invitation, Chung Hee Park visited the White House. The agenda of the meeting was rather predictable.

A flurry of actions that took place led the Johnson administration's taking over the war, making South Korean participation imperative. To start with, Johnson signed National Security Action Memorandum 328, authorizing the U.S. forces in South Vietnam to undertake combat roles. Next, his advisers pushed for increasing American troop strength to 200,000. At the same time, they concluded that SEATO allies would not offer any meaningful assistance and that Korean combat forces must be invited for "reasons of domestic reaction."[25]

When the two presidents met in the White House, Johnson did not conceal his eagerness to discuss their "mutual effort in Vietnam." During their conversation Johnson repeated three times his hope that Korea would "raise the [force] commitment [to South Vietnam] to one division" or 20,000. Park took this as his cue to lash out at what he perceived as America's retreat from the Korean peninsula. He told Johnson that the dispatch of a combat division could "invite further activity from North Korea." He then charged that, while the United States sought Korea's sacrifice in South Vietnam, it schemed to reduce America's commitment to South Korea. "This sort of talk," warned Park, "disturbed" his people, and "made it very difficult [for him] . . . to help in Vietnam." Johnson apologetically assured Park that he would "see to it that . . . troops and money enough will be provided to ensure" Korea's security. Also, as an economic inducement, he promised to lobby Congress to approve a $150 million economic aid package to Korea his administration had proposed.

In August, 1965, three months after Johnson and Park met in Washington, Korea's National Assembly authorized Park to send 20,000 combat soldiers to South Vietnam. As *quid pro quos,* the United States assured the Park government that, first, it had "no present plans" to reduce American forces in Korea, and even if such plans were to be devised later, Washington would not implement them "without prior consultation" with Seoul. Second, the United States guaranteed military aid at a level "necessary to preserve the Korean forces' effectiveness." More specifically, the United States promised to modernize the "firepower, communications and mobility" of Korean forces by providing "tanks, artillery, communication equipment, vehicles, and an improved anti-infiltration system." What did these military *quid pro quos* symbolize? They forced Washington to retreat from the doctrine built around conventional force reduction and the reorientation of a client army into nation builders, at least in South Korea.

The United States also had to compensate individual Korean soldiers sent to South Vietnam. Initially, the United States resisted strenuously rewarding soldiers with cash, for it wanted allies, not hired guns from Korea. Thus, the Johnson administration insisted that "payment of per diem and allowances . . . should be supported" by the Korean government as a "demonstration of [its] willingness" to defend South Vietnam's "independence."[26]

This guideline became irrelevant, however, as South Korea resisted sending anything more than the soldiers, and insisted that the United States remunerate individual soldiers. As the U.S. ambassador to Seoul, Winthrop Brown, advised his superiors in Washington, there was "no point [of] making [financial and material] demands" on Park, which he would "certainly reject," and from which Washington would have to "retreat."[27] Eventually, Washington abandoned all hopes of convincing South Korea to finance its military involvement in South Vietnam. Thus the United States agreed to provide "equipment, logistical support, construction, training, transportation, subsistence, [and] overseas allowances."[28] The two governments agreed on the per diem combat allowance schedule in table 8.1.[29]

Critics of the U.S.-Korean alliance in the Vietnam War have fingered monetary compensations to individual soldiers as the most concrete evidence that the two countries were engaged in mercenary import-export, and that the Koreans were essentially "America's rented troops."[30] White House officials, however, cavalierly dismissed such criticism. In a memorandum to Johnson, his aides wrote, "There are lots of Americans who don't give a damn how much it costs to support foreign soldiers so long as it enables an American boy to stay home." Also, they argued, the Americans had "enough sense" to understand that their allies, some of which had a "$133 annual income per person," could not afford to pay for the military intervention in South Vietnam.[31]

Ironically, war creates markets while it destroys the society. This irony was especially apparent in the Vietnam War because of the exorbitantly large quantity of goods and services that were imported by the United States for its forces in South Vietnam and South Vietnamese. For South Vietnam's consumptive needs, the United States paid for $100 million in goods and services. South Korea, as America's largest third-country ally, sought a share of this market as well as opportunities to supply American procurement needs to earn hard currency. As Ambassador Brown observed, "Material aspects . . . loomed large in Korean calculations, both official and private." He noted that Koreans expected a "substantial benefit from the sale of goods" and "maintenance and repair

Table 8.1. Pay Scale for South Korean Soldiers (per diem)

Rank	Allowance	Rank	Allowance
Colonel	$6.50	Master Sergeant	$2.50
Lieutenant colonel	$6.00	Sergeant 1st class	$2.00
Major	$5.00	Sergeant	$1.50
Captain	$5.00	Corporal	$1.20
1st lieutenant	$4.00	Private 1st class	$1.00
2nd lieutenant	$4.00	Private	$1.00

services."[32] South Korea also desired to sell to the U.S. military, or secure the rights to stock "DOD [Department of Defense] furnished supplies," in Washington's official jargon.[33] William Porter, who succeeded Brown, more succinctly captured the Korean government's desire: it wanted to "participate in the opportunities as well as the risks."[34]

The Park government had a well-formulated rationale for taking material advantage of its participation in the Vietnam War: "if Korea is to help abroad it needs to be strengthened internally."[35] As expected, South Korea launched an all-out effort to extract economic concessions. For example, in January, 1965, the director of Korea's Central Intelligence Agency, Hyung Wook Kim, confided to Chester Cooper, Johnson's special assistant for Far Eastern affairs, that South Korea "was willing to do almost anything that President Johnson requested." In return, Kim demanded that the United States "arrange to have some of the materials (e.g., cement) needed in Vietnam purchased in Korea."[36] In March, 1965, Park's chief of staff, Hu-Rak Yi, submitted a list of economic inducements that Korea expected from the United States including procurement of "goods and services (repair and maintenance) in Korea for Vietnam."[37]

South Korea had paramount needs for export markets. A typical Third World country that had long suffered colonial exploitation, Korea struggled with entrenched, structural economic problems. As one commentator noted rather depressingly, the Korean economy stood out for "a critical lack of capital, technical weakness, and an over-qualified surplus labor force."[38] Joel Bernstein, who served as director of the Agency for International Development (AID) mission in Seoul beginning in 1964, elaborated on Korea's economic problems in another way. First, South Koreans consumed more than they produced, and were thus unable to accumulate capital for investment. The government used American economic aid to support the nation's consumption needs, instead of investing it in long-term economic development. Second, South Korea under-utilized its "human skills and learning and performance capabilities."

Essentially, a large number of Koreans were educated and trained to be, in essence, unemployed or under-employed. Korea, in other words, wasted human and national resources. Lack of opportunities for an educated and trained population, particularly for the younger generation, fostered social discontent. Third, political and social instability and the threat from North Korea scared off foreign investors. The government usually attempted to solve these problems by printing more legal tender, thus precipitating inflation.[39]

Beginning in 1964, AID forced the Park government to accept "radical reforms," including harsh government-spending cuts and tight control over the money supply. These steps initially made the lives of the majority of South Koreans more difficult. David Cole, a senior economic adviser to the AID mission in South Korea in the early 1960s, testified in Congress that the United States imposed on Korea "an extreme set of stabilization measures that did slow the inflation in a hurry, but at [a] considerable" social cost.[40]

In medicine, as well as in economics, a harsh remedy is applied in anticipation of a quick recovery. According to this strategy, once public spending and inflation went down and capital accumulated, the government should invest national wealth in developing the export sector. Then, theoretically, a gradual increase in national income and opportunities generated by exports would relieve the initial hardship caused by the government's retrenchment measures. Economic planners expected the export sector, which would bring in foreign exchange, to fuel economic development, create jobs, and raise the overall standard of living. Naturally, as prescribed by AID, the export industry was promoted as the "leading sector" of, if not the panacea for, the Korean economy. If South Korea failed to export, the economy would falter and the country would have to go on relying on foreign aid. Under these circumstances, Park did not exaggerate when he exhorted the nation in a Patrick Henry–like manner, saying that it was either export or death for Korea.[41]

South Korea's foreign policy embodied this desperation. In January, 1965, Minister of Foreign Affairs Dong Won Lee enunciated what he called an "economic foreign policy" whereby Korea's diplomatic representatives would be mobilized to earn hard currencies for the national treasury. Lee suggested assigning export quotas to Korea's diplomatic missions overseas.[42] At this crucial moment for the export market and hard currency, the Americanization of the Vietnam War created an unprecedented economic boom in the Asia-Pacific region. South Korea, which had 20,000 of its soldiers fighting in the war claimed the right to tap into a $100 million-a-year market for imported goods and services in South Vietnam. It also hoped to furnish some selected goods and services needed by the U.S. forces and AID operation in Vietnam.

U.S. officials were by and large sympathetic to South Korea's desire for economic rewards. For example, Henry Cabot Lodge, whom Johnson sent to Korea in April, 1965, to solicit Korea's military contributions, reported to Washington after meeting with Park, "I recommend rewarding such a staunch ally as [South] Korea by enabling it to gain economic benefits deriving from the Vietnam Situation." He recommended giving "contracts for airfield construction, etc. . . . [to] unemployed Korean ex-servicemen who . . . could take care of themselves militarily."[43] Ambassador Brown in Seoul provided the rationale for keeping Park and his soldiers happy: the "well trained" South Korean soldiers could render "a real contribution to the struggle" and "save" Americans "a great deal in blood and treasure."[44] After all, as Jack Valenti, special assistant to Johnson, argued, "The total cost to [the United States] for equipping and paying for" Korean soldiers was "peanuts compared to what it would be for a comparable number of Americans."[45]

South Korea's trade opportunities in South Vietnam strengthened overall U.S.-Korean relations. As Brown observed, the receipts from exports to South Vietnam promised a "stimulation of [Korea's] local industry" and served as the "maximum political ammunition" to Park who emerged as the most pro-American Korean leader. Also, the Johnson administration could not remain oblivious to South Korea's increasing bitterness that the United States "expects flesh and blood from Korea while concentrating its purchases of war materials in Japan to the advantage of that economy."[46]

In essence, Brown proposed a way to feed four birds with a single crust. The U.S. purchase of goods and services from Korea could silence the political opposition to Park's Vietnam policy; stimulate South Korea's economy; reduce its dependence on American aid; and lessen the popular resentment toward the United States for asking the Koreans to fight in South Vietnam while inviting Japan to trade there.[47] Ultimately, the United States expected these economic rewards to strengthen Korea so it could increase its role in the war. Dean Rusk, the secretary of state, once anguished that if South Vietnam were a "kind of society that is indestructible" within, the war could be won.[48] To Johnson administration officials, economic inducements to Korea were not rewards for mercenaries. Rather, they were resources to make South Korea "indestructible" within, so that it could serve as a partner in containment. McGeorge Bundy had a similar, but more geopolitically oriented rationale for giving material rewards to Korea. He argued that the Korean-American alliance in the war had made South Korea a show case to the world: "Korea's success or failure is a major test of the non-Communist approach to nation-building." He declared, "If Korea should fail to develop into an economically and politically viable nation," then the world would consider it a "U.S. failure as well as a Korean failure."[49]

Table 8.2. Korean Civilian Laborers in South Vietnam

Type of Work	Number of Workers
Machinist	2,775
Electrician	1,461
Heavy Machinery Operator	1,423
Driver	1,344
Common Laborer	1,217
Communication	914
Carpentry	899
Office Work (white collar)	688
Security Guard	349
Architect	335
Cook and Domestic Service	309
Other Services	1,101

These rationales prepared Seoul and Washington psychologically to exchange combat forces for economic resources without feeling that the former was providing soldiers of fortune in exchange for hard currencies. For South Korea's first combat division for South Vietnam, the United States pledged to purchase "construction materials, raw blanket material, POL [petroleum, oil, lubricant]" from South Korea. Also, the United States agreed to procure Korean-made military provisions for the Korean forces in South Vietnam.[50] In 1966, when Korea doubled its force size from one to two divisions, the United States agreed to procure "supplies, services and equipment" for Korean forces in Vietnam and to "direct to Korea selected types of procurement" for the American and Vietnamese forces. In addition, Washington promised to purchase "a substantial amount of goods" needed by the AID for "rural construction, pacification, relief, logistics, and so forth." In terms of services, the United States pledged to give Korean companies "expanded opportunities to participate in various construction projects." Also, it guaranteed the "employment of skilled Korean civilians" in South Vietnam.[51]

The massive and rapid American military buildup in South Vietnam created labor demands that the South Vietnamese could not fill. South Korea provided the largest pool of foreign civilian workers to American and Korean companies contracted by the U.S. government. According to official Korean tabulation, in 1965, before Korea's first division arrived in South Vietnam, only 93 South Korean civilians were employed by American and Korean contractors. In 1966, when the Korean commitment increased to 50,000, 10,204 Koreans gained employment in South Vietnam. In 1967, an additional 5,574 workers arrived in South Vietnam. By mid-1968, a total of 17,758 Koreans found employment in South Vietnam. This number increased to 25,120 in 1970. As of May, 1968, Korean civilian laborers who left for South Vietnam found jobs in the professions listed in table 8.2.[52]

The material *quid pro quos* the United States provided to South Korea produced the desired economic, social, and political effects. Table 8.3 illustrates the magnitude of South Korea's earning from South Vietnam from 1965 to 1968.[53]

South Korea also won U.S. developmental loans as a reward. In responding to Johnson's request for combat forces, Korea demanded that the United States underwrite Korea's long-term economic development. Johnson's top advisers—notably, Robert McNamara, Dean Rusk, Treasury Secretary Henry Fowler, McGeorge Bundy, and Charles L. Schultze, the director of the Bureau of the Budget—supported providing Korea with developmental capital. They agreed that the loans would keep Park "happy" and "make it easier" for him to send troops at "a reasonable price." A refusal, they warned Johnson, would inflict "political damage" on Park and make him "less willing [and] . . . able to play ball" in South Vietnam.[54] They felt that a mix of "sweetener"[55] and "maximum pressure" would beget Korean troops.[56]

Johnson's advisers understood how American loans were critical to Park's development strategy. Rostow, for example, argued that the loans were necessary for Korea's "orderly development," a euphemism for preventing socialist challenges.[57] David Bell, the administrator of AID, went one step further to

Table 8.3. South Korea's Earnings from South Vietnam, 1965–68

	1965	1966	1967	1968
U.S. Forces in Vietnam	184,000	385,000	485,000	536,000
Korean Forces in Vietnam	20,000	46,000	48,000	50,000
Korean Civilian Workers in Vietnam	100	10,200	16,000	20,000
Korean Export to Vietnam	$18.4	$23.9	$22.0	$37.9
Goods and Services Sold to U.S. Military		$8.3	$35.5	$46.1
Construction		$4.5	$8.7	$10.7
Remittance from Korean Laborers Hired by U.S. Companies in Vietnam		$9.7	$39.3	$42.3
Total Civilian Earning	$18.4	$46.4	$105.5	$137
Remittance by Korean Soldiers		$15.2	$37.8	$41.9
Korea's Total Vietnam Earning	$18.4	$61.6	$143.3	$178.9
Korea's Gold and Foreign Exchange Reserve	$146	$245	$356	$391
Total Earnings from Vietnam in Relations to its Gold and Foreign Exchange Reserve	12.6%	25.1%	40.2%	45.7%

Note: All monetary figures are in millions.

note that they were essential to Korea's "economic growth and military security. . . ."[58] Charles Schultze added that the extension of American capital was a "solid investment in Korea's future."[59] William Gaud, who replaced Bell as AID administrator, thus concluded that infusion of capital was "a wise investment" on the part of the United States.[60] Perhaps McGeorge Bundy had best summarized the role of U.S. financial capital in the Korean economy. He projected that American capital would help South Korea "Wipe out trade deficit; eliminate inflation; achieve a continuous, self-sustained GNP [Gross National Product] growth."[61] In 1966 when South Korea increased its forces in South Vietnam to 50,000, Washington provided Seoul with $10 million in program loans and $70 million in project loans. For fiscal year 1967, Korea received $15 million in program and $57 in project loans.[62]

The United States also indirectly funneled its capital to South Korea via the Asian Development Bank (ADB) to which the Johnson administration contributed $200 million at its founding in December, 1965, as a regional cooperative financial institution designed to foster economic growth in Asia. For the first time in history, Asia's developing nations, under the leadership of the United States and Japan—the two largest contributors—established a bank primarily to finance the member nations' developmental projects.[63]

The Johnson administration touted the ADB as "the first step in creating regionalism and cooperation" in the areas of the world where national rivalry had been a dominant force.[64] Johnson himself believed that the American contribution to the bank was his "larger constructive effort in Asia."[65] Contrary to its founding spirit, however, the ADB ended up rewarding American allies that supported Johnson's military policy in Asia. According to Richard de Camp, "More than half of all ADB loans have gone to six member states with large U.S. bases and direct involvement in the Indochina War—South Korea, Taiwan, the Philippines, Thailand, Laos, and South Vietnam." South Korea became one of the largest recipients of ADB loans with $111 million borrowed in total by the end of the 1960s.[66]

The United States also rewarded South Korea with agricultural surpluses. Known as Public Law 480 or Food for Peace, this assistance program allowed South Korea to import agricultural crops with U.S. government loans that Korea paid back in Korean currency. The South Korean *won* (monetary unit) paid to the United States was in turn infused back into the Korean treasury as America's military aid. In other words, America used its agricultural surplus to support Korean military forces.

In the middle of the 1960s, under this program South Korea imported tens of millions of dollars worth of rice, wheat, and cotton from the United States. Secretary of Agriculture John A. Schnittker and William Gaud both supported this program by informing Johnson that "with Korean troop participation in Vietnam," indirect military aid such as P.L. 480 "has become increasingly important to [the] U.S. strategic interest in Asia."[67] In 1966, $53 million worth of agricultural crops were provided to South Korea. In 1967, $47 million was given as indirect military aid through this program.[68]

The exchange relationship between Washington and Seoul—the former providing military and economic rewards for the latter's combat forces—put into motion a Hegelian, dialectical process. Material rewards Korea derived from the alliance energized Korea's productive forces to a point where Korea now required fundamentally different American intervention. At the same time, the heightened importance of South Korea's military commitment forced a realignment in the hierarchical relationship between the United States and Korea. Already in mid-1966, in government and private circles, South Korea's emerging economy was keenly noted. For example, the CIA in its assessment of South Korea reported that "a wide range of export products is being produced. Korean woolen and cotton textiles and automobile tires hold their own in quality with any in the world. Korean construction firms have received contracts for work abroad, and Korean laborers and technicians are being recruited for work in Europe, South America, Canada and Vietnam."[69]

A White House memo noted, "Political instability, economic doldrums, and isolation from its neighbors have given way to [a] robust and relatively stable democracy [and] economic take-off." It concluded, "Korea [is] no longer a fragile and isolated U.S. ward."[70]

Korea's success in economic development was also noted by the international business community. *Business Week* commented, "While war raged in Vietnam," South Korea was "churning with . . . drive to industrialize." It observed that in Seoul, the capital, the "gleaming new buildings" and the chimneys of "modern factories" loomed over "thatched-roof villages." Also, "Hundreds of tiny, primitive manufacturing shops in the cities [we]re humming as never before, with workers turning out garments, textiles, and light manufactures."[71]

Be it airborne, or economic, a "take off" requires a sustained, full throttle. South Korea's expanding economy could not be sustained by the traditional U.S. economic aid aimed at alleviating hunger or keeping the Korean economy afloat. In the second half of the 1960s, Korea's needs for U.S. capital grew to the point where Korea presented an economic development plan devised on the assumption that it would receive $100 million in U.S. aid every year. Such a bold move stemmed from a sense of the "special relationship" Korea felt it had established with the United States by joining the war in Vietnam.

In November, 1966, Korea's minister of finance, Hak-Yul Kim, forwarded to the United States Korea's second five-year economic development plan to start in 1967. The "Summary Proposal for Economic Development of Korea" revealed Korea's economic ambitions, and its increased expectation of U.S. assistance. The list included: (1) "Financial and Technical Assistance for the National Land Development Plan"; (2) "Active U.S. Assistance for the Investment of Social Overhead Capital," namely, transportation, harbor, and highway development; (3) "U.S. Assistance on Korea-Vietnam Economic Cooperation," which meant "more opportunity for Korean firms to bid on U.S. military contracts"; (4) "Increased U.S. Government Promotion of Private Investment in Korea," including "Expansion of various risk guarantees given by the U.S. Government to [American] firms planning to invest in Korea"; (5) lifting of "Import Restrictions on Textile, Manufactured & Agricultural Goods"; and (6) exemption of "Double Taxation of U.S. Investors in Korea."[72] Also, South Korea desired U.S. assistance for projects not included in the second five-year plan, namely the construction of "a 300-megawatt nuclear power station," and more AID loans for the petrochemical industry.[73] To Korea, its alliance with the United States in the Vietnam War had become a lode of wealth and opportunities to which it had rightful claims.

By early 1966, less than six months after the arrival of Korea's first combat division, the United States requested one more division, reflecting America's growing reliance on Korean military contributions. Not only was the Korean contribution militarily valuable, but politically more so because of the pace of American escalation. Without South Korea, the Johnson administration's contention that allies were shedding blood to help the American cause in South Vietnam would seem vacuous.[74] Now, the two allies could no longer fight the war within the framework of the patron-client relations that had governed their relationship since the end of World War II. South Koreans could no longer be content with being under American control. South Korea thus demanded *quid pro quos* that would place it on a more even level with the United States. First, South Korea demanded the right to share decisionmaking with the United States in the Vietnam War and the overall containment policy in Asia. Second, it demanded America's stronger commitment to South Korea's security, for Korea had become a combat-sharing partner of the United States.

South Korea framed the U.S.-Korean alliance in the Vietnam War as a crusade against the communist world in general whose success would lessen the chance of communist challenges beyond Southeast Asia. That is why Park said to the first group of combat soldiers embarking for South Vietnam that their sacrifices would "solidify" Korea's own national security and "contribute toward strengthening the anticommunist front of the free world."[75] American officials understood that sentiment from the very beginning. This is how the State Department interpreted the reason why a weak and threatened nation such as South Korea would want to intervene in a foreign war: "It is evident that the leaders of South Korean government are anxious to assist South Vietnam, in part because they believe that a free world victory in Southeast Asia will prompt a favorable settlement of the Korean problems."[76] As matter of fact, U.S. officials used this logic initially to convince Park to commit forces to the Vietnam War.

Park found it logical that the allies should demonstrate to the enemy side — and especially to Beijing and Moscow, which Park accused of being the source of all his country's troubles — that the free world would collectively resist communist expansionism wherever it took place in Asia. In Park's mind, his troops were not in South Vietnam "just to defend" it, or "just to please Americans." They were there because South Vietnam was "part of [a] bigger problem."[77] A big problem — communist hegemony — of course, required big solutions like a "ringing declaration . . . in the form of [a] Pacific Charter" against the entire communist world.[78] The Pacific Charter, in Park's mind, should emulate the more famous Atlantic Charter of August, 1941, with which, according to one observer, the United States formally accepted "full responsibility for the defeat of Hitler and the establishment of a democratic peace."[79] The proposed Pacific Charter must state, Korea insisted, that the United States and its allies pledge to retaliate collectively against communist aggression in the Asia-Pacific region. Second, the charter must be "a very strong call" for settling the current conflict in Vietnam on an "honorable basis," which meant a peace produced by the near, if not complete, defeat of the enemy.[80]

Park also wanted mechanisms to implement the "Pacific Charter." He proposed three different consultative bodies among the allies: "a standing committee at the ambassadorial level located in Washington to provide continuous consultation on Vietnamese War matters," and "periodic conferences" among foreign ministers to discuss "major policy and strategy matters." Park also proposed a "unified command . . . along the NATO-style" of allied nations fighting in Vietnam. Park wanted his generals to occupy "key positions" in an integrated command headquarters.[81] These measures, Park insisted, would deflect the perception that the Vietnam War was "an American war," and, instead, promote it as the free world's crusade to "bring peace and [a] better tomorrow."[82]

Park's demands showed his one-dimensional reading of the historical meaning and the effects of the Atlantic Charter. In his mind, it served three intentions: first, its symbolized American security guarantee over the English Isles; second, it turned Great Britain and the United States into allies of equal standing in the war against the Axis. Third, it necessitated America's sharing of military resources with Great Britain. This interpretation led Park to insist that the

United States must follow up on the declaration of the Pacific Charter by rendering a more pervasive and immediate U.S. security guarantee to South Korea, and recognition of Korea as America's equal partner with a formal consultative body to govern their relationship. Korea's intervention in South Vietnam, reasoned Park, had turned South Korea into the communist world's most hated enemy in Asia, next to the United States. Therefore, for the risk Korea was undertaking, and its status as America's combat-sharing partner in containment, it deserved better protection from the United States. Park also strove to elevate South Korea's position within its alliance with the United States in the Vietnam War by exercising influence over the long-term direction of the war. He wanted Korea to be treated as the third-largest ally, rather than as one of the third-country contributors to the American war effort.

Park most feared Johnson's acceptance of a peace settlement that meant the defeat of the free world in Vietnam. Just as he believed that America's agreeing to the armistice in 1953 to end the Korean War signified the defeat of the free world and had led to a permanent state of tension in the Korean peninsula, he was convinced that any settlement that would leave Vietnam divided would be viewed and exploited as another victory of the communist world; needless to say, the danger of "another Vietnam" would continuously haunt the free world, argued Park. He therefore insisted on his place at the peace table so that he could exercise veto power against any "dishonorable" peace. He sought an assurance from Johnson that the United States and South Korea would continue the war "until the aggressors and the subversive elements realize that all their attempts are futile," and "an honorable peace is achieved." To Park, the unconditional surrender of the communist forces should be the only war aim of the allies and their condition for peace.[83] The Park government surprised the Johnson administration even more with a demand that Korea and all other allies be made "the principal parties to the negotiation for a peaceful settlement." If a peace settlement was achieved without the "full participation of" the allies, insisted Korea, it should not be recognized.[84] To Park, the Vietnam War would demonstrate to the communist world how much the United States and its allies were willing to invest into resisting communist adventurism. The Vietnam War was a war to avoid future wars.

Park's agenda startled the Johnson administration. Rusk, for example, contemptuously dismissed the Korean proposal for a consultative body among the allies: "We shudder to think of [Korean Ambassador to the United States] Henry Kim as Korea's representative on a [consultative] group here [in Washington], not to mention the Korean Embassy's total lack of security."[85] The United States refused to give Park a role in the future peace process. Worse yet, Johnson heightened Park's anxiety by appearing to be receptive to various international peace proposals forwarded by what Park dismissed as "non-participants." They included proposals from the Vatican, UN Secretary-General U Thant, and the Canadian government. These proposals all called for unconditional cessation of hostility and withdrawal of forces by both sides. These two steps were inimical to Park who insisted that the communist side first stop its military action, and that Hanoi withdraw all of its combatants including the NLF guerrillas, which to him constituted foreign invading forces. The ultimate blow to Park came when Johnson sent a personal message to Ho Chi Minh suggesting unconditional peace talks. For Park, this action was as unthinkable as his writing to Kim Il-Sung of North Korea, whom he blamed for the Korean War, to talk unconditionally on unification. Also, as the White House noted, Park grew even more "apprehensive over reports of secret contacts" between the United States and the Communist side.[86]

In wars, appearing tough is sometimes more important than being tough, argued Park. He warned that the communist forces would take Johnson's peace proposals and gestures as a sign of weakness. The perceived weariness on the part of the United States would produce detrimental military repercussions in Vietnam and elsewhere, notably in the Korean peninsula. Therefore, Park insisted, Korea must be represented at "all stages of peace negotiations."[87]

Park had sympathetic ears in the Johnson administration. Rostow, the national security adviser, for instance, told Johnson that Korea's "sensitivity" toward a premature peace agreement had to be considered. Known as a leading hawk among Johnson's advisers, Rostow added that "personally," he felt that Park "deserve[d] to be listened to more than some of our more assertive advisers in London, New York, Paris, etc."[88] Rostow was sarcastically referring to pressure for peace coming from America's European allies and the United Nations. Also, as Ambassador Brown in Seoul noted, Park had committed more than two divisions to the war; therefore, it was "impossible" for the Koreans to contemplate any future peace negotiations without Park's participation. At least, it was "essential" to give an impression that Park would be "sitting at the peace table."[89]

South Korea had no realistic chance of participating in the peace negotiations. To Hanoi, South Korea was America's puppet and its soldiers, hired guns. Thus it did not deserve to partake in the peace process. To make things worse, the Johnson administration erred in explaining why the United States must leave Korea behind when heading for the negotiating table. For example, U.S. officials explained, illogically, that Korea should not feel rejected because, as a matter of fact, Washington, too, could end up not participating: if Hanoi and Saigon decided to negotiate directly, there could be "a situation in which the U.S. would not be directly represented." This was absurd: Negotiations to end the Vietnam War without U.S. representation, and Hanoi's accepting the Saigon government as the sole negotiating partner were unimaginable.[90]

Johnson remained nonchalant toward Park's anger that the United States was willing to sit down with "non-participants" in an international forum to settle the war and negotiate away the future of South Vietnam, and, by extension, that of Korea. The United States simply refused to allow Korean representation "at any given stage" of the peace process.[91] Park nevertheless continued to protest. For example, during the Manila Conference of October, 1966, where all the free world allies were gathered for a ceremonial show of *esprit de corps,* Park publicly challenged Johnson to be tougher. In his speech Park warned that the war was "not the result of an internal rebellion but a war against external aggression." And, from "the Korean experience," Park intoned, it is "an illusion to count on achieving peace through negotiations with the Communists." He then called stridently for ceasing any peace effort and the "dismemberment" of the National Liberation Front.[92]

When Park continued to protest Washington's pursuit of peace, Johnson himself sent the ultimatum. In a letter drafted by Rusk, Johnson told Park that "the search for a realistic and honorable settlement continues to command [America's] most intense efforts. Even though Hanoi's attitude at the moment is totally negative and its military actions highly menacing, [the United States] must continue to explore possibilities for inducing Hanoi to move toward peace." Washington only promised to "continue to consult" Korea.[93] It became clear to Park that he could not sway Johnson on the long-term strategies. Park understood well the meaning of "consultation" within the context of a patron-client relationship. The United States would notify him of the result of the peace talks and ask Korea simply to comply with the conditions agreed to by the U.S. negotiators.

By early 1968, compounded by his perception of Johnson's haste to come to an understanding with Hanoi and the Americans' unwillingness to retaliate against North Korean provocations in and around South Korea, namely, North Korea's capture of the USS *Pueblo* and the commando raid to assassinate Park, the Park government began to question America's commitment to defend South Korea.[94] He now demanded that the U.S.-Korean defense treaty be strengthened by making American intervention "automatic in the event of aggression," as was the case between the United States and the Philippines.[95] The existing U.S.-Korean treaty only assured that America would render help "in accordance with its constitutional processes." Deletion of this phrase, Park hoped, would "compel an instantaneous U.S. response. . . ."[96] Washington considered such a change "out of the question."[97]

Second, the Park government desired a formal pledge from the United States and its allies to come to South Korea's aid if it were attacked, as they had during the Korean War. Moreover, it wanted a declaration that the allies' actions to defend South Korea would not necessarily be "confined to Korean territory." The implication was that North Korea's patrons would be punished, too. It was obvious that countries such as Great Britain and France would not go along with reaffirming such a blanket security promise to defend South Korea. As a matter of fact, Washington's urging could produce a "minus" result by arousing resentment that the United States was coercing these nations into an alliance against China and the Soviet Union.[98] Johnson administration officials concluded that Park had become "a worried man in a state of some frustration," and that "latent anxiety" over America's commitment to Korea's security overshadowed his thoughts.[99] In this atmosphere, it was only natural that Park turned a deaf ear to Johnson's pleas for more soldiers for Vietnam.

The U.S.-Korean alliance in the Vietnam War had survived initially on material incentives. Washington reinforced Korea's military capabilities, provided cash rewards to soldiers, and infused developmental capital. These material rewards transformed a weak client into a durable partner in containment. However, as the patron's reliance on the client increased, South Korea sought to rise above its inferior position in the alliance. It wanted to participate in long-term strategic planning not only in South Vietnam, but in Northeast Asia as well. Also, it demanded a stronger security commitment from the free world allies because South Korea was fighting for their cause in South Vietnam. As noted, the Johnson administration balked at Park's grandiose world views. Johnson's refusal to consider these demands reminded Park that South Korea was powerless to influence the course of the war to which it had committed heavily at a great risk. It had no voice in the larger effort of containing a communist threat in Asia, of which South Korea was one of the most immediate targets.

After failing to move the United States to modify its superior position *vis-à-vis* South Korea, Park gave up his futile search for political rewards and sought larger economic incentives. Being denied a voice in the conduct of war in Vietnam, and in the larger issue of the containment, Park did not find much else to strive for in the alliance. As the war intensified, Korea demanded that the United States hire Korean paramilitary personnel for pacification and logistics duties and pay them a civilian wage. South Korea essentially attempted to turn the pacification campaign—the effort to rebuild the war-destroyed villages and win the "hearts and minds" of the Vietnamese—and logistic operations into employment opportunities for Korea's mostly unemployed Vietnam War veterans.

In addition, Seoul demanded that the United States hire Korean civilians with military backgrounds to replace American and Korean soldiers on support duties so that they could be sent to combat zones. The Park government named this paramilitary group the Korean Logistics Service Corps (KLSC) and asked $30 million annually for their service. Table 8.4 shows the pay and allowance schedule proposed by Seoul to be applied to the members of KLSC based on their military rank at the time of discharge.[100] The fourth column shows what the Korean soldiers in South Vietnam received for their military duties.[101] In addition, the Park government expected the United States to pay death and disability gratuities and other benefits such as health care, which, together, had "substantial cash value."[102] Johnson's aides were startled at this "exorbitant" demand that could "create serious problems" with the Saigon government and in the U.S. Congress.[103] Korea also offered to send more troops if the United States would provide resources for the construction of Korea's highways.[104]

The United States grew resentful of Korea's brazen efforts to capitalize on America's predicament in South Vietnam. Nevertheless, it bargained for better terms, rather than rejecting them. South Korea's search for material incentives, and America's bargaining for a "reasonable price" demonstrated how the alliance had lost its earlier hue of a crusade and had degenerated into a funnel through which Korea's soldiers were exchanged for what Robert Komer, one of Johnson's key advisers on Vietnam, called "bone[s]" that kept them fighting in South Vietnam.[105] South Korea, the United States came to realize, had a bigger appetite than America could satisfy. Also, Johnson's decision not to seek another term as president weakened the administration's political revolve to win Korea's additional contribution at a "reasonable price." On June 19, 1968, Johnson and his principal foreign advisers met to discuss Korea's additional support for South Vietnam. Rostow's handwritten note recorded on the agenda sheet survives. On it, next to the Korean troop question, he wrote, "15–20," "4–5," and "negotiate." It is not difficult to figure out that the first set of numbers was what Seoul wanted for KLSC in millions of U.S. dollars; the latter set was Washington's offer. Next to these comments, Rostow wrote "put off."[106]

In September, 1968, the Joint Chiefs of Staff informed the White House that Korea's request for an additional contribution was "much too high," so it was "not being pursued at present." Consequently, the military began to "divert" the "equipment for the [Korean] light infantry division . . . to the ARVN [Army of Republic of Vietnam] modernization program."[107] Thus began deescalation of the U.S.-Korean alliance in the Vietnam War and the "Vietnamization" of the Vietnam War.

In the Vietnam War, the United States refused to recognize South Korea as an ally in the conventional sense. Korea was a client state, lacking power to influence the future of the alliance. At this point, Korea had two choices. One

Table 8.4. Monthly Pay for KLSC Members and Korean Soldiers

Military Grade	Number in KLSC	Proposed Monthly Pay and Allowance for KLSC (in $U.S.)	Monthly Pay and Allowance for Korean troops in Vietnam (in $U.S.)*
1	51	700	423
2	225	500	343
3	669	409	128
4	2,666	360	112
5	1,389	330	109

*This figure does not include the death and disability gratuities.

was to end the alliance, which would have caused the entire U.S.-Korean security arrangement to disintegrate. Korea, of course, relied on that relationship for its survival. Or, it had the choice to seek other incentives, namely more opportunities to earn foreign exchange and shipment of weapons. Korea chose the latter. The alliance reached a stalemate when Korea's demands were too expensive for the United States—desperate for soldiers, though it was—to meet.

The U.S.-Korean alliance, of course, failed to save South Vietnam. However, it affected profoundly Korea's political, economic, and military developments. The alliance proved that with the infusion of right resources, even a weak and threatened nation such as South Korea could be transformed into a combat-sharing partner in containment. South Korea's intervention in a losing war, rather than destabilizing the country, facilitated the modernization of Korea's economy and military. Also, the alliance imbued confidence in the ruling regime. These changes, however, produced an unexpected and challenging dilemma for the United States: whether or not to accommodate Korea's growing influence in America's Asian policy? The United States in the end refused to realign the superior-inferior relations between the two countries and accommodate South Korea's aspiration to attain equal status as an ally. From Washington's point of view, accepting South Korea's input in the long-term direction of the war augured that America's strategic policies could be unduly influenced by an excessively belligerent junior partner. As South Korea became more vociferous in demanding a larger share in decisionmaking, Rusk asked the following rhetorical question to Johnson and his colleagues: "How does a great power like the United States avoid becoming a satellite of a small allied power" like Korea?[108] The solution was to compensate South Korea with more material incentives while denying political rewards. In the process, the alliance not only weakened but degenerated into a dollars-for-soldiers exchange.

Chapter 9

Japan and the War in Southeast Asia, 1965–67

HIROSHI FUJIMOTO

In discussing the role of Japan during the Vietnam War, three points of view have been presented that are worth notice.

One viewpoint emphasizes the "complicity" of Japan in the Vietnam War. This viewpoint was typically discussed in the antiwar movements during the war. For instance, the "Tokyo Tribunal," a war-crimes trial held in August, 1967, in Tokyo, gave attention to the fact that the Japanese government was actively cooperating with and participating in the U.S. war in Vietnam.[1]

Second, Professor Thomas Havens concluded in his book, *Fire Across the Sea* (1987)—the most comprehensive analysis ever written in English on this topic—that "it was easy for Japan during the war to satisfy both its conscience and its purse because Vietnam was a fire across the sea."[2] Regarding the "purse," he suggested that through direct and indirect procurements Japan replaced the United States as the leading economic power in Southeast Asia. From his argument, it is clear that the long-term effect of the war provided the basis for Japan's rapid evolution into an economic giant.

Third, Professor Motoo Furuta of Tokyo University, who specializes in modern Vietnamese history, suggested that this correlation between Japanese economic prosperity and the war should be analyzed in the larger context of the Cold War. Furuta stressed that one of the motives of American intervention in Vietnam lay in the fact that in order to preserve its hegemony, the United States sought to form an international environment for Japanese economic prosperity.[3] Several historians have already pointed out that the origins of U.S. involvement in Vietnam, especially during the 1950s, lay in efforts to attain economic recovery in postwar Japan.[4] It should be noted that Furuta's viewpoint is important in that it may lead us to see the war beyond a "fire across the sea." The Cold War context enables us to consider, as Furuta has suggested, Japanese "prosperity" and the "misery" of Vietnam as interrelated outcomes of the war.[5]

The purpose of this paper is to present an overall view of the correlation between Japanese economic prosperity and the Vietnam War in the context of "regionalism" as an American policy toward Asia during the Cold War, incorporating the first and the second viewpoints mentioned above. This paper covers the period from the first talks of January, 1965, between Japanese Prime Minister Sato and President Johnson to the second talks of November, 1967, between the two leaders.

Regionalism as an American Policy and Japan's Role in Asia

Since 1960, when the Japan–United States Security Treaty was signed, the United States government had asked Japan to pursue an active role and responsibility as a regional power in Asia under a U.S.-Japan partnership. As Japanese diplomatic historian Professor Hideki Kan of Kyushu University has pointed out, the American embassy in Tokyo advised the State Department in a cable at the end of December, 1964, that the United States requested Japan to have a consciousness and responsibility as a regional power that had an interest in economic development and political stability in Asia in general.[6] By that time, Japanese leaders had realized that economic development in the developing countries would do much toward their own long-term commercial interests, and that Japan would take a responsible position to cope with political instability in the Asian region. Prime Minister Eisaku Sato, who took office on November 9, 1964, after former Prime Minister Ikeda Hayato resigned for health reasons, had decided to take a positive stance regarding U.S. policy toward Asia.

Prime Minister Sato's first visit to Washington, January 9–14, 1965, was the first official occasion on which the U.S. government pressed the idea of Japan's serving as a regional power, and during which the Japanese government complied with the request. The Sato-Johnson joint communiqué of January 13 emphasized that "the two countries should maintain the closest contact and consultation not only on problems lying between them but on problems affecting Asia and the world in general."[7] With respect to this general statement, it is important to note the following two points.

First, Prime Minister Sato showed his recognition that the security of

Japan was correlated with the security of the Far East. For example, Sato affirmed his commitment to preserve the thirty-eighth parallel as the boundary of the Korean peninsula. Sato and Johnson also recognized "the importance of United States military installations on the Ryukyus and Ogasawara Islands for the security of the Far East," while Johnson agreed with the Japanese desire that "as soon as feasible," control over these islands would be restored to Japan.[8] Vietnam was one of the most important topics in these talks, as Prime Minister Sato endorsed American policy to preserve the Saigon regime in Vietnam. The communiqué emphasized "continued perseverance would be necessary for freedom and independence in South Vietnam."[9]

Second, both leaders emphasized the necessity of economic cooperation with the Asian countries, and they recognized "that the elevation of living standards and the advancement of social welfare are essential for the political stability of developing countries throughout the world and agreed to strengthen their economic cooperation with such countries. . . ." Prime Minister Sato "expressed particular interest in expanding Japan's role in developmental and technical assistance for Asia."[10]

The reason the United States asked Japan to take a more active role in Asia was that by that time the United States attached great importance to regional cooperative frameworks to cope with independent or radical directions taken by some developing countries. In Asia, the United States had been concerned about the domino effect caused by radical nationalism in Vietnam, as well as Indonesia's sympathetic attitude to Communist China. The idea of the regional framework, in connection with the U.S. commitment in Vietnam, was highlighted in the address President Johnson delivered at Johns Hopkins University on April 7, 1965. On that occasion, Johnson emphasized that "the countries of Southeast Asia . . . associate themselves in a greatly expanded cooperative effort for development," on the assumption that poverty and illiteracy were the roots of political instability. President Johnson asked Congress to invest $1 billion for the Mekong River project as well as modern medicine and schools.[11]

The Japanese government welcomed Johnson's speech. In a memorandum to President Johnson on April 10, 1967, Prime Minister Eisaku Sato expressed his great appreciation for Johnson's speech and conveyed his earnest wish that the countries concerned would respond to Johnson's constructive suggestions and would show readiness to enter into discussions as soon as possible. Sato also mentioned that in order to realize and implement Johnson's proposal, "Japan is fully prepared to extend further cooperation to the best of her ability."[12] As is discussed later, Japan would play an important role in promoting regional cooperation for development in Asia at the time of the founding of the Asian Development Bank (ADB).

Japan's Cooperation with the American War in Vietnam

In the meantime, the United States had escalated the war in Vietnam and turned it into an American war. Persistent political instability in the Saigon regime forced the United States to begin gradually intensified air attacks against the North, and this led to the introduction of U.S. ground forces into Vietnam. On March 8, 1965, two battalions of marines landed near Danang. In July Johnson made a fateful decision to make an open-ended commitment to deploy American military forces, increasing American forces to about 180,000 by the end of 1965.

Since April, 1964, the Johnson administration had carried out the "more flags" program to enlist assistance from other free world nations. In the end, over forty nations gave some form of aid to the Saigon regime. Only seven nations — South Korea, Taiwan, the Philippines, Thailand, Australia, New Zealand, and Spain — deployed forces. The main body of combat troops, however, came only from South Korea and the United States.[13]

As for Japan, "the prime minister's endorsement of American policies," historian Thomas Havens has pointed out, "was still almost as guarded as the response of most of the other major allies."[14] The Sato cabinet limited its aid to the Saigon regime mainly to noneconomic programs during 1965–70, continuing Prime Minister Ikeda's policy of giving medical aid to Saigon. Sato was also cautious about the American inclination to solve the problem by force. While the United States had an appreciation of Japan's role in supporting the Saigon regime, policymakers also expressed political frustration. In a memorandum to President Johnson on February 16, 1965, William P. Bundy, assistant secretary of state for Far Eastern affairs, briefly summarized reactions in key countries to U.S. actions in Vietnam. The score card for Japan was "with us tepidly."[15]

Prime Minister Sato's cautious attitude reflected the public mood in Japan. The *Asahi,* one of the leading newspapers in Japan, questioned 3,000 adults throughout the country in early August, 1965, finding that about 75 percent of the respondents disapproved of the air attacks against the North.[16] Most Japanese also feared that Japan might be drawn into the war. Deployment of thirty B-52s from Okinawa to Vietnam in July–August, 1965, caused a negative public reaction. Even leaders in the government, including Sato, expressed their displeasure.[17]

As the Vietnam War escalated, however, the government of Japan expressed more support for American use of the military bases. As Thomas Havens has suggested, it should be noted that the American use of the military bases "confirmed that the main purpose of the security treaty was no longer to protect Japan . . . but instead to pursue American strategy in East and Southeast Asia."[18]

During the war, Japan served as an important rear base for U.S. forces in Vietnam. Foreign Minister Etsusaburo Shiina asserted the basic position of the Japanese government in a reply at a Budget Committee meeting of the Lower House on July 18, 1965: "We have the Japan-U.S. Security Treaty. . . . Japan has an obligation to approve the use by U.S. forces of Japanese facilities and areas in this connection. In this sense, . . . Japan is not placed in a neutral position with regard to the war in Vietnam."[19]

Once the United States escalated the war, a controversy arose over the question of "the Far East clause" and "prior consultation" regarding the Japan-U.S. Security Treaty. When the treaty was signed in 1960, the Japanese government limited the geographical area of "the Far East" to the area north of the Philippines and also maintained that Japan could veto American requests during prior consultation. However, on February 14, 1965, just after the beginning of American air attacks against North Vietnam, Shiina told the Budget Committee of the Lower House that although Vietnam was not formally within the Far East, the security treaty could not be limited to the Far East alone if nearby events threatened Japan's peace and security.[20] Regarding "prior consultation," for example, at a meeting of the Foreign Affairs Committee of the Lower House on April 14, Shiina said: "in case bases in Japan are directly used and operation actions are taken from there, they will continue an object of prior consultation; otherwise, the use in various ways of facilities in Japan for supply and other purposes is what Japan should offer from the standpoint of the [Japan-U.S.] Security Treaty."[21] Thus, the Sato government took a more expansive interpretation of the geography and also almost canceled the need for prior consultation. This meant that the Japanese government would explicitly support such actions of the U.S. forces as the transport of munitions to Vietnam within the framework of the Japan-U.S. Security Treaty.

During the war, there were 264 U.S. military facilities in Japan: 147 on the mainland and 177 in Okinawa. Japan provided combat bases; logistic, supply and repair bases; intelligence and training bases; and recreation and recuperation facilities.[22] The United States could take advantage of Japan's highly developed technical capacity and abundant equipment for the repair of its war and merchant fleets, planes, and for all kinds of supplies and equipment. So John C. Stennis, chairperson of an Armed Services Subcommittee of the U.S. Senate, noted in a report on April 6, 1966, that "the U.S. Navy under orders in the Vietnam War largely depends on the bases of Japan and Taiwan for the repair of its fleets. In particular, operations for fighting the war in Southeast Asia would encounter serious difficulties without Yokosuka and Sasebo."[23] Furthermore, as is well known, U.S. bases in Okinawa, "the keystone of the Pacific," which had been under U.S. military administration, were freely used as some of the most important military bases for the Vietnam War. Professor Havens pointed out the role of Okinawa in the following: "Roughly 50,000 U.S. troops were stationed in the Ryukyus during the conflict, staffing ammunition depots, supply warehouses, training grounds, ports, air bases, missile sites, and communication centers. . . . The Second Logistical Command, headquartered in Okinawa, handled about three-quarters of the 400,000 tons of goods consumed each month by American forces in Vietnam. . . . The 3,750-meter runways at Kadena air base averaged a takeoff or landing every three minutes around the clock, totaling more than a million flight operations during 1965–1973."[24] Admiral U. S. Grant Sharp, commander of the U.S. Pacific Joint Forces, was quoted in the December 10, 1965, *Morning Star*—an official organ of the U.S. forces—as saying that "without Okinawa, we cannot carry on the Vietnam War."[25]

While Japan played an important role in providing a rear base in Vietnam, it also received U.S. special procurements in the 1960s. The total direct and indirect procurements did not exceed 7–8 percent of Japanese exports for any year during the conflict. American purchases did not have so much of a decisive influence on the Japanese economy as in the Korean War, during which U.S. procurements accounted for 63 percent of all Japanese exports in the peak year, 1952. It is estimated, however, that on the average Japan profited at least $1 billion per year from the Vietnam War.[26]

It is important to note that through indirect procurements Japan increased its trade with Southeast Asia as well as with the United States. This lifted Japan to a status of "economic giant" and encouraged her to play a more active role in Southeast Asia. While overall Japanese exports to the United States between 1965 and 1972 grew at an average annual rate of 21 percent, and the bilateral balance of trade with the United States turned in Japan's favor for the first time in 1965, Japan took the place of the United States as the leading economic power in Asia, especially in Southeast Asia.[27] The latter long-term effect was typically shown in Japan–South Korea relations during the Vietnam War.

U.S.–Japan–South Korea Relations during the Vietnam War

As the United States escalated the war and increased its war expenditures, it was forced to cut its aid to other countries, including Korea. The Johnson administration keenly felt it necessary to make efforts to share its burden with Japan in U.S.-Korean relations and put pressure on both Japan and Korea to make the concessions that made normalization between the two countries possible. When William P. Bundy visited Japan and South Korea from September 30 to October 3, 1964, he made it clear that "Japan bears special responsibilities to settle outstanding problems with its smaller and heavily burdened neighbor," and that "the security of Japan is virtually connected with the ability of the Korean people to maintain their independence and to develop a strong and prosperous economy."[28] Eventually, Japanese and Korean foreign ministers initialed a draft treaty on February 20, 1965. In July both countries signed the Treaty on Basic Relations between Japan and the Republic of Korea, including a provision whereby Japan would provide $300 million in grants and $200 million in government loans. Thus, in meeting the American request, Japan and South Korea normalized their relations.

It is worth noting that South Korean President Chung Hee Park's willingness to deploy military forces in Vietnam at the request of the American "more flags" program could serve as leverage to get continued American aid. It is undeniable that American promises to continue aid were a main factor in Korea's decision to normalize relations with Japan.[29] The Korean government first dispatched a 140-member Mobile Army Surgical Hospital (MASH) unit in September, 1964, and then on January 18, 1965, President Park decided to deploy a unit of 2,000 engineers and support troops. By October, 1965, about 21,000 Korean troops had joined a force of 150,000 American troops. As Jiyul Kim points out in his master's thesis, a "Memorandum of Conversation" of the first meeting between Park and Johnson on May 17 clearly illustrates "the intimate and complex ties which were developing rapidly among the issues of the treaty, the war, [and] ROK troops for Vietnam." The following is a part of the record that Kim has reproduced:

> He [President Johnson] felt that conclusion of the Korean-Japan treaty would also assist our mutual effort in Viet-Nam. . . .
>
> President Johnson congratulated President Park on his assistance in the struggle in Viet-Nam, and said, with reference to that aid, that we would keep in Korea a military strength equivalent to that at present so that . . . Korean security would not suffer.[30]

U.S. military expenditures in Korea increased from $97 million in 1965 to $364 million in 1969.[31]

During that time, especially after 1966, one year after the signing of the Japan–South Korea Treaty, Japan took the place of the United States as the largest exporting country to South Korea. Until the early 1960s, the United States shared almost 50 percent of the gross total of Korean imports, but from the late 1960s to the early 1970s, Japan's share of Korean imports increased remarkably and amounted to around 40 percent.[32] The reason for this change lies in the fact that materials used by the South Korean exporting industries were largely imported from Japan. For example, as Professor Thomas Havens has pointed out, one estimate in October of 1966 suggested that about 50 percent of South Korean exports were reexports of Japanese goods.[33] In fact, South Korea largely imported from Japan such materials as clothes and synthetic rubber for manufacturing military uniforms and jungle boots, which were exported by South Korea to the Saigon regime through the special procurements program provided to South Korea by the United States.

Japan's windfalls from the Vietnam War came indirectly, as typically shown in these Japan-Korea relations. Japan profited from exports of materials and supplies not only to South Korea but to South Vietnam's neighboring countries—such as Thailand and the Philippines, which deployed their troops in South Vietnam—through special procurements as well as military and economic aid provided by the United States to these countries. As a result, overall Japanese exports to South Korea, Thailand, the Philippines, Taiwan, and Hong Kong increased from $1,145 million in 1965 to $2,998 million in 1969.[34] As Japan came to replace the United States as the leading exporting country in Southeast Asia during the Vietnam War, this would define the new stage in Japan's relations with Southeast Asia.

Japan's Growing Leadership in Its Relations with Southeast Asia, 1966–67

By mid-1966, the Sato government had strengthened its leadership in Southeast Asia and took concrete steps to expand the cooperative efforts that President Johnson mentioned in his Johns Hopkins address in 1965. On April 6–7, 1966, Japan convened the first Ministerial Conference of Southeast Asia in Tokyo. It was the first official international conference that Japan had convened since World War II. To discuss the matter of economic development, eight countries (South Vietnam, South Korea, Thailand, the Philippines, Indonesia, Malaysia, Singapore, and Taiwan) participated in the conference, in which the Sato government pledged to raise its official development aid to 1 percent of its gross national product. Of equal significance, Japan joined the Asian Development Bank (ADB), which was founded in Tokyo in November, 1966. Japan contributed $200 million to its foundation, the same amount the United States provided. In addition, Japan provided $100 million for a special agricultural development bank fund. Japan also participated in the first meeting of the Asian and Pacific Council (ASPAC), which was organized by President Park of South Korea for reinforcing the political alliance of noncommmunist states. Furthermore, in September, 1966, Japan set up a consortium of eleven nations to solve the debt problem for propping up Suharto's Indonesian military government, which took over after the fall of Sukarno. Japan shared the burden with the United States of supporting the Suharto regime by providing 18 billion yen in new government loans in 1967.

Prime Minister Sato's visits to Southeast Asia in September and October, 1967, were related to Japan's emergence as the leading economic power in the region. A ten-day visit to Burma, Malaysia, Singapore, Thailand, and Laos was followed by a second trip in October to South Vietnam, Indonesia, Australia, New Zealand, the Philippines, and Taiwan.

On several occasions during his visits, Sato gave clear support for American policy toward the war. He declared in Thailand, for instance, that ending the bombing against North Vietnam would not bring peace. Professor Havens has suggested that Sato's intention for his visits was that "visiting Taipei and Saigon would help him persuade Johnson to return the Ogasawaras at once and the Ryukyus very shortly."[35]

Epilogue: The Second Sato-Johnson Talks of November, 1967

Under these circumstances, the Johnson administration recognized by late 1967 that Japan had taken positive and helpful actions over the past few years for a larger share of responsibility in the regional affairs in Asia, as well as for supporting U.S. actions in Vietnam.[36] Based on this recognition, Secretary of State Dean Rusk suggested to the president that the major issues during the coming visit of Prime Minister Sato to the United States in mid-November, 1967, would be two-fold: "first, Japanese willingness to shoulder a greater share of the political and economic burdens of regional responsibility; and second, our response to Japanese desires for forward movement on reversion of the Ryukyu and Bonin islands."[37]

On November 14–15, 1967, just after his visits to Southeast Asia, Prime Minister Sato visited the United States and met with President Johnson and other government officials.

In the talks, Sato declared his forthright support for American policy toward the war by expressing "support for the United States position of seeking a just and equitable settlement." He also said that "reciprocal action should be expressed to Hanoi for a cessation of the bombing of North Vietnam." On the matter of security, both leaders affirmed that they would maintain the Japan-U.S. Security Treaty in order to ensure the security of the Far East as well as Japan. It is important to note that Sato expressed his determination to make "a positive contribution to the peace and security in Asia."[38]

In terms of regional cooperation, on November 15 Secretary of State Rusk conveyed appreciation for Japan's growing role and interest in the ADB and other matters for economic development. The U.S. government also expressed its expectation during the talks that Japan would continue efforts to play an active role. Thus, a joint communiqué of November 15 reads:

> . . . it is the intention of the Government of Japan . . . to continue its efforts to provide more effective bilateral and multilateral assistance to the Southeast Asian region. . . .
>
> Recognizing the need to strengthen economic assistance to the developing areas, particularly to the Southeast Asian countries, the President and the Prime Minister agreed to maintain closer consultation with each other in this field.[39]

In the talks, Japan agreed to share aid for Indonesia equally with the United States and promised to consider providing $1 million in additional funds for the ADB.

Although the Sato government was disappointed that the date of reversion of Okinawa was not mentioned precisely in the communiqué, the Sato-Johnson talks showed the culmination of the "Japan-U.S. partnership" during the war, under which the United States obtained Japan's support for the war and requested that Japan take responsibility as a regional power in Southeast Asia.

Finally, while the Japanese government indirectly supported American policy in Vietnam, Japan had also pursued its efforts in the regional framework to enhance its own political and economic power in Asia. In this sense, Japan ended up as, in Professor Havens's words, the "chief beneficiary"[40] of America's longest war, during which the Vietnamese people suffered tremendously.

Part 3

The World System

Chapter 10

What Difference Did It Make?

Assessing the Vietnam War's
Impact on Southeast Asia

ROBERT J. McMAHON

Southeast Asia, trumpeted the *New York Times* in September, 1993, ranked as "the fastest-growing region on earth"—a rank, the influential daily added, that it had held ever since the early 1980s.[1] The *Times* article appeared, appropriately enough, as the lead story in its business section, not the place readers used to find news about Southeast Asia. But for more than a decade now, that is precisely where the America media has featured news about the region. Indeed, the narrative of Southeast Asia as a capitalist showcase and wondrous success story had, by the early 1990s, become the dominant one. So completely has it eclipsed the earlier narrative of Southeast Asia as a crucial cockpit of great power rivalry and the home of precariously perched dominos, that a Rip Van Winkle awakening during the Clinton years from a twenty-year sleep might well have thought himself in some distant century.

The breadth of contemporary Southeast Asia's economic metamorphosis has been nothing short of phenomenal. Between 1965 and 1990, the Gross Domestic Product (GDP) of the ASEAN states (Indonesia, the Philippines, Malaysia, Thailand, Singapore, and Brunei) increased fourteen-fold. In 1993, the combined GDP of those nations, plus Vietnam, stood at $440 million, with experts projecting that it would reach $1 trillion by 2010. The American stake in these expanding economies grew proportionately, with U.S.-ASEAN trade increasing by more than 100 percent between 1985 and 1995.

The economic progress of individual ASEAN countries, and America's multiplying commercial links with those countries, proved no less impressive. Between 1986 and 1996, Thailand (although it has suffered a sharp economic downturn of late) averaged annual growth rates of over 8 percent, virtually the highest in the world during those years. Malaysia was not far behind, recording average growth rates of nearly 8 percent per annum during that same time period. Along with those high growth rates came expanding markets for American goods. U.S. trade with Malaysia increased by 66 percent between 1992 and 1994. Indonesia, identified by the Clinton Commerce Department as one of the world's top ten "emerging markets," recorded a 113-percent leap in U.S. exports between 1989 and 1994. Singapore, with a population of only 2.9 million, boasted the highest per capita income of any Southeast Asian nation and ranked, rather amazingly, as America's tenth largest export market. Even the Philippines, long the economic laggard within ASEAN, has seen steady economic growth since Presidents Corazon Aquino and Fidel Ramos initiated long-overdue economic reforms in the early 1990s.[2]

Malaysia's decision to begin construction, in 1995, of what would become the world's tallest building provided a fitting symbol of the growing wealth and soaring self-confidence of an entire region. The flow, a year later, of major financial contributions from wealthy, influence-seeking Indonesian and Thai businessmen to Bill Clinton's reelection campaign provided a different kind of symbol of Southeast Asian assertiveness and newfound financial muscle. Not even the serious currency and banking problems that swept Southeast Asia in the summer and autumn of 1997 seemed likely to do much more than slow temporarily the region's amazing economic progress.

The spectacular economic success of Southeast Asia's capitalist states over the past several decades offers the most dramatic of contrasts with the economically stagnant Southeast Asia of the mid-1960s. Equally dramatic, if compared to the conditions that obtained a generation earlier, are the relative political stability enjoyed by most of the region's states today, the strategic equilibrium prevailing throughout contemporary Southeast Asia, and the vitality of ASEAN as a regional association.

When President Lyndon B. Johnson decided, early in 1965, that U.S. interests required massive military intervention to block the imminence of a communist triumph in South Vietnam, he found scant grounds for optimism about the region's future. Genuine political stability and economic growth seemed the most distant of prospects at that time. Quite to the contrary, LBJ worried that an amalgam of nettlesome problems—internal strife, regime instability, and economic stagnation chief among them—made the nations of Southeast Asia exceedingly vulnerable to external pressures. The abiding concern of the American president and his principal advisers was that, absent forceful and immediate U.S. intervention, South Vietnam and Laos would soon "fall" to communist insurgents. Their collapse would then generate, in turn, irresistible pressure on Cambodia, Thailand, Malaysia, Singapore, and Burma.

The fact that Indonesia, home to the world's largest nonruling communist party, also appeared gravitating toward the communist bloc just exacerbated the nightmare scenarios that haunted Johnson's inner circle at that time. For if Southeast Asia succumbed to communist pressures, U.S. policymakers were certain, a major Cold War victory with worldwide implications would have been scored by the Soviet Union and China. And a potentially cataclysmic political, strategic, and psychological loss would have been inflicted upon the so-called "free world."

Some observers have offered a retroactive defense of and justification for America's military commitments in Indochina by positing a direct causal link between U.S. efforts there and the economic, political, and geostrategic achievements of contemporary Southeast Asia. They have gone so far as to depict the Vietnam War as a long-term victory for the United States. The war, according to this view, bought crucial time for the economic development and political maturation of the region's noncommunist states. Hence, the broader goals of U.S. intervention in Indochina—checking communism's spread across Southeast Asia and ensuring the emergence of stable, prosperous, Western-oriented regimes—were actually achieved. Put another way, the United States, according to this viewpoint, lost the battle for South Vietnam but actually won the larger war for Southeast Asia.

Walt W. Rostow, a key Johnson adviser and unrepentant Vietnam hawk, has been advancing this argument forcefully for more than a decade. The American commitment in Vietnam, he argued in a 1986 book, "bought valuable time not only for ASEAN to find its feet but also for an additional decade of extraordinary economic and social progress to occur." Continued Rostow: "ASEAN's total real output was probably more than twice its 1965 level in 1975. More important, this interval of sustained rapid progress, combined with the increasingly serious character of ASEAN, suffused the region with a degree of inner confidence which made the trauma of the take-over of South Vietnam much easier to surmount in 1975 than a decade earlier."[3]

The former national security adviser returned to that theme in 1996 with a stinging critique of Robert McNamara's *In Retrospect*. Rostow insisted that "American intervention and the conflict that followed had [quoting Singapore's long-term leader Lee Kuan Yew, another prominent defender of U.S. intervention] 'broken the hypnotic spell on the other Southeast Asians that communism is irresistible, that it is the wave of history.'" Cutting right to the heart of his dissent from the conventional wisdom about the Vietnam War, Rostow concluded that "we certainly lost the battle—the test of will—in Vietnam, but we won the war in Southeast Asia because South Vietnam and its allies for ten years were [quoting Lyndon Johnson here] 'holding aggression at bay.'" Lest there be any confusion on this point, he concluded: "This was surely not simply a pointless, lost war."[4]

Of course, that view of Vietnam—as the pointless and lost war—was, and is, commonly held by scholars and nonscholars alike. It has been reflected not just in the writings of historians, journalists, former policymakers (such as McNamara), and other opinionshapers, but in the various outpourings of American popular culture. The veritable avalanche of novels, memoirs, films, songs, and television programs touching on the Vietnam experience have invariably characterized it in terms of loss, waste, or (at best) misplaced idealism. Presidential candidate Ronald Reagan was well aware of those deep-set attitudes, and, evidently trying to counter them, provocatively anointed the Vietnam War a "noble cause" in a celebrated 1980 campaign speech. But rocker Bruce Springsteen and filmmaker Oliver Stone have undoubtedly come much closer to the dominant view of Vietnam as a tragic misadventure. Springsteen's wildly popular, and savagely ironic, 1984 anthem, "Born in the USA," poignantly captured the widespread bitterness with and disillusionment about a war that Robert McNamara described, with less emotion, as a tragic mistake.

The "buying time" thesis must, then, be understood within this broader political and cultural context. It forms a small, but significant, part of a much broader project: an effort by a conservative band of intensely nationalistic scholars and polemicists, often referred to as the "Vietnam revisionists," to recapture the moral high ground for the United States by reinterpreting the Vietnam experience. Some of these revisionists have zeroed in on how the war might actually have been won, if only it had been fought differently; others have praised the noble *intentions* of U.S. policy; still others have concentrated on the sordid human rights records of the communist regimes that ultimately triumphed in Vietnam and Cambodia. The Rostow view may be the most radically revisionist of all, though, because it seeks to alter the very terms of the debate and the standards by which we judge success and failure.

Whatever the political motivations that gave rise to the "buying time" thesis, it demands serious scrutiny. For one reason, the thesis has gained currency in certain intellectual and political circles. *U.S. News and World Report*'s editor Marvin Stone, for example, offered a succinct preview of this point of view in October, 1981. After returning from a brief tour of postwar Southeast Asia, he told the readers of his mass-circulation weekly that "whatever the U.S. did not accomplish in Vietnam, its sacrifice there gave countries of the region vital years to build their security—modestly in military terms, more important in political and economic terms."[5] More recently, former Assistant Secretary of State Ernest W. Lefever, writing in the *Wall Street Journal,* echoed that assessment. Our steadfastness in Vietnam strengthened nationalist and anticommunist forces elsewhere in Southeast Asia," insisted the Reagan era diplomat. "Holding the line in Indochina as long as we did," he argued, "eventually led to a balance of power favorable to the states in the region and to us . . ."[6]

An even more fundamental reason why the "buying time" thesis commands our attention is that it poses profound questions, in their own right, about the impact of the war on the region in which it was fought. It is a region that *has* changed dramatically in the past generation. And certainly a war of the ferocity and magnitude of the Vietnam conflict must have left some kind of imprint. But how do we measure that imprint? How *do* we assess the relationship between the Vietnam War and the evolution of contemporary Southeast Asia?

This essay seeks to explore some of those intriguing questions. Unfortunately, there is a dearth of serious scholarship concerning the Vietnam War's legacy to Southeast Asia on which to build. For all the voluminous scholarship covering virtually every aspect of that conflict, and for all the attention devoted to the war's impact *on the United States,* the available literature glosses over the war's regional consequences. Since Rostow and his fellow Vietnam revisionists have, largely by default, held the field up to now, my remaining comments will focus on the categories of analysis, and core propositions, that they have advanced.

The "buying time" school offers three basic, interrelated postulates: first, that U.S. intervention contributed significantly to the political stabilization of Southeast Asia's noncommunist states; second, that it helped foster a geopolitical equilibrium throughout the region; and, third, that it helped spark not just economic development but the soaring growth rates recorded by the ASEAN states over the past several decades.

Each of those propositions is, in my judgment, riddled with dubious assumptions, faulty logic, and gigantic leaps in faith. Each tends to conflate *intentions* with *consequences.* Each, moreover, does grave injustice to the issue of causality.

The *post hoc ergo propter hoc* fallacy is the most common of logical errors and is well in evidence here: the ASEAN states became relatively stable and prosperous *after* the Vietnam War, hence they progressed politically and economically *because* of the Vietnam War. Such causal links need to be carefully demonstrated, not just asserted, and an appreciation for complexity and contingency must be displayed by anyone seeking to make such a case. Otherwise, one could just as easily argue (indeed, some do) that U.S. intervention in Vietnam also hastened the end of the Cold War and the subsequent collapse of the Soviet Union. Or, one might just as casually attribute the success of the U.S. stock market in the 1990s to U.S. exertions in Vietnam—or anything else that has happened over the past thirty years for that matter.

What follows is a brief examination of each of these three core propositions.

The Political Stabilization Argument

One of the most glaring deficiencies of the political stabilization aspect of the "buying time" thesis—replete with untenable *post hoc* logic—concerns Indonesia. At almost the exact same time that Johnson was committing American combat troops to Vietnam, U.S. goals in the region were given a sudden, unanticipated boost by a political transformation of seismic proportions in Indonesia. That transformation was precipitated by the shadowy events that occurred on September 30, 1965. On that date, a group of junior army officers, likely acting at the behest of elements within the Indonesian Communist Party (PKI), assassinated six of the seven top Indonesian military commanders. The so-called "Gestapu," though its precise origins and intent remain a subject of considerable controversy to this day, may have represented the prelude to an all-out bid for power on the part of certain PKI leaders.

One thing is certain: the action brought a dramatically different result from that intended by the conspirators. General Suharto, a second-echelon army commander largely unknown to top U.S. officials, responded with brutal efficiency in crushing the incipient revolt. He then ordered a ruthless purge of the party and presided over the subsequent slaughter of hundreds of thousands of presumed communists and communist-sympathizers. The resulting bloodbath ultimately claimed as many as half a million lives. The conservative, pro-Western Suharto also started easing Sukarno out of power while simultaneously courting Western support and encouraging the influx of Western capital.

The Johnson administration could not contain its glee at this stunning turn of events in Indonesia. "It is hard to overestimate the potential significance of the army's apparent victory over Sukarno," senior NSC staffer Robert Komer wrote Johnson in early 1966. "Indonesia has more people—and probably more resources—than all of mainland Southeast Asia. It was well on the way to becoming another expansionist Communist state, which would have critically menaced the rear of the whole Western position in mainland Southeast Asia," he emphasized.[7] Reflecting decades later on the significance of Indonesia's political earthquake, Robert McNamara mused that it "significantly altered the regional balance of power and substantially reduced America's real stake in Vietnam"—though the defense secretary conceded that he and most other senior officials did not at first appreciate fully the latter connection. "The largest and most populous nation in Southeast Asia had reversed course and now lay in the hands of independent nationalists led by Suharto," McNamara observed. "China, which had expected a tremendous victory, instead suffered a permanent setback."[8]

That, at the very moment when Indonesian-American relations appeared to be spinning dangerously out of control, they would suddenly reverse course almost 180 degrees forms one of the great ironies of America's Southeast Asia policy over the past half-century. The ill-considered actions of Lieutenant Colonel Untung and his fellow conspirators wound up ushering in a new epoch in U.S.-Indonesian relations, providing the Johnson administration with a wholly unexpected diplomatic windfall. However favorable to Washington that outcome proved, though, neither the coup attempt itself nor the army's prompt response to it were influenced to any significant degree by the United States. Rather, those events were determined, as one U.S. diplomat had observed earlier, "by basic forces far beyond our ability to control."[9] Recalled Hugh Tovar, the CIA station chief in Jakarta during the Gestapu: "I was stunned. At the time we did not know what had happened."[10]

Interestingly, the Johnson administration searched—in vain, as it turned out—for evidence that the Indonesian army might have been fortified by the burgeoning U.S. troop commitments in Vietnam. CIA Director Richard Helms admitted to Johnson that his experts could find no such link. To the contrary, the agency concluded that the rise of Suharto and the subsequent destruction of the PKI "evolved purely from a complex and long-standing domestic political situation."[11]

The abrupt change in Indonesia's internal and external direction, arguably the single most important political development in the region during the entire Vietnam War era, thus had almost nothing to do with the United States, nor with the U.S. troop buildup to the north. More than likely the counter-coup, an event that evolved "purely from a complex and long-standing domestic political situation," as the CIA put it, would have occurred even if Johnson had decided *against* intervention in Vietnam. Without a demonstrable causal link between U.S. efforts in Vietnam and the political transformation of Indonesia, it becomes exceedingly difficult to posit a direct causal connection between the Vietnam War and the emergence of a more politically stable Southeast Asia.

Under careful examination, this aspect of the "buying time" argument grows even weaker. If not Indonesia, then which Southeast Asian countries owe their current political stability—such as it is—to the Vietnam War? Certainly not Cambodia, which has been in constant turmoil ever since the ouster of Prince Sihanouk in 1970. Cambodia was, in fact, far more stable *before* U.S. intervention in Vietnam than *after*. One could make a strong case that, had the Johnson administration kept U.S. troops home, allowing the Viet Cong and its North Vietnamese allies to achieve victory, Cambodia would have been much better off. The wily, chameleon-like Sihanouk likely would have managed to maintain a degree of independence, even with a communist neighbor, thereby averting the appalling human toll exacted by the grisly events that followed his overthrow. In the Cambodian case, then, one in which direct causal links *can* be established between American actions and subsequent developments, U.S. actions fostered *in*stability, not stability.[12]

Certainly Myanmar (Burma) cannot be said to have gained political stability from the Vietnam War. Only Cambodia is today more volatile and unstable than Myanmar, which remains under the iron grip of a repressive and ruthless military regime. That country's bizarre experiment in self-isolation, moreover, had been launched well before the U.S. troop buildup of the mid-1960s.

The Philippines, then? This, too, is a difficult case to make because Ferdinand Marcos had come to power *before* the major U.S. troop buildup (a buildup, incidentally, that he initially opposed) and remained firmly in control until well after U.S. troops departed. It is hard to equate his repressive, venal rule, a rule that brought forth its own virulent internal opposition, with stability. By the same token, it is highly problematic to posit a direct, or even an indirect, connection between political developments in the Philippines during the 1960s, 1970s, and 1980s and U.S. intervention in Vietnam. No specialist in modern Philippine history has, to my knowledge, found evidence that the Vietnam War promoted political stability in the Philippines; many have, in fact, argued that the societal divisions fostered by the war worked against that end.[13]

The case for the positive political effects of the Vietnam War must, then, rest on the remaining cases of Thailand, Malaysia, and Singapore. Thailand's ruling elite clearly wanted the United States to take a stand in Vietnam and in Laos. That group supported and encouraged U.S. efforts in Indochina, provided critical base sites to the United States, made available Thai territory as a staging ground for regionwide covert operations, and sent combat forces to South Vietnam. But to infer from the temporary convergence of U.S. and Thai regional interests that the United States helped impart a degree of political stability to Thailand oversimplifies a complex domestic situation, in the process sweeping aside any sense of contingency. It is equally problematic to argue that, absent a vigorous U.S. military buildup in Vietnam, Thailand would have toppled, domino fashion. Were there not alternatives? If the Johnson administration truly wanted to bolster Thailand as a regional ally, surely it could have done so with a bilateral treaty that would have had more teeth than the excessively vague SEATO commitment, with a strong U.S. troop presence, and with firm warnings to North Vietnam, China, and/or the Soviet Union that any military threat to Thailand would be met with an immediate U.S. military response. It simply does not follow logically, in short, that had the United States eschewed a major military commitment to Vietnam then Thailand could not have been "saved." Nor does it follow that Thailand—or Malaysia or Singapore—was "saved" as a result of the U.S. commitment in Vietnam.[14]

Rostow also argues that a strong causal link binds the founding of ASEAN in 1967 to the U.S. military presence in Vietnam. But this contention, too, rests on shaky logic. A critical factor that made ASEAN possible was the demise of Sukarno and the emergence of the Suharto regime in Indonesia. With that development, the Indonesian-Malaysian "konfrantasi" that Sukarno had sparked was defused, making a regional association possible. Yet, as already noted, Indonesian developments occurred independent of U.S. regional commitments.

Another critical factor, and one that Rostow conveniently overlooks, is that ASEAN emerged as an Asian *alternative* to great power meddling and domination. Even those states formally allied to the United States—Thailand, the Philippines, South Vietnam—harbored deep reservations about the presence of over a half-million U.S. troops in the region. They regularly complained, moreover, about the arrogance, callousness, and heavy-handedness of their superpower patron. The nations of Southeast Asia, allies and neutrals alike, shared a strong nationalist consciousness that often manifested itself in various forms of anti-Americanism. The newly emerging states of the region were hardly inclined to replace the colonial dependence of the past for a new form of dependence upon the United States. Rather, they longed for Asian solutions to Asian problems. In April, 1966, Thai Foreign Minister Thanat Khoman told the foreign ministers of Malaysia and the Philippines that it was time "to take our destiny into our hands instead of letting others from far away mold it at their whim."[15] Although continuing to emphasize the need to defeat communist forces in Vietnam, he called the next year for "an Asian peace"—a peace that would spur regional progress, bring an end to Western interference, and lead to the removal of all foreign troops.[16]

To argue, as Rostow does, that the emergence of ASEAN as a vital, regional organization demonstrates the long-term success of America's Vietnam policies misses the mark badly. Yes, the U.S. military presence may have spurred Thailand, the Philippines, Indonesia, Malaysia, and Singapore to form ASEAN. But the United States proved more a negative reference point in ASEAN's formation than a positive impetus.

The Geostrategic Equilibrium Argument

Moving to the second core proposition, can the Vietnam War be said to have fostered a geostrategic equilibrium in Southeast Asia? This aspect of the "buying time" thesis cannot, in fact, withstand careful scrutiny any better than can the first. It assumes a direct causal relationship among quite disparate developments: the U.S. "stand against communist aggression," the gradual diminution of external threats to Southeast Asia's noncommunist nations, and the development of indigenous habits and institutions (read ASEAN here) of strategic cooperation. Yet such relationships prove exceedingly difficult to establish.

The essential argument here, at least on its surface, seems straightforward enough—even to possess a certain superficial appeal. Throughout much of the decade of the 1960s, after all, China appeared to the United States and to certain other nations in the region—especially Thailand, but also Malaysia, Singapore, the Philippines, and, after 1965, Indonesia—as a threatening, expansionist power that aimed to dominate Southeast Asia through its superior size and might, its ideological appeal, and its sizable overseas Chinese communities. By the time the United States withdrew its last contingent of troops from South Vietnam in early 1973, Beijing appeared much less threatening. Indeed, the Nixon administration was by then cultivating it as a strategic partner, one that presumably shared a common commitment to peace and stability in Southeast Asia. More, the ASEAN states had by that time taken some important steps toward regional unity and political cooperation. Why not, then, link this favorable alteration in what might be called the regional balance of power, as the "buying time" theorists do, to the brave and principled stand of the United States in Vietnam? There are numerous reasons why such an attempted linkage falls well short of basic evidentiary and logical requirements. I will address just some of the more glaring ones.

Any scholar who seeks to prove the validity of this thesis must substantiate at least four hypotheses: (1) that China was, in fact, a real threat to the peace and stability of Southeast Asia's noncommunist states in the 1960s; (2) that it ceased to be a serious threat principally *because* of the American military commitment in Vietnam; (3) that ASEAN found a constructive regional role for itself in good part because of the time bought for its member states by U.S. intervention in Indochina; and (4) that each of these favorable developments were not just unintended byproducts of the U.S. decision to fight in Vietnam but an integral result of conscious and deliberate American policy commitments.

Others essays in this volume, especially those by Qiang Zhai and Xiaoming Zhang, deal much more fully with the complex subject of Chinese intentions and capabilities vis-à-vis Southeast Asia during the 1960s. Suffice it to say that their contributions, together with an impressive existing body of literature, cast serious doubt on the image promoted by the "buying time" theorists of an aggressive, expansionist China bent on establishing hegemony over Southeast Asia.

As for the second point, solid evidence has yet to be advanced in support of the notion that China metamorphosed from a predatory, expansionist power to a relatively pacific and cooperative one (if, indeed, it did so metamorphose) not only *during* the Vietnam War era but *because* of the American stand against communism in Vietnam. It would be extraordinarily difficult to develop such a causal link, in any case, because so many other variables affected Chinese foreign policy during this period, foremost among them the deepening Sino-Soviet split and China's internal upheaval. Yet, without persuasive evidence linking changes in Chinese objectives toward Southeast Asia to the Vietnam War, the "buying time" theorists find themselves trapped in another *post hoc* condundrum.[17]

What, then, about ASEAN's emergence? Surely some connection must obtain between the growing strength and vitality of ASEAN in the early and mid-1970s and U.S. actions in Vietnam. Actually, a strong connection between the two probably *does* exist. But it is decidedly not the one identified by Rostow and his associates. The United States, as already noted, served largely as a negative impetus for the states that forged the Association of Southeast Asian Nations in 1967. As much as anything else, those states were searching for an alternative to the massive intervention of powers external to the region and to the widespread death and destruction that had resulted from such interventions. "The continuing tragedy of our time," groused Philippine Foreign Secretary Carlos Romulo in 1971, "is that our affairs are very much shaped by the ill-considered actions of the superpowers."[18] Such sentiments ran deep. When the ASEAN foreign ministers, meeting in Kuala Lumpur in November, 1971, declared a common commitment to establish Southeast Asia as a "Zone of Peace, Freedom, and Neutrality," a zone "free from any form or manner of interference by outside powers," they were seeking to bring peace and security to the region on their own terms. Although plans for implementing the Kuala Lumpur declaration remained exceedingly fuzzy, the neutralization initiative is nonetheless suggestive of an important trend in regional affairs. By the early 1970s, the ASEAN states were increasingly taking the initiative by proposing indigenous solutions to indigenous problems.[19]

Those efforts, it bears emphasizing, were given urgency by America's adoption of a reduced regional role during the late 1960s and early 1970s. Johnson's halting move toward disengagement following the shattering Tet Offensive of 1968, the Nixon doctrine of the following year, the steady removal of U.S. forces from Vietnam, Nixon's dramatic reversal of America's China policy, his watershed trip to the Forbidden Kingdom in 1972, the Paris peace accords of 1973 — taken together, those actions portended a tectonic shift in U.S. interests and policies in Southeast Asia. America's diminished military presence in the area, in tandem with Nixon's sudden embrace of the once-hated Chinese as putative strategic partners, profoundly altered the geopolitical environment within which Southeast Asia's indigenous states operated. Those developments impelled the ASEAN states toward greater cohesion and self-reliance. Long-serving Thai Foreign Minister Thanat Khoman exclaimed bitterly to a New York audience in January, 1970: "We in Asia cannot sit idly by and wait for doomsday to come." The "relevant question" now, he told his American listeners, was "how Southeast Asia will fare when those who have for so long cast their shadows over the region will have gone from the scene."[20]

As the United States lurched from overinvolvement to headlong retreat from empire in the space of a few years, it is hardly surprising that Southeast Asians increasingly came to doubt American reliability. The failure of the Nixon administration to consult in advance with any of its Southeast Asian allies about the impending China policy shift compounded the problem. In August, 1971, a Thai political cartoon acidly captured prevailing elite and popular feelings throughout the region by portraying Nixon dropping a bomb on his Southeast Asian allies from a high-flying jet bound for China.[21]

In short, seeing ASEAN's emergence not only as a positive, but as an *intended,* outcome of America's Vietnam commitments makes little sense. The association can more accurately be seen as an indigenous alternative to a U.S.-dominated regional order, its growing vitality in the 1970s an indigenous adaptation to a rapidly changing regional security environment. The United States intervened in Vietnam, it must be remembered, because of its own global interests. American intervention there was never primarily about Vietnam, nor was it primarily about Southeast Asia. To look at subsequent developments in that region, no matter how favorably some might have turned out from a long-range perspective, as an intended byproduct of U.S. intervention is to misread and distort history badly.

The Economic Development Argument

That leaves, then, the third and final leg of the "buying time" thesis. To what extent did the Vietnam War stimulate the economic development of Southeast Asia's noncommunist states? The *Wall Street Journal* offered its version of the Rostow thesis in a feature article on Southeast Asia that appeared in 1985. "The U.S. war effort—despite its ultimate failure—pumped billions of dollars into the region," the influential business daily reported, "and provided what Asian leaders now call 'breathing room' for their fledgling post-colonial governments to shake down."[22] But securing tight, causal connections between the Vietnam War and the economic success stories that this essay began with—and which the Rostow/*Wall Street Journal* assertions require—remains a highly problematic exercise.

Strikingly few of the political economists, development experts, or economic historians who have analyzed Southeast Asia's recent boom have attributed it, in any appreciable way, to the Vietnam War. Indeed, hardly any of the books and articles produced by specialists in the economic development of Southeast Asia so much as mention the Vietnam War. The dominant strand in the literature—what is typically categorized as the free market, or liberal bourgeois, approach—emphasizes the critical importance of the ASEAN nations' shift in the late 1960s and early 1970s from import-substitution strategies to export-oriented growth, the crucial role played by Japanese investment in the 1970s, the oil boom of that decade, and the influx of South Korean, Taiwanese, and Hong Kong investment in the 1980s. These themes are prominent in the work of such major figures as Richard Robison, E. K. Fisk, J. A. C. Mackie, Donald Crone, Chris Dixon, P. W. Preston, Ian Brown, R. S. Milne, and Diane K. Mauzy.[23]

Several representatives of this free market school of thought also stress the importance of global economic shifts in capitalist modes of production. In his recent survey of Southeast Asian economic history, for example, Ian Brown writes: "An important part of the explanation for modern capitalist South-East Asia's dramatic industrial growth lies in the changes that have taken place in the advanced industrial economies, the effect of which has been to encourage the relocation of entire industries or particular industrial processes to the Third World." The ASEAN countries, with their oversupply of industrious, docile, and cheap workers proved especially alluring to companies looking to cut labor costs by shifting production sites. In addition, the ASEAN states also possessed a treasure trove of natural resources and enough communication, commercial, and administrative networks to support a substantial modern industrial sector. Again, Brown: "Cheap labour, rich natural resources, and, commonly, high quality infrastructures were the crucial pre-conditions that made it possible for the capitalist states of South-East Asia to respond to the new opportunities created by restructuring in the advanced industrial core."[24]

Identifying with any degree of precision the root causes of contemporary Southeast Asia's economic growth remains a complex, elusive, and highly contentious enterprise. A number of prominent Marxist scholars argue, to further complicate the issue, that Southeast Asian development is a phony or "ersatz" form of capitalism that has brought wildly uneven results, a point of view that has gained force with the economic crisis currently plaguing the region.[25] My point here is a simpler one: the Rostow argument may have seeped into popular discourse, especially within certain conservative political circles, but it has had surprisingly little impact on serious scholarly investigations of Southeast Asian development.

There are a few notable exceptions, of course, and at least one deserves mention here. The political scientist Richard Stubbs has argued that the external security environment in the Asia-Pacific region was closely intertwined with, and did contribute positively to, the economic development of the ASEAN states—much as it did in the earlier cases of Japanese, South Korean, and Taiwanese economic growth. To summarize his intriguing argument briefly: U.S. aid to and military spending in Thailand contributed significantly to the growth and development of the Thai economy. Between 1950 and 1975, the United States pumped approximately $650 million in economic aid into Thailand; it provided $940 million in regular military assistance between 1951 and 1971; $760 million in operation costs, in the acquisition of military equipment, and in payments for Thai troops serving in Vietnam; it contributed another $250 million for the construction of U.S. bases there; and it provided still another $850 million in expenditures by U.S. military personnel stationed in Thailand or visiting the country on R&R junkets. Singapore also benefited substantially from the economic activity spurred by the Vietnam War, according to Stubbs, emerging as a center of the local entrepôt trade and as the region's chief petroleum refining center. The value of Singapore's exports to the United States rose from only $52 million in 1966 to $858 million by 1974. The capital influx and increased absorptive capacities traceable directly to the Vietnam War, in his view, thus sparked real growth in both of those states.

But Stubbs also offers some important caveats. He points out that the Vietnam War had little economic impact on Indonesia, Malaysia, or the Philippines. And he stresses that the war, together with certain other external developments (including the earlier conflict in Korea and the later influx of Japanese capital into Southeast Asia), are best seen as necessary, "though by no means sufficient" conditions for the economic growth of certain countries within the region.[26] His overall assessment, then, falls well short of the grandiose claims staked by Rostow and the *Wall Street Journal*. Moreover, Stubbs's modest work would seem a rather weak reed upon which to base the economic dimension of the "buying time" thesis. Surely no one is suggesting that a justification of the Vietnam War can be found in the positive spin-off effects it exerted on the economic development of Thailand and Singapore!

A stronger argument for the positive economic consequences of the fighting in Indochina concerns Japan. As Thomas R. Havens and Michael Schaller have demonstrated, Japan became the chief economic beneficiary of the Vietnam War; it managed to capitalize upon U.S. procurement orders, both directly and indirectly, to push its already soaring economic growth rate ever higher. According to data compiled by its Ministry of International Trade and Industry (MITI), Japan earned at least an additional $1 billion per year from Vietnam War–related export growth. Many of the additional dollars harvested by the Japanese were then circulated back into the Southeast Asian region in the form of investments, grants, and loans, spurring some modest economic growth, especially in Thailand and the Philippines.[27] Again, though, these effects were largely indirect, uneven, and unintended results of American policy in Vietnam—a far cry from the "we won the war in Southeast Asia" claims of Rostow.

The "buying time" thesis, in sum, cannot withstand careful, critical scrutiny. This essay suggests, however, that there has been at least one truly fundamental, if *unintended,* consequence of U.S. intervention in Vietnam for the peoples of Southeast Asia: namely, the emergence of an increasingly assertive and cooperative indigenous regional grouping. ASEAN's historic announcement on May 31, 1997, that Myanmar, Laos, and Cambodia would soon be admitted to full membership in the association serves as but the most recent indication of that association's central role in regional affairs. The decision shattered decisively Southeast Asia's artificial division into communist and noncommunist blocs, with isolationist Myanmar standing apart from both—and ran directly counter to U.S. advice.

"We are complete now," observed Indonesian Foreign Minister Ali Alatas about the decision to admit the outside three to the ASEAN fold. "And we are in a better position to contribute to peace and stability in our region."[28] More than at any time in this century, Southeast Asia's future certainly seemed to lie in the hands of Southeast Asians. And the Vietnam War, ironically, has had much to do with that.

Chapter 11

The 1967 Middle East Crisis

A Second Vietnam?

JUDITH A. KLINGHOFFER

On June 8, in the midst of the Six-Day War, a Soviet informer described Moscow's intentions in inducing the crisis that led to the war thus: "The USSR had wanted to create another trouble spot for the United States in addition to that already existing in Vietnam. The Soviet aim was to create a situation in which the US would become seriously involved, economically, politically, and possibly even militarily and in which the US would suffer serious reverses as a result of its siding against the Arabs."[1]

The Soviet Decision to Create a Second Vietnam

Because the Johnson administration "was not naive," as Walt Rostow noted, this report did not come to it as a great surprise.[2] In fact, this understanding of the origins of the 1967 Middle East crisis was widely shared by many contemporary policymakers, analysts, media, and public. Curiously, though there is no dearth of studies of either the Vietnam or the Six-Day Wars, there are no systematic studies of the close link between the two conflicts.

Even recent declassification of documents filled with cross references have yet to make an impression on the students of the war in Vietnam. Students of the Middle East do make passing references to the influence of Vietnam on the American response to the crisis, but their paltry nature during a 1995 Middle East symposium led Robert Komer (who, like other valuable administration resources, had been transferred from the Middle East to Vietnam) to say:

I have a comment on the subject of parochialism. During the discussion this morning, I was stunned to see that in the Israeli presentation of what the U.S. attitude was going to be and in the Arab responses, there was no discussion of Vietnam. Let me tell you that by May 1967 we had 500,000 men in Vietnam, a half million. If you want to know where the fleet was, it wasn't in the Red Sea; it was over there on Yankee Station off Hanoi. So in the eyes of the president, who spent twenty times as much time on Vietnam as he did on the Arab-Israeli fracas, even at its height, there was no possibility of the United States adopting a military role or intervening militarily or providing a great deal of support."[3]

Former Israeli diplomat and Lyndon Johnson's personal friend, Ephraim Evron, protested that he did "mention" it. In fact, he even admitted to having been "naive" in believing those "including the vice-president" who had assured him that "if the president went to war over Vietnam, surely he's not going to leave you [Israel] in a lurch."[4]

The Arab participants remained silent, though even a cursory examination of their contemporary media reveals its enormous preoccupation with the correct application of the lessons of the Southeast Asian struggle and the effect of the American embroilment in it. Arab politicians (at the urging of "moderate" Habib Bourguiba) redefined the Arab-Israeli dispute into a Palestinian-Israeli one by substituting their call for "the implementation of the UN resolutions" with a call for "the liberation of Palestine." Radical analysts added that because the Palestinians had no territory or army, "armed struggle" Viet Cong style was their sole road to such liberation.

As the American difficulties in Vietnam became more apparent, the number of Arab strategists favoring "armed struggle" grew. By the end of 1966, they began arguing that such a struggle would foster an atmosphere of insecurity that would undermine Israeli development by lowering immigration and increasing emigration; also, concentration on counterinsurgency techniques would damage both the Israeli economy and its military preparedness. Moreover, a combination of American fear of a "second front" induced restraint and Israeli-demonstrated moderation would not only insure that Israel would not respond with a full-fledged war (as it did in 1956), but would also limit the number and scope of its inevitable reprisals to manageable proportions. Indeed, those retaliatory actions would serve to galvanize the Palestinian population and shame Arab states into improving their armed forces and responding more aggressively to retaliatory attacks. They would enable the Palestinians to prove that they too deserved the support of the international community and, most especially, the support of the revolutionary world. Indeed, Palestinians should be sent to Vietnam to study methods of dealing with the defensive measures Americans planned to supply to Israel.

Some Arab strategists wished to turn Jordan into a "second Hanoi," others feared that Amman was more likely to turn into a "second Danang." The latter also argued that Israeli national cohesion prevented a Palestinian liberation army from melting into the population in the manner such an army did in Vietnam. Therefore, rather than trying to constrict the battlefield as in Vietnam, the Arabs should seek to widen it to the entire Arab front. Such a tactic would diminish projected American efforts to contain the war and might even prevent American interference. If the United States did send in forces, the role of the Palestinians would be to carry out guerrilla warfare against them. Widening the war would also undermine the logistical advantages enjoyed by Israel. Indeed, the Israeli army should be lured into the Sinai and the West Bank of Jordan and destroyed there. After all, Arab "admiration" for the Vietnamese people derived not from their specific tactics but "from their iron determination to fight and from their unusual willingness to withstand blows silently," which as contrasted so sharply with Arab "lack of response."[5]

These closely argued articles, published in the Arab press and reprinted in Israeli military outlets, demonstrate that: (1) the American failure in Vietnam served to demonstrate the efficacy of "wars of national liberation"; (2) the Arab world was replete with sophisticated analysts willing and able to take advantage of the opportunities presented by the global power struggle; and (3) Ambassador Richard Parker's observation was valid that "what cries out for explanation now, a quarter-century later, is that a scant three weeks before June 5 no one—statesman, scholar, or soldier, Eastern or Western, Israeli or Arab has predicted a general Arab-Israeli war in June or even in 1967."[6]

Indeed, as analysts freely acknowledged at the time, and continue privately to admit, the only rational explanation for the sudden spring, 1967, crisis was a Soviet wish "to draw the US into the Arab-Israeli conflict, creating a 'Second Vietnam.'" That was the reason Georgiy Kornienko, the 1967 chief of the American department in the Soviet Foreign Ministry, not only spent the symposium organized for the twenty-fifth anniversary of the Six-Day War trying to refute a "Second Vietnam" thesis no one had developed but devoted numerous hours delving into the archives in the same pursuit after its completion. In the end, he was forced to follow in the footsteps of all those who refused to see: "Soviet representatives committed 'blunders,' which, if one wished, could be wrongly interpreted," but the "USSR, neither in 1967 nor at any other point, ever gave its blessing to the Arabs for war with Israel." Those innocent "blunders" included, by Kornienko's own admission, "the *triple* delivery to the Egyptians of information [about Israeli troop concentration near Syria] which as it later turned out was not wholly accurate." Egyptian President Nasser said that information induced him to take the steps that led to the war that has transformed the region and, indeed, the world.[7]

In his biography of Senator William Fulbright, Randall Woods proves that the reluctance of an American historian not to face "unacceptable" facts can parallel that of a former Soviet official. Woods resists a serious consideration of the reasons the senator and his aide viewed the "Middle East crisis through the prism of the conflict in Vietnam." He finds it "incredible" that the two men "saw in the week-long conflagration an opportunity to hammer out a great-power rapprochement that would in turn make possible an end to the fighting in Indochina." In fact, there was nothing incredible in the senator's advocacy of a "package deal." President Johnson advocated such a deal in Glassboro, and Kissinger and Nixon renewed the effort. Fulbright's assertions that it was "hypocritical" for Johnson to demand "restraints" from the Israelis, while attempting to bomb the Vietnamese, even leads Woods to empathize with the Johnson administration. He writes: "Well aware that the vast majority of the American people were pro-Israeli, Fulbright and Stuart Symington declared that the United States was unprepared to mediate in the Middle East and to protect its "vital interests"—a euphemism for Israeli security—because it was bogged down in Vietnam. Johnson, Rusk and McNamara were furious. What an irony, Rusk remarked bitterly; the dove was sprouting talons."[8]

Actually, as Pacificist Rusk freely acknowledged, Fulbright's opposition to the Vietnam War (like that of George Ball) stemmed not from his dovishness, but from his Atlanticism.[9] He knew that the American position in Europe and the Middle East were inextricably linked. Fulbright's reference to American "vital interests" was not a euphemism for Israeli security but for continued Western access to Middle Eastern oil and bases. As Ambassador Richard Parker knows only too well, "the U.S. government's definition of American interests before 1967 was, first, denial of the region to the Soviets and, second, access to its oil on 'reasonable terms.' *After 1967,* the security of Israel was added to this list."[10]

Aware of the ultimate importance of the Middle East to the United States, Brezhnev was sure that serious regional trouble would force Johnson to give up his dogged effort to settle the Vietnam War in 1967 by "bombing North Vietnam into the stone age." As Anatoly Dobrynin's memoirs reveal, the Kremlin did not necessarily object to the American embroilment in Vietnam. Nor was it interested in ending a war that served to "divert Washington's attention from Europe . . ."[11] Indeed, "the Soviet government did not have any clear plan for settling the conflict" apart from "the simple demand" for an end to the bombing of the North.

That demand was anything but simple as it represented Washington's most effective leverage on Moscow as well as Hanoi. The bombing of a communist country seriously damaged Soviet credibility by raising questions (even among its European clients) concerning Moscow's ability to protect effectively its allies. Moreover, it did so at the time the Kremlin faced a serious Chinese challenge to its leadership of the "revolutionary world."[12]

As Leonid Brezhnev angrily told Dobrynin, he was determined to meet the American challenge without sinking "in the swamps of Vietnam."[13] A far better option, he seemed to have concluded, was to open a second or perhaps even a third "revolutionary front." The Kremlin eschewed that option in the 1965 Kashmir conflict in part because it harmed their anti-Chinese ally, India. But, in July, 1966, after Washington bombed Haiphong, Moscow used a routine scenario of Palestinian sabotage followed by Israeli retaliation to serve notice that they might do so in the Middle East.[14]

This was done by initiating a UN Security Council Middle Eastern debate in which its representative Nikolai Fedorenko tied the two conflicts together. Thus, it was in the context of the Middle East that the United States and the Soviet Union carried on a week-long debate on Vietnam at the Security Council.[15] It led an American analyst to write: "Moscow might back a Near East operation carried out by Nasser and left-wing Syrian government. . . . The strategic idea is simple. The U.S. has become so heavily committed—politically and psychologically as well as militarily—in South Asia that its potential for effective response elsewhere is much weakened. The U.S. would have unusual difficulty in counteracting even a modest move in another theater; at the least, a diversionary move would have an automatically depressant effect on the Vietnam effort."[16]

That possibility was far from alien to American decisionmakers. Already in March, 1965, they had listed "sympathetic fires over Berlin, Cyprus, Kashmir, Jordan waters" as one of the "major risks" the United States might incur by its plan to bomb North Vietnam.[17] Moreover, the Joint Chiefs of Staff had warned that without a substantial mobilization of reserves, supplying the needed forces in Vietnam would "further impair US military posture and capability to maintain forward deployment to deter aggression worldwide." Meeting American commitments to NATO and other threatened areas" would mandate "mobilization (and even then dangerously late)."[18]

Since 1965, Washington had tried to appease Moscow by signaling "its interest in improved peaceful relations with the Soviet Union and the European Block."[19] Moscow responded that American officials were laboring "under strange and persistent delusion" if they thought it was possible to improve superpower relations despite the conflict in Vietnam."[20] To quiet growing

Atlanticist concern with the increased Soviet penetration into the Middle East, the president appointed a special State-Defense study group to evaluate the matter, and the North Atlantic Command planned a special meeting in which Washington hoped to convince resistant West Europeans to take over the responsibility for the Mediterranean, if not the Middle East.[21]

Upheavals in China during the winter of 1966–67 made Hanoi temporarily receptive to a negotiated settlement in Vietnam; hence, the Anglo-Soviet mediation attempt. The Kremlin blamed the United States for its failure and demonstrated its fury by instigating a near incident in which "a Soviet oiler attempted to create a collision situation by maneuvering into the path" of an American destroyer in the Black Sea.[22] The British *Economist* understood the hint. Its March, 1967, issue called Morocco-Somalia-Iran the "triangle to watch," because it was about to become the center of the Cold War due to "the change taking place in the relations between Russia and America in *other parts* of the world."[23]

On April 6, Johnson sent a letter to Hanoi via Moscow. The letter was opened, returned, but not acknowledged.[24] So, Washington decided to raise the ante by canceling the bombing prohibition within ten miles of the centers of Hanoi and Haiphong. On April 13 Ambassador Dobrynin was recalled because, according to the Soviet military attaché in Washington, "his policy towards the United States was too soft." He returned after the Six-Day War.[25]

On April 25, at the conference of European Communist Parties in Karlovy Vary, Leonid Brezhnev praised the Vietnamese for undermining American prestige and pinning down a significant portion of the American armed forces. He heralded Algeria, the United Arab Republic, and Syria as examples of the expansion of the "national liberation movements." More importantly, Brezhnev argued that the time had come to aid Third World "liberation struggles" by inflicting a defeat on imperialism "that would be felt everywhere."[26]

Washington debated the precise meaning of the new Soviet mood. John McNaughton and Zbigniew Brzezinski warned of an upcoming Soviet challenge in other parts of the world. Walt Rostow downplayed the danger. Dean Rusk expected the challenge to come in Berlin where the Soviets could control the degree of crisis better, and where their conventional forces enjoyed a significant advantage. But this anticipation overlooked the obvious damage such a move would do to Soviet-French relations, not to mention its potential for strengthening the North Atlantic Treaty Organization at a time when the United States and its allies were in the midst of an argument over who should hold the primary responsibility for the Mediterranean. A move against NATO's southern flank was bound to exacerbate the argument and provide ammunition to those who, as Johnson complained, were "saying that we are overemphasizing Asia."[27]

It also ignored Brezhnev's call "for the demand that the U.S. Sixth Fleet be withdrawn from the Mediterranean to ring out at full strength."[28] American plans to integrate NATO navies in the Eastern Mediterranean under U.S. command did not find favor in the Soviet military, especially after Andrei Grechko replaced Rodion Malinovskii as defense minister in April, 1967. Grechko, who enjoyed Brezhnev's support, had fought in the Northern Caucasus during World War II and consequently possessed an acute appreciation of the strategic value of the Middle East.[29] In short, whether to take advantage of American preoccupation with Vietnam, or to relieve the pressure on Vietnam, the Middle East seemed to have been chosen as the location for "another Vietnam."[30]

If anyone in Moscow had any doubts concerning the efficacy of such a move, the May Greek military coup ended them. The 1965 escalation in Vietnam was followed by the overthrows of Ben Bella, Sukarno, and Nkrumah. Soviet and Third World leaders viewed both the escalation and the coups as part of an American onslaught on "the forces of national liberation." They interpreted the Greek coup as a sign of another such onslaught on the way. Consequently, the coup also provided Moscow with a way to secure the collaboration of the region's central figure, Gamal Abdel Nasser. After all, the Egyptian president, whose best forces were tied down in Yemen, had repeatedly stated that the time was not right to take on Israel. However, no leader was more fearful of a U.S. Central Intelligence Agency–instigated coup than Nasser, and no regime was more vulnerable than Syria's, whose sponsorship of Fatah cross-border raids made it a probable candidate for a major retaliatory attack by Israel.[31]

To convince Nasser that his best hope for survival was to come to Damascus's aid by taking on the United States via Israel, Moscow provided him with (1) a recording of an American agent discussing plans for a Greek-like coup in Arab countries; (2) public and private misinformation indicating the existence of an "immense concentration of Israeli troops on the Syrian border"; (3) a promise to neutralize the Americans; and (4) an assurance that his military (especially his air force) was superior to that of the Israelis.[32]

On May 14, Egyptian troops began marching into the Sinai; Nasser demanded the withdrawal of UN troops and moved his own forces to the vicinity of Sharm-al Sheikh. At the same time, the UAR tightened the screws on Saudi Arabia. For the first time Nasser publicly admitted that his air force had carried out bombing raids within Saudi borders. Ousted King Saud was flown to the Saudi-Yemeni border to await his return to the throne under Egyptian auspices. A Soviet-backed, Egyptian two-prong attack on Western positions in the Middle East commenced.

The Six-Day War: An Antithesis to the Vietnam War?

On June 25, the *New York Times* reprinted a Conrad *Los Angeles Times* cartoon that showed five eyepatch-wearing Joint Chiefs of Staff members à la Israeli Moshe Dayan placing before a startled Lyndon Johnson a map of Vietnam covered with bold attack arrows. The caption read: "Now here's our plan. . . ." Obviously, the tables had turned. Not only did Israel prevent the Middle East from becoming a "second Vietnam," but the American military wished to turn Vietnam into a "second Middle East." In other words, it seemed as if the Soviet plan had badly misfired. Why? The short answer is that neither Moscow nor Washington proved able to control its clients long enough to secure a package deal along the lines described by Senator Hartke of Indiana: "The U.S.S.R. knows that the United States, with huge petroleum investments, is vulnerable in the Islamic world—and vulnerable militarily because of our preoccupation in Southeast Asia. Moscow is bargaining. The price for peace in the Middle East may be backing down in Vietnam."[33]

First, Washington tried to use the nuclear card. It publicized a June, 1965, remark Johnson made to his daughter Lucy to the effect that "he might go down in history as having started World War III." It did not seem to work. *Pravda* haughtily retorted that the story was designed "to scare somebody to show that those in the White House are ready to take any risk," but it warned that "attempts to frighten the Vietnamese people will fail" and, moreover, "these attempts will not frighten *other people either.*"[34]

So, on May 19, a reluctant Lyndon Johnson began the global bargaining process with a letter to Soviet Premier Alexei Kosygin, asking for his cooperation in getting under control "a series of situations" that he blamed on Soviet clients. In Southeast Asia the culprit was North Vietnamese support of the NLF; in the Middle East, the troublemakers were "elements (the Fatah) based in Syria," and in Latin America it was Cuba, which was "engaging in quite open and active support of violent movements." He also expressed his wish to conduct "serious discussions" on bilateral issues such as the antiballistic missile and intercontinental ballistic missile.[35]

To underline his steadfastness, the president did not cancel the first bombing of a Hanoi power plant, which took place on the very day the letter was delivered. Sixteen dovish senators tried to buttress his position with a declaration that, regardless of previous disagreement with the president's policy in Vietnam, they "wanted Hanoi, Peking [Beijing] and Moscow to have very clearly in mind the fact that we do not favor unilateral withdrawal from Vietnam."[36]

The Soviet leadership convened a special meeting of the party's Central

Committee to evaluate the situation.[37] Its response came in the form of a public statement supportive of the "Arab countries in their just struggle for national liberation," which included a warning that any attempt "to unleash aggression" in the Near East "would be met not only with the united strength of the Arab countries but also with strong opposition . . . from the Soviet Union."

Pravda added that "events in the Middle East must not be considered in *isolation*. They are closely connected with . . . the encroachment into the demilitarized zone and the stepping up of the barbarous bombing of Hanoi and with the preparation of new provocations against Cuba."[38] To add muscle to its rhetoric, Moscow notified Turkey of its plan to augment its Mediterranean squadron, which consisted of nuclear and conventional submarines, destroyers and surface-to-surface missile ships. This augmentation turned out to include newly developed amphibious forces with advanced design landing craft and naval infantry units.[39] Nasser upped the ante by announcing the closure of the Straits of Tiran, thereby activating a 1957 American commitment to Israel.

Lyndon Johnson made some chess moves of his own. He sent Kosygin yet another letter, warning that "your and our ties to nations of the area could bring us into difficulties which I am confident neither of us seeks;" issued a public statement declaring the closure of the Straits of Tiran to be illegal; expressed his opposition to any "overt" or "clandestine aggression" and his continued commitment "to oppose aggression" in Vietnam; ordered elements of the Sixth Fleet, carrying marines and landing craft, to sail eastward; and, last but not least, *reinstituted the bombing prohibition within the ten-mile radius from the center of Hanoi.*[40] Round one went to the Soviets. Their diversionary move succeeded in having a depressant effect on the Vietnam War.

In the United States, the public and private debates were marked by general conviction that "a two-front war is very bad and a two-continent war is even worse." But, to the chagrin of administration Pacificists, the balance of power was shifting toward the Atlanticists. At his meeting with the Senate Foreign Relations Committee, Rusk was told that because the Middle East was more important than Southeast Asia, the United States should escalate or deescalate, but get the Vietnamese war over quickly. When Senators Symington and Fulbright made such sentiments public, an angry Johnson remarked that this was just the kind of talk Kosygin wanted to hear.[41]

The military felt that it was payback time. Its representatives repeatedly told the president, the secretary of state, Congress, and the media that the United States neither had the forces needed for a Middle Eastern intervention nor a way to get them there in real time. The Sixth Fleet was under strength, and "Robert S. McNamara's insistence on using up inventories of weapons and supplies and holding down production have strained the regular forces; as officers and members of Congress have warned, there is not much cushion left."[42] In Vietnam, Admiral Grant Sharp complained that "just when the pressure is increasing by virtue of such an air campaign, and the weather is optimum over northern NVN, we must back off." Israel, argued the military, could take care of itself and, not incidentally, of American Middle Eastern interests.[43]

The administration was in disarray. CIA and American military bravado aside, military professionals were far from convinced that Israel would prevail easily. In 1956, Israel had 236 bombers and fighter planes, the Arabs had 277, and the British and French provided Israel with air cover. In 1967, Israel had 247 such planes, the Arabs 571, and no one was about to provide Israel with air cover.[44] So McNamara, who had insisted and continues to insist that the United States had the military capability to fight a two-front war, worried that Israel would get in trouble and need to be resupplied. Rusk preferred to work out a side deal with Nasser. Lyndon Johnson worried about a clash with the Soviet Union, and the Rostows pinned their hopes on an international armada.[45]

But efforts to enlist even symbolic allied support failed miserably. As Johnson complained to Walt Rostow: "Canadians and Europeans will not accept responsibility . . . they say it's not their trouble, and why should they get in the Middle East now, too."[46] In fact, everybody from the Europeans to UN Secretary-General U Thant to the American doves seemed in favor of a package deal.[47] Washington was amenable. So when Rusk heard that the Soviets told British Foreign Minister George Brown that they would participate in French-proposed four-power talks on the Middle East crisis, provided that the "war in Vietnam is QUOTE tackled with similar urgency UNQUOTE," he swiftly cabled his London ambassador: "We would be prepared to explore possibility of early talks (on bilateral repeat bilateral basis) to discuss how tensions can be lessened in both the Middle East and Vietnam."[48]

Satisfied with the manner in which the events were unfolding, Kosygin delayed answering Johnson's letter, Fedorenko downplayed the severity of the Middle East crisis at the United Nations, and Soviet spokesman Leonid Zamyatin held a rare press conference comparing the Middle Eastern and Vietnamese fronts. The West sought UN guarantees for Israel, he argued, just as Washington demanded that Hanoi give it guarantees before agreeing to halt the bombing.[49]

Fearing an imminent Soviet-American deal, which would rob him of anticipated fruits of victory, Nasser agreed to launch an air attack on Israel on May 27. Israeli intelligence got wind of the plan. They told the Americans, who told the Soviets, who scuttled the plan. However, at his May 26 meeting with Abba Eban, Lyndon Johnson did what Moscow was sure he would never do.

He pronounced all past American commitments, including those by President Eisenhower concerning the Straits of Tiran, conditional.[50]

Apparently, unhappy with his options, Johnson decided to gamble on an Israeli victory. The Soviet Union understood as much. At 2:30 that morning, an alarmed Soviet ambassador demanded an immediate audience with Israeli Prime Minister Levi Eshkol. He carried a written appeal from Kosygin "not to create a *new* area of war" and insisted on knowing whether Israel would dare to go to war without American backing. Eshkol, who was fed up with the repeated Soviet references to Vietnam, indicated that he would unless the Soviets repeated their performance during the 1965 Indian-Pakistani War and organized a Tashkent-like conference. Moscow checked with Cairo, but the Egyptians insisted that the Kremlin reject the offer that could have established it as the primary force in the region.[51]

Moscow instantly acted to neutralize the potential war zone. After weeks of ducking American officials, the Soviet chargé d'affaires asked for an "extremely urgent" meeting with Secretary Rusk. Rusk delayed the meeting until the afternoon. The chargé then handed him a letter from Kosygin that claimed "to know" that the Arabs did not "wish a military conflict," threatened "to give aid to the countries attacked, " but held out the possibility that a solution might be found to the problem of the Straits. The secretary read and orally answered the letter on the spot. Thereafter, the two superpowers "exchanged assurances with each other" to stay out of the conflict and to "make a maximum effort to restrain" their clients.[52]

The superpower exchange changed Washington's attitude toward Israeli preemption. Johnson sent Eshkol a letter that stressed Soviet threats, promised to lead an armada to reopen the Straits, and warned that he would consider Israel "the aggressor" if it "went alone." To underline his warning to Israel, and prove his good will toward the Soviet Union, Johnson ordered the Sixth Fleet to leave the eastern Mediterranean.[53]

This action suited the Soviets just fine. A jubilant Marshal Grechko told the Egyptian secretary of defense, Shams Badran, "We received confirmation today that the Sixth Fleet in the Mediterranean returned to Crete the marines it had been carrying on landing vessels. Our fleet is in the Mediterranean, near your shores."[54] Badran also reported Gromyko's urging of Egyptian restraint and Kosygin's references to superpower negotiations.[55]

Talk of those negotiations led China, which was creating yet another crisis center in Hong Kong, to charge Moscow with "selling out" its Arab allies: "The Soviet revisionist clique had once again played the role of chief accomplice in U.S. activities to intimidate the Arab countries by force and exert political pressure on them." Beijing called on the Arabs to stand tall, because the "Vietnamese people's war . . . serves as a powerful support for the Arab people's struggle against U.S. imperialism and, in its turn, the anti-U.S. struggle of the Arab people constitutes a powerful support" for the Vietnamese.[56]

A stung Soviet government officially rejected French proposals for four-party talks, in part "because the US was fighting a war in Vietnam" and ignored American appeals for rhetorical moderation at the Security Council. Fedorenko made clear that Moscow held Washington responsible for Israeli behavior. Moreover, he contrasted American behavior in the Middle East and Vietnam, asking sarcastically: "Are the people of that country (Vietnam) made of different stuff so, in their case, barbarous treatment is permissible?"[57]

A concerned Ambassador Llewellyn Thompson cabled from Moscow, suggesting that the United States further restrict the bombing of North Vietnam in part "for effect it might have on our efforts to obtain Soviet cooperation in the Middle East."[58] Ironically, superpower discussions concerning the Straits were making too much progress to suit Nasser.[59] Increasingly confident of his ability to take on Israel with impunity but unwilling to disregard Soviet admonitions, Nasser set out to provoke an Israeli attack. He did so by letting Jordan, Iraq, and the rest of the Arab states join the Egyptian-Syrian entente and encouraging Iraq to organize a conference of Arab foreign ministers to orchestrate an anti-Western oil embargo for June 4 and 5.[60]

The administration considered such a Nasserification of the region as presenting "the United States and NATO with a security crisis of major, and potentially catastrophic proportions: NATO military positions were being outflanked. Communications between Europe, Africa and Asia were threatened. . . . Oil essential to the European (and Japanese) economies could be used as lever of political coercion."[61] Still, not wishing to appear incapable of restraining its client and confident of the imminence of an Arab attack, Washington too insisted that Israel absorb the first blow.[62]

For Israel, acquiescence to American wishes meant at best getting mired in a Vietnam-type Palestinian people's war. The removal of the United Nations Emergency Force (UNEF) from Gaza had raised the prospects of renewed pre-1956 Palestinian infiltration, especially because seventy-two lookout posts in Gaza were turned over to the Palestinian army. "Nasser permitted Shukayri to get organized," but would "he permit him to act?" That was the question asked in trepidation in Israel and, provocatively, in the Jordanian press. Publicly, the Egyptian answer was that it would: "The Fedayeen are the owners of Palestine and Israel does not have the right to challenge their rights. Had the United States with all her power succeeded in blocking what she calls infiltration into South Vietnam? . . . THE ACTIONS WITHIN THE CONQUERED TERRITORY OF PALESTINE ARE LEGITIMATE."[63]

Bravado aside, during the first two weeks of the crisis, there was a marked absence of Palestinian insurgency. That changed during the third week, and the change signaled a shift in Nasser's thinking. As Nasser told the Egyptian National Assembly, he had succeeded in restoring "conditions to what they were in 1956" and "God" would help him "to restore conditions to what they were in 1948." To provide his campaign with the aura of a war of national liberation, he had to be seen as acting on the Palestinians' behalf. Permitting the Palestinian army to place mines and to open fire on Israeli border settlements was the first step in redefining the nature of the crisis; accepting Jordanian surrender was the other.[64]

On May 21, the Jordanian chief of staff came to Cairo to propose reconciliation between Hussein and Nasser. He was turned away unceremoniously. On May 29, the same day during which Nasser declared his intention to destroy Israel and reactivate the Gaza front, he also signed a mutual defense pact with Jordan. Jordanian forces were weak, but, within a day, Iraq joined the pact and promised to send Iraqi units to Jordan, an Egyptian general was given command over the joint forces, and Egyptian commando units were dispatched to Aqaba. Nasser also insisted that King Hussein permit Shukayri (the man who declared that "to liberate Tel Aviv" the Palestine Liberation Organization had first to "free Amman") to return with him to Jordan. On May 30, Hussein and Shukayri paraded down the main street of Amman; control over the Palestinians was transferred to the PLO, which immediately began to distribute weapons and to train the population at large. The stage was set for an intensified "people's war."[65] As Yitzhak Rabin observed, an Israeli failure to go to war in 1967 "would have led within as a short period of time to a difficult guerrilla war."[66]

On May 28, the Israeli government decided to give the Americans *two to three weeks* to reach a diplomatic solution; Ambassador Walworth Barbour was so notified on May 29. But, on May 30, that timetable was no longer relevant. So, in his letter to Johnson, Eshkol welcomed the American diplomatic efforts and agreed to defer action for *a week or two*.

On June 2, the Joint Chiefs of Staff informed Robert McNamara once again that the U.S. military did not have "the forces needed for any contingencies beyond Vietnam, and that U.S. planes had bombed the Soviet vessel *Turkestan,* anchored in the port of Campha, fifty miles north of Haiphong. The talk in the United Nations had been that Moscow was looking for a "deal" in which the end of the blockade of Aqaba would be repaid with an American promise not to interfere with Soviet supply ships unloading their cargo in North Vietnamese ports. Did the bombing of the *Turkestan* signal that the deal was off?[67]

Fedorenko pointedly asked: "Does the United States not know that it is the criminal aggression of the United States in Vietnam that is posing a direct threat to peace, and *not only in South-East Asia?*" Arthur Goldberg retorted: "If we needed any proof that the Soviet Union's conception of helping relieve tension in the present crisis is to engage in a cold-war exercise, we have just heard it."[68]

The outbreak of the Six-Day War surprised nobody, but the swift Israeli victory, which completely reversed the East-West strategic positions, did. American officials observed with satisfaction that "notwithstanding the scorn Soviets had previously heaped on similar US proposals in Vietnam," they had to agree "to cease fire resolutions which failed to distinguish between 'victim and aggressor.'" Moreover, the war mended NATO fences while shattering Warsaw Pact ones. East Europeans, led by Tito, responded to Nasser's temporary resignation by joining the Chinese in screaming "sell out." Even the Soviet "relationship with Hanoi, Pyongyang and other revolutionaries" was adversely affected by the Mideast fallout.[69]

Consequently, when Israel attacked the Golan Heights, and Moscow threatened to intervene militarily, the newly confident American administration (which had encouraged the attack) reacted forcefully on *both fronts*. It lifted the bombing prohibition within ten miles of Hanoi for the two days of fighting on the Syrian front and ordered the Sixth Fleet to sail toward the eastern Mediterranean. Another cease-fire *in place* cemented the Israeli-Western victory and reemphasized Soviet inability to protect its clients.[70]

Ironically, this Cold War victory left Johnson less than jubilant: The crisis undermined Americans' faith in détente, refocused attention on the Atlantic front, and highlighted the ineffectiveness of the American "step by step" approach in Vietnam. In addition, the media was filled with stories detailing the American betrayal of Israel and the failure of its Mideast policies. Feeling vulnerable politically, the president would have preferred a cooling-down period, but when Alexei Kosygin came to New York, Lyndon Johnson had no choice but to meet with him.

The Glassboro Deal

"YANKS GO HOME AND ISRAELIS GO HOME TOO!" is the graffiti message Kosygin (holding a Glassboro summit menu) was scribbling on the wall, according to Shitton, a *Philadelphia Inquirer* cartoonist. The cartoon was entitled "After-dinner Speech." Indeed, Kosygin came to the summit demanding both American and Israeli withdrawals. Hence, the conditions negotiated for one could not but influence the conditions negotiated for the other. Succumbing to Soviet and Arab demands for an Israeli withdrawal that did not mandate Arab recognition of Israel's right to exist would have grave implication for the American position in Vietnam. There was no real way of separating the two issues. That was, at least, one of the reasons why Johnson instituted "a major shift in American policy towards the Arab-Israeli dispute" by stating that Israeli withdrawal, like American withdrawal, "would take place only in the context of a formal negotiated peace between Israelis and Arabs."[71] After all, as American analysts quickly noted, the post–Six-Day War communist bloc statements used a language "lifted virtually verbatim from standard Moscow statements on China and Vietnam." Not to mention that just two days prior to the summit, the Central Committee of the Soviet Communist Party had passed a resolution stating that the Six-Day War had been the result of an American conspiracy "directed against a detachment of the national liberation movement . . . the vanguard Arab states."[72] Hence, a package deal seemed more a necessity than a mere option for both parties.

Once in Glassboro, Johnson realized that Kosygin, who shared his own preference for focusing on domestic expenditure, wanted to reduce the escalating cost of supporting his Arab and Vietnamese allies. The premier found the closure of the Suez Canal particularly burdensome, as it left Egypt teetering on the brink of economic disaster and raised considerably the price of supplying North Vietnam. Talk of the Israeli lessons for America in Vietnam led Moscow to fear an American ground attack on North Vietnam.[73]

But Johnson came to Glassboro with an ambitious package deal. He suggested that the superpowers act like responsible "big brothers" and settle between themselves the outstanding regional and bilateral issues from Vietnam to the ABM and nonproliferation treaty. Kosygin too came ready to deal. But first he tried to put Johnson on the defensive by accusing Washington of acting in bad faith for failing to prevent an Israel preemption and insisting on a cease-fire in place only four hours after agreeing to a cease-fire plus withdrawal.

These actions left him unable to negotiate on behalf of his allies, Kosygin argued. However, he brought along Nasser's personal emissary to negotiate with Rusk directly. Assuming that Johnson, as a Texan, was partial to oil interests, Kosygin also emphasized that Moscow had no designs on Arab oil.[74] An American or Israeli failure to withdraw, he repeatedly warned, would result in lengthy Arab and Vietnamese wars of national liberation and any progress on bilateral relations, including on the ABM treaty, which Johnson was so anxious to have, would depend on a solution to the Middle Eastern problem.

If a solution to this problem was Kosygin's primary goal, a solution to the Vietnamese problem was Johnson's primary goal. Thus, when Kosygin made a sketch of the Suez Canal, Johnson made one of the DMZ. Kosygin wanted Israel to withdraw from the Canal. The United States specified that "both sides withdraw 10 miles on either side of the DMZ."[75] This apparently came as no surprise to Kosygin, who began the afternoon session by announcing that, in anticipation of the summit, he had contacted Hanoi, and he had just received an answer that amounted to the following: "Stop the bombing and they would immediately go to the conference table." Kosygin even offered to act as an intermediary and offered to meet again so that he could receive and "transmit any reply the President had to make."

Johnson wanted a Soviet commitment to help the United States "obtain an agreement providing self determination for the people of South Viet-Nam." Kosygin refused. He insisted that Johnson formulate his response on paper—"without reference to Mr. Kosygin or the U.S.S.R."—then address them to Hanoi, and give them to Kosygin for transmission. Still, when the two men parted, the expectation of a reciprocal American gesture was obvious.

That night, at a President's Club fund-raising dinner in Los Angeles, Johnson sent a message to centrist "dawks and hoves": " No human being in the world wants peace in Vietnam or in the Middle East more than" he did. However, he added, "I was not elected your President to liquidate our agreements in Southeast Asia. I was not elected your President to run out on our commitments in the Middle East. If that is what you want, you will have to get another President."[76]

However, when the summit reconvened, Johnson presented Kosygin with a written response to Hanoi's message along with a personal note clarifying the American negotiating position in Vietnam. The president assured the premier that he would not send ground troops into North Vietnam and would withdraw all American troops from the peninsula once a settlement was reached. Soviet miscalculation in the Middle East had led him to fear a similar one in Southeast Asia. He then repaid Kosygin by promising to authorize Rusk to be *"flexible"* in "the search for common language" on a UN Middle Eastern settlement, but he warned that Rusk found the Egyptians less flexible than Kosygin had assumed.

Kosygin was no more satisfied than Johnson had been. His primary objective was the reopening of the Suez Canal, which Kosygin mentioned by name *seven times.* In contrast, he showed no interest in a separation of forces on the Syrian front; Johnson was not interested. Afterward, Kosygin grumbled, "We agreed on next to nothing." In fact, within months, even the something they did agree on collapsed.[77]

Later, Henry Kissinger seemed to have been caught off guard by the unpopularity of his linkage policy, but the astute Lyndon Johnson made sure that his never saw the light of day. In fact, when Walt Rostow handed Johnson a sealed envelope containing a transcript of the meetings, he "blew a fuse . . . called both Rusk and McNamara and chewed them" out because "he didn't want anyone to see that transcript." Indeed, for years thereafter no one did.[78]

Johnson promptly instructed Goldberg to be flexible on "common language" at the United Nations. In July, Goldberg and Dobrynin agreed on an "equivocal formula" so favorable to the Soviets that Dobrynin assumed that Goldberg had failed to understand its ramifications. The sole condition for a total Israeli withdrawal was a clause referring to the right of each state to an independent national state. Because Israel was not mentioned by name, Arab countries could have simply claimed that the clause did not apply to Israel and, as the resolution precluded border adjustments, there would be no need for negotiations implying recognition prior to Israeli withdrawal. Israel was ready to cry "sell out," but the Arabs disregarded Soviet advice and held out for an even better deal.[79]

In the following months American foreign policy experts became embroiled in an intense Atlanticist-Pacificist debate: was the United States still fighting an anti-Soviet Cold War and, if so, what was the role of the Middle East in it? In the House, a special subcommittee began a "Review of the Vietnam Conflict and Its Impact on U.S. Military Commitments Abroad."[80] Internally, the debate swirled around the final draft of the State-Defense Study, which stated that Moscow had turned the Middle East into a "field of competition beyond which lie the ultimate targets of Europe and worldwide position of the United States." Pacificist Nicholas Katzenbach dismissed the report as "a Cold War document," while Atlanticist Eugene Rostow supported it. Consequently, the State Department found itself unable to "ready a short memo for the President" on it.[81] Of course, recognition that the Cold War was not over, the Middle East was important, and that regionalism alone could not block a major Soviet thrust had important implications for the future of the administration's Vietnamese policy.

Two factors aided Pacificists in the fall of 1967. Despite drawbacks, the Middle East seemed under control and the Vietnam War was going well. By quickly refurbishing the Egyptian army, the Soviets succeeded in keeping Nasser in office, increasing their influence on his forces and gaining naval bases. Still, the Arab monarchs had defanged Nasser during the August, 1967, Arab summit in Khartoum: The oil-rich monarchs of Saudi Arabia, Kuwait, and Libya undertook to replace the Egyptian and Jordanian revenues lost as a result of the closure of the Suez Canal and the Israeli occupation of the West Bank. In return, Nasser promised to withdraw from Yemen, to permit renewal of oil sales to the United States and Britain, and to direct all his efforts toward preparation for a war against Israel. It went without saying that Nasser's efforts to overthrow monarchies and unite the Arab world ended. It seemed that as long as the Canal remained closed, and Nasser remained dependent on oil producers' money, American Arab clients and interests were safe. So, regardless of

"European concern over the closure of the Suez Canal," the United States "did not encourage" any "action leading towards an early opening" of the Canal at the NATO Council session or anywhere else.[82]

After all, to Johnson's chagrin, Kosygin had failed to deliver Hanoi's answer to the American note. In August, when worry about upcoming Senate hearings on Vietnam led Johnson to lift temporarily the bombing restrictions he had instituted prior to the Six-Day War, Kosygin sent him a "very negative" third-person response to his letter.[83]

On October 20, Washington-Hanoi contacts through intermediaries in Paris ended in failure and, the next day, Egypt used a Soviet radar-controlled missile to sink an Israeli destroyer. Analysts found "no evidence" that Hanoi had such missiles. Israel bombed the Egyptian oil installations near Suez. Moscow sent naval units to Port Said and Alexandria. On October 23, Washington lifted the bombing prohibition within ten miles' radius of Hanoi and Johnson sent Kosygin a tough letter, reiterating that Israel would only withdraw in the context of his five points; he also threatened to renew weapons sales to the region.[84]

During his October 24 appearance before the National Press Club, Foreign Minister Eban was asked whether he could "visualize" the situation in which Port Said or Alexandria would become "a second Haiphong, that is, a privileged sanctuary from bombing?" He chose not to answer.[85] When negotiations concerning a Middle East resolution recommenced, it was clear that because Kosygin had failed him on Vietnam, Johnson was going to fail Kosygin on the Middle East. The United States withdrew its backing of the July resolution. Kosygin appealed to Johnson, but to no avail. The Soviets and the Arabs had no choice but to accept Resolution 242, which linked Israeli withdrawal from "territories" to the termination of the state of belligerency, and mentioned the Jewish state by name. Even a mediator was to be appointed "to help achieve a peaceful and accepted settlement."[86] After all, it made little sense for Washington to pressure Israel to give up its demands for peace and Arab recognition at the time the United States was deploying half a million troops to achieve those same goals for Saigon.

The Choice

To Johnson's dismay, demands that he choose between the two Cold War fronts refused to go away. McNamara noted that growing Soviet ability to project conventional forces was eroding what used to constitute Washington's "most important advantage." Brzezinski warned that the Vietnam War served Soviet interests because its end would "simply free the US to pursue more effectively its policies in Asia and Europe." But Rusk, who shared the belief that the Vietnam War had "reached a peak" and was "beginning to decelerate slowly," retorted that "there will be a hairy period when the Soviets will have to decide whether they will let Hanoi fall without doing more in the way of assistance." In other words, the Vietnam War was about to be won and, therefore, it was not the time to ruffle Soviet feathers.[87]

In any case, a closed Suez Canal limited the efficacy of the new Soviet bases in Egypt and permitted the United States to delay its response. Eventually, the Arabs would come to realize the Soviet inability to retrieve their territories and turn to the United States. The American task was to insure that Israel did not make any "permanent moves in occupied lands," including establishing an independent Palestinian entity, which might dampen Arab hopes of future Israeli concessions.[88] The "Wisemen" concurred in November.

The year 1968 quickly undermined the American assumptions concerning both fronts: The battle of Khe Sanh and the Tet Offensive revealed that, rather than being poised for victory in Vietnam, the United States had become mired in a costly war of attrition. Moreover, the closure of the Suez Canal was insufficient to blunt the Soviet thrust in the Middle East.

In August, 1967, Nasser had agreed to move out of Yemen, but, in December, 1967, the Soviet Union moved in. To make matters worse, the British told the United States in January, 1968, that they had decided to accelerate their disengagement east of Suez. Rostow wrote Johnson: "Don't Mourn, Organize" and promised to "stimulate staff work" on a new regionalist plan for the Middle East and Southeast Asia. Assistant Secretary Luke Battle requested an urgent study "of the naval defense problem in the Arabian Sea." Iran and Saudi Arabia began to fight over the booty that one called the Persian Gulf and the other, the Arabian Gulf, while the Soviets continued to emphasize the Gulf's proximity to their southern frontier and sent vessels to visit Iranian and Iraqi ports. It was "the first Russian naval presence in the Gulf since 1903," American officials observed.[89]

During his final National Security Council Meeting in February, 1968, even McNamara acknowledged "the shortage of US resources" in the Middle East and recommended that it "be given very high priority" for American resources. He believed that "needs could be met largely from existing appropriations," but, if not, the United States "should not let a few dollars" stand in its way. "The President said he would 'not object to a little more money.'"[90] But money was not easy to come by during a worsening gold crisis fueled by balance of payments deficits, and the new secretary of defense, Clark Clifford, quickly reached the conclusion his predecessor had reached: The Vietnamese battle-front was consuming too large a share of the nation's resources.

After all, a China racked by a destructive Cultural Revolution no longer constituted much of a threat, and Southeast Asia was hardly the place to confront the Soviet Union. Johnson disagreed. Soviet behavior caused him to doubt that the Soviets "wanted to live in peace" with the United States. If, as he suspected, they did not, an American exit from Vietnam would solve little, because it "wouldn't be 24 hours" before the United States would face new challenges.[91]

Clifford asked Johnson to reconvene the "Wisemen" and suggested that General Matthew Bunker Ridgway be added to the group in order to enable the general to express his concern that the United States did not have "enough strength to meet a new crisis" in areas where it had "alliances and responsibilities" such as Europe, Latin America, Southeast Asia, and the Middle East. When the "Wisemen" met in March, 1968, Ridgway was there, and Paul Nitze told the assembled that "the time had come to wind down the costly sideshow in Vietnam and return to the center stage, facing the Soviets in Europe." The "Wisemen" could not agree more.[92]

The president, who understood that he had lost the argument, announced his decision not to seek a second full term at the end of a speech in which he did what Clifford insisted he do. He talked not about the war in Vietnam, but about peace in Vietnam. Afterward, to the growing frustration of his Paris negotiators, Johnson refused to make the concessions needed to permit a quick American exit from Vietnam. At Glassboro, Kosygin had conditioned superpower détente on the settlement of the regional conflicts. In his last year in office, Johnson conditioned regional settlements on progress toward superpower détente. His quest for a package deal embroiled him in an eight-month-long battle with Israel, American Jews, Congress and even those in his own Democratic administration who worried that he was intentionally jeopardizing the election prospects of Hubert Humphrey. For Johnson understood that Nixon was more likely than Humphrey to continue his search for such a détente. Nixon had told French President Charles de Gaulle: "I am not a doctrinaire who would oppose the communists as such. One must consider the Communist leaders and judge them as they are. However, the participation by the U.S.S.R. in the development of the Middle East crisis causes one to doubt that these leaders really want detente."[93]

It took Richard Nixon four years to establish the conditions he deemed adequate for leaving Vietnam. During that period, the Arab-Israeli conflict had indeed become awfully similar to the early stages of the Vietnam War. Israel and Egypt became embroiled in a "war of attrition," replete with Soviet advisers and terror-wielding Palestinian "liberation" forces. Once the Vietnam War was over, the Palestinians even replaced the Vietnamese as the galvanizing force of the left. In May, 1967, Charles de Gaulle had warned both Israel and Egypt: "You will fight and in so doing you will become playing pieces in the global contest between the United States and the Soviet Union. Think before you turn your countries into a 'second Vietnam.'" They would not, or could not, listen.[94]

Chapter 12

Vietnam

Toward an International History

H. W. BRANDS

International history is at once voguish, intriguing, and devilishly difficult to do well. The first attribute follows from the second, and the second at least in part from the third. What makes international history so hard is that the international historian has to master multiple bodies of knowledge, usually involving diverse languages, political cultures (including rules of access to documents and other evidence) and historiographies. Yet the payoff can be great, for the international historian gains a perspective on world events unavailable to researchers who examine the same events from the perspective of but one or two participating countries. The advantage is akin to that acquired by the first cartographers to take to the air in balloons and airplanes and apply a third dimension to the two of their charts.

An international approach is particularly appropriate to the Vietnam War. Although a civil war, the conflict in Vietnam was simultaneously a contest among the great powers. It was Vietnam's misfortune to be caught in the iron triangle encompassed by the United States, the Soviet Union, and China; to understand the Vietnam War requires understanding the geometry of that triangle, as well as the geometry that linked Vietnam to fifth, sixth, and seventh countries.

Geometry—theory, if you will—is the subject here. Suppose for the sake of argument that all difficulties of language, access and local knowledge could be waved away; what would an international history of the Vietnam War look like?

Several considerations come to mind. A first has to do with the concept of international history itself. "International," of course, simply means "between or among nations." Which nations? All the nations of the world? Those that had troops on the ground in Vietnam? The first group is too big—not just for this topic but for any other. The second is too small; neither Japan nor West Germany sent troops to Vietnam, but both had much riding on the outcome there. It was for such as the Japanese and especially the Germans that American leaders became obsessed with American credibility and fought so long in Vietnam.

A second consideration involves chronology. The wars for Vietnam filled, in one form or another, much of the twentieth century. Should the proposed international history of the Vietnam War cover this entire period? The period of intense American involvement in the 1960s and 1970s? The era of the Cold War? The age of decolonization? The half-century of communist ascendancy? The so-called American century?

How one answers these spatial and chronological questions naturally depends on how one interprets the connections between the conflict in Vietnam and other contemporaneous events of international affairs. To focus on the most obvious connection for the United States: How was the Vietnam War related to the Cold War? Europeanists at the time, and Europe-oriented scholars since, have often treated Vietnam as a sideshow to what they perceived to be the main event of international affairs during the Vietnam era: namely the Cold War in Europe. Not surprisingly, Asianists have seen things differently. Not unsurprisingly, Vietnamese and Vietnam experts have been inclined to turn the sideshow argument on its head: The fight for Vietnam was the main event; the Cold War in Europe was the distraction from the central issue of Vietnam's fate.

It is worth a reminder that this issue, like those relating to spatial and chronological context, depends not at all on facility with languages or availability of records. These latter matters are hardly unimportant, but they are distinct from the decision any historian must make as to where to center his or her story—where to locate the camera, so to speak. Is the camera in Vietnam? Is it hovering somewhere over Indochina? Is it located in geosynchronous orbit observing the entire earth? Simply stating the question in these terms serves to remind of the tradeoffs involved in international history. Getting the big picture inevitably involves sacrificing detail; capturing detail sacrifices big-picture perspective.

On this point—and in an era when American policies are often criticized for being too parochial—it might also be worth a reminder that the American failure in Vietnam resulted largely from adopting *too* international a perspective, from losing the trees for the forest, so to speak. Americans leaders fought in Vietnam to contain international communism, which may or may not have been a prudent and laudable course. But in concentrating on the international contest with the Soviet Union and China, they lost sight of the national contest for control of Vietnam. The war Americans fought in Vietnam was international; the one they lost was national.

If, for the Vietnamese, the war there is best understood as a slice of national history, rather than of international history, a case can be made for a similar interpretation regarding the United States. The mere word "Vietnam" conjures images for Americans of the first post–World War II generation that the name of no other foreign country does. It exaggerates things only a little to say that the impact of Vietnam on American history was almost as great as the impact of the United States on Vietnamese history. To be sure, the body count in Americans from the war was orders of magnitude smaller than the body count in Vietnamese, but the war shattered assumptions about the world among the American losers in a way it did not among the Vietnamese victors. To put it another way, the Vietnamese Communists emerged from the war with their illusions intact; the Americans did not.

In a similar, although generally less dramatic way, one could examine the impact of the Vietnam War on the other countries involved. The impact of the war on China and the Soviet Union was less transforming than on Vietnam and the United States; the impact on Cambodia was greater. But in each case, one is examining the national implications—that is, the implications for a single nation—of the war in Vietnam.

As to the original question of the Vietnam War as international history: Here the crux of the matter is not the impact of the war on the individual nations involved, but the impact of the war on the international system, and vice versa. (International history and diplomatic history are two distinct fields that overlap, to be sure, in the same way that social and political history overlap. But to argue that international history, which is the study of the history of the international system, is intrinsically more or less important or interesting than diplomatic history, which takes individual nations as the fundamental elements of study, is equivalent to saying that the designated-hitter rule is the end of baseball as we know it—which is to say, it is essentially a theological argument.)

So if the international history of the Vietnam War is, properly speaking, the history of the international system as it pertains to the war in Vietnam, what then?

The most direct approach to an answer is to look at the international system on the eve of the Vietnam War; to look at it again at the end of the war; and to try to figure out how much of the difference was the war's result. Immediately, of course, we once more run into the problem of dating the Viet-

nam War. Which war are we talking about, and which phase of that war? Lest we fall victim to the historian's chronic affliction of endless regression, let us take as a starting point the beginning of significant American escalation: the late Kennedy and early Johnson years. The end will be the standard milepost: the fall of Saigon in April, 1975.

With the target thus bracketed, it immediately becomes apparent that the Vietnam War formed a kind of continental divide between two drainage basins of postwar history. The period just prior to American escalation in Vietnam was the high Cold War, including the Berlin crisis of 1958–61 and the Cuban missile crisis of 1962. The period of American withdrawal from Vietnam and the fall of Saigon was the era of détente, the period of the most constructive relations between the superpowers between 1945 and the late 1980s. In other words, the signature relationship of the international structure during the period of the Vietnam War underwent a major shift during that period. The causal connection between the war and that shift remains to be considered.

But there was something else going on as well during this period. The 1960s witnessed a veritable explosion of new and newly assertive countries, most visibly in the United Nations General Assembly, where the Third World or nonaligned movement became the predominant bloc. This bloc formed a wedge that weakened the hold of the superpowers over international affairs; increasingly, both Washington and Moscow had to modify their approaches to world affairs to accommodate the interests of this growing group.

And finally, the Vietnam era witnessed a loosening of ties within the superpower alliance systems themselves. The most notable manifestation of the loosening in the West was the decision of Charles de Gaulle to pull France out of the NATO unified military structure; but difficulties among West Germany, the United States, and Britain regarding balances of payments, troop levels in Germany, and related matters put additional strains on the NATO alliance. In the same general vein, the emergence of Japan as an economic power required Washington to pay closer attention to Tokyo's concerns.

In the East, the most spectacular instance of the loosening was the definitive rupture between the Soviet Union and China, which by the late 1960s had reached the point of armed clashes along their common border and the reorientation of Soviet threat perceptions—and the redeployment of Soviet divisions—from the Elbe to the Ussuri. Not that Moscow's western front was especially secure: The reforms that constituted the "Prague Spring" of 1968 seemed sufficiently threatening to socialist solidarity for the Kremlin to send in the Red Army, thereby jeopardizing—and in the event setting back—the substantial gains Moscow had made toward achieving recognition of parity and equality with the United States, most notably in the realm of nuclear weapons.

With all these interesting things happening at the same time as the Americanization of the Vietnam War, the question of causality comes to the fore. Was the Vietnam War responsible for this transformation of the international system?

The answer proposed here comes in two parts—a qualified no and an exaggerated yes. The qualified no has to do with the fact that the Vietnam War was, in a fundamental sense, simply a single symptom of the return of the world system to something approaching normality, as the skewing effects of World War II gradually wore off. The single winner of that great contest was the United States; the other Grand Allies—Britain and the Soviet Union—were exhausted by the war (the latter physically more than morally, the former more morally than physically). The United States, by contrast, emerged stronger in every measure of national well-being: economic, moral, military, political. This moment of American supremacy could not last, and it did not. Germany and Japan began to reassert themselves, as did Britain and France after some postcolonial discombobulation. Similarly in the East: the Sino-Soviet alliance, for all the ideological fervor expressed by its architects, was an alliance of convenience, primarily induced by China's post–civil war weakness. After the new emperor in Beijing caught his breath (and especially after Russia's last czar died in 1953), the attractions of Moscow necessarily diminished. And finally, as the former colonies of the now enervated and consequently collapsing European empires—colonies including Vietnam—emerged from their century or so of enforced dependence on the Western metropolises and won their independence, the international system as a whole became more unruly. The imputed Pax Americana never really took hold outside its traditional realm of the Caribbean basin; it certainly never became a substitute for the Pax Britannica and the Pax Gallica—as the Vietnam War demonstrated.

The exaggerated yes of the proposed answer to the question of whether the Vietnam War caused the shift in the international system during the 1960s turns on the fact that even events of seismic scale have triggers, precipitants, catalysts. Did the assassination of the Austrian archduke in June, 1914, cause the Great War that started six weeks later? In the sense of the present argument, it did. This is not to say that a large war between Imperial Germany and its neighbors would not have started eventually had the Black Hand of Serb nationalism not squeezed the trigger that summer day. But that war, at that time, resulted from that assassination. The situation was similar with Vietnam, as will be argued here.

The answer is an *exaggerated* yes, and here is the exaggeration: The Vietnam War did not simply cause the loosening of the international system during the 1960s; it was actually responsible for the end of the Cold War. Or to put it in the terms applied above, Vietnam was not a sideshow; it was not even the main event; it was the ringmaster.

Justifying this argument—which, admittedly, is overstated, on the reasoning that any argument worth stating is worth overstating—requires a reconsideration of when the Cold War ended, which in turn requires a close consideration of what the Cold War was all about. What made the Cold War different from other great-power confrontations was the ideological element: Each side in the contest believed it had an earth-saving mission that the other side's mere existence threatened. In this regard the Cold War ended in 1972, when détente essentially de-ideologized relations between the United States and the Soviet Union. (By this line of reasoning, the Cold War II of the Reagan administration lasted only from 1981 to the beginning of 1984, when Reagan himself extended the olive branch to Moscow, at a time when Mikhail Gorbachev was not even a gleam in the beady eyes of Yuri Andropov or the cloudy eyes of Konstantin Chernenko. This second Cold War was chiefly a failed attempt to generate interest in proto-Vietnam-like ventures in Central America and also an arms buildup, which served principally as a jobs program to cushion the shock of economic air-traffic controller Paul Volcker's hard landing of the American economy.)

Anyway, if a single development in international affairs was responsible for détente, it was the war in Vietnam. Richard Nixon realized that the only way for the United States to exit Southeast Asia with a modicum of respectability and at least a slim chance that Saigon would not collapse directly on the heels of an American withdrawal was for the Soviet Union and/or China to collaborate with Washington in arranging such a withdrawal—much in the way the big communist powers had collaborated in arranging the French withdrawal in 1954. Needless to say, Hanoi was not amenable to American pressure, despite all the bombers Nixon (following Johnson) had been sending over the North for years; but Hanoi *might* be amenable to pressure from its Soviet and Chinese sponsors. The principal immediate aim of détente was to make it worth the while of the big communist powers to apply that pressure.

It should be noted here that Nixon's need to provide cover for an American withdrawal from Vietnam was not the sole cause of détente—the exaggerated yes is not *that* exaggerated. Without the preexisting rift between Moscow and Beijing, détente would have been impossible. But the China card had been in the American deck for ten years; it was Vietnam that prompted Nixon to pick it out and to think he could get away with playing it.

Which raises the other mechanism by which Vietnam triggered the end of the Cold War. The first was by providing the impetus to détente (whose Moscow principles of 1972 constituted the peace settlement of the Cold War); the second was by convincing the American people that the game was no longer worth the candle. Americans had bought into the ideological framework of the high Cold War in the late 1940s when Harry Truman conceptually divided the world into two spheres—of democratic freedom and communist oppression—and pledged to support regimes of the former against challenges from the latter. At the time, certain individuals such as George Kennan worried about taking such liberties with a mere civil war in out-of-the-way Greece, but the Truman administration's perception of need to make its case as strong as possible suppressed such doubts. The line from the Truman Doctrine to the Gulf of Tonkin resolution was direct; the rhetoric and the reasoning changed hardly at all.

The problem was that what cost $400 million in 1947 and had succeeded cost hundreds of times that much in the 1960s and was failing. By the time Americans realized that Vietnam was a lost cause—a working majority of Americans, that is: Some still have not acknowledged today that it was a lost cause—the entire concept of an ideologically driven containment policy had fallen into disrepute. The most striking evidence of this was the equanimity, indeed enthusiasm, with which Americans accepted Nixon's opening to China. It was China—Red China—that heretofore had been the target of American containment efforts in Asia; without China to worry about, it would hardly have occurred to American leaders to get involved in Vietnam in the first place. But now that the Forbidden City was no longer forbidden, containment had lost its raison d'être.

When Franklin Roosevelt in the 1930s designed the Social Security system, he intentionally crafted it to look like the insurance scheme it was not, and although by original motivation it was an antipoverty program, he deliberately drew it to include the middle class, on the reasoning that this one-size-fits-all approach was the only way to guarantee that his handiwork would not be undone by the first Republican Congress to come along. His strategy worked brilliantly—too brilliantly, in the minds of many current-day disentitlement reformers. Harry Truman learned his lesson at FDR's knee and applied the same approach in foreign affairs. He judged that the only way to sell his policy of Cold War containment was in all-or-nothing terms. The defenders of liberty could not pick their fights; eternal vigilance—and ubiquitous effort—were the price of freedom in the post-Munich era. A defeat for freedom anywhere endangered freedom everywhere.

And so it turned out, although not in the way Truman envisaged. The American defeat in Vietnam need not, in theory, have fatally undermined the policy of containment. Americans might have acknowledged a prudential error of application while continuing to embrace the philosophical approach of containment. But having endlessly heard that once containment started to fray, there would be no end to the unraveling, they could hardly be blamed for assuming that the defeat in Vietnam discredited the whole policy. It did not help matters, of course (nor was it entirely coincidental) that they discovered that containment, particularly in Vietnam, had been riddled with deception. Containment had always been based on faith: faith that what the American government said was necessary to halt communist aggression really was necessary; and faith that the consistent frustration of the communists' expansionist goals would, as architects of containment like Kennan said, lead to the eventual undoing of Communist rule in Russia itself. After the publication of the Pentagon Papers in 1971, it was hard for many Americans to summon much faith in government; after the defeat in Vietnam became unavoidable and undeniable, it was difficult to place much faith in containment.

Détente, as designed by Nixon and Henry Kissinger, was a response both to the changing international reality of the decline of the superpowers relative to the other players in the game of nations, and to the diminishing support in America for a continuation of the Cold War—a diminution that was largely a result of the tragic experience in Vietnam. Again, this is not to say that there was something intrinsically unique about Vietnam in this regard. McGeorge Bundy remarked that pretexts for escalation in Vietnam were like streetcars—if you missed one, another would come along soon. Vietnam as a whole was something like that for the United States: If it had not been Vietnam, it might have been the Philippines or Panama or Angola or someplace else. The open-ended nature of American Cold War containment virtually guaranteed that the policy would be pushed to the point of unsustainability. Sooner or later, the costs of enforcing an anticommunist status quo in some particular locale would exceed the benefits that that status quo could be expected to yield. Given the inertia of the American political system, it was a fair bet that the costs would greatly exceed the benefits before American leaders mustered the courage to change course. And given the seamless rationale for containment, it was almost as good a bet that when this happened, the disillusionment that followed would not be confined to the locale in question. The policy of containment had become so wrapped up in American Cold War ideology that unwrapping the policy almost required overthrowing the ideology (which brings to mind the remark attributed to John Adams to the effect that ideology is the science of idiots.) This, to a large degree, is what happened.

So, back to the basic question of the Vietnam War and international history. If the above has any merit, it would appear that the Vietnam War, far from being a sideshow of international history during the post-1945 period, was in fact an absolutely critical contributor to the evolution of the international system. Put differently, any attempt to explain the most important development of the Vietnam era—what here has been called the end of the real Cold War, and what just about everyone accepts as at least the end of Cold War I and the emergence of détente—fails completely without central reference to the war in Southeast Asia. Put still differently, it was Vietnam's fate—and it contributed to Vietnam's tragedy—during the decades from the 1940s to the 1970s to be perceived by the great powers as worth fighting over. A quarter-century after that fighting ended, it ought to be Vietnam's fate to be perceived by historians of the international system as eminently worth studying.

Notes

Introduction by Lloyd C. Gardner

1. "Cabinet Room, Wednesday, July 21, 1965," The Papers of Lyndon Baines Johnson, Meeting Notes File, Box 2.
2. Draft Memorandum, Nov. 3, 1965, *Foreign Relations of the United States, vol. 4, Vietnam: July–Dec., 1965* (Washington: Government Printing Office [hereafter G.P.O.], 1966), pp. 514–18.
3. U.S. Senate, Foreign Relations Committee, *Hearings: Supplemental Foreign Assistance Fiscal Year 1966 — Vietnam,* 89th Cong., 2d sess. (Washington: G.P.O., 1966), p. 77.
4. "Memorandum of a Conversation," Dec. 11, 1967, *Foreign Relations of the United States, 1964–1968,* XIII, pp. 646–48 (hereafter cited *FRUS*).
5. Lloyd C. Gardner, *Approaching Vietnam: From World War II through Dienbienphu* (New York: W. W. Norton & Co., 1988), pp. 57–58.

Chapter 1 by John Prados

1. H. W. Brands, "Vietnam: Toward an International History," ms.
2. Neil Sheehan, et al., eds. *The Pentagon Papers as Published by the New York Times* (New York: Bantam Books, 1971), p. 365.
3. Ibid., p. 432.
4. Frank Costigliola, "The Vietnam War and the Challenge to American Power in Europe," ms., quoted p. 2.
5. Ibid., p. 16.
6. Ibid., p. 12.
7. Lloyd Gardner, "Fighting Vietnam: The Russian-American Conundrum," ms., p. 6.
8. Qiang Zhai, "An Uneasy Relationship: China and the DRV during the Vietnam War," ms., p. 1.
9. Xiaoming Zhang, "Belligerent Allies: China, the Soviet Union, and the Vietnam War," ms., tables 1 and 2.
10. Robert K. Brigham, "Vietnam at the Center: Patterns of Diplomacy and Resistance," ms., p. 18.
11. Robert J. McMahon, "What Difference Did It Make? Assessing the Vietnam War's Impact on Southeast Asia," ms., pp. 5 et seq.
12. Ibid., pp. 17–22.
13. Hiroshi Fujimoto, "Japan and the War in Southeast Asia, 1965–67," ms., p. 16.
14. Kil J. Yi, "A Demanding Ally: South Korea and the Vietnam War," ms.
15. Unfortunately (or otherwise) the War of Jenkins's Ear has largely passed out of currency as a subject of diplomatic historical analysis. For the most part, detailed sources date from the 1950s or 1960s. Recent treatments can be found in M. S. Anderson, *The War of the Austrian Succession, 1940–1748* (London: Longman, 1995),

pp. 11–20; and also, Reed Browning, *The War of the Austrian Succession* (New York: St. Martin's Press, 1996), pp. 16–25, 28–29. These books draw further attention, just by their titles, to the way an escalatory process begun with Jenkins's Ear led to general war.

Chapter 2 by Lloyd C. Gardner

1. *Washington Post,* June 29, 1997, p. CO1.
2. David K. Shipler, "Robert McNamara and the Ghosts of Vietnam," *The New York Times Magazine,* Aug. 10, 1997, pp. 30–35, 42, 50, 56–57.
3. Arthur Schlesinger, Jr., "The Origins of the Cold War," *Foreign Affairs* (Oct., 1967): 22–52.
4. "Memorandum from the Chairman of the National Security Council Working Group," Nov. 24, 1964, in Department of State, *FRUS, 1964–1968,* vol. I, *Vietnam, 1964,* pp. 938–42.
5. Quoted in Robert Johnson, *Improbable Dangers: U.S. Conceptions of Threat in the Cold War and After* (New York: St. Martin's Press, 1994), p. 141. (Emphasis in original.)
6. "Notes Taken at Leadership Meeting on Aug. 4, 1964," *Johnson Papers,* Vietnam Reference File.
7. Ilya Gaiduk, *The Soviet Union and the Vietnam War* (Chicago: Ivan R. Dee, 1996), pp. 12–13. With the war ending the way it did, however, Moscow drew the wrong lessons from American defeat, and plunged ahead into Afghanistan, argues Gaiduk, an important point certainly—but not a suggestion of Soviet manipulation of Hanoi to its own purposes. See pp. 249–50.
8. "Notes Taken at Leadership Meeting on August 4, 1964," *Johnson Papers,* Vietnam Reference File.
9. On this point, see George McT. Kahin, *Intervention: How America Became Involved in Vietnam* (New York: Alfred A. Knopf, 1986), pp. 168–70. It is difficult to assign a proper weight to this motive, because there were several well-known factors involved. Subsequent "interventions" to prevent independent action by Saigon leaders suggests that it was indeed a major consideration.
10. Highly suggestive in this regard is the recent provocative study by Barbara Ehrenreich, *Blood Rites: Origins and History of the Passions of War* (New York: Metropolitan Books, 1997).
11. See, William Stueck, *The Korean War: An International History* (Princeton: Princeton University Press, 1995), for the readiness of American leaders to consider deposing Syngman Rhee for violating this Cold War rule.
12. "Memorandum of Conversation Between Secretary of State Rusk and Prime Minister Khanh," Apr. 18, 1964, *FRUS, 1964,* I, p. 244.
13. Memorandum to Rusk from William Sullivan, with attachment, May 23, 1964, ibid., pp. 351–55.
14. Memorandum of Conversation at Vienna, June 3, 1961, *Johnson Papers,* National Security File, Country File, Box 228. Kennedy's wording is of some interest, as it implied no specific concern about Third World struggles beyond avoiding a direct superpower clash. Khrushchev, however, had made the point during this conversation that it was American "intervention" on behalf of reactionary regimes that drew in outside support, and posed the danger of a confrontation.
15. Memorandum to Walter Jenkins from Leonard Marks, Nov. 25, 1963, ibid., Box

229. How indicative Dobrynin's assertions about Khrushchev's attitude really were, given arguments that the Soviet ruler had placed missiles in Cuba because of a special attachment to Castro as the new revolutionary hero, may be a useful question, but it is not really germane to American considerations of a possible change in Soviet policies—if encouraged by a combination of firmness and receptivity.

16. Two sets of notes on this meeting exist, "President's Talk with Mikoyan," Nov. 26, 1963, ibid., Box 228, and "Memorandum of Conversation," Nov. 2, 1963, *FRUS, 1961–1963,* XI, pp. 894–95. Johnson's pledges to Mikoyan that the United States was not planning an invasion obviously did not cover subversion. The next day, indeed, the president met with CIA Director John McCone to ask "how we planned to dispose of Castro. He said he did not wish any repetition of any fiasco of 1961, but he felt that the Cuban situation was one we could not live with and we had to evolve more aggressive policies." Ibid., p. 896.

17. "Memorandum for the Record," Dec. 3, 1963, *Johnson Papers,* National Security File, Country File, Box 229.

18. "Memorandum for the Record: Lunch with Soviet Ambassador Dobrynin," Dec. 18, 1963, ibid. Unless this was a hint of some sort, Bundy's comments here were disingenuous, for the next day Johnson heard him outline various possibilities of "increasing our pressures" on Cuba with the ultimate aim of removal. "Memorandum of a Meeting with President Johnson," Dec. 19, 1963, *FRUS, 1961–1963,* XI, pp. 904–908.

19. "Lunch with . . . Dobrynin," *Johnson Papers,* Country File, Box 229.

20. "Memorandum for the Record," Dec. 31, 1963, ibid.

21. Anatoly Dobrynin, *In Confidence* (New York: Times Books, 1995), p. 117.

22. Gaiduk, *Soviet Union and Vietnam War,* pp. 30–31.

23. "Summary Record of the 548th Meeting of the National Security Council," Feb. 10, 1965, *FRUS, 1964–1968,* II, pp. 216–20.

24. "Congressional Briefing," Feb. 25, 1965, *Johnson Papers,* Congressional Briefings, Box 1.

25. Gaiduk, *Soviet Union and Vietnam War,* p. 30. "The Pleiku incident and U.S. retaliation destroyed what was left of Moscow's hope to avoid an internationalization of the conflict in Vietnam. As a result, the Soviet Union would be forced to set aside its policy of propaganda and noninvolvement and plunge into a war with unpredictable consequences."

26. Undated (Feb., 1965), untitled memorandum, *Johnson Papers,* National Security File, International Travel, Boxes 28–29.

27. It is not possible in this paper to go beyond speculation on some of these purposes, for example, the utility argument for fighting the war in Vietnam to discredit "new" leftist admiration and "solidarity" with iconic figures from this alien world, Mao, Castro, Ho Chi Minh, Nkrumah. There was a circular dynamic at work here, for the greater the effort to discredit Ho by showing that "nation-building" in South Vietnam was a success, the greater the "alienation" from American methods. And, as we shall see below, the efforts to incorporate Russia into the West by bombing North Vietnam prevented, in the final analysis, any cooperative effort from getting off the ground, and defeated attempts to carry on other diplomatic business as well.

28. "Telcon: Chalmers Roberts, Ball," Apr. 9, 1965, *The Papers of George Ball,* Box 7, LBJL.

29. Rusk to Kohler, July 1, 1965, and Kohler to Rusk, July 2, 1965, *Johnson Papers,*

Country File, Russia, Boxes 220–21. It is worth noting that at this early date, the American representative in Moscow foresaw what Hanoi's attitude to third party approaches would be throughout the war, and which came up at the 1997 conference as the essential American error.

30. Kohler to Rusk, July 13, 1965, ibid.
31. Memorandum of Conversation, July 15, 1965, *FRUS, 1964–1968,* III, pp. 147–52.
32. John C. Guthrie, Minister-Counselor, to Rusk, July 26, 1965, with enclosed memorandum of conversation, *Johnson Papers,* Country File, Russia, Boxes 220–21. Unfortunately, *FRUS* editors did not include the transcript in *FRUS, 1964–1968,* III, where the record of the first conversation can be found. But they did put together a very important editorial note on pp. 179–80 on key elements of the conversation, and the reaction in Washington.
33. Gaiduk, *Soviet Union and Vietnam War,* p. 54.
34. "Memorandum of Conversation: Vietnam," July 19, 1965, *Johnson Papers,* Agency Files, Box 66.
35. Thomas Hughes to Rusk, July 22 and 24, 1965 (copies for Bundy), ibid., Country File, Russia, Boxes 220–21; Gaiduk, *Soviet Union and Vietnam War,* p. 55; *FRUS, 1964–1968,* III, editorial note, pp. 179–80.
36. "Telcon: McCloy, Ball," July 23, 1965, *Ball Papers,* Box 4.
37. Oral History of W. Averell Harriman, LBJL, pp. 12–13. Harriman was scathing about his foes in the State Department, though he apparently did not include McGeorge Bundy, who was the real skeptic, among them. These anonymous opponents believed, Harriman said in loaded phrases, that the Russians were supposed to want to see China diverted to Southeast Asia as well, "just as Chamberlain tried to divert Hitler to the East to Russia, rather than to the West." One was not supposed to talk about the origins of World War II in those terms during the Cold War.
38. Bundy to Johnson, Nov. 25, 1965, with enclosures, *Johnson Papers,* Country File, Vietnam, Box 229. See also, Bundy to Hamilton Fish Armstrong, Nov. 25, 1965, *Hamilton Fish Armstrong Papers,* Box 109, Seely Mudd Library, Princeton University, Princeton, N.J.
39. See Lloyd C. Gardner, *Pay Any Price: Lyndon Johnson and the Wars for Vietnam* (Chicago: Ivan R. Dee, 1995), pp. 271–76.
40. Ibid., and Gaiduk, *Soviet Union and Vietnam War,* p. 84.
41. "Meeting in the Cabinet Room," Jan. 22, 1966, *Johnson Papers,* Meeting Notes File, Box 2.
42. "Meeting in the Cabinet Room," Jan. 28, 1966, ibid.
43. Ibid.
44. Gardner, *Pay Any Price,* p. 241.
45. Jan. 19, 1966.
46. "Meeting in the Cabinet Room," Jan. 28, 1966, *Johnson Papers,* Meeting Notes File, Box 2.
47. Spurgeon Keeny to Robert Komer, Mar. 19, 1966, ibid., Files of Walt Rostow, Box 10.
48. Rostow to Johnson, Apr. 5, 1966, ibid., Rostow Memos for the President, Box 7.
49. Hughes to Rostow, Aug. 6, 1966, ibid., Box 9.
50. Draft, May 10, 1966, ibid.
51. "Memorandum of Conversation: Southeast Asia," May 26, 1966, ibid., White House Central Files, Southeast Asia, Box 66; Komer to Valenti, Mar. 29, 1966, ibid., Rostow, Memos for the President, Box 7.

52. Gaiduk, *Soviet Union and Vietnam War,* pp. 86–87.

53. Ibid., p. 88, and Harriman to Johnson and Rusk, Sept. 16, 1966, *Johnson Papers,* Agency Files, Box 67.

54. Harriman to Johnson and Rusk, Oct. 3, 1966, ibid., Rostow, Memos for the President, Boxes 11–12.

55. "Memorandum of Conversation: Miscellaneous Matters," Oct. 10, 1966, ibid., Country File, Russia, Box 228.

56. Ibid.

57. "Memorandum of Conversation: Non-proliferation," Oct. 10, 1966, ibid., and "Memorandum of Conversation: Non-proliferation," Oct. 17, 1966, ibid., Boxes 220–21. The intense discussions on NPT (Nonproliferation Treaty) prospects are detailed in *FRUS, 1964–1968,* XI, pp. 356–97. Gromyko's anxiousness to get a treaty completed within a few months was apparent to all those American officials who talked with him. The Soviets, read one report of his visit, considered NPT a major objective, "which will be pursued despite Vietnam and other difficulties." Ibid., p. 397. The major hang-up was the question of whether or not it would prohibit the United States from sharing hardware with a currently non-nuclear nation—which meant the Federal Republic of Germany—through the Atlantic Alliance. Also at issue was a stickier matter of whether, in the case Europe achieved a truly federated government, that federation would succeed to the nuclear status of one of its members, e.g., France or Great Britain. Hence Gromyko's visit might well be taken to suggest that Russia would help on Vietnam, should it be assured that all the loopholes against German control of nuclear weapons had been closed. The issue needs much more elaboration than is possible here.

58. Gardner, *Pay Any Price,* pp. 317–18.

59. Ibid., 338–39. Walt Rostow advised Johnson that American diplomats in Vietnam in 1967 would need all the skill and wisdom they could muster to help Ky create a government that could "defeat the VC if they give up the war and enter politics. None of us knows when the South Vietnamese may have to face that test." Obviously, this was super-sensitive stuff, for it had long been Washington's collective nightmare that the war would be "won," militarily, only to see a VC electoral victory. See, also, Memorandum of Conversation with George Brown, British Foreign Secretary, Oct. 14, 1966, *Johnson Papers,* Country File, United Kingdom, Boxes 210–12.

60. Gaiduk, *Soviet Union and Vietnam War,* p. 95. The draft letter, undated, is in *Johnson Papers,* Files of Walt Rostow, Box 10.

61. In *Pay Any Price,* pp. 344–51, I have made an effort—far from conclusive—to identify the various strands, some of which, however, will always remain hidden not in classified documents, but somewhere in LBJ's deepest thoughts and feelings. Johnson's anger and resentment at Bobby Kennedy's new role as would-be savior of the liberal credo, for example, certainly affected his unwillingness to be seen as a "chump" for trying to appease the Martha's Vineyard and Georgetown soiree crowds, though how much it intruded into his calculations in this instance is impossible to say.

62. Gaiduk, *Soviet Union and Vietnam War,* pp. 102–107.

63. *In Confidence,* pp. 155–57.

64. "Memorandum of Conversation," Feb. 8, 1967, *Johnson Papers,* Rostow Memos to the President, Box 13.

65. Dobrynin, *In Confidence,* p. 156.

66. Harriman, "Memorandum for the President," Feb. 8, 1967, *The Papers of W. Averell Harriman,* Box 520, Library of Congress, Washington.
67. Ibid.
68. Thompson to Rusk, Feb. 18, 1967, *Johnson Papers,* Rostow Files, Box 10.
69. Ibid.
70. Rostow to Johnson, Feb. 18, 1967, ibid.
71. Notes, Mar. 13, 1967, *The Papers of Drew Pearson,* Box G 246, LBJL.
72. Thompson to Rostow, Dec. 10, 1966, *Johnson Papers,* Rostow Memos for the President, Boxes 11–12.
73. See Alfred Grosser, *The Western Alliance: European-American Relations since 1945* (New York: Viking Books, 1982), pp. 209–43.
74. "Memorandum of a Conversation," Dec. 11, 1967, *FRUS, 1964–1968,* XIII, pp. 646–48.
75. Harriman to Johnson and Rusk, Apr. 13, 1967, *Harriman Papers,* Box 520.
76. Rostow to Johnson, Apr. 23, 1967, and Rostow to Johnson, Apr. 25, 1967, *Johnson Papers,* Diary Back-Up, Box 62.
77. Johnson to Kosygin, May 19, 1967, ibid., Rostow Files, Box 10.
78. Rostow to Johnson, June 14, 1967, ibid., Country File, Russia, Box 230. Carl Rowan had learned from the Soviet embassy that Kosygin would find it difficult to come to Washington because of the Chinese Communists and the Arabs.
79. Rostow to Johnson, June 17, 1967, ibid., Boxes 220–21.
80. Thompson to Rostow, June 22, 1967, ibid., Box 230.
81. Bundy to Johnson, June 22, 1967, ibid.
82. While Johnson and Kosygin were meeting on June 23, 1967, Secretary Rusk had his own conversation with Foreign Secretary Gromyko. One topic was West German relations with the Soviet Union and Eastern Europe. In keeping with the themes of Glassboro, Rusk tried to draw out his counterpart on the FRG's efforts to improve its relations with Eastern Europe. Gromyko expressed considerable skepticism. Memorandum of Conversation: West German Relations with the USSR and Eastern Europe, June 23, 1967, ibid.
83. Memorandum of Conversation, 11:15 A.M. to 1:30 P.M., June 23, 1967, ibid., p. 295.
84. Memorandum of Conversation, 3:15 P.M. to 4:30 P.M., ibid. The formulation of this statement in the translator's notes is intriguing. Did Kosygin mean to say North Vietnam, or Vietnam? If he actually meant North Korea, he was apparently suggesting that the United States had brought Communist China onto the world scene in the worst way possible, as a regime that had forced one of the great powers to a stand-off after only one year in power!
85. Ibid.
86. Rusk to Johnson, June 24, 1967, ibid.
87. Dobrynin writes that after hearing Johnson's appeal that Moscow act as a third party at the peace table, Kosygin admitted to his colleagues that he was not confident that Hanoi would be prepared to negotiate even if Washington ended the bombing. *In Confidence,* p. 164. It is not clear from this passage in his memoirs, however, whether it was Johnson's argument for Soviet participation, or more broadly, that Hanoi simply was not ready for talks. Certainly, it is clear that he had not persuaded Johnson to reduce American conditions for peace.
88. Ibid., p. 167.
89. Bohlen to Rusk, July 13, 1967, ibid., Country File, France, Box 173.
90. Memorandum of Conversation with Ambassador Dobrynin, ibid., Rostow Files, Box 10.

91. Kornienko to Thompson, as reported to Washington, Aug. 5, 1967, ibid.
92. "Notes of the President's meeting with Harry Reasoner," ibid., Tom Johnson's Notes, Box 1.
93. Robert D. Schulzinger, *A Time for War: The United States and Vietnam, 1941–1975* (New York: Oxford University Press, 1997), pp. 250–52.
94. Jim Jones to Johnson, undated, Nov., 1967, *Johnson Papers,* Meeting Notes File, Box 2.
95. "Stag Dinner for House Members," Nov. 2, 1967, ibid., Congressional Briefings, Box 1.
96. Memorandum of Conversation, Mar. 10, 1968, ibid., Rostow, Memos to the President, Box 31.
97. "Memorandum for the Record, Sunday," Mar. 31, 1968, ibid., Rostow Files, Box 11.
98. Memorandum of Conversation, Apr. 1, 1968, ibid.
99. Ibid.
100. Rostow to Johnson, Apr. 3, 1968, ibid., Country File, Vietnam, Box 96.
101. Rostow to Johnson, May 6, 1968, ibid., DSDUF, Box 4.
102. "Memorandum of Conversation," May 19, 1968, *Harriman Papers,* Box 553.
103. "Notes of the Tuesday Lunch Meeting," May 21, 1968, *Johnson Papers,* Tom Johnson's Notes, Box 3.
104. Rostow to Johnson, June 5, 1968, encl. Kosygin letter, ibid., Rostow Files, Box 10.
105. Johnson to Kosygin, June 11, 1968, ibid.
106. Memorandum of Conversation: Vietnam and Bombing, July 8, 1968, ibid., Country File, Vietnam, Box 229.
107. Bromley Smith to Johnson, July 30, 1968, with encl. draft, ibid., Rostow Files, Box 10.
108. "Notes of the President's Meeting with Foreign Policy Advisers," July 30, 1968, ibid., Tom Johnson's Notes, Box 3.
109. See, for example, Rostow to Johnson, Sept. 17, 1968, ibid., Rostow Files, Box 12.
110. Gardner, *Pay Any Price,* pp. 501–12.
111. Ibid., p. 513.

Chapter 3 by Ilya V. Gaiduk

1. See, Chen Jian, "A Crucial Step toward the Breakdown of the Sino-Soviet Alliance: The Withdrawal of Soviet Experts from China in July 1960," *Cold War International History Project Bulletin* 8–9 (winter, 1996–97): 246, 249–50.
2. Boyevoi Avangard V'etnamskogo Naroda. Instiriia Kommunisticheskoi Partii V'etnama (Militant Vanguard of the Vietnamese People. History of the Communist Party of Vietnam) (Moscow, 1981), p. 130.
3. From the Diary of L. I. Sokolov, "Record of Information Provided by Deputy Minister of Foreign Affairs Ung Van Khiem for Heads of Diplomatic Missions of the Countries of the Socialist Camp," Apr. 15, 1960. Tsentr Khraneniia Sovremennoi Documentatsii (Storage Center for Contemporary Documentation, Moscow), Fond 5, Opis' 49, Delo 347, pp. 107–108 [Hereafter TsKhSD].
4. From the Diary of Georgii M. Pushkin, Reception of Deputy Prime Minister and DRV Minister of Defense Vo Nguyen Giap, May 16, 1960. Arkhiv Vneshnei Politiki Rossiiskoi Federatsii (Archive of Foreign Policy of the Russian Federation, Moscow), Fond 079, Opis' 15, Papka 28, Delo 4, p. 10 [Hereafter AVP RF]. Emphasis added.

5. "Notes on Two Sections of the Theses of the Report of the WPV CC to the third Congress of the Party," June 1, 1960. AVP RF, f. 079, op. 15, p. 30, d. 18, p. 73.

6. Ibid., p. 75.

7. Memorandum of Conversation, chargé d'affaires N. I. Godunov to Ung Van Khiem, July 9, 1960. TsKhSD, f. 5, op. 49, d. 346, p. 165.

8. Ibid., p. 164–65.

9. Draft of the report at the CPSU CC plenum "On the Results of the Meeting of Fraternal Parties in Bucharest and on the Erroneous Positions of the CCP CC Leadership on Some Principal Issues of Marxist-Leninist Theory and Modern International Relations," July 13, 1960. TsKhSD, f. 2, op. 1, d. 458, p. 4.

10. Ibid., p. 14.

11. Ibid., p. 31.

12. Memorandum, "Democratic Republic of Vietnam," prepared by the Southeast Asian department of the Soviet Foreign Ministry in July, 1960. AVP RF, f. 079, op. 15, p. 30, d. 18, pp. 112, 119. Emphasis added.

13. SEA department memorandum, "On Vietnam-China Relations," July 2, 1960. Ibid., d. 20, p. 48.

14. SEA department memorandum "Democratic Republic of Vietnam," July, 1960. Ibid., d. 18, pp. 105, 111.

15. See confirmation in: Survey prepared by Southeast Asian Department of the Soviet Foreign Ministry, "South Vietnam," May 19, 1962. AVP RF, f. 079, op. 17, p. 36, d. 18, p. 35.

16. V. Likhachev to G. Pushkin, Nov. 19, 1960. AVP RF, f. 0570, op. 6, p. 3, d. 5, p. 64.

17. Ibid., p. 63.

18. Memorandum of Conversation, Counsellor I. K. Kisilyov to Pham Van Dong, Dec. 4, 1960. TsKhSD, f. 5, op. 49, d. 445, p. 38.

19. Memorandum of Conversation, N. G. Sudarikov to Chen Yi, Dec. 8, 1960. AVP RF, f. 0100, op. 53, p. 454, d. 8, p. 30–34.

20. Ibid., p. 36.

21. Ibid., p. 53.

22. Memorandum of Conversation, L. I. Sokolov to Vo Nguyen Giap, Jan. 27, 1961. TsKhSD, f. 5, op. 49, d. 445, p. 58.

23. Memorandum of Conversation, L. I. Sokolov to Pham Van Dong, Feb. 2, 1961. Ibid., p. 61.

24. Survey of the Soviet Foreign Ministry, "South Vietnam," May 19, 1962. AVP RF, f. 079, op. 17, p. 36, d. 18, p. 36. The reference to "armed units" is not as clear as one would like. The document does not specify whether these were southern regroupees, northern guerrillas, or units of the Regular People's Army. In fact the implication is that they were the latter.

25. Memorandum of Conversation, N. G. Sudarikov to Zhou Enlai, Apr. 19, 1961. TsKhSD, f. 5, op. 49, d. 436, p. 105.

26. The USSR Foreign Ministry Southeast Asian department's Memorandum, "To the Aide-Memoire of the PRC Government," May 12, 1961. AVP RF, f. 0570, op. 7, p. 5, d. 14, p. 108.

27. USSR Foreign Ministry Memorandum "On Laos," Mar. 14, 1961. AVP RF, f. 0570, op. 7, p. 6, d. 19, p. 1.

28. Pushkin's Report to the meeting of the Collegium of the USSR Foreign Ministry, "On the Activities of the Soviet Delegation at the International Conference on the

Settlement of the Laos Problem," Dec. 27, 1961. AVP RF, f. 0570, op. 7, p. 5, d. 15, p. 255. Emphasis added.

29. Italics added. Memorandum of Conversation, G. M. Pushkin to Zhang Hanhfu, May 16, 1961. AVP RF, f. 0445, op. 1, p. 1, d. 2, pp. 19–20.

30. See: Memorandum of Conversation, N. G. Sudarikov to Chen Yi, July 28, 1961. TsKhSD, f. 5, op. 49, d. 436, pp. 172–73.

31. Memorandum of Conversation, G. M. Pushkin to Nguyen Co Thach, Oct. 10, 1961. AVP RF, f. 0445, op. 1, p. 1, d. 3, p. 41.

32. See, for example, A. Chistiakov, Head of the Southeast Asian department, and Suren Tovmasian, Soviet Ambassador to the DRV, to Georgii Pushkin, Aug., 1962. AVP RF, f. 079, op. 17, p. 35, d. 13, p. 67.

33. Directives to the USSR Ambassador to the DRV, project, top secret, Jan. 22, 1962. Ibid., p. 10.

34. A. Chistiakov, S. Tovmasian to G. Pushkin. Ibid., p. 68.

35. Southeast Asian department memorandum, "Toward developments in South Vietnam," Apr. 14, 1962. AVP RF, f. 079, op. 17, p. 36, d. 18, p. 11.

36. Aide-Memoire signed by A. Chistiakov, Head of the USSR Foreign Ministry Southeast Asian department, "Toward the Question of South Vietnam. Introductory Notes," Dec. 25, 1962. Ibid., p. 198.

37. Memorandum, "Soviet-Vietnamese Relations," June 2, 1962. AVP RF, f. 079, op. 17, p. 35, d. 13, p. 40.

38. Ibid.

39. Memorandum by the USSR embassy in the DRV, "Some Aspects of Vietnam-China Relations," Apr. 10, 1962. Ibid., op. 17, p.36, d. 19, p. 10.

40. Ibid., p. 15.

41. Memorandum of the USSR embassy in the PRC, "On Combination of Internationalism and Nationalism in the Foreign Policy Activity of the CCP," Sept. 30, 1961. TsKhSD, f. 5, op. 49, d. 435, p. 207.

42. For example, on problems of internal reforms in which Hanoi was cautious in following examples of "people's communes" or "great leaps forward." See, Political Letter of the Soviet embassy in the DRV, "Some Issues of the Activities of the WPV CC after the Moscow Meeting of the Communist and Workers' Parties in 1960," Oct. 17, 1961. AVP RF, f. 079, op. 16, p. 31, d. 3, p. 48.

43. "Toward the Question on Soviet-Vietnamese Relations (Brief Memorandum on the Activities of the Referentura on the DRV)," Mar. 6, 1962. AVP RF, f. 079, op. 17, p. 36, d. 19, pp. 1–2.

44. Political Letter, "Some Issues of the WPV CC activities . . . ," p. 55.

45. Political letter of the USSR embassy in the DRV, "Aggravation of the Internal Situation in South Vietnam," Oct. 10, 1961. AVP RF, f. 079, op. 16, p. 31, d. 3, p. 34.

46. "To USSR Ambassador to the DRV S. A. Tovmasian," top secret, Dec. 7, 1961. AVP RF, f. 079, op. 16, p. 31, d. 3, p. 61.

47. "Proposals on Further Development of Political, Economic, and Cultural Relations with the DRV and on Settlement of International Problems," Sept., 1962. AVP RF, f. 079, op. 17, p. 35, d. 13, pp. 75–76.

48. See, on the plenum and Soviet reaction on it, Gaiduk, *Soviet Union and Vietnam War,* p. 9.

49. Memorandum of Conversation, Soviet Ambassador to Cambodia Konstantin Krutikov-Polish representative in ICC Spasovkii, June 5, 1964. TsKhSD, f. 5, op. 50, d. 631, p. 131.

50. Memorandum of Conversation, Konstantin Krutikov to Wilfred Burchett, Mar. 25, 1964. Ibid., p. 93.

51. On the situation in Soviet–North Vietnamese relations on the eve of the Vietnam War: Gaiduk, *Soviet Union and Vietnam War,* chapters 1, 2.

52. On the plenum and the Soviet reaction to it, see Gaiduk, *Soviet Union and Vietnam War,* p. 9.

53. Memorandum of Conversation, Soviet Ambassador to Cambodia Konstantin Krutikov to Polish representative in the ICC Spasovkii, June 5, 1964. TsKhSD, f. 5, op. 50, d. 631, p. 131.

54. On the situation in Soviet–North Vietnamese relations on the eve of the Vietnam War, see Gaiduk, *Soviet Union and Vietnam War,* chapters 1 and 2.

55. USSR Ministry of Defense Memorandum, "On the Vietnam-China Military Cooperation," July 14, 1967. TsKhSD, f. 5, op. 59, d. 416, p. 119–20.

Chapter 4 by Xiaoming Zhang

The author would like to thank Gary Aguiar, Robert Brigham, Ilya Gaiduk, Lloyd Gardner, Lawrence Gelfand, and John Prados for comments and suggestions.

1. The best account based on recently available Soviet resources is Gaiduk, *Soviet Union and Vietnam War,* while Douglas Pike, *Vietnam and the Soviet Union: Anatomy of an Alliance* (Boulder, Colo.: Westview Press, 1987), provides a relatively balanced study from Vietnamese and Soviet perspectives. The study on this subject from a more international dimension can be found in R. B. Smith, *An International History of the Vietnam War.* Vol. I: *Revolution Versus Containment;* Vol. II: *The Kennedy Strategy;* Vol. III: *The Making of a Limited War, 1965–66* (New York: St. Martin's, 1984–90).

2. See Gordon M. Chang, *Friends and Enemies: The United States, China, and the Soviet Union, 1948–1972* (Stanford, Calif.: Stanford University Press, 1990), p. 29; Sergei N. Goncharov, John W. Lewis, and Xue Litai, *Uncertain Partners: Stalin, Mao, and the Korean War* (Stanford, Calif.: Stanford University Press, 1993), pp. 26–35.

3. Zhu Yuanshi, "Liu Shaoqi's Secret Visit to the Soviet Union in 1949," *Dangde wenxian* [Party historical documents] 3 (1991): 76–77; Shi Zhe, *Zai lishi juren shenbian: Shi Zhe huiyilu* [Together with historical Giants: Shi Zhe's memoirs] (Beijing: Central Press of Historical Documents, 1991), pp. 412–13. For an English text in the same line, see Appendix Document 6, "Kovalev Notes re Stalin's Conversation with the Liu Shaoqi Delegation on the Importance of the Chinese Revolution," in Goncharov, Lewis, and Xue, *Uncertain Partners,* p. 232.

4. Goncharov, Lewis, and Xue, *Uncertain Partners,* pp. 71–72; Gary Hess, *Vietnam and the United States: Origins and Legacy of War* (Boston: Twayne Publishers, 1990), p. 37.

5. According to a Chinese source, Stalin told Mao, who was also visiting Moscow, that there had been so many World War II weapons, which were useless for the Soviets, that would be shipped to China, and the Chinese could keep them while transferring some of them to Vietnam if they found proper to do so. Qian Jiang, *Zai shenmi de zhanzheng zhong: Zhonggui junshi guwntuan fu Yuenam zhengzhan ji* [In the course of a mysterious war: Chinese military advisory group in Vietnam] (Zhengzhou: Henan People's Press, 1992), pp. 17–18. Also see, Hoang Van Hoan, *A Drop in the Ocean: Hoang Van Hoan's Revolutionary Reminiscences* (Beijing: People's Liberation Army Press, 1987), p. 259.

6. Chen Jian, "China and the First Indo-China War," *The China Quarterly* 133 (Mar., 1993): 89.

7. In September, 1956, during his talk with an Albanian Labor Party delegation, Mao pointed out that "the success of Soviet revolution brought an intervention from more than ten countries. The imperialists, however, did not intervene us [China] when our nation achieved revolutionary victory. This is because the existence of the Soviet Union rather than their fear of our people . . ." Cited from Chi Aiping, "The Evolution of Mao Zedong's International Strategic Thought," *Dangde Wenxian* [Party historical documents] 3 (1994): 48.

8. This Middle Kingdom mentality refers to the Chinese traditional view of China as the center of the world and their historical experience of not dealing with foreign countries on a equal footing. This view was first advanced by Professor Chen Jian at the 1992 conference, held at the Woodrow Wilson Center. See *Toward a History of Chinese Communist Foreign Relations 1920s–1960*, edited by Michael H. Hunt and Niu Jun (Washington: Woodrow W. Wilson International Center for Scholars, 1993), xii.

9. David J. Daln, *Soviet Foreign Policy After Stalin* (Philadelphia: J. B. Lippincott, 1961), p. 153; Joseph L. Nogee and Robert H. Donaldson, *Soviet Foreign Policy since World War II* (New York: Pergamon Press, 1988), p. 111.

10. Zhai Qiang, "China and the Geneva Conference of 1954," *The China Quarterly* 129 (Mar., 1992): 122.

11. Shi Zhe, *Zai lishi juren shenbian*, pp. 536–65. Also see Shi Zhe, "Random Recollections of the 1954 Geneva Conference," *Xin Zhongguo wiajiao fengyun* [Diplomatic wind and cloud of new China], edited by Waijiaobu waijiao shi bianjishi [Diplomatic history editorial office of foreign ministry], vol. 2 (Beijing: World Knowledge Press, 1991), pp. 29–32.

12. For a detailed analysis about Soviet roles in Sino-American and Sino-British relations at Geneva, see Zhai Qiang, "China and the Geneva Conference of 1954," pp. 113–14.

13. At Geneva, the Chinese leadership was convinced that (1) "all international disputes can be resolved through peaceful consultation"; and (2) "different social systems can coexist peacefully." See He Di, "The Most Respected Enemy: Mao Zedong's Perception of the United States," *Toward a History of Chinese Communist Foreign Relations 1920s–1960*, edited by Hunt and Niu Jun, p. 38.

14. Cited from Chen Jian, "China's Involvement in the Vietnam War, 1964–1969," p. 358.

15. Shi Zhe, *Zai lishi juren shenbian*, p. 569.

16. Mao called Khrushchev's denouncement of Stalin at the Twentieth Congress of the Soviet Communist Party "a war of liberation" to enable the Chinese leadership "to think freely and independently." See Sun Gang and Sun Donsheng, "An Important Meeting at a Turning Point in History," *Dangde wenxian* [Party historical documents] 3 (1991): 11–12.

17. For Mao's personal experience with Stalin, see Shi Zhe, *Zai lishi juren shenbian*, pp. 431–515.

18. For Chinese documents for the emerging disputes between Beijing and Moscow, 1956–58, translated and annotated by Zhang Shu Guang and Chen Jian, see *Cold War International History Project (CWIHP) Bulletin 6–7* (Washington: Woodrow Wilson International Center for Scholars, 1995–96), pp. 148–63.

19. For a thorough English analysis, see He Di, "The Most Respected Enemy: Mao Zedong's Perception of the United States," pp. 41–44.

20. Hoang Van Hoan, "The Reality of Sino-Vietnamese Friendship in Fighting Ought Not to Be Distorted," in *Hoang Van Hoan wenxuan* [Selected Works of Hoang Van Hoan, 1979–1987] (Beijing: People's Press, 1988), p. 20.

21. Wang Xiangen, *Kangmei yuanyue shilu* [A factual account of resisting America and Assisting Vietnam] (Beijing: International Cultural Development Press, 1990), p. 26; also see Gaiduk, *Soviet Union and Vietnam War,* p. 5.

22. Guo Ming, et al., *Zhong Yue guanxi yanbian sishinian,* p. 66.

23. For Chinese military assistance to the DRV during this period, see Zhang Xiaoming, "The Vietnam War, 1964–1969: A Chinese Perspective," *The Journal of Military History* 60 (Oct., 1996): 735–36.

24. Wu Xiuquan, *Huiyi yu huainian,* pp. 335–42.

25. Bo Yibo, *Ruogan zhongda juece yu shijian de huigu* [Recollections of certain major decisions and events] (Beijing: CCP Central Academy Press, 1993), pp. 1142–44.

26. See He Di, "The Most Respected Enemy," p. 48.

27. For Mao's views, see *Mao Zedong waijiao wenxuan* [Selected diplomatic papers of Mao Zedong] (Beijing: Central Press of History Documents, 1994), pp. 529–33.

28. Xiaoming Zhang, "The Vietnam War," pp. 736, 741.

29. Liu Tianye, et al., *Li Tianyou Jiangjun zhuan* [Biography of General Li Tianyou] (Beijing: People's Liberation Army Press, 1993), p. 383.

30. For detailed description of the 1963 Sino-Soviet talk, see Wu Xiuquan, *Huiyi yu huainian,* p. 367–73. Wu, an alternate secretary of the CCP Central Secretariat, was a member of the Chinese delegation.

31. Mao to Ho, Dec. 17, 1963, *Jianguo yilai Mao Zedong wengao* [Mao Zedong manuscripts for the period following the establishment of the country] vol. 10 (Beijing: Central Press of Historical Documents, 1996), pp. 465–67.

32. Douglas Pike, *Vietnam and the Soviet Union,* p. 57.

33. According to Hoang Van Hoan, a member of the VWP delegation, the signing of the joint statement in Moscow was conducted in an abnormal way. When Duan and his delegation was ready to take a regular flight in the Moscow airport, the VWP secretary-general was asked to meet Soviet leaders alone. After he signed the statement, the Soviets arranged a special chartered plane to take the Vietnamese delegation back to Hanoi. See Hoang Van Hoan, *A Drop in the Ocean,* p. 294–95.

34. Ibid., p. 296.

35. This strategy divided China into three fronts. The first and second fronts consisted of the provinces in coastal and central China, where the Chinese economy and industry was concentrated, and the provinces in southwestern and northwestern China made the third front. For a comprehensive discussion of the emergence and development of the Third-front strategy, see Barry Naughton, "The Third Front: Defense Industrialization in the Chinese Interior," *The China Quarterly* 115 (Sept. 1988): 351–88.

36. Sun Dongsheng, "The Great Transformation in the Strategic Planning of Our Country's Economic Construction," *Dangde wenxian* [Party historical documents] 3 (1995): 44.

37. See "Remarks on the Draft of the Chinese Government Statement Protesting America's Invasion of Vietnam," Aug. 6, 1964, *Jianguo yilai Mao Zedong wengao,* vol. 11, p. 120.

38. Huang Yao and Zhang Mingze, *Luo Ruiqing zhuan* [Biography of Luo Ruiqing] (Beijing: Contemporary China Press, 1996), p. 385; Sun Dongsheng, "The Great

Transformation in the Strategic Planning of Our Country's Economic Construction," p. 44.

39. For the Chinese leaders' comment on Khrushchev's fall, see the PRC Foreign Ministry's Diplomatic History Research Office, comp., *Zhou Enlai waijiao huodong dashiji, 1949–1975* [Chronicle of Zhou Enlai's important diplomatic activities] (Beijing: World Affairs Press, 1993), p. 425.

40. Wu Xiuquan, *Huiyi yu huainian,* pp. 378–79. Wu accompanied Zhou to Moscow. Also see Tong Xiaopeng, *Fengyu sishinian* [Forty years of wind and rain] vol. 2 (Beijing: Central Press of Historical Documents, 1996), p. 486.

41. Tong Xiaopeng, *Fengyu sishinia,* pp. 487–88.

42. Hoang Van Hoan, *A Drop in the Ocean,* p. 299.

43. Gaiduk, *Soviet Union and Vietnam War,* pp. 17–18.

44. Oleg Sarin and Lev Dvoretsky, *Alien Wars: The Soviet Union's Aggressions Against the World, 1919 to 1989* (Novato, Calif.: Presidio, 1996), p. 91.

45. Cited from Douglas Pike's *Vietnam and the Soviet Union,* p. 78.

46. Gaiduk, *Soviet Union and Vietnam War,* p.38; Sarin and Dvoretsky, *Alien Wars,* p. 91.

47. Xie Yixian, ed., *Zhongguo waijiao shi: Zhonghua remin gongheguo shiqi, 1949–1979* [A diplomatic history of China: the period of the People's Republic of China, 1949–1979] (Zhengzhou: Henan People's Press, 1988), p. 344.

48. Pike, *Vietnam and the Soviet Union,* p. 63.

49. *Zhou Enlai waijiao huodong dashiji,* p. 438.

50. "The CCP Central Committee's Directive for Strengthening War Preparation Work," Apr. 14, 1965, cited from *Jianguo yilai Mao Zedong wengao,* vol. 11, pp. 359–60.

51. Xiaoming Zhang, "The Vietnam War," pp. 746–53.

52. "Refutation of the New Leaders of the C.P.S.U. on 'United Action,'" *Peking Review* 46 (Nov. 12, 1965): 10–21.

53. This letter was drafted on July 10, and approved by Mao on July 11. *Jianguo yilai Mao Zedong wengao,* vol. 11, pp. 394–95.

54. Li Ke and Hao Shengzhang, *Wenhua dageming zhong de renmin jiefangjun* [The People's Liberation Army during the cultural revolution] (Beijing: Central Press of Historical Documents, 1989), pp. 413–14; Liu Tianye, et al., *Li Tianyou Jiangjun zhuan,* 385.

55. Pike, *Vietnam and the Soviet Union,* p. 63.

56. "Revisionist-U.S. Conspiracy," *Peking Review* 2 (Jan. 7, 1966): 18.

57. Quan Yanchi and Du Weidong, *Gongheguo de mishi* [A secret envoy of the republic] (Beijing: Guangming Daily Press, 1990), p. 193.

58. This situation got even worse in Guangxi, a province adjacent Vietnam, in May, 1968. Zhou Enlai summoned the leaders of the rival factions to Beijing, urging them not to obstruct the shipments to Vietnam. Jiao Hongguang, "Some Records about Zhou Enlai's handling of the Problems in Guangxi during the Cultural Revolution," *Dande wenxian* [Party historical documents] 3 (1996): 73–74.

59. Li and Hao, *Wenhua dageming zhong de renmin jiefangjun,* p. 414.

60. Xiaoming Zhang, "The Vietnam War," p. 737.

61. Li and Hao, *Wenhua dageming zhong de renmin jiefangjun,* p. 412.

62. See Xiaoming Zhang, "The Vietnam War," pp. 744–45.

63. Ibid., pp. 747–51.

64. Wang Xiangeng, *Kangmei yuanyue shilu,* p. 225.

65. Ibid., pp. 225–26.

66. Guo Ming, et al., *Zhong Yue guanxi yanbian sishinian*, p. 102.

67. Wang Xiangeng, *Kangmei yuanyue shilu*, p. 225.

68. For a discussion of the internal debate within the Hanoi leadership on the question of war and peace, see Robert Brigham, "Vietnamese-American Peace Negotiations: The Failed 1965 Initiatives," *The Journal of American–East Asian Relations* 4 (winter, 1995): 377–95.

69. Hoang Van Hoan, *A Drop in the Ocean*, p. 307.

70. *New York Times,* Mar. 7, 1966, section 6, p. 3.

71. In fall, 1966, Nguyen Chi Thanh went to Beijing, and talked with Zhou Enlai about Hanoi's new military, political, and diplomatic strategy. See Hoang Van Hoan, "The Reality of Sino-Vietnamese Friendship in Fighting Ought Not to Be Distorted," p. 25.

72. Hoang Van Hoan, *A Drop in the Ocean*, p. 308.

73. *Mao Zedong waijiao wenxuan*, pp. 580–83.

74. Other examples included that the Soviets always had priority to use ferries or bridges to cross the Red River, even though the Chinese had arrived first. A former Chinese antiaircraft artillery division commander, interview by Xiaoming Zhang, Jan., 1997.

75. For example, in April, 1968, Chinese soldiers detained Soviet military personnel on the charge of spying on their artillery position, and then held a denunciation meeting criticizing the "Soviet revisionists" before releasing them to the local Vietnamese authorities. Wang Xiangen, *Kangmei yuanyue shilu*, pp. 229–35.

76. Christian F. Ostermann, "New Evidence on The Sino-Soviet Border Dispute, 1969–71," *CWIHP* 6–7 (winter, 1995–96): 186–87.

77. Chinese initial response to border incidents was cautious and moderate. After the first serious bloody clash on Qilixin Island in the Ussuri on January 5, 1968, with the deaths of four Chinese fishermen, the CMC ordered to strengthen defense in certain eastern sections of the Sino-Soviet border, while requesting the border troops to continue to carry a forbearing and restrained attitude toward the Soviet provocation. Li and Hao, *Wenhua dageming zhong de renmin jiefangjun*, p. 318.

78. After Czechoslovakia, Mao no longer perceived China's dispute with the Soviet Union as an ideological issue, but a struggle against Soviet "socialist imperialism." See Niu Jun, "A Research Outline of Mao Zedong's 'Three-world' Theory," in Xiao Yanzhong, ed., *Wanlian Mao Zedong* [Mao Zedong in his later years] (Beijing: Spring Autumn Press, 1989), p. 81.

79. Xiong Xianghui, *Lishi de zhujiao—huiyi Mao Zedong, Zhou Enlai and silaoshuai* [Footnotes of history: recollections of Mao Zedong, Zhou Enlai and four old marshals] 2nd edition (Beijing: CCP Central Academy Press, 1996), pp. 173–74.

80. Ibid., pp. 184–88.

81. *Zhonggong dangshi dashi nianbiao* [Chronicle of important events in CCP's history] (Beijing: People's Press, 1974), p. 371; Li and Hao, *Wenhua dageming zhong de renmin jiefangjun*, pp. 255–59.

82. Li Danhui, "The 1969 Sino-Soviet Border Clash: Causes and Consequences," *Dangdai* Zhongguoshi yanjou [Study of modern Chinese history] 3 (May, 1996): 49–50.

83. Xiong Xianghui, *Lishi de zhujiao*, p. 194.

84. Mobilization of China into a war status in 1969 was also due to Mao's domestic consideration to revolutionize Chinese state and society. Particularly, the creation

of a perception that China was facing serious external threats was Mao's way to strengthen the dynamics of revolution at home as well as his authority and controlling position in China's political life. For more discussions of Mao's attempt to use external threats to radicalize China's party, society, and population, see Chen Jian, "China's Involvement in the Vietnam War," pp. 361–65.

85. On November 23, 1969, Zhou talked with the Vietnamese Politburo members, Le Thanh Nghi and Hoang Van Hoan, about the ongoing Sino-Soviet border negotiations. *Zhou Enlai waijiao huodong dashiji, 1949–1975,* p. 546.

86. Qu Aiguo, et al., *YuanYue kangMei—Zhongguo zhiyuan budui zai Yuenan* [Assisting Vietnam against the U.S.—Chinese support troops in Vietnam] (Beijing: Military Science Press, 1995), p. 13.

87. According to Hoang Van Hoan, Zhou Enlai promised the Hanoi leadership that "the Vietnam and Indochina problem must be resolved first in order to normalize Sino-U.S. relations and ease tensions in the Far East. We [the Chinese] do not seek the settlement of the Taiwan issue first, and will do it the next." See Hoang Van Hoan, "The Reality of Sino-Vietnamese Friendship in Fighting Ought Not to Be Distorted," p. 26.

88. According to one Chinese source, between 1971 and 1972, the direct transfer of PLA's arms and equipment to North Vietnam included 14 planes, 3 surface-to-air missile systems along with 180 missiles, 2 warning radar systems, 20 amphibious tanks, 2 pontoon bridge equipment, 204 large caliber field guns along with 45,000 shells. Li and Hao, *Wenhua dageming zhong de renmin jiefangjun,* p. 412.

89. On May 9, 1972, Hanoi's ambassador in Beijing requested the Chinese leadership to help sweep mines in Haiphong Harbor. Zhou realized China's weakness in this regard, and thus responded with the question why the North Vietnamese did not ask the Soviets for assistance inasmuch as their navy was much better equipped and advanced. The Vietnamese side never gave the Chinese an answer but reiterated Hanoi's request. Lai Zhuguang, "Primer Zhou's Management of Mine sweeping Operations in Vietnam," in Qu Aiguo et al., *YuanYue kangMei,* p. 297. Lai was the PLA navy's deputy chief of staff at the time.

Chapter 5 by Robert K. Brigham

I would like to thank George C. Herring, Robert McMahon, Frank Costigliola, John Prados, and Lloyd Gardner for their comments and suggestions.

1. Luu Doan Huynh, former Lao Dong diplomat and senior fellow at Vietnam's Institute for International Relations, interview by Robert K. Brigham, Hanoi, May, 1997.

2. *The Truth About Viet Nam–China Relations Over the Past Thirty Years* (Hanoi: Foreign Ministry, 1979), p. 12.

3. Tran Van Hoanh, former Lao Dong diplomat, interview by Robert K. Brigham, Hanoi, Mar., 1996.

4. Truong Chinh, "Nam vung moi quan he giua chien tranh va cach mang o Viet Nam de hoan thanh thang loi su nghiep chong My, cuu nuoc," [Let us fully understand the relationship between war and revolution in our anti-U.S. resistance war for national salvation of the fatherland] *Hoc Tap* 11 (Sept., 1965): 18–23, and "De thau suot nghi quyet cua dai toan quoc lan thu III cua Dang," [To thoroughly understand the resolution of the III Party congress] *Hoc Tap* 7 (Apr., 1961): 10–36.

5. *Cuoc khang chien chong My, cuu nuoc, 1954–1975: nhung su kien quan su* [The anti-

U.S. resistance war for national salvation of the fatherland, 1954–1975: military events] (Hanoi: Nha Xuat Ban Quan Doi Nhan Dan, 1988), p. 85.

6. David Floyd, *Mao Against Khrushchev: A Short History of the Sino-Soviet Conflict* (New York: Praeger, 1963), p. 68.

7. Donald S. Zagoria, *Vietnam Triangle: Moscow, Peking, and Hanoi* (New York: Pegasus, 1967), p. 58.

8. Ilya V. Gaiduk, "Soviet Policy Towards U.S. Participation in the Vietnam War," Paper Delivered at the Cold War International History Project's conference on the Cold War in Asia, Hong Kong University, Jan., 1996.

9. *The Origin and Development of the Differences Between the Leadership of the CPSU and Ourselves* (Peking: Foreign Languages Press, 1963), pp. 6, 8–15.

10. "Jishi gongchuang you shi chouxing," [Not only an affidavit, but also evil behavior] *Renmin Ribao* 15 (Nov., 1979).

11. George Herring, *America's Longest War: The United States and Vietnam, 1950–1975* Second Edition (New York: Alfred A. Knopf, 1986), p. 55.

12. Bai Noi cu Ho Chu Thich Trong Cuoc Mit Tinh cua Nhan Dan Hanoi Mung Doan Dai Bieu Chinh Phu Lien-Xo," [Text of a Speech by President Ho at a Meeting of the People of Hanoi to Greet a Delegation of Soviet Government Representatives] *Nhan Dan* 4 (Apr., 1956).

13. "Bao Cao cua Dong Chi Truong Chinh o Hoi Nghi Trung Uong Lan Thu 9 mo rong, 20.4.56," [Report by Comrade Truong Chinh at the 9th Enlarged Session of the Central Committee, 20.4.56] *Nhan Dan* 28 (Apr., 1956).

14. Ibid.

15. Le Duan, "Duong loi cach mang mien Nam" [The Path of Revolution in the South], Lao Dong document, circa 1956.

16. *Some Documents of the National Assembly of the Democratic Republic of Viet Nam, 3rd Legislature—1st Session, June–July 1964* (Hanoi: Foreign Languages Publishing House, 1964), p. 74, and Pham van Dong, "Viet Nam Ten Years After Geneva," *Vietnamese Studies* 1 (1964): 48–58.

17. Former Lao Dong officials, interview by Robert K. Brigham, Hanoi, June, 1997.

18. *The Truth About Vietnam-China Relations Over the Last Thirty Years,* p. 33.

19. Viet Nam News Agency, Clandestine Radio Broadcast to Viet Nam, Nov. 11, 1964, 1400GMT, Text in National Archive I, Hanoi.

20. "Peace or Violence," as republished by Peking's Foreign Languages Press, 1963. See also, Victor Funnell, "Vietnam and the Sino-Soviet Conflict, 1965–1976," *Studies in Comparative Communism* 11 (spring/summer, 1978): 146–53.

21. Nguyen Chi Thanh, *Who Will Win in South Viet Nam?* (Peking: Foreign Languages Press, 1963), pp. 8–9.

22. Ibid.

23. Neil Jamieson, *Understanding Vietnam* (Berkeley: University of California Press, 1993), p. 3. The author suggests that "ecological and historical factors have combined to produce very significant regional differences" in contemporary Vietnam.

24. Comments by Dinh Nho Lien, Viet Nam Critical Oral History Conference, Hanoi, June, 1997. See also, General Van Tien Dung, *South Vietnam: U.S. Defeat Inevitable* (Hanoi: Foreign Languages Publishing House, 1967) and General Vo Nguyen Giap, *People's War, People's Army* (Hanoi: Foreign Languages Publishing House, 1961).

25. Truong Chinh, *The Resistance Will Win,* Third Edition (Hanoi: Foreign Languages Publishing House, 1966), p. 125.

26. Tran Quynh Cu, scholar and former Lao Dong official, interview by Robert K. Brigham, Hanoi, June, 1992.

27. Comments by Lt. General Nguyen Dinh Uoc, Vietnam War Critical Oral History Conference, Hanoi, June, 1997.

28. Bui Tin, *Cadre to Exile: The Memoirs of a North Vietnamese Journalist* (Chang Mai, Thailand: Silkworm Books, 1995), p. 43.

29. Nguyen Chi Thanh, "Cang thuoc tu tuong cong viec giua luc luong vu trang va nhan dan o mien Nam va 1965–66 kho mua thang loi," [The ideological task among the armed forces and the people of our South and the 1965–66 dry season victories] *Hoc Tap* 12 (July, 1966): 7.

30. Tung Le, former NLF official, interview by Robert K. Brigham, Ho Chi Minh City, July, 1989.

31. Tuyet thi Vanh, former NLF official, interview by Robert K. Brigham, Ho Chi Minh City, Mar., 1996.

32. *Cuoc khang chien chong My, cuu nuoc, 1954–1975: nhung su kien quan su,* p. 85.

33. People's Army of Vietnam.

34. General Vo Nguyen Giap, *Once Again We Will Win* (Hanoi: Foreign Languages Publishing House, 1966), p. 28.

35. *Cuoc khang chien chong My, cuu nuoc, 1954–1975: nhung su kien quan su,* 85.

36. Anonymous former Lao Dong official, interview by Robert K. Brigham, Hanoi, Mar., 1996.

37. Lu van Loi and Nguyen Anh Vu, *Tiep xux bi mat Viet Nam-Hoa Ky truoc hoi nghi Pa-ri* [Secret Negotiations Between Viet Nam and the United States Before the Paris Meetings] (Hanoi: Vien Quan He Quoc Te, 1990), p. 114.

38. Anonymous Foreign Ministry official, interview by Robert K. Brigham, Hanoi, Jan., 1997.

39. Le Duan, "Cuu nuoc la nghia vu thieng lieng cua ca dan toc ta," [Keep up the protracted war against the Americans for national salvation of the fatherland] *Hoc Tap* 12 (Dec., 1966): 8–16.

40. Hoang Minh Thao, "Quan diem chien tranh nhan dan cua Dang ta," [Our Party's viewpoint of the people's war] *Hoc Tap* 12 (Dec., 1966): 33.

41. "Xu luan," [editorial] *Hoc Tap* 12 (Sept., 1966): 1.

42. "Xu luan," [editorial] *Hoc Tap* 13 (May, 1967): 2.

43. Radio Peking, International Service in English, Dec. 19, 1966, 1600GMT.

44. Ibid.

45. George McT. Kahin, "The NLF's Terms for Peace," *The New Republic,* Oct. 14, 1967, p. 13.

46. Tung Le, former NLF official, interview by Robert K. Brigham, Ho Chi Minh City, July, 1989.

47. "South Vietnam People's Delegation Welcomed in Kwangchow," Douglas Pike Collection, NLF Documents, Document Number 002722, Indochina Archive, University of California at Berkeley.

48. "China and the NLF," Douglas Pike Collection, NLF Documents, Document Number 001495, Indochina Archive, University of California at Berkeley.

49. As cited in, Viet Nam News Agency, International Wire Service Report, Dec. 18, 1966, Text in National Archives I, Hanoi.

50. Viet Nam News Agency, International Wire Service Report, Dec. 10, 1967, Text in National Archives I, Hanoi.

51. Hoang van Hoan, *A Drop in the Ocean,* 329–31.

52. Zhai Qiang, "China and Johnson's Escalation of the Vietnam War, 1964–1965," Paper Delivered at the Cold War International History Project's conference on the Cold War in Asia, Hong Kong University, Jan., 1996. See also, Ralph B. Smith, *An International History of the Vietnam War,* Volume III (New York: St. Martin's Press, 1991), 298–99.

53. Chen Jian, "China's Involvement in the Vietnam War, 1964–1969," *The China Quarterly* 142 (June, 1995): 382.

54. According to Chinese reports, their own railway system was overloaded. Wang Xiangen, *Kang Mei yuanyue shilu* [A factual account of resisting America and Assisting Viet Nam] (Peking: International Cultural Development Press, 1990), p. 226, and Alan S. Whiting, "The Sino-Soviet Split," in Roderick MacFarquhar and John K. Fairbanks, eds., *The Cambridge History of China* (Cambridge University Press, 1987), Volume 14, pp. 478–538.

55. Chen Jian, "China's Involvement in the Vietnam War," p. 383.

56. Ibid.

57. Wang Xiangen, *Kang Mei yuanyua shilu,* pp. 255–56.

58. Hoang van Hoan, *A Drop in the Ocean,* p. 331.

59. Zagoria, *Vietnam Triangle,* p. 60.

60. General Tran Van Quang, interview by Robert K. Brigham, Hanoi, June, 1997.

61. "NLF Thoughts on Peace Negotiations, World Policies: A Cadre's Notes on a High Level 1967 Reorientation Course," in U.S. Department of State, *Vietnam Documents and Research Notes,* Document Number 14 (Saigon: Jan., 1968).

62. "Dong chi Nguyen Chi Thanh da tu tran," [Obituary notice of Nguyen Chi Thanh] *Hoc Tap* 13 (Aug., 1967): 1–8. See also, Douglas Pike, *PAVN: People's Army of Vietnam* (Novato: Presidio Press, 1986), p. 350. There have always been rumors that Thanh was in fact assassinated for his strong viewpoints that often ran contrary to party leaders in Hanoi.

63. Anonymous former Lao Dong official, interview by Robert K. Brigham, Hanoi, Nov., 1995.

64. This date is now confirmed by the highest ranking Viet officials. Vietnam War Critical Oral History Conference, Hanoi, June, 1997.

65. *Tap Chi Lich Su Quan Doi: So dac biet 20 Nam Tet Mau Tan* [Journal of Military History: Special 20th Anniversary Issue on the Tet Offensive] (Feb., 1988).

66. Chien Jian, "China's Involvement in the Vietnam War," p. 384, and John Garver, "The Tet Offensive and Sino-Vietnamese Relations," in Marc Jason Gilbert and William Head, eds., *The Tet Offensive* (Westport: Praeger, 1996), p. 45.

Chapter 6 by Qiang Zhai

1. For detailed discussions of China's involvement in the First Indochina War, see Qiang Zhai, "Transplanting the Chinese Model: Chinese Military Advisers and the First Vietnam War, 1950–1954," *The Journal of Military History* 57 (Oct., 1993): 689–715; Chen Jian, "China and the First Indo-China War, 1950–54," *The China Quarterly* 133 (Mar., 1993): 85–110.

2. Gaiduk, *Soviet Union and Vietnam War,* p. 5.

3. Li Ke and Hao Shengzhang, *Wenhua dageming zhong de renmin jiefangjun* (The People's Liberation Army during the Great Cultural Revolution) (Beijing: Zhonggong dangshi ziliao chubanshe, 1989), p. 409. The two authors were military history researchers at the Military Science Academy of the PLA when they

wrote the book. After its publication, the volume was banned in China because it revealed classified military information.

4. George C. Herring, *America's Longest War: The United States and Vietnam, 1950–1975*, 3rd ed. (New York: McGraw-Hill, 1996), pp. 131–33.

5. Sandra C. Taylor, "Laos: The Escalation of a Secret War," in Jane Errington and B. J. C. McKercher, eds., *The Vietnam War as History* (New York: Praeger, 1990), pp. 73–90; Timothy N. Castle, *At War in the Shadow of Vietnam: U.S. Military Aid to the Royal Lao Government, 1955–1975* (New York: Columbia University Press, 1993), pp. 70–72. Established in Khang Khay in November, 1961, the Chinese Economic and Cultural Mission had been an important instrument of Beijing's policy in dealing with the Pathet Lao. The director of the mission was He Wei, China's ambassador to Hanoi. Aside from its economic and cultural functions, the mission had also directed a group of military advisers attached to the Pathet Lao. See, Liu Chun, "The Bumpy Process of Establishing Diplomatic Relations between China and Laos and My First Mission to Laos," *Waijiao xueyuan xuebao* (Journal of Foreign Affairs College) 2 (1989): 7–14. Liu Chun was deputy director of the mission and became China's ambassador to Laos in October, 1962.

6. The Diplomatic History Research Office of the PRC Foreign Ministry, ed., *Zhou Enlai waijiao huodong dashiji, 1949–1975* (Chronology of Zhou Enlai's Diplomatic Activities, 1949–1975) (Beijing: Shijie zhishi chubanshe, 1993), pp. 410–11.

7. The Diplomatic History Research Office of the PRC Foreign Ministry, ed., *Zhou Enlai waijiao huodong dashiji, 1949–1975,* p. 411; the CCP Central Documentary Research Department, ed., *Zhou Enlai nianpu, 1949–1976* (Chronology of Zhou Enlai, 1949–1976) (Beijing: Zhongyang wenxian chubanshe, 1997), vol. 2, p. 650.

8. Xue Mouhong and Pei Jianzhang, chief eds., *Dangdai Zhongguo waijiao* (Contemporary Chinese Diplomacy) (Beijing: Zhongguo shehui kexue chubanshe, 1988), p. 159; Qu Aiguo, Bao Mingrong, and Xiao Zuyao, *Yuanyue kangmei: Zhongguo zhiyuan budui zai yuenan* (Assist Vietnam and Resist America: Chinese Support Troops in the DRV) (Beijing: Junshi kexue chubanshe, 1995), p. 9. These two sources do not indicate the exact date of the Mao-Van Tien Dung meeting. It is possible that Mao made those remarks during Dung's June 21–22 visit. (Qu Aiguo, Bao Mingrong, and Xiao Zuyao are military history researchers at the Military Science Academy of the PLA).

9. Present at the meetings were Zhou Enlai, Chen Yi, Wu Xiuquan, Yang Chengwu, and Tong Xiaopeng of the CCP; Ho Chi Minh, Le Duan, Truong Chinh, Pham Van Dong, Vo Nguyen Giap, Nguyen Chi Thanh, Hoang Van Hoan, and Van Tien Dung of the VWP; and Kaysone Phomvihane, Prince Souphanouvong, Nouhak Phoumsavan, and Phoumi Vongvichit of the Lao People's Party. The Diplomatic History Research Office of the PRC Foreign Ministry, ed., *Zhou Enlai waijiao huodong dashiji, 1949–1975,* p. 413; Tong Xiaopeng, *Fengyu sishinian* (Forty Years of Winds and Rains) (Beijing: Jiefangjun chubanshe, 1995), vol. 2, pp. 220–21. This book is the second part of a two-volume biography of Zhou Enlai by a long-time associate of the Chinese premier.

10. Li and Hao, *Wenhua dageming zhong de renmin jiefangjun,* p. 408; Qu, Bao, and Xiao, *Yuanyue kangmei,* p. 9.

11. Qu, Bao, and Xiao, *Yuanyue kangmei,* p. 10; Chen Jian, "China's Involvement in the Vietnam War, 1964–69," *The China Quarterly* 142 (June, 1995): 364.

12. Allen S. Whiting, "How We Almost Went to War with China," *Look,* Apr. 29, 1969, p. 76; Melvin Gurtov and Hwang Byong-moo, *China Under Threat: The Politics of*

Strategy and Diplomacy (Baltimore: Johns Hopkins University Press, 1980), pp. 160–61.

13. Gurtov and Hwang, *China Under Threat: The Politics of Strategy and Diplomacy,* p. 162; Herring, *America's Longest War,* pp. 143–45; Gardner, *Pay Any Price,* pp. 168–72.

14. The Diplomatic History Research Office of the PRC Foreign Ministry, ed., *Zhou Enlai waijiao huodong dashiji, 1949–1975,* p. 445; Xue and Pei, *Dangdai Zhongguo waijiao,* pp. 160–61.

15. The strains in U.S.-Pakistani relations as a result of Karachi's deepening ties to Beijing between 1964–65 are covered in detail in Robert J. McMahon, *The Cold War on the Periphery: The United States, India, and Pakistan* (New York: Columbia University Press, 1994), pp. 309–24.

16. The CCP Central Documentary Research Department, ed., *Zhou Enlai nianpu, 1949–1976,* vol. 2, p. 736.

17. Han Huaizhi and Tan Jingqiao, chief eds., *Dangdai zhongguo jundui de junshi gongzuo* (The Military Work of the Contemporary Chinese Armed Forces) (Beijing: Zhongguo shehui kexue chubanshe, 1989), vol. 1, pp. 539–40; Li and Hao, *Wenhua dageming zhong de renmin jiefangjun,* p. 415; Guo Ming, ed., *Zhongyue guanxi yanbian sishinian* (The Evolution of Sino-Vietnamese Relations over the Forty Years) (Nanning: Guangxi renmin chubanshe, 1991), pp. 69–70; Li Ke, "Zhongguo renmin yuanYue kangMei de yeji biaobing qingshi" (The Indelible Mark on History of Chinese Assistance to Vietnam against the United States), *Junshi lishi* (Military History) 4 (1989): 31.

18. Han and Tan, *Dangdai zhongguo jundui de junshi gongzuo,* vol. 1, pp. 539–40; Wang Xiangan, *Yuanyue kangmei shilu* (A Factual Record of Assistance to Vietnam against the United States) (Beijing: Guoji wenhua chuban gongsi, 1990), p. 44; Li, "Zhongguo renmin yuanYue kangMei de yeji biaobing qingshi," p. 31.

19. Wang, *Yuanyue kangmei shilu,* p. 45.

20. Ibid., pp. 35, 44; Li and Hao, *Wenhua dageming zhong de renmin jiefangjun,* p. 422. R. B. Smith dates Ho's meeting with Mao on May 16–17. His source is the diary of Ho's personal secretary. See R. B. Smith, *An International History of the Vietnam War, Volume III: The Making of a Limited War, 1965–66* (New York: St. Martin's Press, 1991), p. 139.

21. Wang, *Yuanyue kangmei shilu,* pp. 46–48.

22. Li and Hao, *Wenhua dageming zhong de renmin jiefangjun,* p. 417.

23. The Ministry of Foreign Affairs of the Socialist Republic of Viet Nam, *The Truth about Vietnam-China Relations over the Last Thirty Years* (Hanoi: Ministry of Foreign Affairs, 1979), p. 33. According to Luu Doan Huynh, a senior research fellow at the International Relations Institute of the Ministry of Foreign Affairs of Vietnam, Beijing informed Hanoi in June, 1965, that it would not be able to defend North Vietnam from U.S. air attacks. Quoted in Allen Whiting, "China's Role in the Vietnam War," in Jayne Werner and David Hunt, eds., *The American War in Vietnam* (Ithaca: Cornell University Southeast Asia Program, 1993), pp. 71–76.

24. *Beijing Review,* Nov. 30, 1979, p. 14; Xue and Pei, *Dangdai Zhongguo waijiao,* p. 161; Qu, Bao, and Xiao, *Yuanyue kangmei,* p. 12.

25. Researchers at the Military Science Academy of the PLA, interview by Robert K. Brigham, Beijing, July 2, 1996.

26. Guo, *Zhongyue guanxi yanbian sishinian,* p. 71; Li and Hao, *Wenhua dageming zhong de renmin jiefangjun,* p. 427.

27. The CCP Central Documentary Research Department, ed., *Jianguo yilai Mao Zedong wengao* (Mao Zedong's Manuscripts since the Founding of the PRC) (Beijing: Zhongyang wenxian chubanshe, 1996), vol. 11, p. 478.

28. Li and Hao, *Wenhua dageming zhong de renmin jiefangjun,* p. 410.

29. Ibid., pp. 412–14.

30. Li, "Zhongguo renmin yuanYue kangMei de yeji biaobing qingshi," p. 31; Guo, *Zhongyue guanxi yanbian sishinian,* p. 69.

31. According to the French scholar Marie Alexanderine Martin, on November 25, 1965, General Lon Nol, chief of staff of the royal Khmer armed forces, visited Beijing on Sihanouk's orders and concluded with Luo Ruiqing a military treaty, which stipulated: "(1) Cambodia would permit the passage and the refuge of Vietnamese combatants in the border regions, granting them protection if necessary and permitting them to establish command posts; (2) Cambodia would permit the passage of material coming from China and intended for Vietnam." Marie Alexanderine Martin, *Cambodia: A Shattered Society* (Berkeley: University of California Press, 1994), pp. 92–93. For a Chinese account of Beijing's use of Sihanoukville to send military supplies to the NLF between 1966–67, see Kang Daisha, "Zai Jianpuzhai de rizi" (My Days in Cambodia), in Cheng Xiangjun, ed., *Nu waijiaoguan* (Women Diplomats) (Beijing: Renmin tiyu chubanshe, 1995), pp. 482–83. Kang Daisha is the wife of Chen Shuliang, who was the Chinese ambassador to Cambodia 1962–67.

32. Anne Gilks and Gerald Segal, *China and the Arms Trade* (New York: St. Martin's Press, 1985), p. 50.

33. For Mao's view of the United States, see his January 12, 1964, statement in support of the struggle of the Panamanian people, in the CCP Central Documentary Research Department, ed., *Jianguo yilai Mao Zedong wengao,* vol. 11, pp. 6–7.

34. For a discussion of foreign policy and China's national identity, see Samuel Kim, ed., *China's Quest for National Identity* (Ithaca: Cornell University Press, 1993).

35. Allen S. Whiting, *The Chinese Calculus of Deterrence: India and Indochina* (Ann Arbor: University of Michigan Press, 1975), p. 186; idem., "Forecasting Chinese Foreign Policy: IR Theory vs. the Fortune Cookie," in Thomas W. Robinson and David Shambaugh, eds., *Chinese Foreign Policy: Theory and Practice* (Oxford: Clarendon Press, 1994), pp. 506–23.

36. John W. Garver, "The Chinese Threat in the Vietnam War," *Parameters* 22 (spring, 1992): 75.

37. On this point, see Zhai, "Transplanting the Chinese Model," pp. 712–13.

38. Wang, *Yuanyue kangmei shilu,* p. 60–68.

39. Ibid., pp. 74–75.

40. Guo, *Zhongyue guanxi yanbian sishinian,* p. 102.

41. Cong Jin, *Quzhe fazhan de suiyue* (Years of Twisted Development) (Zhengzhou: Henan renmin chubanshe, 1989), p. 607. The author is a party history researcher at the Chinese National Defense University.

42. Lowell Dittmer, *Sino-Soviet Normalization and Its International Implications, 1945–1990* (Seattle: University of Washington Press, 1992), p. 334. Between 1965–67, Beijing and Moscow exchanged accusations over whether China had hindered the transportation of Soviet arms to the DRV. Xie Yixian, ed., *Zhongguo waijiao shi: Zhonghua renmin gongheguo shiqi, 1949–1979* (A Diplomatic History of China: The Period of the People's Republic of China, 1949–1979) (Zhengzhou: Henan renmin chubanshe, 1988), pp. 346–48.

43. The CCP Central Documentary Research Department, ed., *Jianguo yilai Mao Zedong wengao,* vol. 11, pp. 394–95.

44. Masaru Kojima, ed., *The Record of the Talks Between The Japanese Communist Party and the Communist Party of China: How Mao Zedong Scrapped the Joint Communiqué* (Tokyo: Central Committee of the Japanese Communist Party, 1980). The volume contains a full text of the joint communiqué, see pp. 190–96.

45. Quoted in Zagoria, *Vietnam Triangle,* p. 112.

46. Ibid.

47. Zhou's talk with Pham Van Dong, Apr. 11, 1967, in the Diplomatic History Research Office of the PRC Foreign Ministry, ed., *Zhou Enlai waijiao huodong dashiji, 1949–1975,* pp. 510–11.

48. Tran Van Tra, "Tet: The 1968 General Offensive and General Uprising," in Jayne S. Werner and Luu Doan Huynh, eds., *The Vietnam War: Vietnamese and American Perspectives* (Armonk, New York: M. E. Sharpe, 1993), pp. 37–65; Gabriel Kolko, *Anatomy of a War: Vietnam, the United States, and the Modern Historical Experience* (New York: Pantheon Books, 1985), p. 279.

49. William J. Duiker, *Sacred War: Nationalism and Revolution in a Divided Vietnam* (New York: McGraw-Hill, 1995), p. 208; Kolko, *Anatomy of a War,* p. 279. New information from Hanoi suggests, however, that the Vietnamese did not intend to carry out the so-called "general uprising," a broad popular revolution throughout South Vietnam, during the Tet offensive. At a Vietnamese-American meeting attended by former policymakers from both sides in Hanoi in June, 1997, Ambassador Nguyen Khac Huynh, retired deputy foreign minister, claimed that the main objective of Tet was to achieve a major victory that would contribute to a "gradual" collapse of the Saigon regime. For a report of the meeting, see John Prados, "Looking at the War from Both Sides Now," *The VVA Veteran* 17 (Aug.– Sept., 1997): 29–31.

50. Mao Zedong, "On Protracted War," in *Selected Military Writings of Mao Tse-tung* (Beijing: Foreign Languages Press, 1967), pp. 187–267. See also John Garver, "The Tet Offensive and Sino-Vietnamese Relations," in Marc Jason Gilbert and William Head, eds., *The Tet Offensive* (Westport: Praeger, 1996), pp. 46–52.

51. Garver, "The Tet Offensive and Sino-Vietnamese Relations," pp. 46–52. For a further discussion of how Hanoi's strategy differed from Mao's military principles, see David W. P. Elliott, "Hanoi's Strategy in the Second Indochina War," in Werner and Huynh, eds., *The Vietnam War,* pp. 66–94.

52. Xie, *Zhongguo waijiao shi,* p. 360. This source does not mention the exact date of Mao's remarks.

53. Zhou's talk with Ho Chi Minh, Feb. 7, 1968, in the CCP Central Documentary Research Department, ed., *Zhou Enlai nianpu, 1949–1976,* vol. 3, p. 217.

54. For further discussions of Beijing's calculations in insisting on a protracted people's war in Vietnam, see Dittmer, *Sino-Soviet Normalization and Its International Implications, 1945–1990,* p. 198; Robert S. Ross, *The Indochina Tangle: China's Vietnam Policy, 1975–1979* (New York: Columbia University Press, 1988), p. 23.

55. Hoang Van Hoan, *Canghai yisu: Hoang Van Hoan geming huiyilu* (A Drop in the Ocean: Hoang Van Hoan's Revolutionary Reminiscences) (Beijing: Jiefangjun chubanshe, 1987), p. 308; idem., "Distortion of Facts About Militant Friendship Between Viet Nam and China Is Impermissible," *Beijing Review,* Dec. 7, 1979, p. 18. Hoan was also in Beijing at the time for a rest cure.

56. "77 Conversations between Chinese and Foreign Leaders on the Wars in Indochina,

1964–1977," Cold War International History Project Working Paper, (forthcoming).

57. Zhou's talk with Xuan Thuy, May 7, 1968, in the Diplomatic History Research Office of the PRC Foreign Ministry, ed., *Zhou Enlai waijiao huodong dashiji, 1949–1975,* p. 524. For a further discussion of China's attitude toward the Vietnam peace talks, see Qiang Zhai, "Beijing and the Vietnam Peace Talks, 1965–68: New Evidence from Chinese Sources," Cold War International History Project Working Paper No. 18 (Washington: Woodrow Wilson International Center for Scholars, June, 1997).

58. Herring, *America's Longest War,* p. 231.

59. During this same period, Hanoi censored China's references to the "peace talks fraud" and the "bombing halt hoax." See Jay Taylor, *China and Southeast Asia: Peking's Relations with Revolutionary Movements,* expanded and updated edition (New York: Praeger, 1976), p. 61; Hoang Van Hoan, "Distortion of Facts About Militant Friendship Between Viet Nam and China Is Impermissible," p. 18.

60. The PRC Foreign Ministry and the CCP Central Documentary Research Department, eds., *Mao Zedong waijiao wenxuan* (Selected diplomatic Works of Mao Zedong) (Beijing: Zhongyang wenxian chubanshe and Shijie zhishi chubanshe, 1994), pp. 580–83.

61. Zhou's talk with Ion Gheorghe Maurer, Sept. 7, 1969, in the Diplomatic History Research Office of the PRC Foreign Ministry, ed., *Zhou Enlai waijiao huodong dashiji, 1949–1975,* pp. 538–39.

62. Li and Hao, *Wenhua dageming zhong de renmin jiefangjun,* p. 426; Qu, Bao, and Xiao, *Yuanyue kangmei,* p. 13.

63. Zhou's talk with Pham Hung and Hoang Van Thai, Apr. 21, 1969, in the CCP Central Documentary Research Department, ed., *Zhou Enlai nianpu, 1949–1976,* vol. 3, p. 293.

64. Li and Hao, *Wenhua dageming zhong de renmin jiefangjun,* p. 416. According to the Vietnamese White Paper, in 1968, when discussing aid to the DRV for 1969, Beijing cut its aid by 20 percent as compared with 1968. The Ministry of Foreign Affairs of the Socialist Republic of Vietnam, *The Truth about Vietnam-China Relations over the Last Thirty Years,* p. 37.

65. Xue and Pei, *Dangdai Zhongguo waijiao,* p. 219; Xiong Xianghui, *Lishi de Zhujiao: Huiyi Mao Zedong, Zhou Enlai ji Silaoshuai* (Historical Footnotes: Remembering Mao Zedong, Zhou Enlai as well as Four Old Marshals) (Beijing: Zhonggong zhongyang dangxiao chubanshe, 1995), pp. 189–90.

66. Xiong, *Lishi de Zhujiao,* pp. 173–204.

67. Daniel S. Papp, *Vietnam: The View from Moscow, Peking, Washington* (Jefferson, North Carolina: McFarland, 1981), p. 160.

68. Zhou's talks with Sihanouk, Mar. 19 and 22, 1970, the Diplomatic History Research Office of the PRC Foreign Ministry, ed., *Zhou Enlai waijiao huodong dashiji, 1949–1975,* p. 549.

69. Papp, *Vietnam: The View from Moscow, Peking, Washington,* p. 161.

70. The Diplomatic History Research Office of the PRC Foreign Ministry, ed., *Zhou Enlai waijiao huodong dashiji, 1949–1975,* p. 552.

71. The Editorial Group of "The Record of Mao Zedong's International Contacts," ed., *Mao Zedong guoji jiaowang lu* (The Record of Mao Zedong's International Contacts) (Beijing: Zhonggong dangshi chubanshe, 1995), pp. 66–68.

72. Xue and Pei, *Dangdai Zhongguo waijiao,* p. 219; Gong Li, *Kuayue honggou: 1969–1979*

nian Zhong Mei guanxi de yanbian (Crossing the Chasm: The Evolution of Sino-American Relations, 1969–1979) (Zhengzhou: Henan renmin chubanshe, 1992), pp. 56–57. The author is a party history specialist at the CCP Party School.

73. As Kissinger pointed out to Nixon at the time, Mao's speech "makes no threats, offers no commitments, is not personally abusive toward you, and avoids positions on contentious bilateral issues." Absent in Mao's address was the usual phrase about China being a "rear area" for the Indochinese struggle. Henry Kissinger, *White House Years* (Boston: Little, Brown, 1979), p. 695.

74. Xue and Pei, *Dangdai Zhongguo waijiao*, pp. 219–20; Gong, *Kuayue honggou*, p. 66.

75. Quoted in Kissinger, *White House Years*, pp. 706–707.

76. Kissinger, *White House Years,* p. 706. Kissinger again noted that Beijing's criticisms "carefully avoided personal attacks on Nixon." See also Raymond L. Garthoff, *Détente and Confrontation: American-Soviet Relations from Nixon to Reagan,* rev. ed., (Washington: The Brookings Institution, 1994), p. 288.

77. Gong, *Kuayue honggou*, p. 69. The official Chinese account of Zhou's visit to Hanoi in March, 1971, however, only lists the issues of Korea, East Germany, Cuba, the Middle East, and Soviet-Japanese relations as on the agenda of his discussions with the DRV leaders. It does not mention Laos. See the Diplomatic History Research Office of the PRC Foreign Ministry, ed., *Zhou Enlai waijiao huodong dashiji, 1949–1975,* pp. 580–81.

78. Garthoff, *Détente and Confrontation,* p. 288.

79. Xue and Pei, *Dangdai Zhongguo waijiao,* pp. 220–21.

80. Gong, *Kuayue honggou*, p. 105. The author does not identify the officials who held the reservations. According to the conventional view in the West, Lin Biao opposed improving relations with the United States because a continuation of the "dual enemy" approach would benefit his constituency, the military. But there is no evidence in the new Chinese sources that supports such a hypothesis.

81. Gong, *Kuayue honggou,* pp. 102–107.

82. Li and Hao, *Wenhua dageming zhong de renmin jiefangjun*, p. 416. George McT. Kahin observed that during his trip to the DRV in September, 1972, nearly all of the hundreds of trucks he saw on the roads between Hanoi and the China border were of the Chinese make, and oil and gasoline pipelines had been constructed across the border deep into Vietnam. George McT. Kahin, "Nixon and the PRG's 7 Points," in Werner and Hunt, eds., *The American War in Vietnam,* p. 66.

83. The Ministry of Foreign Affairs of the Socialist Republic of Viet Nam, *The Truth about Vietnam-China Relations over the Last Thirty Years,* p. 41.

84. The Diplomatic History Research Office of the PRC Foreign Ministry, ed., *XinZhongguo waijiao fengyun* (Episodes of New China's Diplomacy) (Beijing: Shijie zhishi chubanshe, 1991), vol. 2, pp. 41–42; Xue and Pei, *Dangdai Zhongguo waijiao*, pp. 221–22; Zhang Guang, "Dakai ZhongMei guanxi damen de lishi beijing yu jingguo" (The Historical Background and Process of the Opening of Sino-American Relations), *Waijiao xueyuan xuebao* (Journal of Foreign Affairs College) 2 (1991): 59.

85. The Diplomatic History Research Office of the PRC Foreign Ministry, ed., *XinZhongguo waijiao fengyun,* vol. 2, pp. 41–42.

86. Robert S. Ross, *Negotiating Cooperation: The United States and China, 1969–1989* (Stanford: Stanford University Press, 1995), p. 40.

87. The Diplomatic History Research Office of the PRC Foreign Ministry, ed., *Zhou Enlai waijiao huodong dashiji, 1949–1975,* p. 596.

88. The Ministry of Foreign Affairs of the Socialist Republic of Vietnam, *The Truth about Vietnam-China Relations over the Last Thirty Years*, p. 40.

89. Kahin, "Nixon and the PRG's 7 Points," pp. 47–70; Luu Doan Huynh, "The Seven-Point Proposal of the PRG (July 1, 1971) and the U.S. reaction," in Werner and Huynh, eds., *The Vietnam War*, pp. 198–202.

90. Cited in Papp, *Vietnam: The View from Moscow, Peking, Washington*, p. 166.

91. John W. Garver, "Sino-Vietnamese Conflict and the Sino-American Rapprochement," *Political Science Quarterly* 96 (fall, 1981): 454.

92. Papp, *Vietnam: The View from Moscow, Peking, Washington*, pp. 164–65. Whitlam met with Zhou Enlai in Beijing on July 5, 1971. The Diplomatic History Research Office of the PRC Foreign Ministry, ed., *Zhou Enlai waijiao huodong dashiji, 1949–1975* (p. 595) mentions their meeting but provides no detail about the conversation.

93. The CCP Central Documentary Research Department, ed., *Zhou Enlai nianpu, 1949–1976*, vol. 3, pp. 469–70.

94. Seymour M. Hersh, *The Price of Power: Kissinger in the Nixon White House* (New York: Summit Books, 1983), p. 442. Hersh's account was based on his interview with North Vietnamese Deputy Foreign Minister Nguyen Co Thach in Hanoi in August, 1979. Thach had been present with Pham Van Dong in Beijing in November, 1971.

95. The CCP Central Documentary Research Department, ed., *Zhou Enlai nianpu, 1949–1976*, vol. 3, p. 497.

96. Yun Shui, *Chushi qiguo jishi: jiangjun dashi Wang Youping* (Record of Diplomatic Missions to Seven Countries: General Ambassador Wang Youping) (Beijing: Shijie zhishi chubanshe, 1996), p. 136. This book is based primarily on the recollections of Wang Youping. After the first formal discussion with Pham Van Dong on November 21, Zhou Enlai blamed Deputy Foreign Minister Han Nianlong, who was in charge of arranging the visit of Dong, for not including in the agenda of the meeting China's appreciation for the DRV's support for the PRC's representation in the United Nations. Ibid., pp. 136–37.

97. Ross, *Negotiating Cooperation*, p. 49; Vernon A. Walters, *Silent Missions* (Garden City, New York: Doubleday, 1978), pp. 545–46.

98. The Diplomatic History Research Office of the PRC Foreign Ministry, ed., *XinZhongguo waijiao fengyun* (Diplomatic Turbulence of New China) (Beijing: Shijie zhishi chubanshe, 1994), vol. 3, pp. 71–82.

99. Ross, *Negotiating Cooperation*, p. 49.

100. The Diplomatic History Research Office of the PRC Foreign Ministry, ed., *XinZhongguo waijiao fengyun*, vol. 3, pp. 73–75.

101. In early February, 1972, the Soviet embassy in Hanoi reported to Moscow that the Chinese had pressed the DRV for approval of their plan to discuss the issue of Indochina with Nixon. Later Moscow was relieved when Hanoi resisted the Chinese pressure. Gaiduk, *Soviet Union and Vietnam War*, p. 232.

102. Zhang, "Dakai ZhongMei guanxi damen de lishi beijing yu jingguo," p. 62.

103. Kissinger, *White House Years*, p. 1087.

104. Yun Shui, *Chushi qiguo jishi*, p. 138.

105. Guo, *ZhongYue guanxi yanbian sishinian*, pp. 102–103.

106. The Ministry of Foreign Affairs of the Socialist Republic of Vietnam, *The Truth about Vietnam-China Relations over the Last Thirty Years*, p. 41.

107. Yun Shui, *Chushi qiguo jishi*, p. 138.

108. Duiker, *Sacred War,* p. 234.

109. William S. Turley, *The Second Indochina War: A Short Political and Military History, 1954–1975* (Boulder: Westview, 1986), pp. 138–39; Duiker, *Sacred War,* pp. 234–35.

110. Herring, *America's Longest War,* pp. 271–73; Robert D. Schulzinger, *A Time for War: The United States and Vietnam, 1941–1975* (New York: Oxford University Press, 1997), pp. 295–96.

111. Zhou's talk with Nguyen Tien, Apr. 14, 1972, the Diplomatic History Research Office of the PRC Foreign Ministry, ed., *Zhou Enlai waijiao huodong dashiji, 1949–1975,* p. 627.

112. *Haijun shi* (History of the Navy) (Beijing: Jiefangjun chubanshe, 1989), p. 178.

113. *Peking Review,* May 19, 1972.

114. *Haijun shi,* pp. 178–82.

115. Garthoff, *Détente and Confrontation,* p. 290.

116. Gaiduk, *Soviet Union and Vietnam War,* pp. 236, 290n; Kissinger, *White House Years,* p. 1151.

117. Hersh, *The Price of Power,* p. 502.

118. Garthoff, *Détente and Confrontation,* p. 291.

119. Duiker, *Sacred War,* pp. 235–37; Schulzinger, *A Time For War,* pp. 298–99.

120. Hersh, *The Price of Power,* p. 442; Duiker, *Sacred War,* p. 234. According to Luu Doan Huynh, Mao advised Pham Van Dong that Thieu should be kept in office and negotiated with. See Kahin, "Nixon and the PRG's 7 Points," p. 66. See also Garver, "Sino-Vietnamese Conflict," pp. 459–60.

121. Quoted in Garver, "Sino-Vietnamese Conflict," p. 460.

122. Garthoff, *Détente and Confrontation,* p. 292.

123. Mao's talk with Nguyen Thi Binh, Dec. 29, 1972, in Chen Donglin and Du Pu, eds., *Zhonghua renmin gongheguo shilu: disanjuan (xia) Neiluan yu kangzheng— "Wenhua dageming" de shinian, 1972–1976* [A Factual Record of the PRC: Volume 3 (Part 2), Internal Disturbance and Rebellion—The Ten Years of the "Great Cultural Revolution," 1972–1976] (Changchun: Jilin renmin chubanshe, 1994), p. 878.

124. Zhou's talk with Truong Chinh, Dec. 31, 1972, in the Diplomatic History Research Office of the PRC Foreign Ministry, ed., *Zhou Enlai waijiao huodong dashiji, 1949–1975,* p. 659.

125. Zhou's talk with Le Duc Tho, Jan. 3, 1973, in ibid., p. 660.

126. Zhou's talk with Penn Nouth, Feb. 2, 1973, in ibid., p. 663.

127. Hoang Van Hoan, "Distortion of Facts About Militant Friendship Between Viet Nam and China Is Impermissible," p. 19. See also Garver, "Sino-Vietnamese Conflict," p. 461.

128. Garver, "Sino-Vietnamese Conflict," p. 462.

129. Glenn H. Snyder, "The Security Dilemma in Alliance Politics," *World Politics* (July, 1984): 461–95. Hope M. Harrison has made a similar discovery of the entrapment and abandonment syndrome in the Soviet–East German alliance. See Hope M. Harrison, "Ulbricht and the Concrete 'Rose': New Archival Evidence on the Dynamics of Soviet–East German Relations and the Berlin Crisis, 1958–1961," Cold War International History Project Working Paper No. 5 (Washington: Woodrow Wilson International Center for Scholars, May, 1993).

130. The Soviet role in connecting the DRV with the West and the UN is chronicled in Gaiduk, *Soviet Union and Vietnam War,* pp. 75–78.

131. For further discussions of Hanoi's approach to negotiations, see Gareth Porter, *A Peace Denied: The United States, Vietnam, and the Paris Agreement* (Bloomington:

Indiana University Press, 1975), pp. 1–33; Allan E. Goodman, *The Lost Peace: America's Search for a Negotiated Settlement of the Vietnam War* (Stanford: Hoover Institution Press, 1978), pp. 11–12; Duiker, *Sacred War,* pp. 191–92.

132. For detailed accounts of the circumstances surrounding the Trinh remarks, see Wallace J. Thies, *When Governments Collide: Coercion and Diplomacy in the Vietnam Conflict, 1964–1968* (Berkeley: University of California Press, 1980), p. 198; George C. Herring, *LBJ and Vietnam: A Different Kind of War* (Austin: University of Texas Press, 1994), p. 108; Don Oberdorfer, *Tet!* (Garden City, New York: Doubleday, 1971), pp. 68–69.

133. According to Huynh Kim Khanh, the designation of the Indochinese Communist Party was imposed by a Comintern instruction in late 1929 and adopted reluctantly in 1930 by the previously separated communist units in Vietnam. Huynh Kim Khanh, *Vietnamese Communism, 1925–1945* (Ithaca, New York: Cornell University Press, 1982), pp. 123–29. See also MacAlister Brown, "The Indochinese Federation Idea: Learning from History," in Joseph J. Zasloff, ed., *Postwar Indochina: Old Enemies and New Allies* (Washington: The Foreign Service Institute of the U.S. State Department, 1988), pp. 85–86.

Chapter 7 by Frank Costigliola

1. Dean Acheson to the President, Mar. 16, 1965, Dean Acheson Papers, box 88, Harry S. Truman Library, Independence, Mo. (hereafter HSTL).

2. Acheson, "Memorandum on the Draft of Message dated Dec. 11, 1967," box 88, Acheson Papers, HSTL.

3. Brussels Embassy to Department of State, May 11, 1964, International Meetings and Travel File, NSF, LBJL.

4. "U.S. Policy Toward Europe," enclosed in Acheson to the President, Nov. 25, 1964, Box 88, Acheson Papers, HSTL.

5. Sixth Meeting of the Steering Committee, Atlantic Policy Studies, Oct. 29, 1963, vol. III, RG, CFR.

6. Sixth Meeting of the Steering Committee, Atlantic Policy Studies, Oct. 29, 1963, vol. III, Records of Groups, Council on Foreign Relations Archives, New York City (emphasis added).

7. Draft letter, Johnson to Wilson, May 20, 1966, box 7, Memos to the President, Walt W. Rostow Files, LBJL.

8. Acheson, "United States Policy Toward Germany," Dec. 5, 1963, box 87, Acheson Papers, HSTL.

9. Acheson to Robert McNamara, Sept. 16, 1963, box 22, Dean Acheson Papers, Yale University, New Haven, Conn.

10. "Lyndon B. Johnson, Germany, and the 'End of the Cold War,'" Warren Cohen and Nancy Tucker, eds., *Lyndon B. Johnson Confronts the World* (Cambridge University Press, 1994), pp. 173–210.

11. George Ball conversation with the President, June 14, 1965, box 6, George Ball Papers, LBJL.

12. Eugene Rostow to the President through William R. Tyler, Apr. 10, 1965, box 171, NSF, Country File France, LBJL.

13. Summary Record of National Security Council Meeting No. 532, May 15, 1964, 12:00 noon," box 1, Meeting Notes, LBJL.

14. John T. McNaughton to McGeorge Bundy, Dec. 4, 1965, box 17, files of McGeorge

Bundy, NSF, LBJL; Johnson to General Franco, Jan. 13, 1967, box 4, files of Francis Bator, LBJL.

15. Ball telephone conversation with Henry Fowler, July 29, 1965, 10:20 A.M., box 6, Ball Papers.

16. Rusk to the President and Acting Secretary, Dec. 16, 1965, box 172, Country File, France, NSF, LBJL. For the German record, see Gespräch des Bundesministers Schroder mit dem amerikanischen Aussenminister Rusk in Paris, Dec. 15, 1965, in Hans-Peter Schwarz, et al., eds., *Akten zur Auswartigen Politik der Bundesrepublik Deutschland 1965* (Munchen: R. Oldenbourg Verlag, 1996), pp. 1899–1900. See also Chester Cooper to McGeorge Bundy, Apr. 29, 1965, "Free World Assistance to Vietnam," box 18–19, files of McGeorge Bundy, LBJL.

17. W. W. Rostow to E. V. Rostow, with message from the President, Nov. 19, 1966, box 11, Rostow's Memoranda to the President, LBJL. See also Ball memorandum of telephone conversation with Schaetzel, Mar. 17, 1965, box 6, Ball Papers.

18. Summary Notes of 566th NSC Meeting, Dec. 13, 1966, Meetings File, box 2, NSF, LBJL.

19. Memorandum by Adelbert de Segonzac, "de Gaulle," May 4, 1964, enclosed in McGeorge Bundy to the President, May 11, 1964, box 1, NSF, Aides Files, LBJL.

20. Bohlen to Department of State, Feb. 2, 1965, no. 1977/327D, Declassified Documents Reference System (hereafter DDRS); Henry Cabot Lodge to the President, Feb. 22, 1964, box 1, NSF, Aides Files, Memoranda to the President, LBJL.

21. William R. Tyler and Robert Schaetzel, "NATO Ministerial Meeting, The Hague, May 12–14, 1964, box 33–34, NSF International Meetings and Travel File, LBJL.

22. Ambassador Lodge to President Johnson, Feb. 22, 1964, box 1, Aides Files, Memoranda to the President, NSF, LBJL. See also Anne E. Blair, *Lodge in Vietnam* (New Haven: Yale University Press, 1995), pp. 91–93, 105–106.

23. President Johnson to Ambassador Bohlen, Feb. 25, 1964, no. 1975/97C, DDRS; Bohlen to President Johnson, Feb. 26, 1964, 1975/98B, ibid.

24. Lodge to President Johnson, Feb. 22, 1964, box 1, Aides Files, Memoranda to the President, NSF, LBJL; Bohlen to President Johnson, Feb. 26, 1964, 1975/98B, DDRS.

25. David Klein to McGeorge Bundy, July 23, 1964, box 170, Country File, France, NSF, LBJL.

26. Memorandum of Conversation between the President and Couve de Murville, Feb. 19, 1965, no. 1978/274C, DDRS.

27. George Ball memorandum of telephone conversation with the President, Mar. 6, 1965, box 6, George Ball Papers, LBJL.

28. Bohlen to Secretary of State, Aug. 27, 1965, no. 1978/276A, DDRS.

29. Bohlen to the Secretary of State, June 3, 1965, NSF, box 171; Bundy to the President, June 12, 1965, box 3, Aides Files, LBJL.

30. Frank Costigliola, *France and the United States: The Cold Alliance Since World War II* (New York: Twayne/Macmillan, 1992), pp. 141–44.

31. Bohlen to Secretary of State, May 20, 1965, box 171, NSF, LBJL.

32. Botschafter Klaiber, Paris, an das Auswärtige Amt, Feb. 8, 1965, in Schwarz, et al., *Akten zur Auswärtigen Politik 1965,* p. 279.

33. Gespräch des Bundeskanzlers Erhard mit Staatspräsident de Gaulle, June 11, 1965, in ibid., p. 1005.

34. Gespräch des Bundeskanzlers Erhard mit Staatspräsident de Gaulle, June 11, 1965, in ibid., 1007–1008.

35. Gespräch des Bundesministers Schröder mit dem französischen Aussenminister Couve de Murville in Paris, Feb. 7, 1966 in Hans-Peter Schwarz, et al., *Akten zur Auswärtigen Politik der Bundesrepublik Deutschland 1966* (Munchen: R. Oldenbourg Verlag, 1997), p. 164.
36. J. Ward to Foreign Office, Jan. 4, 1966, PREM 13/1271, Public Record Office, London.
37. Gespräch des Bundesministers Schröder mit dem französischen Aussenminister Couve de Murville, July 21, 1966, *Akten zur Auswärtigen Politik 1966*, pp. 945–46.
38. Leonard H. Marks to the President, Oct. 23, 1967, box 229, EX ND19/CO312, White House Central Files, LBJL.
39. Costigliola, *France and the United States*, pp. 149–58.
40. Costigliola, "Lyndon B. Johnson, Germany, and the 'End of the Cold War,'" pp. 207–209.

Chapter 8 by Kil J. Yi

1. South Korea's involvement in the Vietnam War began in the fall of 1964, when it dispatched a 120-member Mobile Army Surgical Hospital (MASH), and 10 martial arts instructors. In the early spring of 1965, South Korea added 3,000 army engineers to its expeditionary forces in Vietnam. Although some combat soldiers were included in the contingent to provide security, its duties were non-combat.
2. U.S. Congress, Senate Committee on Foreign Relations, *United States Security Agreement and Commitment Abroad, Republic of Korea: Hearings before a Subcommittee on United States Security Agreement and Commitments Abroad*, 91st Cong., 2nd sess., 1970, 1542–43. [Hereafter *Security Agreement*.]
3. Cable 1008 from Seoul, Apr. 15, 1965, "NODIS-LOR, Vol. II, 3/65–9/65," Box 46, Vietnam, Country File, National Security File, LBJL [Hereafter Vietnam Country File.]
4. Ibid.
5. Cable 931 from Seoul, Mar. 10, 1965, "NODIS-LOR, Vol. II, 3/65–9/65," Box 46, Vietnam Country File.
6. Cable 1008 from Seoul, Apr. 15, 1965, "NODIS-LOR, Vol. II, 3/65–9/65," Box 46, Vietnam Country File.
7. David C. Cole and Princeton N. Lyman, *Korean Development: Interplay of Politics and Economics* (Cambridge: Harvard University Press, 1971), pp. 13–14.
8. Presidential Task Force on Korea Report to NSC, June 5, 1961, Box 4, Vice-President Security File, National Security File, LBJL, discussion, 12.
9. Ibid.
10. Robert Komer to Lyndon B. Johnson, July 31, 1964, "Memos, Vol. II, 7/64–8/65," Box 254, Korea, Country File, National Security File, LBJL. [Hereafter Korea Country File.]
11. Johnson wrote his ambassadors who were seeking help for South Vietnam from the host countries that "The American people should not be required to continue indefinitely, alone and unassisted, to be the only champions of freedom in Viet Nam today." He argued that the "allies and associated nations" that had received America's help "in the past should not for their own long-range interest, consider their responsibility and their security in terms of immediate national and local concerns." Circular Telegram 14, July 2, 1964, "Cables, Vol. XIII, 6/64–7/64," Box 6, Vietnam Country File.

12. Fearing a setback to his liberal nation-building in South Korea and elsewhere, President Kennedy briefly contemplated initiating a counter coup.

13. This is an untitled, secret memorandum dated Dec. 7, 1963, filed in "Memos, Vol. 1, 11/63–6/64," Box 254, Korea Country file. It is believed to be a summary of McNamara's position on South Korean troop reduction issue.

14. Ball to Kennedy, May 13, 1963, Foreign Economic Policy, Vol. IX, 1961–1963, *Foreign Relations of the United States,* pp. 373–77.

15. Ibid.

16. Untitled, Dec. 7, 1963, "Memos, Vol. 1, 11/63–6/64," Box 254, Korea Country file.

17. Edwin O. Reischauer, *Beyond Vietnam: The United States and Asia* (New York: Alfred A. Knopf, 1968), p. 105.

18. Thomson, Jr., to Johnson, May 17, 1965, "Park's Visit Briefing Book," Box 256, Korea Country File.

19. Cable 915 to Seoul, Mar. 30, 1965, "Cables, Vol. II, 7/64–8/65," Box 254, Korea Country File.

20. Memorandum of Conversation, Feb., 29, 1964, "Memos, Vol. I, 11/63–4/64," Box 250, Japan, Country File, National Security File, LBJL [Hereafter Japan Country File.] After the treaty was ratified, Japan's Prime Minister Sato sent an "off-the-record" message thanking Johnson for "the moral support you have given us in the course of these negotiations." Cable 4387 from Tokyo, June 24, 1965, "Cables, Vol. II, [2 of 2], 9/64–10/65," Box 250, Japan Country File.

21. Bundy to Reischauer, Aug. 3, 1964, "Memos, Vol. II, [2 of 2], 5/64–11/64," Box 250, Japan Country File.

22. Cooper to Watson, Mar. 16, 1965, "Park Visit, 6/65," Box 256, Korea Country File.

23. Korea, Dec. 12, 1965, "Non Committee," Box 15, Files of McGeorge Bundy, National Security File, LBJL [Hereafter Files of McGeorge Bundy.]

24. Thomson, Jr., to Johnson, May 17, 1965, "Park's Visit Briefing Book," Box 256, Korea Country File.

25. Cable 2131 to Saigon, Mar. 30, 1965, "Cables, Vol. XXXI, 3/12–31/65," Box 14, Vietnam Country File. The Johnson administration understandably preferred to have the SEATO allies first pledge help. For example, it wanted to approach Australia and New Zealand, first, then seek "participation [of] other countries in" Asia. Nevertheless, U.S. officials knew that Korea and Philippines were the most likely source of assistance. Cable 2273 to Saigon, Apr. 10, 1965, "Cables, Vol. XXXII, [2 of 2], 4/1–20/65," Box 16, Vietnam Country File.

26. *Security Agreement,* 1551.

27. Cable 552 from Seoul, Dec. 19, 1964, "Cables, Vol. II, 7/64–8/65," Box 254, Korea Country File.

28. Korean Military Assistance to the Republic of Vietnam, [Mar., 1967,] "PM Chung Il-Kwon Visit, 3/14–15/67," Box 257, Korea Country File.

29. *Security Agreement,* 1569.

30. The dean of the "mercenary school" is historian Frank Baldwin who writes that Korean soldiers in South Vietnam well deserved "the appellation of mercenary" because America "secretly paid a high price of dollars and military and economic aid" for their service. He also stated that "all aspects of U.S. official involvement in South Korea were engaged in the various forms of payments." See Frank Baldwin, "America's Rented Troops: South Koreans in Vietnam," *Bulletin of Concerned Asian Scholars* 7 (Oct.–Dec., 1971): 33–39.

31. Memorandum for the President, Jan. 5, 1968, "5D(1) Allies: Troop Commitments; Other Aid (General Material) 3/67–1/69," Box 85–91, Vietnam Country File.

32. Ibid.

33. South Korea first forwarded its list of *quid pro quos* on Apr. 29, 1965, three weeks before Park's scheduled visit to Washington for a summit meeting with Johnson. Cable 1101 from Seoul, May 1, 1965, "Cables, Vol. II, 7/65–8/65," Box 254, Korea Country File.

34. *Security Agreement,* p. 1545.

35. Cable 931 from Seoul, Mar. 30, 1965, "NODIS-LOR, Vol. II, 3/65–9/65," Box 46, Vietnam Country File.

36. Memorandum of Conversation, Jan. 14, 1965, "Memos, Vol. II, 7/64–8/65," Box 254, Korea Country File.

37. Cable 861 from Seoul, Mar. 12, 1965, "Cables, Vol. II, 7/64–8/65," Box 254, Korea Country File.

38. Sang Cho Shin, "Hanil Gukkyo Jungsanghwanun Hanguk Kyongjeui Yesokul Kajoonda (Korea-Japan normalization will cause a subjugation of the Korean economy)," *Business Review* (Sept., 1965): 13.

39. There were historical reasons for South Korea's economic difficulties. During its colonial rule over Korea, Japan concentrated on developing industries in the northern half of the peninsula, whereas the south was left to remain mostly agricultural for expropriation of foodstuffs. Also, the North was richer in terms of natural resource deposits.

40. U.S. Congress, House Committee on International Relations, *Investigation of Korean-American Relations: Hearings before a Subcommittee on International Organizations,* 95th Cong., 2nd sess., 1978, pp. 36–45; The economic stabilization program included the devaluation of the Korean currency against the U.S. dollar. A cheaper Korean *won* made imports from other countries more expensive while making South Korean products cheaper and more attractive to foreign buyers. David Cole, a leading authority on Third World development who later taught economics at Harvard University, argued that this strategy was "a step away from an unhappy dependence on the United States and a generally pessimistic attitude regarding a South Korean state, and a step toward an aggressive policy of economic growth, more international diplomacy, and clear expression of national self-confidence." See *Korean Development, The Interplay of Politics and Economics* (Cambridge: Harvard University Press, 1971), p. 97.

41. Dong Won Lee, "Saehae OeKyojungchyaekui Chongsajin (Blueprint for the New Year's Foreign Policy)," *Gukhoebo* 40 (Jan., 1965): 19–21.

42. Ibid.

43. Lodge, without consulting Washington, instructed American embassy staff in Seoul to prepare for a situation in which Japanese workers had to be replaced by Koreans. See Visit to Pacific and Asian Countries, May 4, 1965, "Lodge Mission (Third Country Assistance)," Box 193, Vietnam Country File.

44. Cable 40 from Seoul, July 10, 1965, "Cables, Vol. II, 7/64–8/65," Box 254, Korea Country File.

45. Valenti to Johnson, Feb. 25, 1966, "CO 151, 6/2/65–8/8/66," Box 49, EX CO 151. Confidential File, White House Central File, LBJL.

46. Ibid.

47. Johnson's advisors were aware of Korea's resentment toward America's large pro-

curement of goods and services from Japan for the forces in South Vietnam. Henry Cabot Lodge, for example, wrote "When the going gets rough," Tokyo would pull out its nationals from South Vietnam. He, therefore, proposed giving more opportunities to South Korea. See Visit to Pacific and Asian Countries, May 4, 1965, "Lodge Mission (Third Country Assistance)," Box 193, Vietnam Country File.

48. Quoted in Herring, *America's Longest War: The United States and Vietnam, 1950–1975,* 2nd ed. (New York: Wiley, 1979), p. 158.

49. "Korea," Dec. 12, 1965, "Non Committee," Box 15, Files of McGeorge Bundy.

50. Korean Military Assistance to the Republic of Vietnam, [Mar., 1967,] "PM Chung Il-Kwon Visit, 3/14–15/67," Box 257, Korea Country File.

51. *Security Agreement,* p. 1534.

52. "Daewolnam Suchul Jinhung Banane Kwanhan Yongu (Research on the ways to promote exports to South Vietnam)," *Muyokyongu* 1 (Mar., 1969): 281–82; Young Jin Hyun, "Wolnamkyonggi Chongkyolsan (Complete tabulation of Vietnam economic boom)," *Wolganjungang* (Mar., 1972): 192.

53. Young Jin Hyun, "Wolnamkyonggi Chongkyolsan (Complete tabulation of Vietnam economic boom)," *Wolganjungang* (Mar., 1972): 190, 192.

54. Bator to Johnson, Dec. 28, 1965, "CO 151 6/2/65/–8/8/66," Box 49, EX CO 150, Confidential File, White House Central File, LBJL.

55. Bundy to Johnson, Feb. 3, 1966, "Vol. 19, 1/19–2/4/66," Box 6, McGeorge Bundy, Memos to the President, National Security File, LBJL [Hereafter Bundy Memos to the President.]

56. Bell to Johnson, May 17, 1966, "Vol. 5, May 27–June 10, 1966," Box 8, W. W. Rostow, Memos to the President, National Security File, LBJL [Hereafter Rostow Memos to the President.]

57. Rostow to Johnson, June 6, 1966, "Vol. 5, May 27–June 10, 1966" Box 8, Rostow Memos to the President.

58. Bell to President May 17, 1966, "Vol. 5, May 27–June 10, 1966," Box 8, Rostow Memos to the President. Johnson's advisors did not fail to remind him that the loans were justified by "the difficult step" Park had taken by pledging 20,000 additional Korean combat troops to Vietnam "at our [Americans'] urging." Rostow, too, pointed out that the loans come "at a time when the Koreans have doubled their Vietnam troop commitment." See Rostow to Johnson, June 6, 1966, "Vol. 5, May 27–June 10, 1966," Box 8, Rostow Memos to the President.

59. Schultze to Johnson, Apr. 21, 1967, "Vol. 27, May 1–15, 1967," Box 16, Rostow Memos to the President.

60. Gaud to Johnson, Apr. 21, 1967, "Vol. 27, May 1–15, 1967," Box 16, Rostow Memos to the President.

61. "Korea," Dec. 22, 1965, "Non committee," Box 15, Files of McGeorge Bundy.

62. Hughes to Johnson, Feb. 23, 1967, "Vol. IV, 1/67–8/67," Box 255, Korea Country File.

63. Initially, Johnson was skeptical of the utility of a regional development bank in Asia to be established mostly by recipients of American aid who would seek America's financing of their economic development projects. Skepticism turned into support after Johnson promised in his Johns Hopkins University speech to help Vietnam and its neighbors with economic development and social modernization. Johnson often cited the ADB as a proof of America's commitment to these goals throughout America's involvement in the Vietnam War.

64. Jones to Johnson, Sept. 12, 1967, "Box 2, Meeting Notes File, Special Files, LBJL [Hereafter Tom Johnson's Notes of Meetings.]

65. Lyndon B. Johnson, *The Vantage Point, Perspectives of the Presidency 1963–1969* (New York: Holt, Rinehart and Winston, 1971), p. 356.

66. Richard de Camp, "The Asian Development Bank: An Imperial Thrust into the Pacific," in *Remaking Asia: Essays on the American Uses of Power,* Mark Selden, ed. (New York: Pantheon Books, 1971), pp. 81, 83. ADB loans to South Korea continued well into the Nixon administration.

67. Gaud and Schnittker to Johnson, Mar. 6, 1967, "Filed by LBJ Library," Box 256, Korea Country File.

68. Hughes to Johnson, Feb. 23, 1967, "Vol. IV, 1/67–8/67," Box 255, Korea Country File.

69. "South Korea Moves Ahead Under Pak Chong-Hui," June 24, 1966, "Memos, Vol. III, 11/65–12/66," Box 255, Korea Country File.

70. Memorandum to Rostow, June 24, 1966, "Vol. 7, June 21–30, 1966," Box 8, Rostow Memos to the President.

71. *Business Week,* May 7, 1966, p. 171.

72. "Summary of Proposal for Economic Development of Korea," [Nov. 1966,] "Vol. 15, Nov. 1–30, 1966," Box 11, Rostow Memos to the President. This is part of the memorandum of a conversation between Rostow and Korea's minister of finance Had Yul Kim in Seoul on Nov. 1, 1966.

73. Memorandum of Conversation, Nov. 1, 1966, "Filed by the LBJ Library," Box 256, Korea Country File.

74. Korean soldiers' toughness was confirmed by Harry McPherson, counsel to the president, who visited South Vietnam in June, 1967, He summarized his impression of Korean soldiers by writing: "God, they are a tough bunch." They used a "seal-and-search" method that was "epitome of war psychology," continued McPherson. He also noted that Koreans' *ruse de guerre* was "slow, harrowing, and effective" so he only wished that he might never meet Korean soldiers "in a rice paddy some night without the right set of credentials." See McPherson to Johnson, June 13, 1967, "Vietnam-1967 (Part 2)," Box 29, Files of Harry McPherson, Office Files of the White House Aides, LBJL. In another testimony to Korean soldiers' "combat effective" *modus operandi* in the Vietnam War, David Ross, who served in Vietnam from May, 1969, to May, 1970, as a warrant officer in a Canadian force, recalled that "Koreans were excellent soldiers." He testified that "we would put them into an area for 15 to 30 days. We would bring in and out medical supplies, weapons, etc. One thing we found that was noticeably different about the Koreans —we never brought out prisoners." Fred Gaffen, *Unknown Warriors: Canadians in the Vietnam War* (Toronto, Canada: Dundurn Press, 1990), p. 199.

75. *Security Agreement,* pp. 1549–50.

76. Hughes to Rusk, Aug. 28, 1964, "Memos, Vol. XVI, 8/16–31/64," Box 7, Vietnam Country File.

77. Cable 1747 from Seoul, Oct. 4, 1966, "Manila Conference and Asian Trip, Vol. IV, Backup Material [IV]," Box 46, National Security Council Histories, National Security File, LBJL [Hereafter National Security Council Histories.]

78. Cable 1707 from Seoul, Oct. 1, 1966, "Manila Conference and Asian Trip, Vol. IV, Backup Material [IV]," Box 46, National Security Council Histories.

79. Thomas A. Bailey, *A Diplomatic History of the American People,* 9th ed. (Englewood Cliffs, New Jersey: Prentice-Hall, 1974), p. 729. The Atlantic Charter can be read differently; for example, Lloyd Gardner writes that the charter "pledged the two leaders of the English-speaking world to the restoration of sovereign rights and self-government to those nations that had been deprived of them and to the estab-

lishment of conditions that would allow all states access to the trade and raw materials of the world." Lloyd C. Gardner, *Imperial America: American Foreign Policy Since 1898* (New York: Harcourt Brace Jovanovich, 1976), 159. Park seemed to have concluded that the Atlantic Charter enunciated the liberation of all the territories under Axis control as the war aim.

80. Cable 1707 from Seoul, Oct. 1, 1966, "Manila Conference and Asian Trip, Vol. IV, Backup Material [IV]," Box 46, National Security Council Histories.

81. Ibid.

82. Cable 1807 from Seoul, Oct. 6, 1966, "Manila Conference and Asian Trip, Vol. IV, Backup Material [IV]," Box 46, National Security Council Histories.

83. Cable 1999 from Seoul, Oct. 14, 1966, "Manila Conference and Asian Trip, Vol. IV, Backup Material [IV]," Box 46, National Security Council Histories.

84. Ibid.

85. Cable 59565 to Seoul, Oct. 4, 1966, "Manila Conference and Asian Trip, Vol. IV, Backup Material [IV]," Box 46, National Security Council Histories.

86. "Visit of Prime Minister Il Kwon Chung . . . Scope Paper," [Mar., 1967]," PM Chung Il-Kwon Visit Papers 3/14–15/67," Box 256, Korea Country File. The three major peace proposals from "non-participants" had very little chance of being adopted by Hanoi. For example, in February, 1967, UN Secretary-General U Thant proposed the following three-step procedure: "a general cease fire; preliminary talks; the reconvening of the Geneva Conference." In April, Canada forwarded another four-step proposal: "demilitarization of DMZ; no increase in military activity or reinforcements; cessation of hostilities; return to the cease fire of the Geneva settlement." Hanoi's precondition, of course, was the unconditional withdrawal of foreign forces. When Johnson responded to these international calls for negotiation by proposing a "balanced reduction in military activity," Park protested against it as a concession. For history of "major peace initiatives" to end the Vietnam War, see Johnson, *Vantage Point*, pp. 579–89.

87. Copy of Cable 5094 from Seoul, Mar. 23, 1967, "Vol. IV, 1/67–8/67," Box 255, Korea Country File.

88. Rostow to Johnson, Mar. 24, 1967, "Vol. IV, 1/67–8/67," Box 255, Korea Country File.

89. Cable 2110 from Seoul, Oct. 18, 1966, "Manila Conference and Asian Trip, Vol. IV, Backup Material [IV]," Box 46, National Security Council Histories.

90. Copy of Cable 5094 from Seoul, Mar. 23, 1967, "Vol. IV, 1/67–8/67," Box 255, Korea Country File.

91. Ibid.

92. "Summary Record of the Second Session Summit Conferences," Oct. 24, 1966, "Manila Conference and Asian Trip, Vol. II," Box 45, National Security Council Histories, pp. 3–5.

93. Draft of cable to Seoul, [Cleared for transmission on May 14, 1967,] attached to Read to Rostow, May 14, 1967, "Filed by LBJ Library," Box 256, Korea Country File.

94. On January 21, 1968, North Korean commandos launched what South Korea recognized as a "matchlessly brilliant" assassination attempt against Park. The commandos infiltrated deep into Seoul and nearly reached their target, the presidential palace. They were stopped by South Korean forces at a high cost. Two days later, on the 23rd, in Korea's eastern waters, (or the Sea of Japan), North Korea captured the American intelligence-gathering vessel, the USS *Pueblo* with eighty-six crew members on board. Pyongyang accused the *Pueblo* of being an "armed spy

ship," and threatened to put the crew on trial for "military provocation" and espionage. The *Pueblo* became, according to historian Larry Berman, "the first U.S. vessel captured since the USS *Chesapeake* in 1807—during the Napoleonic wars." When the United States agreed to talks proposed by North Korea to negotiate the return of the ship and crew members without South Korean representatives, and to exclude North Korea's attempt to assassinate Park from the agenda of the meeting, Park accused the United States of protecting its own interest at the cost of South Korea's. See Cable 3624 from Seoul, Jan. 25, 1968, "Vol. 5, 9/67–3/68," Box 255, Korea Country File; Larry Berman, *Lyndon Johnson's War: The Road to Stalemate in Vietnam* (New York: W. W. Norton, 1989), p. 144.

95. "Honolulu Meeting with President Park, Major Topics," [Apr. 1968,] "Meeting with President Park, 4/68," Box 21, International Meetings & Travel File, National Security File, LBJL [Hereafter International Meetings and Travel File.]

96. "ROK Desire for Amendment of Mutual Defense Treaty," [Apr., 1968], "Meeting with President Park, 4/68," Box 21, International Meetings & Travel File.

97. "Honolulu Meeting with President Park, Major Topics," [Apr., 1968,] "Meeting with President Park, 4/68," Box 21, International Meetings & Travel File. See also "ROK Desire for Amendment of Mutual Defense Treaty," [Apr., 1968], ibid.

98. "Honolulu Meeting with President Park, Major Topics," [Apr., 1968], "Meeting with President Park, 4/68," Box 21, International Meetings & Travel File. See also, "ROK Desire for Reaffirmation of 1953 Declaration by the Sixteen Korean War Participants," [Apr., 1968], "Meeting with President Park, 4/68," Box 21, International Meetings & Travel File.

99. "President Park's Probable Concerns," [Apr., 1968], "Meeting with President Park, 4/68," Box 21, International Meetings & Travel File.

100. Cable 3103 from Seoul, Dec. 23, 1967, "5D(3) Allies: Troop Commitments; Other Aid (Korea–United Kingdom) 1967–69," Box 91, Vietnam Country File.

101. South Korea initially requested $400 as monthly pay plus allowance for the lowest ranking KLSC personnel. In the negotiation, it was brought down to $330. Cable 3466 from Seoul, Jan. 18, 1968, "5D(3) Allies: Troop Commitments; Other Aid (Korea–United Kingdom) 1967–69," Box 91, Vietnam Country File.

102. Ibid.

103. For Bunker's objection see Cable 16410 from Saigon, Jan. 19, 1968, "5D(3) Allies: Troop Commitment; Other Aid (Korea–United Kingdom) 1967–69," Box 91, Vietnam Country File. For Rusk's comments see Cable 102815 to Seoul, Jan. 23, 1968, Ibid. Washington risked appearing to openly recruit mercenaries—ex-veterans doing military tasks for civilian pay—by negotiating for the Korean Logistics Service Corps. The negotiation fell apart only because Washington could not meet Korea's demand on pay scale, not because of possible political repercussions.

104. Cable 3104 from Saigon, Dec. 23, 1967, "5D(3) Allies: Troop Commitments; Other Aid (Korea–United Kingdom) 1967–69," Box 91, Vietnam Country File.

105. Komer to Johnson, May 1, 1967, "Memos(A), Vol. 70, 4/25–5/8/67," Box 43, Vietnam Country File.

106. "Lunch Meeting with the President . . ." June 19, 1968, "Meetings with President, May–June, 1968 [1]," Box 2, Walt Rostow File, National Security File, LBJL.

107. Joint Chiefs to Smith [Bromley], Sept. 7, 1968, "5D(3) Allies: Troop Assistance; Other Aid (Korea–United Kingdom) 1967–69, Box 91, Vietnam Country File.

108. "Notes of the President's Meeting with the Senior Foreign Affairs Advisory Council," Feb. 10, 1968. Box 2, Tom Johnson's Notes of Meetings.

Chapter 9 by Hiroshi Fujimoto

This is almost the same version of my paper presented at the conference titled "Vietnam: International Perspectives," which was held at the LBJ Library on October 17–19, 1997. This essay is mainly based on secondary sources. For the revised and expanded version of this essay, based on archival research at the LBJ Library after the conference, see Hiroshi Fujimoto, "Betonamu Sensōto Nichibei Kankei [The Vietnam War and the Japanese-American Relations], 1965–1967," *Shakaikagaku-ronshuu* [The Review of Social Sciences] 37 (1998): 137–72.

1. Betonamu ni okeru America no Sensō Hanzai Chousa Iinkai ed., *Jenosaido* [Genocide] (Tokyo: Aoki Shoten, 1967).

2. Thomas R. Havens, *Fire Across the Sea: The Vietnam War and Japan, 1965–1975* (Princeton, N.J.: Princeton University Press, 1987), p. 260. For major works in English on Japan and the Vietnam War, see John W. Dower, "The Superdomino in Postwar Asia: Japan in and out of the Pentagon Papers," in *The Pentagon Papers: Critical Essays* [The Senator Gravel Edition, Vol. 5], Noam Chomsky and Howard Zinn, eds. (Boston: Beacon Press, 1972), pp. 101–42; K. V. Kesavan, "The Vietnam War As an Issue in Japan's Relations with the United States," *International Studies* [India] 16:4 (1977): 501–19; J. A. Clarke, "Japanese Foreign Policy and the War in Vietnam, 1964–1969." Ph.D. diss., University of Sheffield [UK], 1986; Masaya Shiraishi, *Japanese Relations with Vietnam, 1951–1987* (Ithaca, N.Y.: Cornell University Southeast Asia Program, 1990). Walter LaFeber and Michael Schaller each have recently published monographs on the history of U.S.-Japanese relations, which include valuable insights on Japan's role in the Vietnam War. Walter LaFeber, *The Clash: U.S.-Japanese Relations throughout History* (New York: W. W. Norton, 1997); Michael Schaller, *Altered States: The United States and Japan since the Occupation* (New York: Oxford University Press, 1997).

3. Motoo Furuta, *Rekishi toshiteno Betonamu Sensō* [The Vietnam War as History] (Tokyo: Otsuki Shoten, 1991), pp. 171, 176–77. There were many contemporary articles and essays in Japanese journals and daily newspapers during the Vietnam War, but after the end of the war, besides Furuta's book, there have been only a few works written in Japanese on Japan's role in the war. Among them are Shigeo Hayashi, "Betonamu Sensōto Nihon" [The Vietnam War and Japan] in *Betonamu Sensō no Kiroku* [The Documents of the Vietnam War] (Tokyo: Otsuki Shoten, 1988), pp. 266–71; Minami Yoshizawa, *Betonamu Sensōto Nihon* [Japan and the Vietnam War] (Tokyo: Iwanami Shoten, 1989); idem., "Betonamu Sensōto Nikkan Jouyaku [The Vietnam War and the Japan-Korea Treaty]," in *Nihon Dōjidai-shi* [History of Contemporary Japan], Rekishigaku kenkyukai, ed., vol. 4 of 5 (Tokyo: Aoki Shoten, 1990), pp. 75–114.

4. See, for example, William Borden, *The Pacific Alliance: United States Foreign Economic Policy and Japanese Trade Recovery, 1947–1955* (Madison: University of Wisconsin Press, 1984); Andrew J. Rotter, *The Path to Vietnam: Origins of the American Commitment to Southeast Asia* (Ithaca, N.Y.: Cornell University Press, 1987); Thomas J. McCormick, "American Hegemony and the Roots of the Vietnam War," in *Vietnam: Four American Perspectives,* Patrick J. Hearden, ed. (West Lafayette, Ind.: Purdue University Press, 1990), pp. 83–107.

5. Furuta, *Rekishi toshiteno Betonamu Sensō,* p. 176.

6. Department of State Policy on the Future of Japan, National Security File [NSF], Country File, Japan, Reischauer to Rusk, cable 2013, Dec. 23, 1964, Sato's Visit,

memo & cables [1 of 2], LBJL, quoted in Hideki Kan, "Betonamu Sensōto Nichibei Ampo Taisei [The Vietnam War and the U.S.-Japan Security System]," *Kokusai Seiji* [International Relations] 115 (May, 1997): 79, 91.

7. *The Department of State Bulletin,* Feb. 1, 1965, p. 134.
8. Ibid., p. 135.
9. Ibid.
10. Ibid.
11. *The Department of State Bulletin,* Apr. 26, 1965, p. 608.
12. Memorandum, Prime Minister Eisaku Sato to President Lyndon B. Johnson, Apr. 10, 1965, NSF, Country File, Japan, Box 250, LBJ Library. See also Takashi Itō, ed., *Sato Eisaku Nikki* [The Diary of Eisaku Sato], vol. 2 of 6 (Tokyo: Asahi Shimbunsha, 1998–99), p. 260.
13. For the "more flags" program, see Robert M. Blackburn, *Mercenaries and Lyndon Johnson's "More Flags": The Hiring of Korean, Filipino and Thai Soldiers in the Vietnam War* (Jefferson, N.C.: McFarland & Company, Inc., Publishers, 1994).
14. Havens, *Fire Across the Sea,* p. 25.
15. Memorandum, Assistant Secretary of State for Far Eastern Affairs (W. Bundy) to President Johnson, Feb. 16, 1965. *Foreign Relations of the United States, 1964–1968, Vol. II, Vietnam, January–June, 1965* (Washington: G.P.O., 1996), p. 292. For a thirteen-page attached memorandum dated February 16, which is not printed, see "Reactions of Non-Communist Countries to US Actions in Vietnam," NSF, Country File, Vietnam, Box 13, LBJL.
16. Asahi Shinbun, Aug. 24, 1965; Havens, *Fire Across the Sea,* p. 50.
17. Kan, "The Vietnam War and the U.S.-Japan Security System," p. 85.
18. Havens, *Fire Across the Sea,* p. 84.
19. Quoted in "Combined Testimonies on the Complicity of Japan in the Vietnam War, testimony by the Japanese Committee," in *Against the Crime of Silence: Proceedings of the Russell International War Crimes Tribunal,* John Duffet, ed. (Flanders, N.J.: O'Hare Books, 1968), p. 589.
20. Havens, *Fire Across the Sea,* p. 28.
21. Quoted in "Combined Testimonies," p. 588.
22. Havens, *Fire Across the Sea,* pp. 84–92. See also Shigeo Hayashi, "Betonamu Sensō to Nihon."
23. Quoted in Betonamu niokeru, *Jenosaido,* p. 115. See also Havens, *Fire Across the Sea,* p. 85.
24. Havens, *Fire Across the Sea,* pp. 87–88.
25. Quoted in "Combined Testimonies," p. 595.
26. Havens, *Fire Across the Sea,* pp. 93, 96.
27. Ibid., p. 95. On windfalls for Japan from the Vietnam War, see also Schaller, *Altered States,* pp. 198–202; Yoshizawa, *Betonamu Sensōto Nihon,* pp. 35–42.
28. Quoted in Jiyul Kim, "U.S. and Korea in Vietnam and the Japan-Korea Treaty: Search for Security, Prosperity and Influence," M.A. thesis, Harvard University, 1991, p. 36. I would like to thank Professor Lee Jong Won of Rikkyo University, Tokyo, Japan, for permitting me to use a copy of Kim's thesis.
29. See Lee Jong Won, "Kan-Nichi Kokko Seijou-ka to Amerika [The United States and the Normalization between Japan and Korea], 1960–1965," in *Sengo Gaikōno Keiksei* [Making of Postwar Diplomacy], Kindai Nihon Kenkyukai, ed. (Tokyo: Yamakawa Suppansha, 1994), pp. 295–98. For more detailed analysis in Japanese on South Korea's role in the Vietnam War, see Park Kun Ho, *Kankoku no Keizai-*

hatten to Betonamu Senso [Economic Development of Korea and the Vietnam War] (Tokyo: Ochanomizu Shobo, 1993); Masashi Kimiya, "1960nen-dai Kankoku niokeru Reisen to Keizai-kaihatsu [The Cold War and South Korea's Economic Development in the 1960s]," *Hogaku-shirin* 92, no. 4 (Mar., 1995).

30. Department of State, Memorandum of Conversation, May 15, 1965, NSF, Country File, Korea, Box 254, LBJL. Quoted in Kim, "U.S.-Korea in Vietnam and the Japan-Korea Treaty," pp. 172–73.

31. Kiyoko Imura, *Gendai Nihon Keizai-ron* [The Modern Japanese Economy], p. 239.

32. Park, *Kankoku no Keizai-hatten to Betonamu Sensō*, pp. 68–69.

33. Havens, *Fire Across the Sea*, p. 104.

34. Imura, *Gendai Nihon Keizai-ron*, p. 236.

35. Havens, *Fire Across the Sea*, p. 132.

36. See, for example, Memorandum, B. Reed [Executive Secretary of the National Security Council] to Walt Rostow [National Security Adviser to President Johnson], "Check List of Helpful Japanese Actions: Past and Anticipated," Nov. 6, 1967, NSF, Country File, Japan, Box 252, LBJL.

37. Memorandum, Dean Rusk to the President, Oct. 27, 1967, NSF, Country File, Japan, Box 253, LBJL.

38. *The Department of State Bulletin*, Dec. 4, 1967, p. 745.

39. Ibid.

40. Havens, *Fire Across the Sea*, p. 97.

Chapter 10 by Robert J. McMahon

1. *New York Times,* Sept. 12, 1993, III, p. 1.

2. These figures have been culled from the following: *Direction of Trade Statistics Yearbook* (Washington: International Monetary Fund, 1995); U.S. Department of Commerce, *The Big Emerging Markets* (Washington: G.P.O., 1996); John Bresnan, *From Dominoes to Dynamos: The Economic Transformation of Southeast Asia* (New York: Council on Foreign Relations Press, 1994), pp. 14–28; *New York Times,* Feb. 2, 1996, p. C-1, and Mar. 9, 1996, III, p. 7.

3. W. W. Rostow, *The United States and the Regional Organization of Asia and the Pacific, 1965–1985* (Austin: University of Texas Press, 1986), p. 143.

4. W. W. Rostow, "Vietnam and Asia," *Diplomatic History* 20 (summer, 1996): 467–71.

5. Marvin Stone, "Southeast Asia Revisited," *U.S. News and World Report* 91 (Oct. 12, 1981): 90–92. In a similar vein, see Geoffrey Walker, "Saigon's Fall Masked a U.S. Victory in Vietnam," *Wall Street Journal,* Apr. 28, 1983, p. 28.

6. Ernest Lefever, "Vietnam's Ghosts," *Wall Street Journal,* May 21, 1997, p. 14.

7. Quoted in H. W. Brands, *The Wages of Globalism: Lyndon Johnson and the Limits of American Power* (New York: Oxford University Press, 1995), p. 178.

8. Robert McNamara, *In Retrospect: The Tragedy and Lessons of Vietnam* (New York: Times Books, 1995), p. 214.

9. Quoted in H. W. Brands, "The Limits of Manipulation: How the United States Didn't Topple Sukarno," *Journal of American History* 76 (Dec., 1989): 798.

10. Hugh Tovar, "The Indonesian Crisis of 1965–1967: A Retrospective," *International Journal of Intelligence and Counterintelligence* 7 (fall, 1994): 324. See also Paul F. Gardner, *Shared Hopes, Separate Fears: Fifty Years of U.S.-Indonesian Relations* (Boulder, Colo.: Westview, 1997), pp. 213–29; Marshall Green, *Indonesia: Crisis and Transformation, 1965–1968* (Washington: Compass, 1990).

11. Quoted in Brands, "Limits of Manipulation," p. 805.

12. See, for example, David P. Chandler, *The Tragedy of Cambodian History: Politics, War, and Revolution since 1945* (New Haven: Yale University Press, 1991).

13. Among other important works that cover the Marcos era are H. W. Brands, *Bound to Empire: The United States and the Philippines* (New York: Oxford University Press, 1992); Stanley Karnow, *In Our Image: America's Empire in the Philippines* (New York: Ballantine, 1989); Raymond Bonner, *Waltzing with a Dictator: The Marcoses and the Making of American Policy* (New York: Times Books, 1987).

14. See, for example, McMahon, *Limits of Empire.*

15. *New York Times,* Aug. 4, 1966, p. 1.

16. Ibid., Apr. 12, 1967, p. 6.

17. Qiang Zhai's forthcoming book on Chinese-Vietnamese relations during the Vietnam War, a preliminary copy of which the author kindly shared with me, details the multiple influences shaping Chinese foreign policy during this period.

18. *Far Eastern Economic Review* 74 (Dec. 11, 1971): 18.

19. Ibid., 74 (Dec. 4, 1971): 5–6; Leifer, *ASEAN and the Security of South-East Asia* (London: Routledge, 1989); Ronald D. Palmer and Thomas J. Reckford, *Building ASEAN: 20 Years of Southeast Asian Cooperation* (New York: Praeger, 1987); Michael Antolik, *ASEAN and the Diplomacy of Accommodation* (Armonk, N.Y.: M. E. Sharpe, 1990).

20. *Far Eastern Economic Review* 67 (Mar. 27, 1970): 25–26.

21. Ibid. 73 (Aug. 14, 1971): 14; *Washington Post,* May 5, 1972, p. 1.

22. *Wall Street Journal,* Mar. 14, 1985, p. 1.

23. Richard Robison, *Indonesia: The Rise of Capital* (Sydney: Allen and Unwin, 1986); Richard Robison, Kevin Hewison, and Richard Higgott, *Southeast Asia in the 1980s: The Politics of Economic Crisis* (Sydney: Allen and Unwin, 1987); E. K. Fisk, "Development in Malaysia," in *The Political Economy of Malaysia,* E. K. Fisk, ed. (Kuala Lumpur: Oxford University Press, 1982); J. A. C. Mackie, "Economic Growth in the ASEAN Region: The Political Underpinnings," in *Achieving Industrialization in East Asia,* Helen Hughes, ed. (Cambridge, Eng.: Cambridge University Press, 1988); Donald Crone, *The ASEAN States: Coping with Dependency* (New York: Praeger, 1983); Chris Dixon, *South-East Asia in the World Economy* (Cambridge, Eng.: Cambridge University Press, 1991); P. W. Preston, *Making Sense of Development* (New York: Routledge and Kegan, 1986); Ian Brown, *Economic Change in South-East Asia, 1830–1980* (Kuala Lumpur: Oxford University Press, 1997); R. S. Milne and Diane K. Mauzy, *Singapore: The Legacy of Lee Kuan Yew* (Boulder, Colo.: Westview, 1990). For an incisive review of this literature, see Richard F. Doner, "Approaches to the Politics of Economic Growth in Southeast Asia," *Journal of Asian Studies* 50 (Nov., 1991): 818–49.

24. Brown, *Economic Change in South-East Asia,* pp. 260–64.

25. The most influential work in this vein is probably Kunio Yoshihara, *The Rise of Ersatz Capitalism in Southeast Asia* (Singapore: Oxford University Press, 1988).

26. Richard Stubbs, "Geopolitics and the Political Economy of Southeast Asia," *International Journal* 44 (1989): 517–40.

27. Thomas R. Havens, *Fire Across the Sea: The Vietnam War and Japan, 1965–1975* (Princeton, N.J.: Princeton University Press, 1987), pp. 84–102; Michael Schaller, *Altered States: The United States and Japan Since the Occupation* (New York: Oxford University Press, 1997), pp. 198–202.

28. *New York Times,* June 1, 1997, p. 6; *Economist* 343 (June 17, 1997): 37–38.

Chapter 11 by Judith A. Klinghoffer

1. CIA Report, June 8, 1967, NSF, M.E. Crisis, Box 18, p. 185, LBJL.
2. Walt Rostow, telephone interview by Judith Klinghoffer, Oct. 3, 1997.
3. Richard B. Parker, *The Six-Day War: A Retrospective* (Gainesville: University of Florida Press, 1996), pp. 229–30.
4. Ibid., pp. 129–30.
5. Salach Shaval, "New Strategy for the Liberation of Palestine," *Maarchot,* May, 1967, p. 26. *Al Dafah,* Nov. 15, 1966, "Flexible action plan—in light of experience, (an Israeli intelligence analysis of new Arab strategic thinking on the Palestinian issue)," *Hedim Utguvot,* March 23, 1967, and *Al Charia* (Lebanon), Jan. 9, 1967, DCSS.
6. Parker, *The Six Day War,* p. 3.
7. Georgiy Kornienko, "The Cold War: Testimony of a Participant" (Moscow: 1994), pp. 129–33, as translated in Parker, *The Six Day War,* pp. 71–72.
8. Randall Bennett Woods, *Fulbright: A Biography* (Cambridge: Cambridge University Press, 1995), pp. 454–55.
9. Dean Rusk, interview by Judith Klinghoffer, Augusta, Ga., Aug. 2, 1991.
10. Parker, *The Six Day War,* p. 2.
11. Dobrynin, *In Confidence,* p. 136.
12. Gaiduk, *Soviet Union and Vietnam War,* pp. 18, 258.
13. Dobrynin, *In Confidence,* pp. 143–44.
14. *The Washington Post,* July 25, 1966.
15. *Security Council Official Records.* 1293rd Meeting. Aug. 1, 1966, p. 18.
16. James Burnham, "The Kremlin Move?" *The National Review,* Aug. 23, 1966, p. 822.
17. *Pentagon Papers,* Gravel, ed., III, p. 698.
18. *Pentagon Papers,* IV, pp. 346–47 and 385.
19. "Memorandum for the President, July 1, 1965, NSF, Box 18, 113, LBJL.
20. *Pravda,* Oct. 16, 1966.
21. Lyndon Johnson, *Vantage Point,* p. 288.
22. The American Sixth Fleet and the Soviet so-called "Red Fleet" had been keeping an eye on each other for at least two years but, as the navy reported, "no embarrassing or dangerous incidents occurred." Weekly Report, DoD Feb. 28, 1967. Soviet UN representative Fedorenko mentioned these incidents in his May 29 Security Council speech. From Walt Rostow to the President, May 29, 1967, NSF, Middle East Crisis, Box 17, LBJL.
23. *The Economist,* Mar. 25, 1967.
24. Johnson, *Vantage Point,* pp. 578 and 587.
25. Janos Radvanyi, *Delusion and Reality* (South Bend, Ind.: University of Notre Dame Press, 1978), pp. 232–36.
26. *Pravda,* Apr. 25, 1967. This change of heart was also evident in Latin America, where guerrillas were beginning to receive promises of material support from Moscow.
27. Memorandum, Subject: The US—The Soviet Union—and Detente, Apr. 14, 1967, NSF, Country File, USSR, Box 223, 229, 132a; Memorandum for the President from W. W. Rostow, May 6, 1967, *Pentagon Papers,* IV, p. 476; "The McNaughton Draft Presidential Memorandum," May 19, 1967, *Pentagon Papers,* IV, p. 485; NSC Meeting, May 3, 1967, Box 2, Vol. 4, Tab 5, LBJL, *The Washington Star,* Apr. 5, 1967; *Congressional Record—Senate,* Apr. 27, 1966, 10996-8; and Dean Rusk and Zbigniew Brzezinski, interviews by Judith Klinghoffer, Washington, D.C., July 29, 1991.

28. *Pravda,* Apr. 25, 1967.

29. Vassiliev, *Soviet Policy in the Middle East* (Reading, N.Y.: Ithaca Press, 1993), p. 111.

30. Ben Tsur, *Gormim Sovietiim Lemilchemet Sheshet Hayamim* (Tel Aviv: Sifriyat Hapoalim, 1975), p. 155; Weit, *Eyewitness: The Autobiography of Gomulka's Interpreter* (London: Deutch, 1973), pp. 139–40; and Vassiliev, *Soviet Policy in the Middle East,* p. 111.

31. Following the demise of Ben Bella, Nasser told Zhou Enlai, Sukarno, and Ayub Khan that what happened to Ben Bella could easily happen to other Afro-Asian leaders and that the UAR would be a victim because the "Soviets were cowards." Sukarno "was shaken" because he believed that he "probably" would be next. CIA Intelligence Information Cable, June 27, 1965, Country File, UAR, p. 159, LBJL.

32. Moshe Gilboa, *Shesh Shanim Veshisha Yamim* (Tel Aviv: Am Oved, 1968), p. 86. See also, Radio Czechoslovakia in Arabic, *Hedim Utguvot,* June 23, 1967.

33. *Congressional Record—Senate,* May 19, 1967.

34. *Washington Post,* May 17, 1967, and Eugene Rostow, interview by Judith Klinghoffer, Washington, D.C., Oct. 15, 1991.

35. Dept. of State to Amembassy Moscow, May 19, 1967, NSF, M.E. Crisis, Box 17, p. 27.

36. *Congressional Record—Senate,* May 19, 1967.

37. Richard Parker, *The Politics of Miscalculation in the Middle East* (Bloomington: University of Indiana Press, 1993), p. 31.

38. *Pravda,* May 22, 1967, and *New York Times,* May 24, 1967.

39. "Near East, North Africa and the Horn of Africa: A Recommended American Strategy," The Special State-Defense Study Group, July 1, Vol. I, p. 28, and Vol. II, B-5, B-6 and *New York Daily News,* June 1, 1967.

40. *Pentagon Papers,* IV, p. 187. [Author's note: The link between U.S. bombing in Vietnam and the Middle East was brought to my attention by Benjamin Read, the executive secretary of the State Department.]

41. Summary, Secretary Appearance before the SFRC, May 23, 1967, M.E. Crisis, Box 17, p. 99; Lucius Battle, interview by Judith Klinghoffer, Aug. 28, 1991; and *New York Times,* May 24, 1967.

42. NSC Meeting, May 24, 1967, Box 2, p. 2, *New York Times,* May 25, 1967.

43. *Pentagon Papers,* IV, p. 187.

44. Arie Brown, *Moshe Dayan and the Six Day War* (Tel Aviv: Yediot Aharonot, 1996), p. 110.

45. Parker, *The Six Day War,* p. 49, and Robert McNamara, telephone interview by Judith Klinghoffer, Oct. 31, 1991; Rusk and Rostow interviews.

46. *Daily Diary,* May 25, 1967, and Remez to Levavi, May 25, 1967, "Six Day War—Diplomatic cables," Yad Eshkol.

47. Parker, *Politics of Miscalculation,* p. 232, and *Christian Science Monitor,* May 25, 1967.

48. Dept. of State to Amembassy Moscow, May 25, 1967, NSF, Country file, USSR, Box 223, 229, p. 31, LBJL.

49. *New York Times,* May 27, 1967.

50. Parker, *Politics of Miscalculation,* 252n and Memorandum of Conversation, Appointment book, May–June, 1967, Box 66, 1d, LBJL.

51. Memorandum of Eshkol and Chuvakhin conversation, Oct. 11, 1966; Memorandum of Semyonov and Israel Katz conversation, Nov. 9, 1966; a Soviet oral declaration, Apr. 21, 1967, "Israeli-Soviet Relations," Yad Eshkol; interviews with Israeli sources and *Maariv,* Oct. 4, 1967.

52. Dean Rusk, *As I Saw It* (New York: W. W. Norton, 1990), pp. 385–86, and Memorandum of Conversation, May 27, 1967, NSF, M.E. Crisis, Box 17, p. 61, LBJL.
53. Outgoing Telegram, Dept. of State, May 27, 1967, NSF, M.E. Crisis, Box 17, p. 70.
54. An Egyptian memorandum of conversation cited in Parker, *The Politics of Miscalculation*, p. 32.
55. As Printed in Theodore Draper, *Israel and World Politics* (New York: Viking Press, 1967–68), pp. 224–31.
56. *People's Daily,* May 29, 1967, reprinted in the *Peking Review,* June 2, 1967, pp. 34–35.
57. From Embassy Paris to Jerusalem, May 29, 1967, "Six Day War—Diplomatic cables," Yad Eshkol. *Security Council Official Record,* 1343rd Meeting, May 29, 1967, p. 20.
58. Dept. of State, from Amembassy Moscow, May 29, 1967, NSF, USSR, Box 223, 229, p. 10, LBJL.
59. Memorandum of Conversation at Luncheon, June 25, 1967, NSF, Country File, USSR (Glassboro Memcon) 6/67, p. 10, LBJL.
60. *Davar,* May 29, 1967.
61. Eugene V. Rostow, "The Middle Eastern Crisis in the Perspective of World Politics," *International Affairs* 47 (Apr., 1971): 280–81.
62. Dean Rusk asserted that it was important that Israel accept American advice "on such an important matter." Robert McNamara, Dean Rusk and Meir Amit, interviews by Judith Klinghoffer, Ramat Gan, Israel, Jan. 8, 1992.
63. Radio Cairo, May 19, 1967 (emphasis in original), Indar Jit Rikhye, *The Sinai Blunder* (New York: Frank Cass, 1980) p. 163; 967. *Maariv,* May 22, 1967; and *Tamzit Shidurim,* May 19, 1967. Ahmed Shukayri was the chairman of the Palestine Liberation Organization.
64. Nasser, as printed in Draper, *Israel and World Politics,* p. 232.
65. "Ashaf," *Maarchot,* Oct., 1968, p. 25.
66. *Maariv,* June 2, 1972.
67. Memorandum for the Secretary of Defense, June 2, 1967, JCSM-310-67, NSF, M.E. Crisis, Box 18, 36, *Maariv,* June 4, 1967; and Memorandum of Conversation with Mr. Gely Skirtski of the Soviet Embassy, June 6, 1967, Country file, USSR, Box 223, 229, p. 140a, LBJL.
68. *Security Council Official Records,* June 3, 1967, pp. 15–23.
69. Amembassy Moscow to the Department of State, June 15, 1967 NSF, U.S.S.R., Box 230, 46a, LBJL; K. S. Karol, "Angry Men in the Kremlin," *New Statesman,* June 16, 1967, p. 820.
70. Nicholas Katzenbach, interview by Judith Klinghoffer, Princeton, N.J., July 15, 1991; Eugene Rostow interview; and Arkady Shevchenko, *Breaking with Moscow* (New York: Ballantine Books, 1985), pp. 177–78.
71. Donald C. Bergus, "View from Washington," in Parker, *The Six Day War,* p. 194.
72. *Pravda,* June 12 and 22, 1967; Amembassy Moscow to the Dept. of State, June 15, 1967, NSF, USSR, Box 230, p. 46a.
73. *Pravda,* June 19 and 23, 1967.
74. Shevchenko, p. 163, and Memorandum of Conversation between President Johnson and Alexei Kosygin, June 23 and 25, 1967, NSF, Addendum, CF, USSR (Glassboro Memcons), LBJL.
75. Talking Points for Meetings with Prime Minister Pearson, NSF, Presidential Appointment File, May–June, 1967, Box 66, p. 1c.
76. *Public Papers of the Presidents, Lyndon B. Johnson,* June 23, 1967, p. 281.
77. Shevchenko, p. 181.

78. Benjamin Read, LBJ-OH, Tape I, p. 25.
79. Vassiliev, *Soviet Policy in the Middle East,* p. 73; Abba Eban, *Personal Witness* (New York: G. P. Putnam's Sons, 1992), p. 453; Gideon Rafael, *Destination Peace* (London: Weidenfeld and Nidlson, 1991), pp. 178–82; Mahmoud Riad, *The Struggle for Peace* (London: Quartet Books, 1981), p. 47.
80. U.S. Congress, Special Subcommittee on National Defense Posture of the Committee of the Armed Services, Interim Report, Dec. 13, 1967 (Washington: 1968), p. 49.
81. "A Recommended American Strategy," Special State-Defense Study Group, July, 1967, Vol. I, State Department archives; For Mr. Rostow from Hal Saunders, Aug. 17, 1967, NSF, Agency File, Box 34, NSC, Vol. 2, p. 7, LBJL.
82. David A. Korn, *Stalemate* (Boulder: Westview Press, 1992), pp. 78–89; Cable from Ambassador Cleveland (Paris, 3224), Sept. 13, 1967, NSF, CF, France, Box 173, p. 92, LBJL. Fifty percent of the oil the United States used in Vietnam came from Saudi Arabia.
83. Read remembers the message coming in late July, but he says it followed some heavy bombing in the Hanoi area, which started only on August 8. Read, LBJ-OH, p. 25.
84. "The threat of the guided-missile patrol boat," CIA Special Report, Nov. 24, 1967, NSF, CF, Israel, Box 138. *Congressional Record—House,* Oct. 23, 1967, p. 29614. Tom Johnson's Tuesday lunch notes, Oct. 23, 1967, Box 1, LBJL.
85. *Congressional Record—House,* Oct. 31, 1967, p. 30603.
86. Lawrence L. Whetten, *The Canal War* (Cambridge, Mass.: The MIT Press, 1974), pp. 52–55.
87. Memorandum on China, the Soviet Union and Vietnam, Nov. 27, 1967, NSF, NSC Meeting, Box 2, p. 5, LBJL.
88. NSC Meeting, Nov. 29, 1967, NSF, NSC Meeting, Box 2, p. 3, "Talking Points for Prime Minister Eshkol," Jan. 5, 1968, NSF; Memos for the President, Box 15, LBJL; and Rafael, *Destination Peace,* p. 179.
89. Administrative History, pt. 4, ch. 4, Sec. F and Memorandum to the President, Jan. 16, 1968, NSF, Name File, Walt Rostow, Box 7, p. 31, LBJL.
90. NSC Meeting on the Near East, Feb. 21, 1968, NSF, Box 2, p. 2, LBJL.
91. "Memorandum of Conversation, Feb. 7, 1968, NSF, CF, Box 140, 141, 148, LBJL.
92. Tom Johnson Tuesday lunch notes, Mar. 19, 1968, Box 2. LBJL; Walter Isaacson and Evan Thomas, *The Wise Men* (New York: Simon and Schuster, 1986), p. 689; David L. Dileo, *George Ball* (Chapel Hill: University of North Carolina Press, 1991), p. 235n; and Clark Clifford, *Counsel to the Presidents* (New York: Random House, 1991), p. 519.
93. Amembassy Paris to Secstate, June 29, 1967, NSF, CF, France, Box 173, p. 183a, LBJL.
94. *Maarive,* May 29, 1967.

Contributors

H. W. Brands is professor of history and coordinator of the Program in Foreign Relations and the Presidency, Center for Presidential Studies, George Bush School of Government and Public Service, Texas A&M University.

Robert K. Brigham has written several articles on the policies of the National Liberation Front and is preparing a book on that subject.

Frank Costigliola is professor of history at the University of Connecticut and has written extensively on American relations with Europe.

Hiroshi Fujimoto is a specialist on Japanese-American relations and is professor of international relations at Aichi University of Education, Japan.

Ilya V. Gaiduk has written the first account of Russian policy in Vietnam.

Lloyd C. Gardner has written two books on American policy in Vietnam.

Judith A. Klinghoffer has written a book on the triangle of American Jewry, the Johnson administration, and Israel.

Robert J. McMahon specializes in U.S. relations with Southeast Asia, particularly Indonesia.

John Prados is an independent scholar and writer who has written extensively on both political and military aspects of the Vietnam War.

Kil J. Yi, of Bergen Community College, is preparing a book on Korean participation in the Vietnam War.

Qiang Zhai teaches at Auburn University at Montgomery and is the author of several articles on Chinese military policy and Vietnam.

Xiaoming Zhang is a specialist on China's foreign policies in the communist bloc.

Index

cerns about, 208–209; E. Rostow on Soviet goals in, 220; and the Glassboro conference, 49, 217–19; linked to Vietnam, 6; and Resolution 242, 221; similarities to Vietnam, 223–24; Soviets reject French proposal for conference, 215

"Middle Kingdom mentality," 79, 138, 245n 8

Mikoyan, Anastas, 85

"more flags" campaign, 156–57, 179, 263n 11

Moto Furuta, cited, 176–77

multilateral force, 34, 39

Myanmar (Burma), 196

Nasser, Gamal Abdel: air strength of, 213; Brezhnev promises to assist, 209; ceases to threaten Arab monarchies, 220; closes Straits of Tiran, 212; fears CIA coup, 210, 275n 31; mobilizes support of Iraq and Jordan, 216; national liberation movements, 115; seeks to provoke Israeli attack, 215

NATO: a front for U.S. influence, 145–46; members chided by Rusk, 46–47; resents U.S. role in Vietnam, 143–44; U.S. credibility in, 6–7

Ngo Dinh Diem, 27; anticommunist campaigns of, 100

Nguyen Chi Thanh, 71; argues for armed struggle, 101; argues for decisive military engagements, 103; criticizes USSR and peaceful coexistence, 105; death of, 106; strategic views of, 99

Nguyen Co Thach, 70

Nguyen Van Thieu, 135

Nie Rongzhen, 125

Nixon, Richard: doubts USSR wants détente, 223; and the formation of ASEAN, 200; meets Zhou Enlai, 131; seeks rapprochement with PRC, 124–31; and the Sino-Soviet split, 24–25; withdraws from Vietnam, 230

Nixon Doctrine: DRV criticizes, 129

NLF: courts PRC, 105

North Vietnam. See DRV

nuclear nonproliferation treaty, 37, 41, 42–43, 239n 57

Nyerere, Julius, 111–12

Ogasawara Islands, 178

Okinawa, 6; importance of, to U.S. effort in Vietnam, 181

pacification, 173

"Pacific Charter," 169–70

Paris peace talks, 54; DRV goals at, 123; PRC critical of, 54, 122–23; surprise Ho Chi Minh, 93; SVN backs out of, 56; Zhou Enlai criticizes, 123

Park, Chung Hee: attempts to reverse U.S. disengagement, 157; a Cold Warrior, 168–69; demands increased economic incentives, 173–74; demands role in peace process, 170–71; demands U.S. guarantee S. Korean security, 172–73, 268n 94; political vulnerability of, 155; rebuffed in demand of role in peace talks, 172; seeks a "Pacific Charter," 169–70; suspicious of a peace settlement in Vietnam, 170, 171, 268n 86; visits Washington in 1965, 159

Parker, Richard, 206

"pen pals" correspondence, 28

Pham Van Dong: asks PRC to cancel Nixon visit, 130; attends 23d CPSU Congress, 119; favors a pro-Soviet line, 71, 101; and the Laotian crisis, 66–67; and the ouster of Khrushchev, 86

Philippines, 190

Phoumi Nosavan, 66–70, passim

PL 480. See Public Law 480

Pleiku incident, 30

Porter, William, 161

PRC: aid clogs DRV transportation system, 114; alarmed at growing friendship of DRV and USSR, 92; border strategy of, 72; continues aid to DRV despite détente with U.S., 96, 249n 88; critical of Paris peace talks, 93, 122–23; criticizes Soviet Middle East policy, 214–15; declines DRV request for pilots, 90; declines to assist in peace process, 130; discussed at Glassboro, 49, 240n 84; and DRV, 15–16; DRV policy of, summarized, 96–97; early advice to DRV, 81–82; early views on reunifying Vietnam, 80; encourages DRV to pursue armed struggle, 71–76 passim;

PRC (*cont.*)

evaluates its role vis-a-vis the USSR, 79–80, 245*n* 7; fears war with U.S., 84, 246*n* 35; general policy of, 4; growing fears of conflict with USSR, 94, 248*n* 77, 248*n* 78; hinders aid to DRV from USSR, 89, 106, 247*n* 58, 252*n* 54; increases aid to DRV in 1972, 127, 258*n* 82; Kosygin warns U.S. about, 44; and the Laotian crisis, 67–70, 109–10, 253*n* 5; "Middle Kingdom" mentality of, 79, 245*n* 8; at 1954 Geneva Conference, 80, 245*n* 13; 1963 military talks with DRV, 83; in 1968–69, 257*n* 64; number of troops sent to DRV, 113; policy toward DRV, summarized, 135–39; prefers protracted warfare, 122; prepares for war with U.S., 87; promises aid to DRV in 1965, 112; rapprochement with U.S., 124–31; rationalizes détente with U.S., 127–29, 258*n* 80; reacts to invasion of Cambodia, 125–26, 258*n* 73; reacts to invasion of Laos, 126, 258*n* 77; reacts to ouster of Khrushchev, 85; reacts to Paris agreement, 135–36; reacts to Tonkin Gulf incidents, 110–11; reassures DRV after Kissinger visit, 95, 249*n* 87; refuses to provide pilots to DRV, 113, 254*n* 23; rejects Soviet offer of summit meeting, 118; rejects Soviet overtures, 86–87, 88; revisionist errors about, 198–99; scale of aid sent to DRV, 113; sends aid through Cambodia, 114, 255*n* 31; sends troops to DRV, 87; signs military agreement with DRV, 75; sources of friction with DRV, 116–17; troops in DRV, 117; unimpressed with Khrushchev, 81; U.S. fears of, 4, 5, 231; volume of aid to DRV, 89–91, 109, 114. *See also* Mao Zedong; Zhou Enlai

Public Law 480: in S. Korea, 166–67

Pushkin, G. M.: on Soviet goals in Laos, 69–70

regionalism, 177–78

Resolution 242, 221

Rolling Thunder, 30. *See also* bombing; bombing halt

Romulo, Carlos, 199

Rostow, Eugene, 147; on Soviet goals in Middle East, 220

Rostow, Walt: advises reassessment of Middle East in early 1968, 222; asks LBJ to reassure FRG, 47; believes Moscow has little leverage on DRV, urges escalation, 37; downplays fear of new Soviet challenges around the world, 209; encouraged by Sino-Soviet split, 45; favors a role for S. Korea in the peace process, 171; favors economic aid to S. Korea, 165; and Glassboro, 47–48; on the long-term effects of the Vietnam War, 191–92, 197; and the Paris peace talks, 54; records decision to put off KLSC, 174; and the Tashkent agreement, 38; views of, endorsed, 192–93

Rusk, Dean: chides NATO allies, 46–47; on a complete bombing halt, 56; confers with Gromyko during Glassboro, 48, 240*n* 82; criticizes Fulbright, 207; decries ambiguity in U.S.-USSR communications, 55; on Japan–S. Korea relationship, 158; links bombing to infiltration, 38; meets with Dobrynin, 29; and NATO, 7; on the PRC, 3, 5; presses FRG to help in Vietnam, 148; ready to link negotiations on Vietnam and the Middle East, 213; rejects Korean role in Vietnam peace process, 170; responds to Senator Hickenlooper, 26–27; and Sato 1967 visit, 184; sees new Soviet challenges in 1967, 209–10; sees S. Korea as a model for SVN, 51; sees success in Vietnam, 222; and Sino-Soviet split, 30; talks with U Thant, 33; view of USSR's position, 30

Ryukyu Islands, 178

SAM (surface-to-air missiles) units: first deployed to DRV, 88–89

San Antonio formula, 51–51

Saragat, Giuseppe, 152

Sato, Eisaku: agrees with LBJ's concept of regionalism, 177–78; declares support for U.S. policy, 184–85; 1967 visit to U.S., 184–85; shows caution in giving aid to SVN, 179

Schaller, Michael, cited, 203
Schnittker, John A., 166–67
Seaborn, Blair, 27–28
SEATO: disappoints LBJ in Vietnam, 156–57
Sharp, U.S. Grant: on the role of Okinawa, 181
Shiina, Etsusaburo, 180
Sihanouk, Prince, 125, 196
Sihanoukville, 114
Singapore, 190; economic impact of Vietnam War on, 202
Sino-Soviet split, 15, 117–18; and the Bucharest Congress, 62; encourages Rostow, 45; facilitates détente, 230; Ho Chi Minh seeks to mediate, 83; intensifies at Bucharest Conference, 82; origins of, 82–97 passim, 100, 229; PRC rejects Soviet overture, 86–87, 88; Soviets recall experts in PRC, 59; USSR lists errors of PRC, 62
Six-Day War: immediate results of, 217; LBJ insists on negotiated peace, 218; and Resolution 242, 221. *See also* Middle East; Israel; Nasser, Gamal Abdel
Snyder, Glenn, cited, 136–37
Southeast Asia: economic growth of, 189–90
Southeast Asia ministerial conference, 183
South Korea: beginnings of prosperity, 167; begins de-escalation in SVN, 174; civilian laborers in SVN, 164–65; earnings of, in SVN, 165; economic reform in, 162; economic weaknesses of, 161–62, 265n 39; establishes relations with Japan, 158, 181–82; first commitments of troops to SVN, 182; general position of, 5–6; impact of Vietnamese War on, summarized, 17; "mercenary" issue, 160, 163, 264n 30; a model for SVN, 51, 163; number of troops sent to SVN, 154, 263n 1; and pacification in SVN, 173; and PL 480, 166–67; quality of troops, 168, 267n 74; recent history summarized, 155–56; re-exports Japanese goods, 182–83; relations with Japan, 158–59, 181–83; second Five-Year Plan, 167–68; seeks share of wartime markets, 161–63, 164; U.S. agrees to pay troops, 160; U.S. asks for a second division of troops, 168; U.S. guarantees security of, 159–60, 182; U.S. loans to, 165–66; Vietnam experience of, summarized, 174–75

Souvanna Phouma, Prince, 65–70 passim
Spring Offensive of 1972, 132–34
Springsteen, Bruce, 192
Stalin, Josef, 78–79
Stennis, John C., 180
Stone, Marvin, cited, 192
Stone, Oliver, 192
Straits of Tiran, 212
Stubbs, Richard, cited, 202
Sudarikov, Nikolai, 66
Suez Canal, 218, 219, 222
Suharto: coup analyzed, 194–95
surface-to-air missiles. *See* SAM (surface-to-air missiles) units

Taiwan: linked to Vietnam, 127–28
Tashkent agreement, 38
Tet Offensive: contradicts Mao's doctrine, 120–21; Lao Dong Party and, 107
Thailand, 190; effect of Vietnam War on, 196–97; U.S. aid and spending in, 202
Thanat Khoman, 200
Thompson, Llewellyn: advice of, at Glassboro, 48; and the London peace feeler, 44–45; presses Kosygin's case to LBJ, 56; suggests bombing restriction, 215
Tokyo Tribunal, cited, 176
Tonkin Gulf incidents: PRC reacts to, 110–11
Tovar, Hugh, 195
Tran Quang Co: says U.S. misunderstood DRV aims, 23
Tran Tu Binh, 71
Truman, Harry: shapes Cold War assumptions, 231
Truman Doctrine, 7
Truong Chinh, 71; changes stance to favor people's war, 102–103; strategic views of, 99, 100

Ung Van Khiem, 60, 61–62
United States: fears about PRC, 4, 5;

United States (*cont.*)
general policy of, 3–4, 5, 9–12, 17, 24–25; impact of Vietnam War on, 227
U.S. News and World Report, 192
USSR: dilemma of, summarized, 73–76; DRV policy of, summarized, 97; early advice and aid to DRV, 81–82; early military aid to NLFSV, 74; early view of the PRC, 78–79; favors conference on Laos, 66–67; general policy of, 3–4, 13–14; at Geneva conference on Laos, 69–70; increases military aid to DRV in 1965, 86; and the Laotian crisis, 65–70; and a Laotian-type conference on Vietnam, 70–71; links Vietnam to Middle East, 208; lists errors of PRC; at the 1954 Geneva Conference, 80; nudges Nasser toward war, 210, 275*n* 31; proposes summit with PRC, 118; reacts to DRV decision for armed struggle, 61; reacts to Spring Offensive of 1972, 133–34; reinforces border with PRC, 94; rejects French proposal for Middle East conference, 215; resents DRV secrecy, 64–65, 73; sends SAM units to DRV, 88–89; and the Six-Day War, 204–24 passim; stance on reunification of Vietnam, 33; suggests joint USSR-PRC program for DRV, 88; volume of aid to DRV, 89–91; warns U.S. against action in the Middle East, 212
U Thant, 33

Valenti, Jack, 163
Van Tien Dung, 110
Vo Nguyen Giap: declares ICC an inconvenience, 60; emphasizes main force warfare in 1971, 132; and the Laotian crisis, 67

Wall Street Journal, 193, 200–201
Walters, Vernon, 130
Wang Youping, 130
War of Jenkins' Ear, 17–19
Whitlam, Gough, 129
Wilson, Harold, 43
Wise Men: January, 1966, meeting, 35–36; November, 1967, meeting, 52; on Six-Day War settlement, 222
Woods, Randall, cited, 207

Xuan Thuy, 71
Xu Xiangqian, 125

Yang Chengwu, 112
Yao Wenyuan, 129–30
Ye Jianying, 125

Zhang Chunqiao, 129–30
Zhou Enlai: chides Le Duan for pro-Soviet behavior, 92; counsels patience to DRV, 135; critical of Paris peace talks, 123; declines Haig's request to press the DRV, 131; July, 1964, visit and advice to Lao Dong Party, 110; meets Nixon, 131; promises PRC intervention, 110, 113; reacts to mining of Haiphong harbor, 133; reassures DRV in wake of Kissinger visit, 128; recommends mobile warfare to DRV, 121–22; urges aid for the Pathet Lao, 66, 68; urges DRV to seek a settlement, 135; visits USSR in 1964, 85; warns U.S. through Julius Nyerere, 111–12
Zorin, Valerian, 54